MATTHEW

MATTHEW

MATTHEW

NICOLE WILKINSON DURAN AND JAMES P. GRIMSHAW, EDITORS

Fortress Press
Minneapolis

MATTHEW

Texts @ Contexts series

Cover image: Christian Hugo Martin, *Composition*, Burn paper work, 340,5×143, 5 cm. 2006/10

Cover design: Laurie Ingram

Library of Congress Cataloging-in-Publication Data

Matthew / Nicole Wilkinson Duran and James P. Grimshaw, editors.
pages cm. – (Texts @ contexts)
Includes bibliographical references and index.
ISBN 978-0-8006-9934-5 (print : alk. paper) — ISBN 978-1-4514-2634-2 (ebook)
1. Bible. N.T. Matthew–Criticism, interpretation, etc. I. Duran, Nicole Wilkinson, editor of compilation. II. Grimshaw, James P., 1963- editor of compilation.
BS2575.52.M377 2013
226.2'06–dc23
2012044787

This book was produced using PressBooks.com, and PDF rendering was done by PrinceXML.

CONTENTS

Part III. Disability and Culture

Part IV. Laborers and Empire

Part V. Community and Borders

Other Books in the Series

Athalya Brenner and Nicole Wilkinson Duran
Series Editors
Editorial Committee
Hebrew Bible
Athalya Brenner, Cheryl Kirk-Duggan, Kari Latvus, Archie Chi-Chung
Lee, Gale A. Yee
New Testament
Nicole Wilkinson Duran, James P. Grimshaw, Yung Suk Kim, Teresa
Okure, Daniel Patte, Volumes
Hebrew Bible
Genesis
Exodus and Deuteronomy
Leviticus and Numbers
Joshua and Judges
New Testament
Matthew
Mark
John
First and Second Corinthians

List of Contributors

Sharon Betsworth is the associate professor of New Testament at Oklahoma City University, in Oklahoma City, Oklahoma. She received her Ph.D. from the Graduate Theological Union in Berkeley, California, and is the author of *The Reign of God Is Such as These: A Socio-Literary Analysis of Daughters in the Gospel of Mark* (2010). Betsworth is actively involved with the Society of Biblical Literature's Children in the Biblical World section and is currently working on a book on children in the Gospels and infancy Gospels.

Jeannine K. Brown is professor of New Testament at Bethel Seminary in St. Paul, Minnesota. She received her Ph.D. from Luther Seminary in Minnesota; her dissertation on Matthew's disciples was published as *The Disciples in Narrative Perspective*. Her recent works include *Scripture as Communication* (2007) and *Becoming Whole and Holy* (2011; with C. Dahl and W. Corbin Reuschling). Brown has been the regional coordinator of the Society of Biblical Literature for the Upper Midwest Region since 2009.

Lung-pun Common Chan is an assistant professor of New Testament at the Chinese University of Hong Kong. Born in Hong Kong, Chan received a Th.D. from the University of Heidelberg, Germany. He is the author of *Eine sozialwissenschaftliche Untersuchung der Metapher des Lammes in der Johannesapokalypse* (forthcoming). His research interests relates particularly to the apocalypses and early Christian texts. Chan is actively involved with the Society of Biblical Literature's Mind, Society, and Tradition section.

Stephanie Buckhanon Crowder, preacher, scholar, and teacher, received a Ph.D. in New Testament from Vanderbilt University. Dr. Crowder has contributed to numerous publications, including *The Chalice Introduction to the New Testament, True to Our Native Land: An African American New Testament Commentary*, and *The African American Lectionary*. Her work on womanist maternal thought can be found in *Mother Goose, Mother Jones, Mommie Dearest: Biblical Mothers and Their Children*, found in Brill's Semeia Studies series. She is on the editorial board of *Feasting on the Gospels and on Scripture*, an online contextual commentary featured on the *Huffington Post*.

Febbie C. Dickerson is a Ph.D. candidate at Vanderbilt University. She received the M.Div. degree from Vanderbilt and a B.A. degree in telecommunications from the University of Georgia. Dickerson is also ordained clergy in the United in Christ Worldwide Fellowship of Atlanta, Georgia, and currently serves as a minister at the Ray of Hope Community Church in Nashville, Tennessee. Her research interests include the special Lukan material and the depiction of women in Luke's Gospel.

Jonathan A. Draper is senior professor of New Testament at the School of Theology, University of KwaZulu-Natal, Pietermaritzburg, where he has taught for twenty-five years. Born in South Africa, he completed his graduate studies in New Testament at Cambridge University in 1983. He has published numerous articles on the *Didache*, including editing *The Didache in Modern Research* (1996). He is author (with Richard A. Horsley) of *Whoever Hears You Hears Me: Prophets, Performance, and Tradition in Q* (1999) and editor of *The Eye of the Storm: Bishop John William Colenso and the Crisis of Biblical Interpretation* (2003), *Orality, Literacy, and Colonialism in Southern Africa* (2003), and *Orality, Literacy, and Colonialism in Antiquity* (2004). He is also editor of the journal *Neotestamentica*.

Nicole Wilkinson Duran is currently the New Testament series editor for the Texts@Contexts series. She is the author of *Having Men for Dinner: Deadly Banquets and Biblical Women* and *The Power of Disorder: Ritual Themes in Mark's Passion Narrative*, as well as various articles on Hebrew Bible and New Testament topics. She served on the editorial board of *The Global Bible Commentary* and has been editor and coeditor of a number of other collections of essays. She is currently an independent scholar outside of Philadelphia.

James P. Grimshaw is associate professor of religion at Carroll University in Waukesha, Wisconsin. Grimshaw received his Ph.D. from Vanderbilt University in 2005. He is author of *The Matthean Community and the World* (2008) and is actively involved with the Society of Biblical Literature Contextual Biblical Interpretation group.

L. J. Lawrence is senior lecturer in New Testament Studies at the University of Exeter, United Kingdom. Lawrence received her Ph.D. from Exeter in 2002. She is the author of *An Ethnography of the Gospel of Matthew*

(2003), *Reading with Anthropology* (2005), and *The Word in Place* (2009). She is a member of the British New Testament Society and Society of Biblical Literature, where she has been involved in Contextual Bible Study, Social-Scientific Criticism, and Disability Studies panels and seminars.

Sung Uk Lim is a Ph.D. candidate in the New Testament and Early Christianity program at Vanderbilt University. As a native of South Korea, Lim received an M.Div. from Seoul Theological Seminary in Bucheon and a M.A.B.L. from the Graduate Theological Union in Berkeley. His dissertation applies narrative criticism to the characters in the Gospel of John through a postcolonial, deconstructive lens. His publications include: "Jonah's Transformation and Transformation of *Jonah* from the Bakhtinian Perspective of Authoring and Reauthoring," *Journal for the Study of the Old Testament* (2008); "*Speak My Name*: Anti-Colonial Mimicry in John 4:1-42," *Union Seminary Quarterly Review* (2010); and "The Myth of Origin in Context through the Lens of Deconstruction, Dialogism, and Hybridity," *Journal for the Study of Religions and Ideologies* (2011).

Tsui-yuk Louise Liu is a lecturer of New Testament and research fellow at the Chinese University of Hong Kong. Born in China, Liu received a Th.D. from the University of Heidelberg, Germany. She is the author of *Herodes als Symbol von Fremdherrschaft im Matthaeusevangelium* (forthcoming). Her research interests include family and children in relation to the Gospels and early Christian texts. Liu is actively involved with the Society of Biblical Literature's Children and Families in the Ancient World unit.

Francisco Lozada Jr. is Charles Fischer Catholic Associate Professor of New Testament and Latino/a Church Studies at Brite Divinity School, in Fort Worth, Texas. Among his publications are *A Literary Reading of John 5: Text as Construction* (Peter Lang, 2000) and, as coeditor, *New Currents Through John: A Global Perspective* (2006).

James A. Metzger received his Ph.D. in New Testament and early Christianity from Vanderbilt University. He has taught courses in religion at Vanderbilt University Divinity School, Luther College, and East Carolina University, where he is currently completing an M.A. in English. He is the author of *Consumption and Wealth in Luke's Travel Narrative* (2007) and *Dim: A Novel* (2011).

Lidija Novakovic is an associate professor of religion (New Testament) in the Department of Religion at Baylor University, Texas. Born in former Yugoslavia, Novakovic received a Ph.D. from Princeton Theological Seminary. She is the author of *Messiah, the Healer of the Sick: A Study of Jesus as the Son of David in the Gospel of Matthew* (2003). Novakovic is a member of the steering committee for the Matthew section of the Society of Biblical Literature.

Elaine M. Wainwright is professor of theology and head of the School of Theology at the University of Auckland, New Zealand. She is a New Testament scholar specializing in the Gospel of Matthew and contemporary biblical hermeneutics: feminist, postcolonial, and more recently ecological. She has published widely in these areas, and her publications include three books and numerous scholarly articles. She is a longtime member of the Society of Biblical Literature and is currently a member of its International Program committee.

Dorothy Jean Weaver is professor of New Testament at Eastern Mennonite Seminary, Harrisonburg, Virginia. She holds a Ph.D. in New Testament from Union Theological Seminary, Richmond, Virginia. Her publications include *Matthew's Missionary Discourse: A Literary Critical Analysis* (1990) and *Bread for the Enemy: A Peace and Justice Lectionary* (2001). From 2004 to 2009, Weaver cochaired the Society of Biblical Literature Matthew section. She coleads regular Israel/Palestine study tours for Eastern Mennonite Seminary and Israel/Palestine work groups for Virginia Mennonite Missions. Weaver has taught New Testament courses in Beirut, Lebanon; Bethlehem, Palestine; Cairo, Egypt; and Debre Zeit, Ethiopia.

Gerald West is professor of Old Testament and African biblical hermeneutics in the School of Religion, Philosophy, and Classics at the University of KwaZulu-Natal, South Africa. He is the coordinator of the Contextual Bible Study programme of the Ujamaa Centre, and has written extensively on the collaboration between socially engaged biblical scholars and ordinary readers of the Bible in contexts of struggle for social justice.

John Yieh is a professor of New Testament at Virginia Theological Seminary in Alexandria, Virginia. Born in Taiwan, Yieh received a Ph.D. in religious studies from Yale University. He is the author of *One Teacher: Jesus' Teaching Role in Matthew's Gospel Report* (2004), *Making Sense of the Sermon on the Mount* (2007), and *Revelation* (with Henry Brinton, 2010). He has served as president of the Mid-Atlantic Regional Society of Biblical Literature, and is currently president of the Ethnic Chinese Biblical Colloquium.

Sithembiso Zwane is completing his master's degree in theology in the School of Religion, Philosophy, and Classics at the University of KwaZulu-Natal, South Africa. He is the coordinator of the Theology and Economic Justice Programme of the Ujamaa Centre and has conducted a series of workshops on the Bible and economy. His research interests are theology and economic justice. He is an ordained minister in the N.D.J Ethiopian Catholic Church in Zion, an African Independent Church (AIC) based in Estcourt, KwaZulu-Natal, South Africa.

SERIES PREFACE, UPDATED: TEXTS IN/ AT LIFE CONTEXTS

> Myth cannot be defined but as an empty screen, a structure. . . . A
> myth is but an empty screen for transference.[1]

> שבעים פנים לתורה ("The Torah has seventy faces")[2]

The discipline of biblical studies emerges from a particular cultural context;
it is profoundly influenced by the assumptions and values of the Western
European and North Atlantic, male-dominated, and largely Protestant
environment in which it was born. Yet like the religions with which it is
involved, the critical study of the Bible has traveled beyond its original context.
Its presence in a diversity of academic settings around the globe has been
experienced as both liberative and imperialist, sometimes simultaneously. Like
many travelers, biblical scholars become aware of their own cultural rootedness
only in contact with, and through the eyes of, people in other cultures.

The way any one of us closes a door seems in Philadelphia nothing at all
remarkable, but in Chiang Mai, it seems overly loud and emphatic—so very
typically American. In the same way, Western biblical interpretation did not
seem tied to any specific context when only Westerners were reading and
writing it. Since so much economic, military, and consequently cultural power
has been vested in the West, the West has had the privilege of maintaining this
cultural closure for two centuries. Those who engaged in biblical studies—even
when they were women or men from Africa, Asia, and Latin
America—nevertheless had to take on the Western context along with the
discipline.

But much of recent Bible scholarship has moved toward the recognition
that considerations not only of the contexts of assumed, or implied, biblical

authors but also the contexts of the interpreters are valid and legitimate in an inquiry into biblical literature. We use *contexts* here as an umbrella term covering a wide range of issues: on the one hand, social factors (such as location, economic situation, gender, age, class, ethnicity, color, and things pertaining to personal biography) and, on the other hand, ideological factors (such as faith, beliefs, practiced norms, and personal politics).

Contextual readings of the Bible are an attempt to redress the previous longstanding and grave imbalance that says that there is a kind of "plain," unaligned biblical criticism that is somehow "normative," and that there is another, distinct kind of biblical criticism aligned with some social location: the writing of Latina/o scholars advocating liberation, the writing of feminist scholars emphasizing gender as a cultural factor, the writings of African scholars pointing out the text's and the readers' imperialism, the writing of Jews and Muslims, and so on. The project of recognizing and emphasizing the role of context in reading freely admits that we all come from somewhere: no one is native to the biblical text; no one reads only in the interests of the text itself. North Atlantic and Western European scholarship has focused on the Bible's characters as individuals, has read past its miracles and stories of spiritual manifestations, or "translated" them into other categories. These results of Euro-American contextual reading would be no problem if they were seen as such; but they have become a chain to be broken when they have been held up as the one and only "objective," plain truth of the text itself.

The biblical text, as we have come to understand in the postmodern world and as pre-Enlightenment interpreters perhaps understood more clearly, does not speak in its own voice. It cannot read itself. *We* must read it, and in reading it, we must acknowledge that our own voice's particular pitch and timbre and inflection affect the meaning that emerges. Biblical scholars usually read the text in the voice of a Western Protestant male. When interpreters in the Southern Hemisphere and in Asia have assumed ownership of the Bible, it has meant a recognition that this Euro-American male voice is not the voice of the text itself; it is only one reader's voice, or rather, the voice of one context—however familiar and authoritative it may seem to all who have been affected by Western political and economic power. Needless to say, it is not a voice suited to bring out the best meaning for every reading community. Indeed, as biblical studies tended for so long to speak in this one particular voice, it may be the case that that voice has outlived its meaning-producing usefulness: we may have heard all that this voice has to say, at least for now. Nevertheless, we have included that voice in this series, in part in an effort to hear it as emerging from its specific context, in order to put that previously authoritative voice quite literally in its place.

The trend of acknowledging readers' contexts as meaningful is already, inter alia, recognizable in the pioneering volumes of *Reading from This Place* (Segovia and Tolbert 1995; 2000; 2004), which indeed move from the center to the margins and back and from the United States to the rest of the world. More recent publications along this line also include *Her Master's Tools?* (Vander Stichele and Penner 2005), *From Every People and Nation: The Book of Revelation in Intercultural Perspective* (Rhoads 2005), *From Every People and Nation: A Biblical Theology of Race* (Hays and Carson 2003), and the *Global Bible Commentary* (*GBC*; Patte et al. 2004).

The editors of the *GBC* have gone a long way toward this shift by soliciting and admitting contributions from so-called third-, fourth-, and fifth-world scholars alongside first- and second-world scholars, thus attempting to usher the former and their perspectives into the *center* of biblical discussion. Contributors to the *GBC* were asked to begin by clearly stating their context before proceeding. The result was a collection of short introductions to the books of the Bible (Hebrew Bible/Old Testament and New Testament), each introduction from one specific context and, perforce, limited in scope. At the Society of Biblical Literature's (SBL) annual meeting in Philadelphia in 2005, during the two *GBC* sessions and especially in the session devoted to pedagogical implications, it became clear that this project should be continued, albeit articulated further and redirected.

On methodological grounds, the paradox of a deliberately inclusive policy that foregrounds differences in the interpretation of the Bible could not be addressed in a single- or double-volume format because in most instances those formats would allow for only one viewpoint for each biblical issue or passage (as in previous publications) or biblical book (as in the *GBC*) to be articulated. The acceptance of such a limit may indeed lead to a decentering of traditional scholarship, but it would definitely not usher in multivocality on any single topic. It is true that, for pedagogical reasons, a teacher might achieve multivocality of scholarship by using various specialized scholarship types together; for instance, the *GBC* has been used side-by-side in a course with historical introductions to the Bible and other focused introductions, such as the *Women's Bible Commentary* (Newsom and Ringe 1998). But research and classes focused on a single biblical book or biblical corpus need another kind of resource: volumes exemplifying a broad multivocality in themselves, varied enough in contexts from various shades of the confessional to various degrees of the secular, especially since in most previous publications, the contexts of communities of faith overrode all other contexts.

On the practical level, then, we found that we could address some of these methodological, pedagogical, and representational limitations evident in previous projects in contextual interpretation through a book series in which each volume introduces multiple contextual readings of the same biblical texts. This is what the SBL's Contextual Biblical Interpretation Consultation has already been promoting since 2005 during the American annual meeting; and since 2011 also at the annual international SBL conference. The consultation serves as a testing ground for a multiplicity of readings of the same biblical texts by scholars from different contexts.

These considerations led us to believe that a book series focusing specifically on contextual multiple readings for specific topics, of specific biblical books, would be timely. We decided to construct a series, including at least eight to ten volumes, divided between the Hebrew Bible (HB/OT) and the New Testament (NT). Each of the planned volumes would focus on one or two biblical books: Genesis, Exodus and Deuteronomy, Leviticus and Numbers, Joshua and Judges, and later books for the HB/OT; Mark, Luke-Acts, John, and Paul's letters for the NT.[3] The general HB/OT editor is Athalya Brenner, with Archie Lee and Gale Yee as associate editors. The general NT editor is Nicole Duran, with Daniel Patte and Teresa Okure as associate editors. Other colleagues have joined as editors for specific volumes.

Each volume focuses on clusters of contexts and of issues or themes, as determined by the editors in consultation with potential contributors. A combination of topics or themes, texts, and interpretive contexts seems better for our purpose than a text-only focus. In this way, more viewpoints on specific issues will be presented, with the hope of gaining a grid of interests and understanding. The interpreters' contexts will be allowed to play a central role in choosing a theme: we do not want to impose our choice of themes upon others, but as the contributions emerge, we will collect themes for each volume under several headings.

While we were soliciting articles for the first volumes (and continue to solicit contributions for future volumes), contributors were asked to foreground their own multiple "contexts" while presenting their interpretation of a given issue pertaining to the relevant biblical book(s). We asked that the interpretation be firmly grounded in those contexts and sharply focused on the specific theme, as well as in dialogue with "classical" informed biblical scholarship. Finally, we asked for a concluding assessment of the significance of this interpretation for the contributor's contexts (whether secular or in the framework of a faith community).

Our main interest in this series is to examine how formulating the content-specific, ideological, and thematic questions from life contexts will focus the reading of the biblical texts. The result is a two-way process of reading that (1) considers the contemporary life context from the perspective of the chosen themes in the given biblical book as corrective lenses, pointing out specific problems and issues in that context as highlighted by the themes in the biblical book; and (2) conversely, considers the given biblical book and the chosen theme from the perspective of the life context.

The word *contexts*, like *identity*, is a blanket term with many components. For some, their geographical context is uppermost; for others, the dominant factor may be gender, faith, membership in a certain community, class, and so forth. The balance is personal and not always conscious; it does, however, dictate choices of interpretation. One of our interests as editors is to present the personal beyond the autobiographical as pertinent to the wider scholarly endeavor, especially but not only when *grids of consent* emerge that supersede divergence. Consent is no guarantee of Truthspeak; neither does it necessarily point at a sure recognition of the biblical authors' elusive contexts and intentions. It does, however, have cultural and political implications.

Globalization promotes uniformity but also diversity, by shortening distances, enabling dissemination of information, and exchanging resources. This is an opportunity for modifying traditional power hierarchies and reallocating knowledge, for upsetting hegemonies, and for combining the old with the new, the familiar with the unknown—in short, for a fresh mutuality. This series, then, consciously promotes the revision of biblical myths into new reread and rewritten versions that hang on many threads of welcome transference. Our contributors were asked, decidedly, to be responsibly nonobjective and to represent only themselves on the biblical screen. Paradoxically, we hope, the readings here offered will form a new tapestry or, changing the metaphor, new metaphorical screens on which contemporary life contexts and the life of biblical texts in those contexts may be reflected and refracted.

Notes

1. Mieke Bal 1993: 347, 360.
2. This saying indicates, through its usage of the stereotypic number seventy, that the Torah—and, by extension, the whole Bible—intrinsically has many meanings. It is therefore often

used to indicate the multivalence and variability of biblical interpretation, and does not appear in this formulation in traditional Jewish biblical interpretation before the Middle Ages. Its earliest appearances are in the medieval commentator Ibn Ezra's introduction to his commentary on the Torah, toward the introduction's end (as in printed versions), in Midrash *Numbers Rabbah* (13:15-16), and in later Jewish mystical literature.

3. At this time, no volume on Revelation is planned, since Rhoads's volume *From Every People and Nation: The Book of Revelation in Intercultural Perspective* (2005) is readily available, with a concept similar to ours.

Introduction

James P. Grimshaw

Matthew's favored place in the tradition calls out for contextual readings. Its stories are familiar and its pages well worn, but it can benefit from fresh perspectives. Matthew's place in the canon is privileged, but its traditional readings need not be. It is often called the church's book, but Matthew is read both by wildly diverse Christian traditions and by those outside the church. Matthew ends with instructions to teach the nations, yet the many nations of the world have much to say about it. And so, sixteen essays have been gathered from a variety of cultures and perspectives around the world to have a conversation that takes seriously both the ancient text and its many contemporary contexts.

These conversations between text and context take different forms. Four scholars highlight conversations with ordinary readers, listening to others read the text such as the Palestinian protestors, the Deaf community, day laborers, and child-care workers. Six authors read with and advocate for their own cultures, religious traditions, or perspectives (African American, Latina/o, Croatian, Oceanian, Mennonite, and those with disabilities). Five contributors read in dialogue with their cultures and religious traditions but push back to challenge them (readers from South Africa, China, Hong Kong, South Korea, and the American evangelical tradition). And one interpreter reads from outside the culture but invites those within the culture to read Matthew and curb the absence of the culture's interpretations. As can be seen already, the primary context is often culture, sometimes religious traditions, and many times a combination of the two. But other contexts come to the foreground as well, such as work conditions, disabilities, ecological trauma, nonviolent resistance movements, post-Communism and globalization, single mothers and preacher's kids, womanism and masculinity studies.

The sixteen chapters not only provide wonderfully diverse readings but also, perhaps surprisingly, connect well with each other around specific themes, texts, and cultures. While the hope is that readers of this volume will make these many connections, for the sake of organization, this volume has gathered the essays into five groupings: community and beginnings, children and family, disability and culture, laborers and empire, and community and borders.

1

Two essays begin at the opening of the Gospel. Lidija Novakovic, from Croatia, reads Matthew's genealogy in light of post-Communist Croatia in order to explore the theme of community identity. As Croatian leaders after the wars in the 1990s reinterpreted their Communist past in order to create a new, democratic, national identity, so also Novakovic explores how Matthew's genealogy provides clues to the way the Matthean community remembered its Jewish past to shape its new identity. Jonathan Draper, a white South African, reads Matthew's genealogy in conversation with the Zulu people and diverse members of the Anglican Church to explore community identity in African cultures in the postapartheid era. As Matthew's genealogy both affirms the traditions of Israel and opens up the promises of the Abrahamic covenant to all the nations of the earth, so Draper explores how indigenous African cultures might be affirmed amid a colonized past and yet also open up to an inclusive transcultural identity in the future.

Five scholars take an interest in the topic of parents and children; the first four focus on mothers and the last one on fathers. Sharon Betsworth met with other Euro-American women who work with children's ministries in the state of Oklahoma (a state that ranks low in the United States regarding childhood health and well-being) to discuss Jesus as a child in Matthew 1–2 and Jesus' teaching with and about children in Matt. 18:1-5. She argues that Jesus begins as a vulnerable and threatened child yet is protected by his parents and God, a situation familiar to the women interpreting this passage. Jesus then becomes an adult who cares for vulnerable and threatened children, only later to again become vulnerable and dependent on God.

Both Febbie Dickerson and Stephanie Buckhanon Crowder interpret the story of the Canaanite woman (Matt. 15:22-28) as African American women. Dickerson is single and without children and stands in solidarity with single, African American mothers raising children in the African American church tradition. The Canaanite woman is marginalized as single mothers are marginalized in the African American church. Dickerson provides a liberative reading of the account of the Canaanite woman in order to critique the dominant image of family as the patriarchal family and to welcome a variety of family models. As Matthew suggests that family includes those beyond biological kin, so Dickerson suggests the family model does the same.

While Dickerson connects the Canaanite woman with single mothers and the view of family, Crowder reads the Canaanite woman as a working mom. She explores a variety of vibrant images of black working mothers and their place in society as women and ethnic minorities. Crowder identifies her own grappling with working while mothering her children. The Canaanite woman is a mother who goes to work outside the home on behalf of her sick daughter and who also challenges racial and gender boundaries in the larger society. The story of the Canaanite women, interpreted from a womanist, maternal, theological approach, raises questions about intersections of family and career, class issues between black women, and child-care issues.

Tsui-yuk Louise Liu also addresses working mothers, but in the context of the international city of Hong Kong. She explores the unique uses of mother in Matthew in light of the disenfranchisement of mother-child intimacy in the Hong Kong church and larger society. In Hong Kong, the fertility rate is low, the demand for women in the labor force and for foreign domestic helpers is increasing, and breastfeeding rates are low. Matthew also exhibits the disenfranchisement of mother-child intimacy with the massacre of the boys in Bethlehem and the death of Mary's son, but the book also shows the intimacy and protection that mothers provide for their children.

Switching from mothers to fathers, Sung Uk Lim examines Jesus' suffering in Gethsemane from the perspective of the emotional suffering of a pastor's kid in a patriarchal Christian family in Korea. Drawing from the structural semiotic model of A. J. Greimas and from the Korean concepts of *han* ("suffering") and *jeong* ("power of healing or reconciliation"), Lim explores how a reader might come to understand Jesus' transformation from the feeling of sorrow to his decision to obey his father's will and the realization of his father's love. So also a pastor's kid in Korea might see how his own *han* is transformed into reconciliation with his father (the pastor) through the discovery of his father's *jeong*.

Two chapters address disability and culture. James Metzger and James Grimshaw, from different perspectives, read several healing stories in Matthew that focus on characters with chronic pain (several of which are in the context of father-son relationships, as Lim discusses). Metzger, who has a rheumatic condition, appreciates Jesus' sensitivity and responsiveness to those characters with aversive chronic pain. He finds troubling, however, the lack of attention given to the experience of the disabled, the portrayal of the impairment as a deficit to be remediated, and the reinforcement of the link between sin and disability. Grimshaw, a male caregiver whose wife has rheumatoid arthritis, perceives an emphasis on hypermasculinity as Jesus and male caregivers take extreme measures to eliminate the disabilities instead of learning to manage them in community. He connects with the caregivers, however, in their concern and tenacity to find relief for those they care for. L. J. Lawrence, a hearing academic who has worked among Deaf groups, interprets the Gospel of Matthew from the perspective of Deaf culture. She first offers a resistant reading and identifies many aspects of Matthew as audiocentric, which serves to marginalize the Deaf community. But she then turns toward a more sympathetic reading and finds several key features in the Gospel that can affirm Deaf culture: vision and sight, minority culture status, strong collective identity, and storytelling elements.

Readings from South Africa, Hong Kong, and China examine laborers and empire. Gerald West and Sithembiso Zwane read Matt. 20:1-16 with casual workers in South Africa. Taking seriously both the details of the text and their own experiences of the socioeconomic inequalities in their country, they explore two primary readings of the text. One interpretation views the parable as an egalitarian socialist vision. A second interpretation is a critique by Jesus of the arbitrary and discriminating practices of "capitalist" landowners. Instead of favoring one reading over another, they value each reading as it helps them imagine and plan for transformation.

Lung-pun Common Chan recontextualizes the Matthean apocalypse in globalized Hong Kong. In Matthew 24–25, Chan see a critique of the larger, Roman imperial context (for example, the materialistic temple and the exploitation of workers and slaves) and a challenge to prepare for Jesus' return and the new world. Chan, then, critiques the global economic and political context of Hong Kong and challenges Hong Kong middle-class churches to be a force for social change by responding to the devastating problems of economic globalization (for example, global structural poverty and abuse of foreign domestic helpers).

From the perspective of a Chinese Christian scholar, John Yieh interprets two passages from the Sermon on the Mount in light of China's growing global economy and accompanying challenges of greed and exploitation. Yieh reads the passages on loving your enemies (5:38-48) and trusting God (6:19-34) in a tug-of-war dialectical process with the original context, historic interpretations, and China's cultural and socioeconomic contexts. His goal is to see how Jesus' teaching on these passages may be a helpful resource for confronting the social and economic challenges of China and may likewise challenge those in the Christian West on social ethics and economic justice.

While the first section of the volume acknowledges the importance of beginnings to revive communities, the final section negotiates the borders that threaten communities. The first two authors discuss issues around land and disputed boundaries. Dorothy Jean Weaver, like Yieh, interprets Matt. 5:38-42. As part of the North American Mennonite community, Weaver is interested in questions of violence and nonviolence, and she traveled to the West Bank and Jerusalem to interview Palestinian Christians on their view of the Matthean Jesus' commands "do not resist the one who is evil" and "love your enemies." These conversations took place in the midst of walls and roadblocks and military checkpoints that separate religious communities. Elaine Wainwright's ecological reading interprets Matt. 4:1-11 in light of the devastating effects of climate change in Oceania, where she lives. Her reading challenges the artificial and unjust boundaries that are often articulated among God, humans, and the earth. For example, "God with us" is God with the earth community, not just the human community. Refocusing the reading process toward the earth can lead to a greater consideration of just interrelationships between God and earth (which includes humanity) and can lead to ethical action.

The final two essays examine strained borders within the Americas. Francisco Lozada explores the process of translation from a Latino/a perspective with a focus on the Lord's Prayer (Matt. 6:9b-13). Between two cultures himself, Lozada examines the complex and often uncomfortable intersection of translation, language, identity, and culture—an intersection that usually involves a hierarchical dynamic. In the act of translation, different sets of borders are crossed. Translation occurs between two cultures and even subcultures, is influenced through history, and involves a complex relationship between translator and text. Jeannine Brown assesses how her own tradition of white, middle-class, evangelicals in the United States interprets Matt. 25:31-46, the parable of the sheep and the goats. She questions the individualistic interpretations of her own tradition of maintaining boundaries and separation between those with power and the "least of these," while other voices, some emerging within her own tradition, emphasize solidarity between us and other.

Over a two-year period, these readings on Matthew emerged through many presentations and discussions at the Society of Biblical Literature meetings. This volume could be used in a variety of ways—and we hope it is. It might be a good conversation starter for the classroom, helping students see how readers from different cultures and perspectives read the same theme or even read the same texts. For example, Novakovic and Draper both read the genealogy. The story of the Canaanite woman is interpreted quite differently by Crowder and Dickerson. Betsworth and Liu interpret the mother-and-child relationship in Matthew 1-2. The same healing stories are read by Metzger and Grimshaw from different life circumstances. And Yieh and Weaver discuss the same passage in the Sermon on the Mount.

The volume can also be used to demonstrate once again that the contexts of interpreters matter. Perhaps this volume provides a small glimpse of how

Matthew, the church's book, has already become the world's book that it seems to have wanted to be.

PART I

Community and Beginnings

Rereading the Past

Memory and Identity in Post-Communist Croatia and the Genealogy of Jesus in the Gospel of Matthew

Lidija Novakovic

INTRODUCTION

The relationship of groups and individuals to their own history is a complex process. As much as "we investigate and analyze our past in order to understand who we are in the present" (Williams 2002: 105–6), our understanding of who we are in the present influences the way we investigate and analyze our past. Moreover, we have access to the past only as the past has been remembered by various groups and individuals. As we access the available historical records, we engage in the process of their reinterpretation, especially as we assess their significance for the present. This assessment includes not only an evaluation of the existing evidence but also a selection of the data that will be moved to the center of our historical consciousness and that will be consequently pushed to its margins.

In stable environments, we might not always be aware of such selection and reevaluation of the past. But in times of transition, when the old ways of life and understandings of the world are being replaced by new ones, the selective task inherent in historiographical enterprise is more noticeable (Hajdinjak 2006: 2). I come from Croatia, a country that has recently gone through a transition from Communism to democracy. Although I now live and work in the United States, I continue to take a keen interest in social and political changes that are taking place in my home country. This interest makes me more attentive to other transitional processes and the role that the reinterpretation of the past plays in them. Jesus' genealogy in the Gospel of Matthew is one such text, one that bears witness to a transition from early Judaism to emerging Christianity.

Its placement at the beginning of Matthew's Gospel, and eventually at the beginning of the New Testament canon, reinforces its transitional character. It functions as a bridge between the old and the new, and it accomplishes this task through the rereading of the past.

In this article, I explore the Matthean genealogy of Jesus from the perspective of the insights gained in post-Communist Croatia, particularly with regard to the transformation of its collective memory and identity. The categories of social and collective memory are slowly, but persistently, making inroads into Gospel studies (Schröter 1997: 462–66; Kirk and Thatcher 2005; Horsley, Draper, and Foley 2006; Barton, Stuckenbruck, and Wold 2007). In his study of the role of social memory in the Matthean community, Samuel Byrskog calls attention to "the dynamics involved as the early Christians struggled to find their identity in relation to the history which they cherished and performed" (Byrskog 2006: 320–21). He concludes that the retelling or reoralization of the Markan narrative created the sense of belonging and internal cohesion of the group (Byrskog 2006: 335–36). The topic of this article is somewhat different. Rather than asking about how the social context of the Matthean community shaped its memory of Jesus' ministry, death, and resurrection, I wish to focus on the question of how the Matthean community remembered its distant past, that is, the history of Israel and its relation to the birth of Jesus. Such activity presumes the availability of various, primarily written, records and an evaluative process of their selection. Jesus' genealogy, strategically placed at the beginning of Matthew's narrative about his life, death, and resurrection, offers a window into the way the collective memory of Israel's past shaped the identity of the Matthean community.

I will begin my analysis by offering a brief survey of various strategies of rereading the past that have been employed in post-Communist Croatia. I believe that this context offers a modern, albeit odd, analogy to the strategies of rereading the past practiced in the Matthean community. I will then turn to the reinterpretation of Israel's history in the Matthean genealogy. Special attention will be given to the question of how the memory of several extraordinary women who are mentioned in the genealogy shapes the identity of the Matthean community.

MEMORY AND IDENTITY IN POST-COMMUNIST CROATIA

Croatia, like other post-Communist countries, experienced a rapid transformation of its social and political structures. The modification of shared memory played a significant part in the transition from Communism to democracy. Such intentional revision of group memory was nothing new for people in the Balkans. During the Communist regime, state propaganda officially "erased" the memory of ethnic tensions between various national groups living in former Yugoslavia and imposed the memory of "Brotherhood and Unity" as a universally accepted truth. During the wars of the 1990s, unresolved ethnic tensions among Serbs, Croats, and Muslims were mercilessly exploited by various nationalistic leaders with the help of resurrected memories of each group's victimization by other group(s).

After the war, Croatian leaders engaged in a radical reevaluation of the past, in order to modify the common perception of national belonging and identity. This reinterpretation of the collective heritage included setting aside existing memories and substituting new, more appropriate memories for them. These new traditions, as Marko Hajdinjak notes, are typically based on "traditions popular before the regime just overthrown took power, preferably in the society's 'Golden Age.' Thus all traces of the *ancien regime* are erased and the successor legitimized" (Hajdinjak 2006: 3). Hajdinjak adds that

> members do not have to perceive the myth to be historically accurate. It is enough that they accept the content and the message of the myth and the myth will successfully perform its main task of establishing the connection between members of the society. . . . Myths and mythic histories bring the collective heritage back to life and are therefore essential in identifying "who we are." (Hajdinjak 2006: 3)[1]

As a result, a new symbolic world was created with the purpose of legitimizing the new regime and making a clear break between Communist and democratic Croatian national identity. This was accomplished through a variety of means, such as the creation of new myths, the renaming of streets and city squares, the erection of new monuments, the rewriting of history textbooks, and public recognition of the victims of Communism.

One of the most popular ways, especially in the 1990s, of using certain historical events for the purpose of shaping national identity was to present specific periods of Croatia's heroic past as the golden age. Anthony Smith explains that the past events selected to serve this function must be authentic, inspirational, and repeatable. They must not only provide the citizens with a sense of national pride but also inspire them to act in a certain way in order to re-create the past glory (Smith 1997: 55–59). For example, in his speech to the Croatian Parliament delivered on December 22, 1990, President Tudjman emphasized that the Croatian state had never ceased to exist from its formation as an independent medieval kingdom until it became a part of the kingdom of Serbs, Croats, and Slovenes in 1918. He also drew a sharp distinction between the West-oriented Croats and the half-Oriental Serbs (Trifunovska 1994). Likewise, the Croatian constitution links the declaration of Croatian sovereignty to a "millennial national identity of the Croatian nation and the continuity of its statehood" for more than 1,300 years.[2]

Another way of shaping national identity in post-Communist Croatia was through the renaming of streets and squares. For example, "The Square of the Victims of Fascism" became "The Square of the Croatian Heroes." A large statue of *Ban* ("governor") Josip Jelačić on a horse, originally erected in 1866 by the Austrian authorities at the central square of the city of Zagreb and then removed in 1947 by Yugoslav Communist authorities, was returned to its original location in 1990 by the new Croatian government as a memorial of Croatian national identity. The square itself, originally named after Ban Jelačić, was renamed during the Communist regime as "Republic Square." With the reinstallation of the Ban Jelačić statue in 1990, the name of the square was again changed to its former designation, "Ban Jelačić Square." Because of Jelačić's antirevolutionary stance during the 1848 revolution in the Austro-Hungarian Empire, the Communist regime denounced him as an Austrian collaborator. Yet, because of his desire—even if miscalculated—to maintain Croatian autonomy, in post-Communist Croatia his statue at the main city square became a memorial to all past longings for independence and a powerful symbol of their realization in the present (Tanner 1997: 90–93). New holidays such as "Independence Day" and "Statehood Day" replaced the old ones, such as "Republic Day," "Fighter's Day," and "Day of Uprising in Croatia," which celebrated the formation of Yugoslavia and antifascist resistance during World War II.

These changes in the perception of the Croatian distant and recent past have also affected historiography. Some Croatian historians, such as Neven Budak, believe that "the communist period influenced historical writing only marginally" so that no significant revision is needed (Budak 2004: 128). Others, such as Jure Krišto, argue that history books need to be revised in light of Croatian independence (Krišto 2001: 165–89). These differences in the assessment of Croatian historiography are partially the result of an ongoing competition between the Department of History, whose members are sometimes accused of having Communist backgrounds, and the Croatian Institute of History, which is sometimes regarded as a center of nationalism and historical revisionism (Budak 2004: 155–58). As time passes, however, it is becoming increasingly clear that different voices in the interpretation of history are welcome. While in the 1990s the political abuse of historiography was a common occurrence, Croatian historians are now more aware of the danger of interpreting history for purely ideological and/or political purposes (Senjković 2002).

One aspect of the rereading of the Croatian past is particularly worth mentioning: the rehabilitation and new appreciation of the victims of Communism. The case of Croatian archbishop (later cardinal) Aloysius Stepinac illustrates the complexity of such a process.[3] During World War II, Archbishop Stepinac helped numerous Jews and other victims of fascism escape Nazi persecution, either by direct action or by instructions given to Croatian clergymen. Yet, the new Communist government under Josip Broz Tito used Stepinac's initial tolerance of the Ustashi-led Independent State of Croatia during World War II as a pretext for accusing him of collaboration with the Nazis and complicity in the forced conversion of Orthodox Serbs to Catholicism. Despite objections from the pope and numerous members of the Jewish community, Stepinac was tried and then sentenced to sixteen years of imprisonment. Because of his poor health, he was moved in 1951 from prison to house arrest. The following year, he was declared cardinal by Pope Pius XII. He died in 1960. During the entire Communist period, he was always described as a Nazi collaborator. At the same time, however, an alternative memory of his role in World War II—one that stressed his resistance to fascism and cherished him as a martyr of Communism—was kept alive by the Catholic Church. In post-Communist Croatia, this alternative memory acquired significant visibility. In 1992, the Croatian Sabor passed a declaration that condemned the court decision against Stepinac and claimed that the true reasons for the trial and eventual verdict were Stepinac's criticism of Communist crimes and his refusal to allow the Catholic Church in Croatia to break with Rome. In 1998, Pope John Paul II declared him a martyr and beatified him. In 2007, the municipality of Marija Bistrica began to build pilgrimage paths linking places significant to his life. In the same year, the Aloysius Stepinac Museum was opened in Zagreb. In February 2010, on the fiftieth anniversary of Stepinac's death, several Masses were celebrated in his memory: in Zagreb, in Krašić, and in Rome.

One of the most helpful theoretical models for understanding the changes in post-Communist Croatia pertaining to the perception of its own past is provided through the concepts of social, collective, and cultural memory as developed by Maurice Halbwachs and Jan and Aleida Assmann (Halbwachs 1925; 1992; Assmann 2006b: 1–30; 2006a: 67–82). Halbwachs claimed that memory is socially conditioned and socially mediated. Jan Assmann, who further refined the communicative aspect of social memory, explained that

> for a functioning communicative memory, forgetting is just as vital as remembering. This is why it is not "photographic." Remembering means pushing other things into the background, making distinctions, obliterating many things in order to shed light on others. This is what brings horizon and perspective into individual memory spaces, and these perspectives are emotionally mediated. (Assmann 2006b: 3)

Yet, on a communal level, it is not sufficient to speak merely about the social or communicative aspect of individual memory, but also about the memory that provides a collective sense of identity to the members of a given group. Assmann calls this memory "collective memory," and points out that this type of memory "is particularly susceptible to politicized forms of remembering." Unlike social memory, which develops and then disappears gradually, collective memory is a willed memory, "a projection on the part of the collective that wishes to remember and of the individual who remembers in order to belong" (Assmann 2006b: 7). This endeavor consists of an examination of cultural traditions, symbols, and myths, including the great stories of the past that can be reactivated or deactivated intentionally in a group's collective memory. Not surprisingly, then, Assmann describes this memory as a "memory of the will" and further qualifies it as "cultural memory." Its repertoire is not limited to a horizontal memory that encompasses only two to three generations, but includes long-term traditions stretching vertically through multiple generations, which are preserved in all kinds of historical records (Assmann 2006b: 7–8). In written cultures, this repository of the past includes numerous written records that can be revisited at will, allowing a selection between the information that is needed and the information that is no longer needed in a given moment. Aleida Assmann calls the information about the past that is needed in the present "functional memory" and the information about the past that is no longer needed "stored memory," and alleges that constant shifting between the two is "the precondition of the possibility of change and renewal" (Assmann 1999: 136).

The concept of collective/cultural memory is easily applicable to the reinterpretation of history in post-Communist Croatia. Typically, the individuals who are brought to collective consciousness are those who struggled, even if unsuccessfully, to achieve Croatian independence. What makes them especially interesting for the present study is the fact that some of them, such as Aloysius Stepinac, have been, and remain, quite controversial in the wider public perception. Yet there is a persistent effort to clear them of false accusations, to bypass their potentially embarrassing deeds, and to present them as Croatian heroes. Alongside the public endeavors to elevate selected personalities and events from Croatia's glorious past to functional memory are systematic efforts to forget Croatia's most immediate past—the one under the Communist regime. The events that took place during the Communist era are, in terms of collective memory, relegated to stored memory. What shapes collective consciousness and identity is a reactivated memory of the events that led to Croatian independence, not the memory of the events that detracted from this goal. One can therefore say that the rereading of the past in modern Croatia takes place from the perspective of an ultimate realization of its ancient dreams.

MEMORY OF THE PAST IN THE MATTHEAN GENEALOGY

I wish to propose that a similar understanding of history—one that rereads the past from the perspective of its ultimate realization in Jesus the Messiah—is operative in the Matthean genealogy of Jesus. Some interpreters presume that the primary purpose of the genealogy is to justify Jesus' questionable birth and claim to messiahship. Such apologetic aims are certainly suitable for polemical contexts, in which one group has to defend its truth claims against charges of distortion raised by a rival group. Indeed, in view of the tension, even hostility, between the Matthean community and an emerging rabbinic Judaism, these objectives cannot be excluded (Overman 1990: 72–149). It is, however, questionable whether sexual irregularities associated with the four women mentioned in the genealogy could really provide compelling arguments for Mary's defense in the controversies surrounding Jesus' birth. As several scholars have noted, it is more likely that they would have provoked such controversies rather than assuage them (Johnson 1969: 148; Harrington 1991a: 32; Levine 1998: 340). It is therefore arguable that the primary purpose of the Matthean genealogy is not to defend but to explain the past from the perspective of an already achieved goal. It is written for insiders, not outsiders, who share the conviction that their hope for a Davidic Messiah has finally been realized. In this role, the genealogy restructures collective memory by moving some individuals from Israel's past to the foreground, while pushing others to the background. With this, certain parts of Israel's history are moved to functional memory, while others are relegated to stored memory.

The above comments presume that Jesus' genealogy in Matt. 1:2-17 functions not only as his family tree but also as a mnemonic device that points to a larger narrative of Israel's past. Strictly speaking, the main task of genealogies, as a distinct literary genre, is to explain the origin of persons by providing their lineage. The Matthean genealogy belongs to a subgroup of linear genealogies, which link an individual to an earlier ancestor through a vertical list of names. Yet, unlike Jesus' genealogy in Luke 3:23-38, which exemplifies a pure form of linear genealogy, the Matthean genealogy contains several extraneous features that indicate an interest in more than mere ancestry. First, the genealogy is formally structured into three sections of equal length, each consisting of fourteen generations.[4] Second, it follows the royal Davidic line, providing the list of David's ancestors in the first division, and the lists of his descendants in the second and third divisions. Third, the qualification "the king," added after David's name in Matt. 1:6, functions as a divider between the first and the second section, while the comments "at the time of the deportation to Babylon" (1:11) and "after the deportation to Babylon" (1:12) create a dividing line between the second and the third section. Fourth, most of the names that appear in the first and the second sections of the genealogy belong to prominent personalities from Israel's sacred history. It is, for example, difficult to imagine anyone familiar with Israel's Scripture who would not hear echoes of patriarchal narratives at the mention of the names of Abraham, Isaac, and Jacob, or who would fail to recall David's rise to power and God's promise of the permanency of the Davidic dynasty at the mention of David's name. Fifth, the genealogy expands the straightforward vertical line of descendants by three horizontal extensions: Matt. 1:2 adds that Jacob was the father not only of Judah but also of his brothers, Matt. 1:3 adds that Judah was the father of Perez and Zerah, and Matt. 1:11 adds that Josiah was the father of Jechoniah and his brothers. These expansions indicate that Jesus belongs not only to a particular family but also to Israel as a nation. Sixth, four women are added to the list of Jesus' male ancestors. These women are not the well-known matriarchs of Israel's past, but are of a decidedly ambiguous reputation, either because of their irregular and potentially scandalous sexual unions or because of their non-Jewish origin. Finally, the genealogy ends with another woman, Mary, and the remark that she gave birth to Jesus, "who is called the Messiah." Each of these supplementary features contributes to the overall impression that the Matthean genealogy offers not only Jesus' lineage but also a distinctive reinterpretation of Israel's history (Smit 2010: 194; Nolland 1997: 529).

Matthew's interest in Israel's history is in continuity with biblical interest in history. Yosef Hayim Yerushalmi explains:

The biblical appeal to remember . . . has little to do with curiosity
about the past. Israel is told only that it must be a kingdom of priests
and a holy people; nowhere is it suggested that it become a nation
of historians. Memory is, by its nature, selective, and the demand
that Israel remember is no exception. . . . The fact that history has
meaning does not mean that everything that happened in history is
meaningful or worthy of recollection. (Yerushalmi 1982: 10)

By the time of the writing of Matthew's Gospel, the accounts of the selected,
and thus meaningful, events of Israel's past had become part of the sacred
texts that had already achieved a relatively fixed form, as well as scriptural
status. The literature produced in the Second Temple period and in early
rabbinic Judaism indicates that Jews continued to interpret the stories of their
sacred past. The New Testament authors engaged in a similar endeavor, as
they tried to articulate the relationship of early Christian communities to their
Jewish heritage. Matthew's genealogy of Jesus offers us a glimpse into the way
his community reread the past. It selectively remembered those individuals
and events that prefigured the appearance of Jesus. The central place in the
genealogy belongs to Israel's and, after the schism, Judah's golden age, that is,
the appearance and glory of the Davidic monarchy. The best-known kings
from the Davidic line are evoked. Moreover, some adjustments are made,
such as making Josiah the father of his grandson Jechoniah (Matt. 1:11), in
order to make the total number fit the overall scheme of fourteen generations.
Matthew is clearly not interested in producing comprehensive historiography
but rather a selective memory of Israel's past. Equally central to his assessment of
history is the loss of past glory. In the economy of words that characterizes the
genealogical genre, Matthew's double mention of the deportation to Babylon
(vv. 11-12) catches the reader's attention. In view of the prominence given to
the Davidic monarchy, the mention of its demise raises a theological question
that most likely underlies Matthew's summation of Israel's history: If God
promised David an everlasting kingdom, why does it no longer exist?
Matthew's answer is relatively simple: the disappearance of the Davidic
monarchy was only temporary. God has remained faithful to his promises to
David and has fulfilled them, once for all, in the appearance of Jesus, the Davidic
Messiah.

Women in the Genealogy and the Identity
of the Matthean Community

The above conclusion must be qualified in light of one of the most striking features of the Matthean genealogy: the mention of five women, four from Israel's distant past and one from the community's recent experience. Even though women rarely appear in genealogies, they are sometimes included to clarify a particular genealogical line or to emphasize a person's distinguished birth. Neither of these reasons seems to be operative in the Matthean genealogy. The four women from Israel's distant past are associated with objectionable sexual behavior and/or perceived as gentiles. Tamar, either a Canaanite or an Aramean,[5] dressed as a prostitute and seduced her father-in-law Judah in order to get pregnant. Rahab, a Canaanite, was a former prostitute.[6] Ruth, a Moabite, enticed Boaz before he took her in marriage. The reference to Bathsheba, which identifies her as "the wife of Uriah," reminds the reader that she was wife of a foreign mercenary, a Hittite, when she committed adultery with David. Yet, none of this directly applies to the fifth woman, the mother of Jesus. She conceived a child without a male partner, and she was Jewish.

Various explanations have been offered for why these women are included. Some proposals seek to discover similarities between the first four women and Mary, while others relate specific traits that characterize them individually or as a group to the character of the Matthean community. Many scholars focus on the irregularities in these women's relationships and argue that they anticipate the irregularity in Mary's pregnancy. According to Peter-Ben Smit, who has offered the most recent version of this theory, the concept of "irregular relationships" enables scholars to describe the common denominator of all five women "in neutral terms" (Smit 2010: 194–95). A theological version of this explanation is that the irregular and potentially scandalous behavior of these women, especially their extraordinary initiative in overcoming various obstacles, demonstrates that God sometimes uses unconventional means to achieve his goals in this world—even as he did to bring about the birth of the promised Messiah (Waetjen 1976: 215–16; Davies and Allison 1988, 1:171–72; Brown 1999: 74). Jane Schaberg and Elaine Wainwright interpret the irregular relationships of the women in Matthew's genealogy as specific acts that endanger patriarchal structure (Schaberg 1990: 32–33; Wainwright 1991: 61–69, 156–71). Each woman takes steps outside of the legitimate patriarchal framework, which defines women in relation to men. Their actions are against the prevailing norms and thus subversive. Amy-Jill Levine, in turn, interprets the irregular relationships of the women in the genealogy in terms of the social categories of marginals and elites. Unlike the powerful males who fail to fulfill their responsibilities in the salvation history, the women, a socioeconomically powerless group of characters, become the examples of "higher righteousness" demanded by Jesus in Matt. 5:20 (Levine 1988: 80–88). In contrast, scholars who focus on the ethnic background of Tamar, Rahab, Ruth, and Bathsheba emphasize that their gentile origin anticipates the inclusion of gentiles into Matthew's predominantly Jewish Christian community (Johnson 1969: 153–55; Luz 2007: 84–85).

None of these explanations entirely satisfies. The differences among the women in the genealogy weigh against their similarities (Luz 2007: 84). A gentile origin of all four women is difficult to establish. To speak about their irregular relationships is too general. Only Tamar's twins were conceived out of wedlock. Regardless of their questionable past, the other three women were married when they became pregnant with the children mentioned in the genealogy. It is therefore not surprising that some scholars hesitate to offer a single explanation and claim that more than one solution is possible (Carter 2000: 61). Indeed, it is not very convincing to suggest that there is only one reason for the inclusion of these women in Jesus' genealogy. Without an accompanying narrative, a mere list of names of otherwise ambiguous characters will always evoke a variety of associations depending on the prior knowledge and presumptions of the audience. In what follows, rather than offer yet another interpretation of the inclusion of the women in the genealogy, I wish to offer another perspective from which the previously proposed solutions might be viewed.

If Matthew "views Israel's history both in the light of Jesus and Jesus in the light of the history of Israel" (Smit 2010: 202), then the ending of the genealogy sheds light on the women in the genealogy as much as they shed light on the ending. It is quite striking that, in addition to the irregular nature of their sexual unions and their non-Jewish origins, the first four women are not evenly distributed—they appear only in the segment that begins with Judah and ends with David and Solomon. The irregularities that are associated with the relationships of the first four women are thus channeled through the royal Davidic line. Matthew's scheme is certainly strengthened by the already existing traditions about these women, most of whom were cleared of any guilt and were even praised in contemporary Jewish literature.[7] These four women, suspected yet vindicated, directly bring about the appearance of David "the king." One could say that without them, the kingdom of David and Solomon would not have arisen. Mary appears at an equally strategic place in the genealogy. Her irregular pregnancy brings about the appearance of the Messiah, the "Son of David," who will finally fulfill God's promise of the permanency of the Davidic dynasty. By overcoming different obstacles, each of these women contributed to the realization of history's ultimate goal.

At the same time, however, there is an aspect of the Matthean genealogy that has only occasionally been considered. As the "enlarged footnote" (Stendahl, 1960: 61) of the genealogy (Matt. 1:18-25) indicates, Mary's irregular pregnancy puts her and her unborn child in a dangerous position. Joseph, suspecting adultery, "resolved to divorce her quietly" (Matt 1:19). Beverly Roberts Gaventa notes that "Joseph poses a threat to Mary (and, by implication, to Jesus as well), just as circumstances have threatened several significant women in Israel's history (and, by implication, their offspring and the line of David)" (Gaventa 1999: 31). Even after Joseph abandons this plan and eventually adopts the newborn, another danger befalls "the child and his mother" (Matt. 2:13-14, 20-21). King Herod and then his son Archelaus seek to kill the infant Jesus. Only with the help of divine guidance is the life of the royal child preserved. If the endangered existence of the infant Jesus in Matthew reflects the endangered existence of the Matthean community vis-à-vis the emerging rabbinic Judaism and Roman imperial propaganda, it might offer us another glimpse into the perspective from which the members of the Matthean community reread the past. As much as they were convinced that the promises to David had been finally realized in the appearance of Jesus, the Davidic Messiah, they were not oblivious to the perils of their actual existence. Mary's baby is indeed the royal child, but his life is threatened by the powers that be.[8] If so, the four women from Israel's distant past prefigure not only the irregularity of Mary's pregnancy but also the threat to her life and the life of her son (Gaventa 1999: 38–39). Past events that anticipate the current community's experience are relocated to functional memory, elucidating present circumstances and shaping the community's sense of identity in relationship to Israel's sacred history. If Matthew's Gospel, as a whole, "legitimates a *marginal* identity and way of life for the community of disciples," as Warren Carter suggests, then the visibility given to five endangered women legitimates the alternative identity of the Matthean community, which is shaped by tension with a synagogue community and imperial Rome.[9] By reaccentuating the basic outline of Israel's past, Matthew incorporates the experience of his own community into the movement of Israel's history toward its ultimate goal.

The last question to be considered here is the question of omissions. If some women were included, why were others, better known and more respected, passed over in silence? Sarah, Rebekah, Leah, and Rachel have also shown initiative in overcoming the obstacles on their path to motherhood. Yet none of them is named in the genealogy. Carter suggests that the omission of their names carries no particular significance because the naming of the four women that appear in the genealogy "reminds the audience of other unnamed women like Sarah, Rebekah, Leah, and numerous others who played important roles in Israel's history but are not named specifically in the genealogy" (Carter 2000: 59). Likewise, Irene Nowell argues that four women in the genealogy "remind us to look at *all* the women in the line that leads to Jesus" (Nowell 2008: 2).[10] She adds eight more women to Matthew's four: Sarah, Rebekah, Leah, and Athaliah, who belong directly to Jesus' family tree, and Jezebel, Naamah, Lot's daughters, and Lot's wife, who belong indirectly to Jesus' family tree. Nowell contends that these women share several commonalities with the four that are explicitly mentioned: many of them were considered sinners and foreigners; they struggled with pregnancies and childbirth issues; they were endangered and rejected; and they used unconventional means, even disguise and deceit, to achieve their objectives. She concludes "that the four women in Matthew's genealogy are there not because they are different but because they are representatives of all Jesus' great-grandmothers: women who have endured discrimination and false judgment, who have suffered through difficult pregnancies and childbirth, and who know how to use devious means to achieve their purposes" (Nowell 2008: 15).

One wonders, however, whether Matthew's audience would have been able to catch so many intertextual echoes as Nowell suggests. Her thesis requires an extraordinarily well-versed reader who is able to evoke an entire web of associations about various biblical personalities who are related to each other, however loosely. Yet readers typically pay attention to what the text explicates and disregard what the text leaves out. If the things that are passed over in silence belong to a repository of knowledge that is otherwise available to the reader, such as the biblical records, they will not be entirely forgotten but only relocated to a stored memory. I propose that the absence of other women's names in the genealogy functions in exactly this way. The stories about the patriarchal wives, most of whom struggled with barrenness and childbearing, belonged to the stored memory of the Matthean community and as such had no direct formative influence on its identity.[11] What shaped the identity of Matthew's readers was the functional memory of several endangered, mostly foreign, women whose irregular relationships brought about the appearance of the Davidic kingdom and, after its temporary downfall, effected its final realization in the Messiah, the Son of David.

Conclusion

In what ways, then, does the rereading of the past in post-Communist Croatia shed light on the rereading of the past in Matthew's genealogy? The analysis of the various forms of reshaping collective memory that took place in the transition from Communism to democracy helps us better recognize the various forms of reshaping collective memory in other transitional processes, such as the emergence of early Christianity. The methods employed in Croatia were far-reaching and thorough, with the purpose of making a radical break with the Communist past. The erasure of the names of the Communist heroes from public buildings and streets was one of the most effective means of facilitating public forgetting. That does not mean that the Communist past had been erased from history books, state archives, or public discourse. But a removal of public memorials of this part of Croatia's history significantly reduces its power in shaping Croatian collective identity. Memories that are reactivated are the memories of the events and persons from the heroic past that anticipated Croatia's political independence. Even if some of these individuals had controversial reputations during the Communist regime, their current visibility exonerates them in the public eye and highlights their contribution to Croatian national identity.

Jesus' genealogy in the Gospel of Matthew is far less radical in its configuration and purpose. Matthew's community undeniably saw its own history in continuity with Israel's history. There are, it seems, no conscious efforts to erase certain periods of the past, even the most painful and embarrassing ones. And yet, one cannot overlook a number of devices employed by the author, which either emphasize or deemphasize certain aspects of Israel's history. One of the most noticeable aspects of the genealogy is the central place given to the Davidic dynasty and the individuals, including four controversial women, who led to its realization. In this way, the ambiguities related to their sexual conduct and/or gentile origin are productively utilized in the service of the genealogy's ultimate purpose—to demonstrate that Israel's entire history led to the birth of Jesus, the Davidic Messiah. This, however, does not mean that the author regards everything in Israel's history to be equally important for the realization of this goal. The struggles with barrenness of the patriarchal wives are, although not entirely forgotten, certainly deemphasized. Instead, the anxieties experienced by four extraordinary women, who acted beyond the prescribed framework of normalcy, are evoked through the mention of their names in an otherwise exclusively male family tree. Their stories prefigure not only the unusual pregnancy of the fifth woman in the genealogy but also the experience of the Matthean community. By bringing to mind certain individuals and overlooking others, the author restructures the collective memory of his community and creates what Aleida Assmann calls "the precondition of the possibility of change and renewal" (Assmann 1999: 136). Through the process of transferring selected events from Israel's past to functional memory and relocating others to stored memory, the Matthean community developed its distinctive identity over against the emerging rabbinic Judaism.

Notes

1. See also Smith 1986: 202.

2. "Constitution of the Republic of Croatia," in Trifunovska 1994: 251–52.

3. For a discussion of Stepinac's attitude during WWII, see Rychlak 2009: 367–83.

4. This is, at least, what the author claims in Matt. 1:17. In reality, however, the third division of the genealogy consists of only thirteen generations. For various explanations of this anomaly, see Novakovic 2003: 46–50.

5. *Jub.* 41:1 and *T. Jud.* 10:1 identify Tamar as a "daughter of Aram."

6. The unusual spelling of Rahab's name in the genealogy (Ραχάβ), unattested in other Greek sources, has generated some controversy regarding the identity of the person designated by it. Jerome D. Quinn (1981: 225–28) argues that this is an unknown woman and not the prostitute Rahab mentioned in Scripture. For a rebuttal, see Brown 1982: 79–80. Another problem related to Rahab is that her marriage to Salmon and parentage of Boaz is mentioned nowhere in the Old Testament or early Jewish literature. Richard Bauckham (1995: 323) proposes that Rahab's marriage to Salmon reflects the midrashic desire to find husbands for those female figures whose husbands are not specified in the Bible.

7. In Ruth 4:12, Tamar is mentioned with respect as the mother of the house of Perez. According to *T. Jud.* 12:1–3, she dressed herself as a bride and not as a prostitute and acted according to custom. A lengthy midrash in *Tg. Neof.* Gen 38:25 emphasizes God's involvement in Tamar's justification. Philo, *Congr.* 124–26, describes Tamar as a prototype of virtue and chastity. Pseudo-Philo, *Liber antiquitatum biblicarum* 9:5, points out that Tamar's motive was not fornication but avoidance of defilement through sexual relationship with gentiles. Rahab's faith and hospitality are emphasized in Heb. 11:31 and Jas. 2:25. According to Josephus, *Ant.* 5.1.2, Rahab was not a prostitute but an innkeeper. Josephus, *Ant.* 5.9.3, emphasizes Ruth's obedience to her mother-in-law and explains that nothing scandalous happened during the nocturnal encounter between her and Boaz.

8. This aspect of Matthew's infancy narrative is even more noticeable when compared with Luke's account of Jesus' birth. Even though the Lukan Jesus is born in modest circumstances and is visited by one of the lowliest social groups (the shepherds), his safety is not endangered. Joseph does not ponder divorce, and nobody seeks the life of the newborn. The Lukan baby Jesus might be poor, but his life is not jeopardized.

9. According to Carter (2000: 43–45), Matthew's community "lives as participants in the wider society, but in tension with, over against, as an alternative to its dominant values and structures."

10. See also Wainwright 1997: 463.

11. Matthew's lack of interest in the patriarchal wives is even more apparent if Ruth 4:11-12, 17-18 served as a source for his genealogy, because this text does include Rachel and Leah. Under this assumption, the omission of the names of Rachel and Leah, two well-known matriarchs, would have been intentional.

2

A South Africa Contextual Reading of Matthew 1:1-17

Jonathan A. Draper

INTRODUCTION

Raymond Brown, who begins his massive commentary on the birth narratives in Matthew and Luke with an examination of the genealogy in Matthew 1:1-17, comments:

> To the modern reader there are few things in the Bible less meaningful than the frequent lists of descendants or ancestors. Those who read the Bible from cover to cover tend to develop an elastic conscience when they come to the first nine chapters of I Chronicles. Genealogies often become the butt of risqué humor, as in the mockery from "Finian's Rainbow": once Adam and Eve ate from the apple tree, "they began the begat." (Brown 1999: 64)

Beyond the debate over the historical (in)accuracy of the genealogy, scholars find little to interest them.[1] This is not surprising, since genealogical myths construct a counter-reality to Western historicism, "Le travail sur le mythe est en quelque sorte une dénonciation de notre lecture de l'histoire et de notre façon de concevoir la réalité" (Decharneux 2008: 99).[2] As a contrast to the Western cultural prejudice against genealogies, we might cite the surprise expressed by the first missionaries to the Batswana people in the early nineteenth century, when they discovered that biblical genealogies were of great interest to African people. John Campbell, a director of the London Missionary Society, made a tour of inspection in 1812–1813 and reports on discussions with Chief Mothibi. The latter was unimpressed when told that the Bible explained the origin of all things, but he and his followers paid immediate and close attention once the list of Israelite ancestors Abraham, Ishmael, and Isaac began. Commenting on this, Gerald West observes:

> What impressed the Chief's uncle and his colleagues was not this claim to an all-encompassing origin, but the naming, maybe, of the missionaries' ancestors, Abraham, Ishmael, and Isaac, which is why "this appeared to them very interesting information, and they all tried to repeat the names we had mentioned, over and over again, looking to us for correction, if they pronounced any of them wrong. Muaneets, and the others who joined the company appeared anxious to have them fixed on their memories." Here then is another hint at how the Bible may have been apprehended by the Tlhaping: the book—the Bible—may have appeared , from the perspective of the Tlhaping, to contain the names of the missionaries' ancestors, and hence would have been a book of great value. (West 2004: 269–70)

This is to be expected, since veneration of the ancestors, understood as a continuing mutual relationship between the living and the living dead in an unbroken chain, is one of the central features of many, if not most, African cultures. It is no accident that the first book in isiZulu by a Zulu person, Magema Fuze's, *Abantu Abamnyama: Lapa Bavela Ngakona* (1922, the English translation by H. C. Lugg [much] edited by A. T. Cope is titled, *The Black People and Whence They Came* [1979]) is essentially concerned with origins and is replete with genealogies of the Zulu people and their leaders—which evoked distaste in colonial readers but much praise from his Zulu contemporaries, an evaluation that continues until today. The gap between reading the genealogy in the West and reading it in Africa is a stark reminder of the role of the context of the reader and, above all, the culture of the reader, in the production of meaning from a text.[3] Providing an "African reading" as a white South African male will, inevitably, open me up to well-justified critique and perhaps even ridicule. However, my own reading horizon is irrevocably shaped by a lifetime of living with, working with, and listening to Zulu people as a priest, as a lecturer, and as a friend, however imperfectly this has been done. My hope is that this study will be viewed simply as a voice in an ongoing conversation between the rich cultural tradition of Africa and the biblical text, which did not originate with me and will not end with me.

CONTEXT FOR AN AFRICAN READING OF MATTHEW 1:1-17

To be human is to be rooted in community, as is affirmed in the widespread saying in various languages of Africa, "A human being is a human being through other human beings." This belief is the core African value of what in Zulu and Xhosa is called *Ubuntu*, humanness, with its requisite ethical value of humane behavior. This community encompasses not only the present generation but also the previous ones. Knowledge of who one's ancestors are locates a person in a web of relationship to self and others, living and departed. Ogbu Kalu has noted that

> the reality of the dead-among-the-living attracts so much religious devotion that in many African societies the ancestors occupy more devotional attention than God/Supreme Being. In some communities, no cultic attention is paid to the divinities; in others the divinities are scions of the ancestral spirits for prediction and control of space-time events. (Kalu 2000: 54–55)

The obligation to remember and honor the ancestors necessitates the preservation of genealogies in various artistic forms, but above all in oral praise poetry, which is framed in a mnemonic fashion to facilitate performance. In Zulu and Xhosa culture, every person has his or her own praise names, beginning with ancestral praise names, which grow as the person acquires his or her own reputation and honor. However, the official performance of the praise poems of clans and chiefs requires professional expertise beyond the skill of ordinary praise.

In any case, the important thing is that genealogies are inherently linked to the veneration of the ancestors, the central "master myth" of (southern) African culture (Gee 1996: 86). This master myth underpinned the symbolic universe of African people, providing coherence, integration, and an ethical framework for human behavior and use of the environment. Breaches of taboos, community, customs, and morals were (are) held to be punished by ancestors with the intention of restoring community and equilibrium. Ancestor rituals and sacrifices provide(d) the means for reconciliation and renewal. It was also a belief and practice that Christian missionaries, whose conquest of African soil was accompanied by a conquest of African culture, condemned unequivocally. Some missionaries even equated the ancestors with harmful demonic spirits and forbade the practice of ancestor rituals, especially sacrifice (Dube 1999). This misunderstanding or even deliberate misrepresentation of the nature of ancestor veneration on the part of missionaries created a lasting social rupture and cultural dislocation for Africans, with associated ethical problems. The majority of Africans south of the Sahara today profess Christianity in some form or other—something like 80 percent of the South African population, at least—and may follow such official policies of the churches in public. But many continue to consult the ancestors through diviners and continue to sacrifice animals in their honor—to please or placate them or to obtain their intervention for healing or well being. Many African Initiated Churches openly seek to integrate traditional practice of the ancestral cult with Christian faith, but even where it is explicitly rejected, the ancestral cult finds its way into African church culture in other forms (for example, lists of ancestors read out at Mass in commemoration of the faithful departed on All Souls Day among Anglicans and Catholics, at least in South Africa).

While the belief in and practice of rituals having to do with ancestors cement communities together and provide continuity that is so essential to a practice of *Ubuntu*, they can also create problems by their limitation to particular family and clan loyalties. Their protection and benevolence is limited to their own kin. (The ancestors "acted as sub-patrons and protectors of individual families and clans" [Mafico 2000: 487].) Indeed, the isiZulu word for ancestors *amadlozi* means "sperm" in the closely related isiXhosa language, which highlights the quasi-physical nature of the relationship. Nevertheless, this is ameliorated in practice, since an adopted child, as indeed a bride, may be ritually "introduced" to the ancestors and become a part of the descent of the clan. However, this remains a problematic and debated element in African genealogies, at least if the discussions I have had with students in university seminars over many years are anything to go by. While Kwesi Dickson may argue that it is legitimate to describe and interpret Jesus as the "great Ancestor" and use that as a christological pivot point, others regard this as impossible, since he is not biological kin! (Dickson 1984).

For our purposes in interpreting Matt. 1:1-17, I would like to point to a few features of African genealogies, which may provide a context for an African interpretation. First, African genealogies are, of course, oral in composition and performance—at least in Africa south of the Sahara. Nevertheless, as Ruth Finnegan insists, there can be no rigid separation between orality and literacy. Instead there is considerable overlap and interaction, so that "the idea of pure and uncontaminated 'oral culture' . . . is a myth," and "the idea that the use of writing *automatically* deals a death blow to oral literary forms has nothing to support it" (Finnegan 1977: 23–24; cf. Opland 1983: 193–232). In the case of genealogies, there are official productions designed to validate the power holders of society of the "grand tradition," but there are also the continuing oral performances of genealogies by people of the "little tradition" often presenting a counter interpretation and counter-claims of the same material (Scott 1977:1–38, 211–46; cf. Vansina 1985: 98). Matthew's performance clearly draws on the written genealogies of the Hebrew Scriptures ("the great tradition"), but seems to share many of the characteristics of the orally performed family genealogies by which peasant families like those of Jesus formulated their identity and claimed their place in the heritage of Israel.

Second, studies of genealogies in oral cultures in Africa by Jan Vansina show that they are "notoriously unreliable" and that their interest is not historical or chronological or factual but social (Vansina 1985: 178). Moreover, the actual names given are largely irrelevant, except for the beginning and end of the genealogies, while "in the middle, one can omit or add names, without any consequences resulting" (Vansina 1985: 181). Moreover, in a largely oral context (as opposed to official lists in royal archives), genealogies are ever changing:

> Cumulative Accounts are accounts such as lists or genealogies which have to be continually updated. They form a basis for the local chronology by providing epochs, units of duration used to evaluate how far in the past something happened. But this is not why they exist. They are of direct relevance to the social structures today. Genealogies show what the relationships between contemporary groups and between individuals today are and when these change they are manipulated to reflect the new relationships. Hence their transmission has a strikingly different dynamic from that of other accounts and not only because names have to be added at birth. Lists of rulers exist to prove the continuity and to legitimate the institution of chieftainship, and justify why X occupies that office today and why he has the authority of the office. (Vansina 1985: 24)

This fluidity is apparent in the genealogy of Matthew (especially in comparison with that of Luke), as we shall see.

Third, performances of genealogies are highly formalized and stylized in order to facilitate memory and fluency, so that they are tightly linked to the vernacular culture:

> The requirements of genre mold the expression of the message. By knowing the genre well the historian will realize what is conventional in the expression and what is not, that is, on what he

or she should put weight and what should be considered general embroidery. When an item does not belong in a certain genre, but nevertheless occurs there, the message acquires unusual significance. (Vansina 1985: 81)

The unusual keys the hearer in to the particular message of a particular performance of the same tradition. Who is included in the list of ancestors and who is excluded and what is said about them is highly significant. So, for instance, Magema Fuze provides a genealogy of Shaka in which a praise song composed by one member of the lineage is held to prophesy the advent of Shaka and his construction of a major kingdom, but he also at the end gives the names of the two brothers of Shaka who succeeded him to the throne, Dingaan, who murdered him and Mpanda:

> I have already stated that Malandela begot Ntombela, Ntombela Zulu, Zulu Nkosinkulu, Nkosinkulu Mageba, Mageba Phunga, Phunga Ndaba. When Ndaba was still a boy who herded cattle along with the other boys of his age, he made a prediction through the song that he composed for himself and his age group, as follows: "Ndaba is a king! Oye! Ha! Oye!" But the song has since been changed and chanted as follows: "Ha! Oye! Ji ji ji!" All the words used in singing it have been dropped.[4] It was composed by Ndaba while still a herd-boy, foretelling that there would come forth from his descendants one who would rule many clans. And he, Ntaba begot Jama, Jama begot Senzangakhona, Senzangakhona begot Shaka, Dingane, Mpande, and other numerous sons. The advent of Shaka was as follows. . . . (Fuze 1922)[5]

Fuze often uses the philological derivation of the names to bring out the significance of their role in history, something not uncommon in Hebrew genealogy also. Hlonipha Mokoena comments on this feature of Fuze's genealogies:

> What is important is that Fuze was convinced enough by his method to repeat it and to reinforce its efficacy by continuously elaborating on the symbolism of names and naming. Moreover, this resort to onomastics is not about describing an immutable fatalism. Rather, Fuze used the names of kings to comment on the agency and political choices of the Zulu people and nobles. . . . In fact, one could argue that Fuze's histories of Zulu kings are about this tension

between fate and free will; or put differently, the pull between ancestry and innovation. (Mokoena 2010: 194–95)

This is, of course, very suggestive in terms of Matthew's methodology, where the genealogy concludes with the same "tension between fate and freewill" and concludes with the same use of onomastics.

In Zulu and Xhosa praise poems (*izibonga*), which combine genealogical material and short stylized narrative of associated deeds and circumstances, the performance of a genealogy or praises of a particular powerful person can contain considerable elements of social criticism or even personal rebuke, and may insert the critique from the little tradition into the performance of the great tradition. This is not unusual, and is even expected of good praise poets. Loyalty to the office of the chief trumps loyalty to the particular occupant of the day and permits an *imbongi* ("praise singer") to comment on affairs and even criticize his patron in the "semi-ecstatic" state of performance, without being held responsible (Opland 1983: 51). The performance of genealogical praise poetry has a power of its own, since it invokes the ancestors of the family, clan, and nation:

> Basically then, izibongo are names of individuals, and naming an individual and his ancestors in this particular form strengthens the living individual through ensuring the protective sympathy of his ancestors and promotes continuing intercourse between the living and the dead. The performance of an izibongo thus *does* something; uttering the words of a poem makes something happen. (Opland 1983: 132)

Since everyone from the individual to the family to the clan and to the nation has their own locus in genealogy and praise poem, the importance of reciting genealogies and the power of their performance is obvious even today, when the oral elements of culture are retreating.

Fourth, although African societies are largely highly patriarchal in their social organization, genealogies may be either patrilineal or matrilineal, but not both. Matrilineal genealogies do not signify social emancipation from patriarchy for women, but reckon descent from the female line. This is important in terms of familial association, and matrilineal societies are also usually accompanied by the residence of the husband in the family domicile of the wife. Genealogies are linked to power and social control, in that they legitimate the primacy and ordering of clans and families and the claim of chiefs to legitimacy. They also usually reenforce gender roles and hierarchies. This was also true for genealogies in first-century Palestine, where proof of legitimacy was a prerequisite for public office and prominent families kept genealogies for this purpose (see already Strack and Billerbeck 1922: 2–6).

Finally, it is important to note that the performative economy of the oral praise poetry and genealogy means that short phrases, even individual words, may bring into play a whole world of referential signification shared by the performer and hearers. John Miles Foley describes this immanence of oral performance as "the set of metonymic, associative meanings institutionally delivered and received through a dedicated idiom or register either during or on the authority of traditional oral performance" (Foley 1995: 7). This is particularly true in the form of a genealogy, in which interpretive signals are restricted to a minimum and metonymic reference becomes key to interpretation. Then unexpected interruptions to the recital of a genealogy become clues to the reason for reciting it and interpreting it in a particular instance.

If we conclude this brief overview of African genealogy and praise poetry by repeating that, while it expresses the core value of *ubuntu*, the interconnectedness of life present and departed, it nevertheless indicates a limitation of *ubuntu*. It is very much bound up with the local, the family, clan, nation. To what extent it can transcend these limitations and become a universal principle is, to my mind, an open and burning question. Africa has more than its share of warfare and examples of inhumanity—enough at least to ask whether the link between *ubuntu* and the ancestors does not undermine its value as an ethical principle and whether it might face not only an affirmation but also a challenge from a careful contextual reading of the genealogy in Matthew's Gospel.

The Text of Matthew 1:1:1–25

What role, then, do ancestors play in the text of Matthew's genealogy? First, Jewish society in the time Matthew was writing was clearly patriarchal in structure and also patrilineal, reckoning descent from the male line.[6] Nevertheless, if the rabbis are a guide to anything as early as Matthew's Gospel, membership in the covenant people in the case of mixed marriages or irregular unions was reckoned through the mother. Such is the ruling in the Mishnah in *m. Qiddushin* 3:12, which states that in normal circumstances of legitimate unions between Jews, the "standing of the offspring follows that of the male," but in abnormal circumstances, descent follows the line of the mother. *B. Qiddushin* 68b is even more specific: an interpretation by Rabina of a ruling by R. Johanan on the authority of R. Simeon b. Yohai (T3) rules that it is the mother who determines the status of the child, and a child of a Jewish mother by a gentile father is a Jew, whereas the child of a gentile mother by a Jewish father is a gentile. There is no proof that this ruling was in existence in the first century; nevertheless, the logic of Paul's argument in Acts 16:1-5 seems to depend on it, since Timothy has a Greek father and a Jewish mother but Paul is described as circumcising him. This implies that a Jewish mother established membership of Israel in such circumstances in the first century ce, regardless of whether the incident happened as Luke describes it or not.[7] Whether this complication plays a role in Matthew's account is not certain, but is both likely and suggestive since, by Matthew's account, Jesus has a mother but no father, and the implications of this need to be explored. By the rabbinic reckoning, one is either born a Jew—minimally through a Jewish mother—or one is a Jew by conversion to Judaism.

Second, while nothing quite parallel to ancestor veneration (that is, the slaughter of animals in veneration of the ancestors) can be found in first-century-ce Palestine, genealogies were certainly related to the connection between the living and the departed. It has even been suggested that the plural name of God, *'elohim*, derives from multiple local gods perhaps related to ancestor cults (see Lewis 1997; Mafico 2000). Whether this is the case or not, it does seem that earlier phases in the history of Israel placed far more emphasis on ancestors, even practicing household ancestor cults, such as the cult of the *terephim* (Gen. 31:19, 34-35; 1 Sam. 19:13, 16; Judg. 17:5; 18:14, 17, 20; Hos. 3:4-5; Ezek. 21:21). Matthew 22:31-32 (and parallels) indicates that the departed ancestors were regarded as living and as being a proof of the resurrection. The implication of this saying is that most people in his community would have regarded his argument as convincing: "But regarding the resurrection of the dead, have you not read that which was spoken to you by God, saying, 'I am the God of Abraham, and the God of Isaac, and the God of Jacob'? He is not the God of the dead but of the living."[8]

Matthew's genealogy of Jesus is tightly structured into three epochs, of Abraham, David, and the Messiah, given chiastically before and after the genealogy itself, and then fleshed out in three sets of fourteen generations.[9] Just as Abraham, the father and founder of Israel, begins the genealogy, so also David, the founder of the Davidic dynasty, begins the second, while the birth of the Messiah concludes the third. Even though the end of the Davidic epoch and the beginning of the third epoch of the Messiah is given as the deportation to and return from Babylon, its significance is that the third epoch is the period in which the Davidic dynasty, which God promised would last forever, had failed. The birth of the Messiah then fulfills the promise, restores the line of David, and initiates the beginning of the new, eschatological time. Between David and Jesus the Messiah lies the middle period of the "floating gap" identified by Vansina, in which there is little and uncertain information, and the names are given in stereotyped fashion, since the emphasis falls on the beginning and end:

> For recent times there is plenty of information which tapers off as one moves back through time. For earlier periods one finds either a hiatus or just one or a few names, given with some hesitation. There is a gap in the accounts, which I will call the floating gap. For still earlier periods one finds again a wealth of information and one deals here with traditions of origin. (Vansina 1985: 23)

In order to facilitate our analysis of the text, the visual structure of the text is displayed as follows:

MATTHEW 1:1–18

A An account of the genealogy **of Jesus** *the Messiah*
   B the son of **David**,
      C the son of **Abraham**.

       C` **Abraham** was the father of Isaac
          and Isaac the father of Jacob
          and Jacob the father of Judah *and his brothers*
          and Judah the father of Perez *and Zerah by Tamar*
          and Perez the father of Hezron
          and Hezron the father of Aram
          and Aram the father of Aminadab
          and Aminadab the father of Nahshon
          and Nahshon the father of Salmon
          and Salmon the father of Boaz *by Rahab*
          and Boaz the father of Obed *by Ruth*
          and Obed the father of Jesse
          and Jesse the father of *King* David.
     B` And **David** was the father of Solomon *by the wife of Uriah*
        and Solomon the father of Rehoboam

and Rehoboam the father of Abijah
and Abijah the father of Asaph
and Asaph the father of Jehoshaphat
and Jehoshaphat the father of Joram
and Joram the father of Uzziah
and Uzziah the father of Jotha,
and Jotham the father of Ahaz
and Ahaz the father of Hezekiah
and Hezekiah the father of Manasseh
and Manasseh the father of Amos
and Amos the father of Josiah
and Josiah the father of Jechoniah *and his brothers*
    at the time of the deportation to Babylon

A` *And after the deportation to Babylon* Jechoniah was the father of Salathiel
and Salathiel the father of Zerubbabel
and Zerubbabel the father of Abiud
and Abiud the father of Eliakim
and Eliakim the father of Azor
and Azor the father of Zadok
and Zadok the father of Achim
and Achim the father of Eliud
and Eliud the father of Eleazar
and Eleazar the father of Matthan
and Matthan the father of Jacob
and Jacob the father of Joseph *the husband of Mary*
    of whom **Jesus** *was born who is called* **the Messiah**

C` So all the generations from **Abraham** to David are fourteen generations
B`and from **David** to the deportation to Babylon, fourteen generations
A` and from the deportation to Babylon to **the Messiah**, fourteen generations

Now the birth of Jesus *the Messiah* took place in this way

When his mother *Mary had been engaged* to Joseph
    but before they lived together
        she was found to be with child from the Holy Spirit

Bold print indicates the three key figures and pivot points of the genealogy, while italics indicate what would not be expected—that is, where the genealogy departs from the form and norms of a genealogy. It has often been noted that the genealogy of Matthew does not square at all points with the information in the Hebrew Scriptures. This is true enough, but it must also be said that no one without access to a great city library such as Jerusalem (which was destroyed by the time Matthew wrote), Alexandria, Antioch (where Matthew was probably located), or Caesarea could have access to all of these books, since they circulated independently in scrolls. Moreover, even with access to a great library to obtain all that data would be a labor of research beyond the reach or interests of most writers, so that to construct his genealogy, Matthew relied on memory and such writings as he had access to (a large number, considering his promise-and-fulfillment citations), as well as oral traditions and invention. In any case, as we have noted, the real interest in a genealogy is the beginning and the end, with, in Matthew's case, an additional interest in David as the midpoint of the genealogy and also the founder of the interrupted dynasty that Jesus is to inherit and restore.

As far as the three-times-fourteen structure of the genealogy is concerned, we note that Abraham begins the first, David the second, but that Jechoniah is marginalized in the beginning of the third. It is not Jechoniah who is significant in the division of the epochs, but the deportation to Babylon and the discontinuation of the Davidic dynasty in seeming contradiction of the explicit promise to David that an heir would always sit on the throne (2 Sam. 7:13-16; 1 Kgs. 2:4, 45). The importance of David as founder of the royal dynasty is highlighted by the addition of *King* to the inclusion of David in the genealogy. The contradiction of promise is removed by the final figure in the fourteen generations of the third epoch—namely, Jesus the Messiah—repeated in an *inclusio* in verses 1, 16, and 17. This is the real purpose of the genealogy, to establish the new point in the history of Israel, the emergence of the Messiah Jesus to restore the kingdom.

However, the beginning point of the genealogy also has importance for Matthew. Abraham is the father of Israel through Isaac and the twelve patriarchs; and indeed, that is the point of the first intrusion into the genealogy: "Judah *and his brothers*," since Abraham is ancestor of the twelve brothers who are founders of the twelve tribes. Hence, Abraham is the ancestor of the totality of Israel, and not just Judah. So the significance of David and hence of Jesus the Messiah holds true in Matthew's understanding for all Israel and not just the kingdom of Judah. However, Abraham has significance beyond the foundation of Israel since, through him, "all the families of the earth shall be blessed" (Gen. 12:3), and, for Matthew, this promise is fulfilled in Jesus the Messiah, whose kingdom extends beyond the confines of Israel.[10] So "Do not presume to say to yourselves, 'We have Abraham as our ancestor'; for I tell you, God is able from these stones to raise up children to Abraham" (Matt. 3:9); and "I tell you, many will come from east and west and will eat with Abraham and Isaac and Jacob in the kingdom of heaven while the heirs of the kingdom will be thrown into the outer darkness, where there will be weeping and gnashing of teeth" (Matt. 8:11). God's purpose in sending Jesus the Messiah includes the gentiles in the promise to Israel: "Go therefore and make disciples of all nations, baptizing them in the name of the Father and of the Son and of the Holy Spirit, and teaching them to obey everything that I have commanded you" (Matt. 28:19-20). So Matthew's affirmation of Abraham as the father of Israel must always be understood in terms of Abraham as the father through whom all the nations are blessed, transcending the local, the tribal, and the particular.

The second of the intrusions into the genealogy has a strong metonymic reference, "*and Zerah by Tamar*," calling to mind the scandalous episode in the life of the patriarch Judah and his sons Er and Onan (Gen. 38:6-30). Er, the oldest of the children, is so wicked that God puts him to death. According to the rules of levirate marriage, Onan is required to take his brother's wife, Tamar, and impregnate her with a son for his dead brother. Instead, knowing that such a son would inherit away from him, he spills his sperm on the ground during intercourse to prevent conception, and, as a consequence of such wicked behavior, God kills him also. Judah now fears for the life of his only remaining son, Shelah, and indefinitely postpones allowing him to marry Tamar. Realizing this, Tamar sets herself up as a prostitute beside the road and seduces Judah, so that she conceives twins, Perez and Zerah (who struggle for precedence inside her womb at the time of birth). When Judah tries to put her to death for adultery, she sends him the pledges she had taken from him as proof he would pay her, forcing him to acknowledge the legitimacy of the children and his own culpability. This complicated genealogical trajectory utilizing incest between father and daughter-in-law, problematizing descent by sperm, is an indication ahead of time that membership of the covenant people passes through the women and that the behavior of the menfolk in this incident, including the father (Lev 18:15), constitutes a "blemish" on the descent in terms of *halakah*, a blemish that requires the standing of the woman to be taken into account. Women are seldom mentioned in Jewish genealogies, so that the mention of Tamar (and that of the other women) is doubly irregular and significant (Strack and Billerbeck 1922: 15).

Next, an intrusion *by Rahab*, another woman who takes the initiative, is brought into the genealogy, this time a gentile and a prostitute. Rabbinic interpreters made many attempts to redeem or even sanctify Rahab, as did the Epistle of James,[11] but Matthew will have none of it: Salmon, the great-great-great-grandfather of David, marries the prostitute Rahab from Jericho, who had entertained and protected the two spies sent by Joshua when they came to examine the defenses of the city before its conquest by Israel (Josh. 2:1-24). As a sign of her faithfulness and courage in protecting them, Rahab receives a promise that she will be spared the destruction of Jericho and is incorporated into Israel. Already, then, if membership of the people of Israel is reckoned through the female, then Boaz is not a trueborn Israelite at all, reckoned by sperm alone, but illegitimate—except by means of the conversion and faith of Rahab, by which she becomes incorporated into Israel and by which her children are reckoned legitimate Israelites. This blemish of Rahab in the genealogy is repeated in the levirate marriage of Boaz, whose son Obed, the father of Jesse and grandfather of David, is *by Ruth* the Moabitess, who follows her mother-in-law from Moab to Naomi's homeland Israel and takes her mother-in-law's people as her own people and Naomi's God as her own God. Again, reckoned by sperm, Obed would be illegitimate according to the rabbis, for whom a child of an Israelite by a gentile woman is illegitimate, except by virtue of the conversion and faith of the Moabitess Ruth in her own standing.

A key intrusion comes in that David fathered Solomon "*by the wife of Uriah*," again a metonymic reference that every Jew would recognize instantly (2 Sam. 11:1-27). Struck by her naked beauty, which he saw from the rooftop of his palace, David sends his soldiers and forcibly takes Bathsheba while her husband, Uriah the Hittite, is away on military service on David's behalf—to make matters worse, she is still unclean from her monthly period (2 Sam. 11:4). When his various stratagems to cover up his rape and adultery by tricking Uriah fail, David has Uriah murdered and takes Bathsheba—if not herself a gentile, then the wife of a gentile—as his favorite wife and makes sure her son Solomon succeeds him as king by crowning him before he himself dies. It could be that, married to a Hittite, Bathsheba was herself a Hittite, though this cannot be established from the text. Nevertheless, as the child of David by a wife he obtained through adultery, rape, and murder of a gentile husband, Solomon's conception and birth must be held to be a blemish on the male line, and Solomon's descent should pass through the mother on her own standing.[12] The blemish is so serious that Luke even takes the genealogy of Jesus away from Solomon and makes it pass through another son of David, Nathan, one of four brothers born to David by Bath-shua, daughter of Ammiel (1 Chron. 3:5). On the basis of the allusions Matthew makes in this brief way, it must be said that the line of David was characterized by inconsistencies and "blemishes" from the beginning, and yet God continues to honor his promise that one of his descendants would sit on the throne of David forever.

Until, that is, the intrusion into the genealogy of "Josiah the father of Jechoniah *and his brothers at the time of the deportation to Babylon,*" signifying a breach of the dynastic succession through the destruction of Jerusalem and the exile of the elite in Babylon, including not just Jechoniah but all his brothers. Probably the reference is to the uncertainty over the exact lineage of David from this unsettled period onward. Indeed, at this point, Matthew's genealogy parts company with our other evidence in the Hebrew Scriptures, in which Jechoniah is the son of Jehoiakim son of Josiah (1 Chron. 3:15; Jer. 24:1). Only one brother, Zedekiah, is mentioned in the Hebrew Bible (1 Chron. 3:16). We are here in what Vansina calls the "middle period" of inaccuracy and lack of interest in a genealogy. The throne is vacant until the arrival of Jesus the Messiah.

Finally, the major intrusion into the genealogy comes at the end: in rather contorted fashion, the readers/hearers of the genealogy are given the information that Jesus himself was born irregularly: "and Jacob the father of Joseph *the husband of Mary of whom Jesus was born who is called the Messiah.*"[13] Joseph is the legal husband of Mary by betrothal and in that sense inherits the genealogy from Abraham through David. Yet Joseph did not beget Jesus by his sperm. Instead, we are informed subsequently that "before they had sex [*synelthein,* literally "came together"] she was found to be with child from the Holy Spirit" (1:18). So there is again an irregularity in the genealogy, since Joseph is not the father and there is no way of determining who was the father, whether by rape or seduction or adultery, the membership of Israel and descent must be held to pass through the woman in her own standing and not by sperm. In the final analysis, the child of Mary and Joseph is *from the Holy Spirit,* is the child of promise and fulfillment—just like the whole genealogy, of which he is the rightful heir. This intrusion of innovation and change, cutting across the affirmation of the tradition embodied in the genealogy, is expressed by Matthew's use of onomastics, mirroring the practice of the Zulu author Magema Fuze, as we have already suggested. The angel tells Joseph, "the husband of Mary of whom was born Jesus the Messiah," whose name is included but whose sperm is now excluded from the genealogy, "She will bear a son; and you shall give him the name Jesus, for he will save his people from their sin" (1:21). Again, he is given the name "Emmanuel," from the enigmatic prophecy in Isa. 7:14, a name that means "God is with us." Once more, sperm alone as the basis for the genealogy of God's promise to his people is rejected, since Matthew specifically comments that Joseph "had no intercourse with her until her son was born" (1:25).[14]

At the end of a long and stylized genealogy, full (like every genealogy in oral recitation) of gaps and problems, we can conclude that Matthew both affirms the importance of genealogy, of ancestors who give us our biological and cultural identity and our place in the social universe, and also criticizes the Davidic house, problematizes its genealogy and ancestors. It is important for Matthew that Jesus the Messiah is son of David and son of Abraham: his culture and his identity within Israel and the line of David are confirmed and affirmed. But the intrusions into the genealogy also confirm and affirm that his place does not depend on sperm alone but on promise. The same may be said of David and Solomon and of every member of the lineage of David. The same may also be said of the people of Israel as a whole, their ancestry and genealogy; their descent from "Jacob the father of Judah *and his brothers*" is confirmed and affirmed but also problematized, in that the promise through Abraham was through faith and extended to all through faith in that "through him all the nations of the earth will be blessed."

Finally, the importance of women in fulfilling God's promise to Abraham that his seed would be as the sands of the sea and then to David that his lineage would never fail problematizes the patrilineal nature of the genealogy. It forcibly reminds Matthew's hearers/readers that women are not only silent but necessary instruments of male descent; they also take vital initiatives for the sake of their families and clans, even initiatives that may constitute a "blemish" on the male descent and may mean that the status of the child depends on her own standing and not that of the father of the child.

DIALOGUE BETWEEN MATTHEW 1:1–18 AND THE (SOUTHERN) AFRICAN CONTEXT

There are a number of aspects of this reading of Matthew that speak clearly to African traditions of ancestor veneration. In the first place, Matthew confirms and, by his genealogy, promotes the importance of ancestors in providing a person with her or his social and personal identity. As such, Matthew confirms the significance of that web of interconnectedness that constitutes humanness or *ubuntu* in (southern) African cultures and that has been downplayed and even lost in many Western societies that emphasize the individual, the nuclear family, or even no family. However, as Matthew provides the genealogy, he also severs the biological chain of being at the vital moment of the birth of Jesus the Messiah. Joseph is not the father, but only the husband of Mary, of whom is born Jesus the Messiah, in her own standing as a woman of faith: Jesus is a child of the Holy Spirit and not of sperm. Indeed, Matthew shows that this is the culmination of a number of such interventions by women, interventions that break the line of descent. There are counter-indications to an overemphasis on descent by sperm alone in African culture as well, since children from another family or clan may be adopted and "introduced to the ancestors," thereby becoming part of the clan, with their children also being regarded as part of the clan, though ambivalence toward such a person may remain. Caring for such children would be regarded as an act of *ubuntu*. In any case, though, our reading of Matthew provides a biblical basis for a rejection of the devaluation of ancestor veneration, which was enforced by the missionaries and which has had a devastating effect on modern Africa.

While this provides both space and the imperative for a revaluation of African culture and tradition by African Christians to counter the "missionary position," it also provides a challenge to an overemphasis on the family, the clan, and the nation in terms of biological descent and patriarchy. Jesus the Messiah draws his identity and culture from the people of Israel, the house of Judah, and the line of David, but he also transcends the local, the clan, and the nation. As the descendant and heir of Abraham, he is the fulfillment of the promise that in him all the nations of the earth would be blessed. As the descendant of David, he draws his identity from Tamar, Rahab, Ruth, Bathsheba, and Mary the wife of Joseph and so transcends the male and the patriarchal. African Christian reappropriations of the culture and cultic importance of ancestors need to take account of these twin challenges. Love of the neighbor cannot be limited to biological kin; recognition of the genealogies needs to ensure the inclusion of women and the recognition of their equal importance in the interconnectedness of life and relationship, which underpins the core humane values of African *ubuntu*. This is how I interpret what Mokoena calls the "pull between ancestry and innovation" for Africa today (Fuze 1922: 195).

South Africa in the postapartheid era has been given a near miraculous space to reshape the way we do things and understand things. One of the priorities is the rescue and proper valuation of many aspects of traditional African culture that had been devalued or even suppressed in the colonial encounter. Veneration of the ancestors was one of these traditions, deeply rooted and still vibrant. Yet while it binds communities together and gives impetus to social ethics, in some circumstances it could lead to nepotism, xenophobia, sectional violence, and sexism. The human-rights-based national

Constitution of South Africa challenges South Africans to forge a new identity and practice not based on kinship, gender, and tribal loyalties, to practice an inclusive ethics that does not discriminate against people on the basis of gender or race or sexual preference or class or religion. In short, to affirm individual rights and liberties, which may liberate oppressed people but may also cut across community goals and understandings. How to affirm both individual and collective rights and values is one of our biggest challenges—how also to affirm the local as well as those things that transcend the local and bind humanity together.

Matthew the Jew faced some of the same kinds of challenges in forging a new Christian identity, one that both affirmed the patriarchs and genealogies of the people of the covenant promise of God with Israel and those things that limited it. The messiah belongs to Israel, but not only to Israel: His lineage and the heritage of the patriarchs are affirmed, but the genetic link is cut or at the very least compromised. The goal of God's act through the Holy Spirit in the conception of Jesus by Mary was not only that Israel and Torah would be affirmed according to the Scriptures but also that all the nations of the earth would be blessed through the covenant with Abraham, which is fulfilled in Jesus. Matthew was only partly successful in his hermeneutical endeavor. His challenge to his own people to see God's call to open up the promise to non-Israelites was later misunderstood by gentile Christians to be a rejection of Israel and was used to persecute and murder Jews. However, the adoption of his Gospel and a genealogy affirming the tradition, the Torah, and the covenant promise to Israel, by gentiles who had no kinship right to the inheritance of Israel, is a sign that he succeeded in much also. This should be both an encouragement and a warning to South African Christians seeking to contribute to the building of an alternative and humane new society.

In my own contextual exegetical model, I insist that the successful outcome of the process of "conversation with the text" in appropriation involves more than head knowledge; it involves new praxis, by which I do not mean walking out of the room and into the picket line, though it may mean that. Fundamentally, it should involve some kind of reorientation of engagement with reality: new attitudes and orientations as well as new concrete actions where appropriate. In my own personal conversation with this text, my understanding emerging from the reading is an acknowledgment that Matthew's Gospel both affirms and problematizes our need to acknowledge our ancestors. My South African context is a multicultural society wrestling with an oppressive past, which either gave a negative valuation to indigenous African cultures or exploited them to justify separation and privilege for European settlers. Culture and identity have become key issues. So has the need to move not just toward the affirmation of cultures subjugated by colonialism and imperialism but also toward the construction of an inclusive transcultural identity. The two are not incompatible, as I believe Matthew's genealogy has shown. They can stand in a constructive and fruitful tension. This has led me to the conviction that a conversation with and around this text could assist South African Christians to move forward by engaging with "subjugated knowledges" between the rooted self and the alienated other. I have explored this by facilitating the reading of the text with a group of about eighty clergypersons of my own Anglican Church in a diocesan clergy school. The participants of this school were as diverse in culture and gender as any in our very diverse country, and for various reasons there was a high level of barely suppressed conflict. I had been invited to give a series of addresses on "interpreting the Bible." Small multicultural groups of six people discussed this text using the contextual Bible study method advocated by Gerald West.[15] After an introductory plenary introduction and "brainstorm," they shared in small groups their own reading of the text and how their experiences of their ancestors affected who they were and how they negotiated life. They also discussed how the affirmation of and limitations of the importance of spermatic ancestry, along with the recovery of the central role of women suggested by the biblical text, might help them to negotiate their identity in relations with people of different gender and different cultural backgrounds.[16] Most found that it was a very positive aid to a new encounter with each other. A particular sign of hope was the way the groups, each in their own particular way, moved from suspicion and at times negative sentiments about what they were being asked to do, to interest, and even to excitement. Discussing their own personal and particular cultural, gender, and family identities concerning ancestors in a supportive group context deepened their understandings of who they were and who others were and why it mattered. All of them in some way found that, since the gospel both affirms and problematizes these things, they had neutral space to speak frankly about their own diversity and the need to transcend it without negating it.

APPENDIX A: QUESTIONS FOR GROUP STUDY OF CLERGY ON MATTHEW 1:1-18

Instructions: Appoint a chairperson/facilitator not to dominate but to help everyone to share. Make sure everyone has a chance to speak/share. There are no right or wrong answers, only explorations. Respect everyone's experiences and answers. Let someone prepare to report back to the whole group.

1. Do you find a table of descent meaningful and interesting? Have you ever done a Bible study on this passage? Why or why not? Why do you think Matthew puts it at the beginning of his Gospel? (Compare Matt. 3:9; 8:11; 22:32.)

2. What role do your ancestors/family trees play in your own culture? Does it make a difference who your parents, grandparents, great-grandparents, and extended family were/are? Do they continue to play a role in the lives of the living? (e.g., *ukubuyisa/umsebenzi*; roots, psychotherapy; genetic/socialization characteristics). How do these cultural dynamics influence you in reading this passage?

3. Women are mentioned at key points in the table. Is it significant? What kind of women are mentioned? How does their mention and historical roles affect the table of descent?
   ... and Judah the father of Perez and Zerah by Tamar
   ... and Salmon the father of Boaz by Rahab
   ... and Boaz the father of Obed by Ruth
   ... and David was the father of Solomon by the wife of Uriah
   ... and Jacob the father of Joseph the husband of Mary, of whom Jesus was born

4. If Joseph was not the biological father of Jesus, as the text suggests, does this invalidate his ancestral lineage? Does this text affirm the importance of ancestors, or does it challenge it, or both?

5. Has sharing in a cross-cultural group opened up new dimensions for you? Could biblical texts be a meeting place for people from different South African cultures, religions, or no religion to explore their commonalities or differences? How or how not?

6. What practical possibilities for changed attitudes or actions might come from the group's reading?

Notes

1. For further discussions of the genre of the Matthean genealogy, see also Luz 1989: 112–13; Allison 2005: 57–62.

2. "The work of myth is in a way an indictment of our reading of history and of our way of conceiving reality" (editors' translation).

3. I do not intend to provide a discussion of my methodology, but those who wish to follow the unfolding of my own hermeneutical framework can trace it through successive phases in Draper 1991; 2001; 2002; 2008. For a critique of my meanderings, see West 2009.

4. This probably means that Ndaba's boastful praise poem was not performed in full, but the chant accompanying it continued to be used by his regiment (*impi*).

5. The English translation is from Fuze 1979: 43.

6. See the summary of Jewish Private Law in Safrai and Stern 1974: 504–34.

7. For a discussion of the incident from a Jewish perspective see Segal 1990: 218–21.

8. All quotations from the Bible are taken from the New Revised Standard Version.

9. A symbolic and evocative number in Israelite tradition, which is concerned to anchor the lineage of Jesus in a sacred numerology of three and fourteen, doubly attested in the Torah and the Prophets, according to Decharneux 2008: 108; though note Luz's (1989: 110–11) reservations about this. However, if sacralization of Jesus' ancestry is the main purpose of Matthew, it is hard to understand why he introduces five shameful moments into the genealogy linked to the (nevertheless salvatory) role of women in Israel's tradition. Only the suggestion of a divine plan can be drawn for certain from the numeric sequence.

10. Luz (1989: 110) rightly observes that the genealogy has a "universalistic overtone" in that Jesus as son of Abraham is also father of proselytes in rabbinic tradition. He is less convinced of the effort to link them together as four gentile women, a move many commentators make, e.g., Keener 1999: 80–81, since they then cannot be linked to Mary, who is clearly not gentile.

11. The evidence is usefully set out in Charles 2011.

12. This interpretation could be questioned, since although the original child of rape, Solomon's brother, died as God's punishment to David (2 Sam. 12:15–23), we are told that after this "David consoled Bathsheba his wife" and that God "loved" the resultant child, Solomon (12:24). However, for Matthew, Bathsheba remains "the wife of Uriah" and not of David, even at the time of Solomon's birth.

13. Luz (1989: 109) notes the intrusion of Tamar, Rahab, Ruth, and Bathsheba and rightly observes that "a divine 'irregularity' is a common denominator among the four women," which connects them to Mary. However, he finds this link problematic, since none of the suggested connections between the four apply to Mary (that all four OT women are instruments of the Holy Spirit; that all are sinners; that all are gentiles).

14. Allison (2005 163–72) demonstrates that first-century Jews seemed to share the Stoic disapprobation of sexual relations during pregnancy, since sexual intercourse was deemed to be not for pleasure but for procreation. Hence Joseph's behavior in abstaining from intercourse confirms that he was a "righteous man" (1:19). Be that as it may, the failure to have sex until after birth confirms the spermatological break in the genealogy.

15. See appendix A at the end of this paper for the group worksheet. Sadly, there is no space in this article to provide the rich data summarized in the reports of the group, but it is available and forms the basis of what has been said here.

16. I did not use this deliberately provocative term "spermatic ancestry" in the Bible study worksheet or discussion.

PART II

Children and Family

3

What Child Is This?

A Contextual Feminist Literary Analysis of the Child in Matthew 2

Sharon Betsworth

INTRODUCTION

Contextual biblical interpretation takes context into account in two ways.[1] First, it brings to the foreground the social context of the interpreter. Different authors emphasize various aspects of their social location. Second, context also applies to the text's social context and conditions under which it was written or the time in which it was written (Bailey 2010). My essay will follow this conceptualization of contextual biblical interpretation. In particular, I will interpret as an educated, Euro-American woman, reading from a feminist and primarily literary perspective. I grew up in the midwestern region of the United States in a predominately white, middle-class, Protestant town. Methodologically, I locate myself within the reading practices that take women's experience seriously (Schottroff 1995: 61–65). The focus of this essay is the second chapter of the Gospel of Matthew and the relationship between the depiction of Jesus as "the child" in chapter 2 and Jesus' teaching with and about children in 18:1-5. My interest in children in the Gospels evolves from my experiences of working with children in a variety of contexts: public schools, summer camps, local churches, and most recently on the board of a nonprofit, Project Transformation, which focuses on children's literacy.

Seeking to bridge the gap between the world of the academy and the world of the church, for which these texts are Scripture, I invited a group of women who are involved in children's ministries to discuss this passage with me.[2] Their context is similar to my own: all of them are educated women and are working in United Methodist Churches or related ministries in Oklahoma.

All are Euro-American women except one, whose father is from India. When I asked them about their context, they were clear that their religious preference is that of progressive Christianity, in a state that is known to be religiously conservative. This makes them somewhat of a minority in their geographic location. Not all of the members of the group, myself included, are Oklahoma natives, but we are all from the middle or western regions of the United States.

All of us are concerned for children because of the many justice issues that pertain to children, especially in the state of Oklahoma. Oklahoma ranks low (in the forties) among the fifty states and Puerto Rico on a variety of indicators of childhood health and well-being including poverty, infant mortality, and food insecurity.[3] Although most of the women in our group do not at this time have children of our own, we are all concerned for the children of our state and their well-being. The group was eager to read Matthew 2 and 18:1-5 taking our context and that of the children to whom we minister into account.

TRADITIONAL READINGS OF MATTHEW 1 AND 2

I will begin with an overview of how interpreters have traditionally read the opening chapters of Matthew's Gospel, then consider how others have read chapter 2 contextually, before discussing our examination of the passage. Chapters 1–4 of the Gospel of Matthew are, according to Dale Allison (2001: 846), an extended introduction that tells "*who* Jesus was (1:1-18; 2:1, 4; 3:11, 17; 4:3, 6), *where* he was from (2:6), *how* he came into the world (1:18-25), *why* he came into the world (1:21, 2:6), *when* he came into the world (1:17, 2:1) and *what* he proclaimed (4:17)." The section is rich with biblical quotations and allusions, which function to foreshadow themes that will arise later in the Gospel and establish for the reader Jesus' identity as Messiah. Commentators often note that Matthew 1 focuses on who Jesus is, while Matthew 2 is more concerned with from where Jesus has come (Hagner 1995a: 23; Harrington 1991a: 46). When scholars discuss Matthew 2 in particular, several themes come to the fore. First, Matthew draws distinct parallels between the story of Jesus and the story of Moses (Allison 2001: 850; Davies and Allison 1988: 227, 253). As an infant, Moses' life was endangered by Pharaoh, who was threatened by the proliferation of the Israelites and demanded that all Hebrew baby boys be killed (Exod. 1:8-22). Likewise, Jesus' life is in danger due to Herod's fear of the newborn "king of Jews" (Matt. 2:16). As an adult, Moses takes refuge in a foreign land when Pharaoh seeks to kill him (Exod. 2:11-15). Similarly, when Jesus' life is threatened by Herod, Joseph takes him to a foreign land for safety

(Matt. 2:13-15). Both Moses and Jesus are then called out of the place of refuge to return to the land of their birth after the respective rulers, who sought to kill them, die (Exod. 4:19; Matt. 2:19-21).

A second theme scholars often mention is the similarities between Joseph in Matthew 2 and Joseph in Genesis. In both cases, each man's dreams lead him to Egypt. In Genesis, Joseph brings his family to Egypt to save them from the threat of death by starvation. In Matthew, Joseph takes the child Jesus to Egypt to save him from the threat of death by Herod (Kennedy 2008: 126). Third, commentators often discuss Herod and the potential historicity of the murder of the children in Bethlehem (France 1979: 98–120; Hagner 1995a: 37). Although the incident in Matthew is not found anywhere outside of the Gospel, Josephus's accounts of Herod suggest that the action is in keeping with Herod's behavioral patterns. He was known as a paranoid ruler, who killed those whom he felt were a threat to his rule, including his own family members, notably his wife Mariamne and some of his sons (Josephus, *Ant.* 15.5.2; 15.7.4; 16.11.1-6). Fourth, the Scripture-fulfillment statements often function to demonstrate that Jesus' life was consistent with God's will as it is outlined in the Scripture. In this chapter, quotations from Mic. 5:2, Hos. 11:1, and Jer. 31:15 emphasize the providential nature of the unfolding events (Carter 2000: 70). Finally, Matthew 2 foreshadows several themes that arise later in the Gospel: the title "king of the Jews" (2:2 and 27:11, 29, 37), the secret meeting of authorities to conspire against Jesus (2:7 and 26:4-5), and the plot on the part of the elite to seek Jesus' death (2:16 and 26:4) (Allison 2001: 849; see also Davies and Allison 1988: 254; Hagner 1995a: 27; Luz 2007: 115). In addition, the magi in Matthew 2 indicate that the gentiles will be a part of this unfolding story of Jesus.

These themes and motifs are certainly important to the story in Matthew 2. Yet commentators often focus on them to the exclusion of the main character of the Gospel narrative. Their concerns often revolve around the adult male characters—Herod, the magi, and Joseph. Attention to these characters often eclipses the one who is the catalyst for their actions, the child Jesus. Keith White notes this as well, stating aptly, "It is as if there is no room for the child in the inn of theology (to borrow an image from Luke's birth narrative)" (White 2008: 357). Although, as mentioned above, some scholars have noted connections between Matthew 2 and the passion of the adult Jesus (Davies and Allison 1988: 254), few connect the child Jesus in Matthew 2 to the adult Jesus' teachings about children in Matt. 18:1-5. Jesus as "child" is simply not a theme of primary concern for many who study this text.

Contextual Interpretations of Matthew 2

Approaching the text from a contextualized perspective, however, allows the concerns of Jesus the child to come to the fore. I will summarize two such readings. One contextual analysis of Matthew 2 is an essay by Aquiles Ernesto Martínez, who describes Matthew 2 as an example of "compulsory migration" (Martínez 2006: 85). Martínez argues that in Matthew 2, Jesus appears as an immigrant child or a political refugee. As such, his experience is analogous to the experiences of many immigrants who have been forced to migrate from their homes to unwelcoming countries (Martínez 2006:86). For Martínez, "Jesus' exile . . . is a *hermeneutical lens*" through which the compulsory migrations of millions can be assessed (Martínez 2006: 87). In turn, Matthew's story may be read from the vantage point of their experiences. By seeking to kill Jesus, Herod is the one who instigates the exile, pushing the family to Egypt. God, however, is ultimately the one in control, pulling the family through the trial safely. Many immigrants can readily relate to the family's experience, since it is often politically abusive and power-hungry systems that compel people to migrate. They too may have a sense that, deep within their circumstances, God is at work to bring about a better life (Martínez 2006: 90). In Matthew's story, Joseph, Mary, and Jesus are powerless characters. They cannot control or change the decrees of Herod. Therefore, God protects them and guides them (Martínez 2006: 105). God guides the main characters of the story—watching over Jesus before, during, and after the exile, and directing Joseph and the magi in dreams—while dismantling Herod's plans to destroy the child. Even so, as Martínez rightly states, we readers are very disappointed that God does not protect the children of Bethlehem in the same manner (Martínez 2006: 106). Martínez then applies Matthew 2 to the debate over immigration and undocumented immigrants in the United States.

Alejandro Alberto Duarte also interprets Matthew 2 contextually, considering issues of injustice and complicity. He reads from the context of an Argentinean who experienced the murder of eleven close friends at the hands of the military dictatorship of the late 1970s and early 1980s in his country. That was a time in which many persons were "disappeared," and as Duarte states, referring to Matt. 2:18, they were "no more" (Duarte 2004: 350). The killing of the baby boys in Bethlehem in chapter 2 particularly resonates with Duarte. As a result of his context, he is always aware of the "'little ones' (10:42; 18:1-14) [who] are exploited, marginalized, and excluded." He finds this theme of the "little ones" first in chapter 2 and then again in Jesus' teachings about the little ones in chapter 18, where Matthew presents the organization of the community (Duarte 2004: 350). Finally, in the resurrection, "Jesus is at the service of the little ones with whom he will be 'to the end of the age' (28:20)" (Duarte 2004: 351). A parallel theme in the Gospel is the promise of "God with us." It arises first in the birth narrative, but is also present in chapter 2. The theme is found again in chapter 18 and finally in the last speech in chapter 28 (Duarte 2004: 352). That "God with us" is first articulated "against the backdrop of those who are no longer with us, those who have disappeared and 'are no more' (2:18)," presents the central conflict the Gospel needs to address if it is to be good news (Duarte 2004: 356).

A central issue in the injustice of the children's murder in Bethlehem is the complicity of the religious leaders, who tell Herod where the Messiah will be born according to the Scriptures. Their action has the effect of misusing Scripture for political reasons. They readily give the information to Herod, a direct response to their close relationship to and need to appease the power structures of their day. The murder of the children in Matthew 2 then demonstrates that there is no neutrality in the use of Scripture. One must bear the responsibility for the result of "one's use of scripture and its symbolic power" (Duarte 2004: 359). In the case of both Martínez and Duarte, the child, representing those who are on the margins, is placed in the center of the interpretation.

Though I come from a different context from Martínez or Duarte, our privileged academic positions notwithstanding, I am also concerned for the marginalized ones in Matthew's Gospel, in particular the child and children. In the remainder of this essay, I will reinterpret Matthew 2 from a feminist contextual perspective. First, I will begin with some insights from Elaine Wainwright's feminist rereading of Matthew 1 to set the context for my discussion of Matthew 2. Second, I will recontextualize Matthew 2 with readers from my social context. Third, I will then demonstrate how "the child" in Matthew 2 is linked literarily and thematically to "the child" in Matt. 18:1-5. Finally, I will show how the child in Matthew 2 becomes both the model for Jesus in his later life and for the disciples to follow, as Jesus admonishes them to become like children.

REREADING MATTHEW 1 AND 2

In chapter 1, Matthew places Jesus firmly within the story of God's people Israel and establishes him as the Messiah, the divinely begotten Son of God. The opening genealogy, however, does not convey the sense that this is a child's family tree. This is the ancestry of a mover and shaker in the history of Israel. Nevertheless, even within this high-powered genealogy are telltale signs that not everyone in this history is on the level of patriarchs (or matriarchs) and kings. The five women listed in the genealogy, Tamar, Ruth, Rahab, the wife of Uriah, and Mary, suggest another side to the story of this one who will save his people. As Elaine Wainwright discusses, the genealogy demonstrates that Jesus is not just born into the male patriarchal structures but also into a family in which the women's stories disclose an alternative to those dominant structures (Wainwright 1998: 56). Each of the women in the genealogy is a marginalized woman. As those outside of the patriarchal power structures, each woman uses her own ingenuity to secure her future. Like Jesus' female ancestors, Mary is also a marginalized woman. Yet, unlike her foremothers, Mary is passive in Matthew's story. Until the point at which Joseph accepts the child and his mother into his home and kinship network, Mary lives precariously on the edge, as a woman whose pregnancy is apparently not yet legitimate (Wainwright 1998: 59). Despite Joseph's actions, however, when Mary's child is born, the child becomes just as marginalized as Mary herself was.

Indeed, chapter 2 describes a vulnerable, humble, human child, dependent on God and his adoptive father, Joseph, for safety. Matthew draws the reader's attention to the vulnerable nature of this newly born one, by omitting his name and referring to him only as "the child" throughout the Gospel's second chapter. In contrast to chapter 1, in which Jesus is named five times—at the opening and closing of the genealogy (1:1, 16); in the annunciation (1:18); and when the angel tells Joseph what the child's name will be and in the announcement that he will be named Jesus (1:21, 25)—chapter 2 uses the name "Jesus" only once, in the first verse. The first words of the chapter are a genitive absolute construction, *tou de Jesu gennethentos*, "after Jesus was born," allowing Matthew to name Jesus first in the chapter. The phrase also links the following material with that which has immediately preceded it (Davies and Allison 1988: 225). It is the last time Matthew will use the name "Jesus" until 3:13, when Jesus comes to John for baptism. Another common epithet for Jesus in Matthew's Gospel, "son," *huios*, is likewise only found once in this chapter (2:15).

Instead of being called by name or being referred to as the son, the hero of the Gospel narrative is designated as "the child," *to paidion*, a total of nine times in Matthew 2. Four times "the child" is used alone (2:8, 9, 13b, and 20b), and five times it is used together with "his mother" (2:11, 13a, 14, 20a, 21). In the instances in which "his mother" (only in 2:11 is she named Mary) is included, Jesus is always identified first. As a result, even when the mother is present in the narrative, the child is the focus of the attention and the emotional center of the story. The phrase "the child and his mother" also functions to keep Joseph in the background, reinforcing 1:16-25, which indicates Jesus has no human father (Davies and Allison 1988: 248). Yet while the actions in chapter 2 revolve around the young boy, he is very much a child in an adult world. His early life is shaped by the adult males around him, especially Joseph, Herod, and the magi. The boy is "powerless in contrast to the political and socio-religious power of Herod and the magi" (Wainwright 1998: 58). Nevertheless, this child, according to the magi, has been born "king of the Jews." Matthew contrasts him with Herod, the reigning "king of the Jews," who is also named nine times in the chapter (2:1, 3, 7, 12, 13, 15, 16, 19, 22). The distinctions between the two are stark: a murderous client ruler of the Roman Empire residing in Jerusalem is threatened by an infant boy from an insignificant village.

RECONTEXTUALIZING MATTHEW 2

As noted at the beginning of this essay, scholars often overlook the child Jesus when they interpret chapter 2 of the Gospel of Matthew. While much is written about Herod and the magi and their respective actions, commentators often neglect to discuss the child, the infant who grows into the man about whom the Gospel is told. Even Matthew, one could argue, seems relatively unconcerned with his main character, by omitting his name from a seemingly important portion of the story. This one who has been named "Jesus" and designated as one who will save his people becomes simply "the child" throughout Matthew 2. This way of referring to Jesus, however, has it own impact on the reader and links this chapter to Jesus' teaching about children in 18:1-5 in ways in which naming Jesus would not.

To help me recontextualize this text in the twenty-first century for real flesh-and-blood readers, I discussed the text with a group of women for whom justice for children is a passion. As we read Matthew 2 together, our first impression was that the storytelling lacks emotion. Only two characters display any emotion: Herod, who is described as "troubled" when he hears of the child (2:3) and becomes "exceedingly angry" when he realizes he has been duped by the magi (2:16), and the magi, who "rejoice with exceedingly great joy" when they find the child (2:10).[4] No affective reaction is depicted over what one would expect to be very emotional events: the birth of a child and the murder of as many as twenty infants in a single village (Hagner 1995a: 37; France 1979: 114). We struggled with the matter-of-fact manner in which the narrative was recounted. While the quotation from Jeremiah suggests a lament from the women of Bethlehem, there was still not the personal attribution of emotion as is true of Herod and the Magi. I did point out to the group, though, that Matthew is careful not to imply that God was responsible for the killing of the baby boys, by avoiding causal language in the scriptural-fulfillment quotation (Hagner 1995a: 37). In particular, Matthew avoids using a strong purpose conjunctive such as *hina*, "in order that," or *hypos*, "so that," as in 2:5, 15, and 23. Moreover, as readers, we have the right to resist the narrator's implication that God does not care as much for those children as God cares for and protects Jesus.

We also examined the role of Mary in the unfolding story. Like Jesus, she is passive and is only the object of the actions of others. She is depicted as isolated and distanced from any other women. Unlike Luke's nativity story, in which Mary joins with Elizabeth to celebrate her pregnancy (Luke 1:39-56), Matthew depicts Mary as a woman alone. We wanted to know how the community reacted to her pregnancy. How did they react to her fleeing with a baby to Egypt? Was she able to find a community there? How did the other parents in Bethlehem react to the murder of their babies? The text does not answer any of these questions.

As we turned to discuss "the child," we recognized that the omission of Jesus' name and the use of "the child" to describe him affected how this group of readers identified with him and the characterization that Matthew continues to develop of him in chapter 2. On one hand, the epithet "the child" has an objectifying effect. There is a sense in which Jesus is simply "a kid" being "shuttled around like a football."[5] Twice, an angel of the Lord tells Joseph to "take the child" (2:13, 20). Joseph obeys each time: "Then he got up and took the child" (2:14, 21). We also noted an emotional distance that the term "child" evokes. For some of these readers, "the child" dissociated them from the story. It added aloofness to the narrative. Even the angel, who gave Jesus his name, calls him "the child." In this way, Matthew's use of "the child" may in fact diminish the importance of Jesus in this chapter in favor of the one who is named as many times as "the child" is, specifically, Herod. Yet the reigning "king of the Jews" is depicted as conniving and homicidal, demonstrating the need for a king who will rule justly. It may be hard for the reader to imagine that this "child" could be that just king.

On the other hand, the use of "the child" also enabled us as readers to identify more fully with Jesus in the story than if he had been named. When asked with whom they identify in a Gospel story, women do not often claim to identify with Jesus (Levine 2009). However, our group readily identified with "the child" and attributed a variety of characteristics to him. The child in the story is one of low status. Both the fact that the child is an infant and the use of *paidion*, "little child," which is semantically related to *pais*, "child or slave," convey the sense of one who lacks choice and is powerless. The child is vulnerable in this story and very much in need of the care provided by his parents. We may not have associated these attributes with Jesus if his name were used in this narrative.

As discussed above, often the role of the quotations from the Hebrew Bible in Matthew demonstrates that Jesus' life was consistent with God's will as it is outlined in the Scriptures. However, we were also able to see how Matthew uses the scriptural quotations to continue constructing the identity of Jesus. Again, by not using his name, we as readers were able to create our own understanding and image of Jesus, rather than filling in the blanks with preconceived notions that the name "Jesus" may evoke. The quotation in Matt. 2:6 from Micah suggests that this child will become a leader, a shepherd of God's people, Israel. The passage in 2:15, from Hosea, emphasizes the child's special relationship to God; he is God's own son. The passage in 2:18, from Jeremiah, links the child to the despair of the exile followed by the joy of the return. It is as if the child is a blank slate on whom all of these attributes are written, augmenting the identity Matthew has already constructed in chapter 1, as he builds his case for why Jesus is the Messiah.[6]

Our final considerations about the narrative did not have to do with what Matthew was doing with the story, as much as what we could do with it in our contexts of children's ministries. How could we teach about "the child" in this passage to children? We agreed that the lesson, however constructed, needed to be age appropriate. One simply would not discuss the killing of babies with very young children. Depending on the age of the children, however, themes for a lesson could arise from the centrality of the child in the story, demonstrated through the measures taken to protect him, and the way those in the story care for the child. For example, one point to discuss with children could be the way Joseph cares for Jesus and seeks to keep him and his mother safe. Children who have only one parent, or who are adopted, may find hope and feel a sense of importance from the fact that Joseph adopts Jesus and cares for him. For children who do not experience the loving care of parents, God is always present, seeking to keep Jesus safe.

"THE CHILD" IN MATTHEW 18:1-5

With these understandings of Matthew 2 in mind, we also considered how "the child" in that chapter relates to "the child" and children in Matt. 18:1-5. Before I discuss the groups' findings, however, a word about Matthew's use of language regarding children and the connection between the two passages is in order. Jesus' teachings in the Gospel of Matthew are replete with references to children, and a variety of words in Greek are used to describe or identify children. *Teknon*, "child," is used fourteen times in the Gospel in both singular and plural forms (Matt. 2:18; 3:9; 7:11; 9:2; 10:21 [twice]; 15:26; 18:25; 19:29; 21:28 [twice]; 22:24; 23:37; 27:24). In all of but two cases, Jesus uses the word *teknon* while he is teaching. (The two exceptions are 2:18 and 27:25.) In only one case does *teknon* refer to another character in the Gospel narrative. Jesus calls the paralyzed man "child" when he heals him (9:2-8), even though the individual does not seem to be a juvenile but an adult: first, no parents are mentioned in the story as they are in the healing stories that are clearly about children (9:2-8; 15:21-28; 17:14-20); rather, an indefinite "they" bring the man to Jesus; and second, he then goes to "his house" after he is healed. *Pais*, "child or slave/servant," is used eight times, the majority of which refers to a slave or servant (Matt. 8:6, 8, 13; 12:18; 14:2). It refers only three times to a child or children (2:16; 17:18; 21:15). *Thygater*, "daughter," is used five times (Matt. 9:18, 22; 14:6; 15:22, 28) to refer to girls, and *korasion*, "girl," is used three times to refer to female children (9:24, 25; 14:11). Matthew uses *mikros*, "little one," five times in reference to persons, though there is some ambiguity as to whether it refers to children, the disciples, or simply "the least" (Matt. 10:42; 18:6, 10; 11:11, 14). *Huios*, "son," is only used once in the singular to refer to a child other than Jesus, in particular the epileptic boy in 17:15.

The word used most commonly for children in the first Gospel is *paidion*, "little child," the diminutive of *pais*. It is used eighteen times, only six of which are in the plural form (Matt. 11:16; 14:21; 15:38; 18:3; 19:13, 14). The majority of the time, *paidion* is in the singular in Matthew's Gospel: it is found nine times in Matthew 2, and all refer to Jesus (Matt. 2:8, 9, 11, 13 [twice], 14, 20 [twice], 21). The remaining three times in which *paidion* is used in the singular form are in 18:1-5 in response to the disciple's question, "Who is the greatest in the kingdom of heaven?" (Matt. 18:2, 4, 5). Jesus calls a child and sets the child among them declaring that they must change and become like children in order to enter the reign of heaven. Then Jesus declares, "Whoever becomes humble like this child is the greatest in the kingdom of heaven. Whoever welcomes one such child in my name welcomes me" (Matt. 18:4-5 NRSV).

In sum, Matthew employs a variety of words to speak about children in the Gospel, including *paidion* in both the singular and plural. The singular of *paidion*, however, is used only in chapter 2 in reference to Jesus, and in chapter 18 as Jesus discusses the child in relationship to the reign of heaven. It is clear from this word choice that Matthew is drawing a connection between the child Jesus and the child who is greatest in the reign of heaven. Thus, just as chapter

2 foreshadows events that Matthew depicts later in the Gospel, so too does "the child" in Matthew 2 anticipate Jesus' teaching with a child as the premier example of membership in the reign of heaven.

As the women's group began examining the Matt. 18:1-5, we first wondered where Jesus and his disciples are that a child is nearby. The broader literary context of the passage indicates that Jesus and his disciples have arrived back in Capernaum, where Jesus made his adult home, after a preaching and healing tour in the region. Matthew 17:24-27 recounts an interaction between Peter and a tax official, after which Peter goes home. There Jesus' disciples come to him, and they ask, "Who is greatest in the kingdom of heaven?" Thus presumably Jesus and the disciples are in Peter's home. It is likely that the home was also that of the child. Like the magi, who find the child Jesus at home with his mother (2:11), so too does this child appear to be at home. Perhaps then the child was Peter's child, since Matthew indicates that Peter was married in 8:14 by referring to his mother-in-law.

One of the group members remarked that the disciples' question was rather childlike, a "who's best?" type of question. As we reflected on this further, however, we concluded that the question is actually more typical perhaps of older children or teenagers. Very young children do not concern themselves with questions of social order. They bond together on the basis of interests or playthings rather than social concepts. In this regard, there is a sense then in which the child as the model for the kingdom of heaven is exactly right. Traditional human social concepts and ordering are turned upside down in the reign of God. If we understand the reign of God to be what life would be like if God were the ruler and the domination systems of the world were not, then the child's sense of community may be right on the mark.

The group wondered about the status of children in that social-historical context. I shared that, on one hand, the Hebrew Bible teaches that children are a sign of divine blessing (Gen. 13:16; 15:1-16; Ps. 127:3-5; 128:3-6). They embody "the hope of the family, or the people, for a meaningful future" (Carroll 2001: 124; see also Grassi 1992: 904). Yet the Hebrew Bible also advocates harsh discipline for children (Prov. 3:11-12; 13:24; 22:15; see also Sirach 30). In the broader Greco-Roman context of the first century, children were at the bottom of the social, political, and economical scale. They were considered "weak, irrational, ignorant [and] unpredictable" and were valued primarily for their later contributions to society as adults (Carter 2000: 80). While most families certainly cared for their children, in many areas of the empire exposure of newborns was commonplace, especially among girls and children born disabled

(Seneca *On Anger* 1.15.2; Osiek and MacDonald 2006: 100). Many children died as infants or young children from a variety of causes (Pomeroy 1999: 80).

One of the group members then reflected that in a real way, both literally and figuratively, children were "left out" of the society: some were left out to die or to be picked up by strangers, and otherwise they generally were not of great significance. Jesus was concretely demonstrating that God does not leave children out of the reign of heaven. In relation to the disciples, Jesus could be telling them that even though society chooses to exclude some, the reign of God is all-inclusive, even of children. Finally, another woman stated that there is a sense of changing to become like a child rather than just acting like a child; it is about not just acting as a child acts but also becoming as a child is.

But what does it mean to become as a child is? Jesus does not elaborate on this point. He does not tell the disciples what aspects of this particular child or children they are supposed to emulate. Though Jesus does not explicate this point, Matthew does. By referring to Jesus only as "the child" throughout chapter 2, Matthew constructs an image of who the child is or will be in the remainder of the Gospel. This image evolves in three ways.

First, as the women's group discussed, the child in Matthew 2 is vulnerable, as all children were, to a variety of dangers. Having endured the perils of childbirth and the crucial first year or two of life, he is uprooted from his home and taken to another land. He becomes a refugee at a young age, exiled to a country that is not his own. He is shuttled from his homeland to a place of refuge and back to the homeland, but the family settles in another region of that land. Second, this child is threatened with death. Indeed, the threat of death was a reality for all children at that time. This child in Matthew is specifically threatened with death by King Herod. He perceives that the child whom the magi have called "king of the Jews" is a threat to his rule, and the ruler responds by seeking to kill the child. Third, this child is completely dependent on others. His safety depends on Joseph's obedience to God's instructions in dreams. An angel of the Lord tells Joseph that Herod is about to kill the child and commands him to take the child and his mother to Egypt. Once Herod has died, the angel then tells Joseph to get up and take the child back to Israel. The child has no will of his own but rather relies on the goodness of his adoptive father, Joseph, and Joseph's obedience to God. The similarities between the story of the infant Jesus and that of the infant Moses reinforce this characterization. In the Septuagint, Moses is referred to as "the child," *paidion*, several times (Exod. 2:3, 6-9). Moses was also vulnerable to the whims of the ruler Pharaoh, threatened by Pharaoh with death, and protected by his mother and an adoptive parent, Pharaoh's daughter (Exod. 2:1-10). Thus a child in Matthew's narrative world is one who is vulnerable, threatened with death, and completely dependent on others, including God.[7]

The child in Matthew 2 can then direct our reading of the Gospel of Matthew in three ways: first, the child in 2:1-23 shapes the role of children in the Gospel from chapters 3–17; second, the child in chapter 2 provides the characteristics of the child the disciples are asked to emulate in 18:1-5; and third, chapter 2 proleptically illustrates Jesus' teaching in 18:5, "Whoever welcomes one such child in my name welcomes me."

This depiction of the child in Matthew is reinforced through the stories of three children whom Jesus heals. In 9:18-26, the daughter of the leader of the synagogue has died, and the leader comes to Jesus asking him to restore the girl to life. In 15:21-28, the daughter of the Canaanite woman is ravished by a demon. In 17:14-20, an epileptic boy also "suffers terribly" from a demon-induced affliction. The boy's father initially asks Jesus' disciples for help, but it is Jesus who eventually casts out the demon. In each case, a child is vulnerable to an illness, disorder, is dead, or threatened with death. The child is completely dependent on her or his parent. The parent, however, is unable to help and in turn depends on Jesus, God's agent, to heal the affliction. Jesus indeed heals each child. The table has now turned: The one who was once the vulnerable, threatened, dependent child is now the adult savior who heals the vulnerable and afflicted children.

Jesus' healing of and teaching about children also anticipates his passion. Although Jesus has the power to heal and do miracles in the Gospel, he himself will model the kind of vulnerability that his infancy demonstrates and his later teachings describe. In chapters 17–20 of the Gospel, Jesus' teachings about children are interspersed with three predictions of his impending suffering and death. The first passion prediction is found in 16:21. Shortly after this, in 17:14-20, Jesus heals the boy with a demon. Immediately following that narrative is the second passion prediction, in 17:22-23. Chapter 18 opens with Jesus teaching, "Who is the greatest in the reign of heaven?" In 19:13-15, Jesus blesses the children, and Matt. 20:17-19 is his final passion prediction.

The passion predictions indicate that it is the ruling elites who will put Jesus to death. The first time Jesus predicts his death, he names Jerusalem as the place and the elders, chief priests, and scribes as those under whom he would suffer. Jerusalem was the center of the religious and political elites. The elders were lay members of the Sanhedrin, while the chief priests and scribes were a part of the governing class (Carter 2000: 342). They are also named in the third passion prediction. While Jesus is quite sure that his death will be at the hands of these groups, the passion predictions also acknowledge God's role in the unfolding events. Each time Jesus speaks about his death, he also says that he "will be raised" (16:21; 17:23; 20:19). The use of the passive here suggests that God is the agent who will raise Jesus. Thus, by the end of this narrative block, the tables seem to have turned again: the one who has healed the vulnerable and afflicted children becomes the one who is vulnerable to the ruling powers, threatened with death, and reliant on God.

Second, the characteristics of the child in chapter 2 are those whom the disciples are supposed to imitate in their life of discipleship. From 18:1—19:20, children become a central image for the disciples, the adults who are following Jesus, regarding what members of God's reign are to be. However, 19:13 makes it clear that the disciples have not understood Jesus' teachings about children. The disciples' lack of clarity, however, is understandable. They equate wealth and prestige with being saved (Matt. 19:16, 25). They cannot grasp that God's saving presence in the reign of heaven could be equated in any way with children. They are concerned with the social ordering of the world, which as one of the women in the study group pointed out, children are not. Thus Jesus tells his disciples to be like the child he has called and placed before them. Though Jesus does not explain which attributes of the child they are to imitate, Matthew has provided the model: as Jesus sets the child before them, he is setting before them the example of his own life. They are to be vulnerable as he was, threatened with death as he was, and reliant on God as he was. In short, his disciples are to become like the child he was and also like the vulnerable and threatened adult he will become. By changing and becoming like children in this way, the disciples will also become humble like the child. To be humble was to be of low status, which, as mentioned above, children are. Vulnerability and dependency are also characteristics of those who are of low status. In this way, then, becoming as the child is also to embody the humility of the child.

Finally, the second chapter of Matthew's Gospel anticipates Jesus' teaching in 18:5 that welcoming the child equals welcoming him. The Greek word *dechomai*, which the NRSV translates as "welcome" can also mean "receive" or "accept." It can have the connotation of "greet" or "worship" as well (Liddell and Scott 1996: s.v. *dechomai*). The magi, by worshiping Jesus, seem to welcome or receive the child/Jesus. Herod, however, in seeking the life of the child, clearly does not receive or accept the child/Jesus. The disciples do not understand Jesus' teaching about children, as 19:13 demonstrates. They do not accept or receive the parents bringing their children to Jesus, but instead rebuke them. This may lead the reader to wonder if the disciples accept the child/Jesus either.

CONCLUSION

Reading Matthew 2 from a feminist contextual perspective in conversation with women whose primary ministry is with children sheds new light on the chapter and how the phrase "the child" affects the reader. The almost anonymous youngster is vulnerable, threatened with death, and yet is protected by his parents and God. This depiction of a child would ring true for Matthew's first-century hearers just as it did for the twenty-first-century women who read this text with me. Matthew then takes this image of the child constructed in chapter 2 to structure the Gospel's teachings about children. Jesus' healing of children illustrates how Jesus as an adult takes care of the vulnerable and threatened children, thereby protecting them. Through the passion predictions, Matthew discloses that as an adult, Jesus has himself again become vulnerable, threatened, and reliant on God. In 18:1-5, Jesus then presents a child to his disciples as he instructs them in the ways of the reign of heaven. Those who would follow Jesus are asked to be humble like the child—vulnerable, threatened, and dependent on others and God. Indeed, for the Gospel of Matthew, to become like the child is to become like Jesus.

Notes

1. This essay is a revised and expanded version of my article "The Child and Jesus in the Gospel of Matthew," which appeared in the *Journal of Childhood and Religion* 1/4 (June 2010): 1–14, http://www.childhoodandreligion.com/JCR/Volume_1_(2010)_files/ Betsworth%20June2010.pdf, and is used by permission.

2. The group consisted of eight women: Erin Floyd, Ann Hochman, Chris McDougal, Trina Bose North, Shannon Rodenberg, Briana Tobey, Emily Valles, and Teranne Williams. They are all currently working with children and youth ministries or have in the past. I am grateful for the time the group spent with me discussing these passages.

3. "Kids Count Data Center," The Annie E. Casey Foundation, http://datacenter.kidscount.org/, accessed May 2, 2011.

4. My own translations.

5. In the words of group member Chris McDougal.

6. This phrase comes from our discussion. Chris McDougal remarked that "this tiny little blank slate is all of these things."

7. Duarte (2004: 355) draws a similar conclusion.

The Canaanite Woman (Matthew 15:22–28)

Discharging the Stigma of Single Moms in the African American Church

Febbie C. Dickerson

The context from which I write is that of a Christian, single, African American woman without children who stands in solidarity with single, African American women with children in the African American church tradition.[1] In the United States, women constitute 60 percent of those attending church. In the African American church, single mothers are viewed as second-class citizens, suffering a double marginalization because of gender and family structure (Dube 2000: 122).[2] This double marginalization engenders marginal treatment because women and men view single mothers negatively. On the one hand, married women and women with significant others often view single women with children as a threat to their marital and intimate relationships. While growing up in the church, I heard older women tell younger married women to be on guard for the single woman with children: she is "seeking a man to be the caretaker" for her family. On the other hand, some men view single women with children as helpless and in need of a male figure to help with the care of their children, especially male children. In churches today, men are encouraged to take time with children who don't have a father at the church. Though the intent is good-natured and acknowledges the importance of a male presence in children's lives, it presumes a neediness on the part of the single mother that may not be there.[3] With this assumption, the single mom may find herself voiceless concerning who establishes relationships with her children.

Exacerbating the stigma of single mothers in African American churches is the authority of the Christian tradition that promulgates the "God-ordained model of family" as hierarchal, male-ruled families advocating marriage and children, and opposing divorce.[4] Communities of faith are generally concerned with Christian faith and lifestyle and refer to the Bible and Christian tradition because of ecclesial authority and societal influence (Schüssler Fiorenza 1984: 9, 23). The image of the church as the household of God has inspired not only the advocates of womanhood, who cast women in a certain role of the family, but also patriarchally controlled associations of church women (Schüssler Fiorenza 1984: 126). The women of the church become a patriarchally controlled association, whose main objective is to protect the "status" of being a married woman. As a result of double marginalization undergirded by church authority, single mothers are constantly reminded that they have fractured families (Riggs 2003: 39).[5] A friend who is a single mother once said that she is not aware she is a single parent until she comes to church. Thus a fundamental problem for single moms in the African American church tradition is that their family structure does not mirror what is thought to be the proper model of family. Moreover, the theological issue for the African American church tradition is what determines the proper family structure for community members. Church tradition promulgates the family model as hierarchal and male-ruled. The contemporary praxis of family shows a multitude of family models not only in society but also within faith communities. This monolithic ideal of family stands in stark contrast to the considerable pluralism surrounding American family life, including extended families consisting of kin, both blood and fictive, that extend beyond the nuclear family and are often multigenerational. American family life may also include egalitarian roles and households whose productive functions often extend beyond immediate physical boundaries into interhousehold exchange networks (Dickerson 1995: x–xi).[6] Thus the African American church tradition may be struggling to theologically understand the changing place of single mothers in the church.

Viewing this life context in light of the Gospel of Matthew, I contend that faith communities have made the idea of "sameness" an idol. The dominant fraction of a community has determined that their status and existence is the only path for proper living. Some within communities of faith have imposed their ideas on others within and outside of the community and announced that their ideas are what God has approved. The Matthean writer reveals that the true nature of family extends beyond biological kinship. Matthew proposes that whoever does the will of the father is a brother, sister, or mother (12:50). Therefore, in the eyes of God, a family is more than a wife and husband with biological children. A family is connected with the presence of God and offers that presence to others.

MOTHERHOOD

Single mothers are bound by a construction of motherhood whose form and content are shaped by religious and theological understandings and are politically reinforced in society through public policy that illumines a certain image of the good and bad mother. The notion of motherhood resides in the dichotomy of the ideal versus the reality (Miller-McLemore 1999: 281–303).[7] The ideal mother points beyond concrete existence toward an ultimate fantasy of motherhood that becomes inscribed as the reality of motherhood. Hence, the ideal as formulated by religious institutions constructs the institution of motherhood in service to patriarchy, which seeks to promote a category of motherhood that solely operates in the realm of wife, purity, nurturer, and caretaker. The institution of motherhood also promotes the family as heterosexual and male-dominated. As head of the household, the male as husband and father has ultimate authority over the family, though the female as wife and mother may have full responsibility for all domestic matters as well as shared economic responsibility for keeping the family going (Cooey 1999). The proper depiction of a mother as declared by Christianity is a nurturer of children who is bound to the family by way of marriage to a man. This framework for motherhood necessarily marginalizes single mothers as it communicates that they are not acting in the proper sphere of mother. The woman with children but without a husband is thus viewed as deviant and lacking in the skills of true motherhood.

The role of mother is reified in both the Hebrew Bible and the New Testament. Proverbs 31:10-31 paints the picture of the super wife and mother. This woman is the heart of her husband and does him good and not harm (31:11-12). She works with willing hands and rises while it is still night and provides food for her household (31:13, 15). This woman looks well to the ways of her household and does not eat the bread of idleness (31:27). Her children and husband call her blessed (31:28). Likewise in the New Testament, the household codes are understood to provide guidelines for the workings of a Christian household. Wives are encouraged to be subject to or accept the authority of their husband (Col. 3:18; Eph. 5:22; 1 Pet. 3:1a). Guidelines for behavior suggest that young women should love their husbands and be self-controlled (Titus 2:4-5), while ideals of reverence and purity are invoked to set an example for wayward husbands (1 Pet. 3:1b-2). In both cases, the ideal and duties of womanhood and motherhood are presented so as to eliminate the idea of single mothers.

The castigation of single mothers is a continuous phenomenon even outside of religious institutions. Political policies such as welfare and welfare reform continue the negative evaluations of single mothers. Linda Gordon in *Pitied but Not Entitled: Single Mothers and the History of Welfare 1890-1935* (1994) examines the political consequences of single motherhood through the lens of the welfare system in the United States. She asserts that women alone with children reinforced all that was perceived as negative because the stigmas of welfare and of single motherhood intersect; hostility to the poor and to deviant family forms reinforced each other (Gordon 1994: 6). The sense that single mothers signify deviant family forms is engendered by the moral intensities that consume a society concerned with the sexuality and reproductive functions of women and women's roles as caretakers of the family. The single mother is thus perceived as being sexually out of control. In our political consciousness as it relates to welfare, sexually out of control women produce more children that the public must then take care of. The category of single mother worked in many ways to degrade any woman found with children and without a husband (Gordon 1994: 24–28).[8]

While other societal problems disproportionately affect African American single mothers, those in the African American church tradition not only must look beyond the normative defamation of single mothers by society but also must not participate in that defamation under the guise of religion (Dickerson 1995: xvi).[9] Cultural influences and the worldview of the dominant fraction of society have long shaped the discourse about and stigma of single motherhood. These social stigmas, along with the ideal of motherhood created by religious institutions, have oftentimes pushed single mothers to the margins of church and society.

WHAT'S THE SOLUTION?

The way forward for a single mother in the African American church tradition is to liberate African American faith communities from the idolatry of viewing the patriarchal family model as an absolute rather than as a cultural construct, which is at the root of an ideological sin that marginalizes single mothers. There must be a new vision of the church as the true *ekklesia*, the public assembly, the household of faith that will bring solidarity among its members, including single mothers. The church as *ekklesia* is ideally the gathering of all those women and men who, empowered by the Holy Spirit and inspired by the biblical vision of justice, freedom, and salvation, struggle against all odds for liberation from patriarchal oppression in society in general and religion in particular (Schüssler Fiorenza 1984: xiv). It is essential that this ideal faith community view the marginalization of single mothers as an ideological sin—that is, a sinful perception of the relationship between members of the community—a sin that suggests single mothers are less worthy than married women because they lack a husband. While the hierarchal, male-ruled family is one model of family, it cannot be presented as the only family model. The Matthean Jesus suggests that family extends beyond biological kinship and rests with those who are true disciples of Christ doing the will of God (12:50). Jesus declares that it is not what goes into the mouth that defiles but that which comes out of the mouth (15:11). It is not single mothers who defile the church. It is the church's *marginalization* of single mothers that defiles the church. Thus the Gospel of Matthew, and specifically the Canaanite woman pericope (Matt. 15:21-28), promulgates a dual message: (1) liberation of single mothers in the church from their doubly marginalized status and (2) a corrective vision for the church that single mothers are viable members of God's family. The Beatitudes (Matt. 5:1-11), the account of the Canaanite Woman (15:21-28), and Jesus' discourse on living in community (18:1-7), sometimes called the church discourse, open new vistas for a shift in the vision of African American churches.

THE GOSPEL OF MATTHEW

The Gospel of Matthew has been considered one of the most highly treasured accounts of Jesus' life among the early Christians. It preserves the teachings of Jesus as the memorable sayings of the Sermon on the Mount, including the Beatitudes, the Golden Rule, and the Lord's Prayer, teachings that have inspired Christian readers through the ages and convinced them of Jesus' genius as a teacher of religious principles (Ehrman 2008: 101). The Gospel, written circa 80–90 ce, raises the issue of how a church rooted in Judaism should relate to the larger gentile world (Meier 1992: 4:625). Some scholars surmise that gentiles were joining the Christian church well before Matthew wrote his Gospel. In fact, there may have been more gentiles who claimed to be followers of Jesus than Jews (Ehrman 2008: 115). Therefore, Matthew engenders a theme of a church struggling to work through transition. However, as the church attempts to manage change, Matthew's Jesus is presented as the one who rightly interprets God's law and teaches others to follow. Here, God's law is the way to walk and be in relationship with others. Jesus did not come to abolish the law or the prophets but to fulfill the law (5:17). Following God's law is not viewed as burdensome but is a spiritual practice that benefits all. Thus Jesus instructs individuals how to live among one another (the Beatitudes), demonstrates a shift in vision toward an "outsider" (Canaanite woman), and instructs the church on how it should welcome and receive others (church discourse).

A contemporary application of Matthew can speak to African American church traditions in transition who are grappling to handle the cultural shifts that transform society's ideas and modes of being. Matthew's Canaanite woman demonstrates, first, that gentiles were entering the spaces of the people of God and, second, that gentiles should receive benefits from the power of Jesus. The Beatitudes (5:1-11) and the establishment of church order (18:1-14) allow Matthew's narrative of the Canaanite woman to point both to the liberation and inclusion of the other into the community of God and to a shift in vision for the faith community.

METHODOLOGY

Using the Gospel of Matthew as instructive for discharging the stigma of single moms in the African American church tradition, I employ literary analysis in examining three passages of Scripture, which will aid in shifting the vision of those within African American faith communities. The primary pericope is the account of the Canaanite woman, which depicts a marginalized woman obtaining liberation from the ecclesial leader Jesus by speaking for herself and refusing to be categorized as an outsider of the house of Israel. The secondary passages are the Beatitudes, which promote a household ecclesiology that instructs persons how to live among one another, and the church discourse, which provides guidance on welcoming and receiving others. The Beatitudes represent the warrant for liberation of single mothers and African American church members by affirming the place of single mothers in the church and by demonstrating that other members of African American church traditions are no different from single mothers. Thus the Beatitudes negate dominance and subordination in the household. The church discourse sets out the ideals of a community that understands the importance of welcoming and receiving others. The literary reading strategy is bolstered by the ideals of liberation so that single mothers may experience full inclusion without stigma in their church communities. I also include an application of Victor Turner's theory of liminality as a ritual by which liberation may not only be envisioned but also obtained for an entire church community. Each biblical passage and Turner's theory of liminality call for the African American church tradition to shift from its ideological sin that suggests single mothers are less worthy than married women because of the lack of a husband.

Liberation for African American Churches

As I noted above, the Gospel of Matthew promotes a new type of family that extends beyond the boundary of biological kinship. In Jesus' new family of disciples, blood means nothing. What counts is being a disciple who does the will of the heavenly Father (Crosby 1988: 60, 145).[10] The Beatitudes, found in the Sermon on the Mount, can be considered the pathway to a household spirituality that involves fulfilling the command to love God, others, and self (22:37–40) (Crosby 2005: 11). Thus the Gospel writer promotes a household ideology in which a number of persons may be fully included in the sphere of God. Moreover, these modes of being instilled within the household promote a vision for how all family members are to be accepted and respected. For the African American church tradition and other contemporary readers, Jesus has put forward an ecclesiology that envisions an *ekklesia* of women and men honoring and accepting all persons as equals in the community.

Although the Canaanite woman is often read as a discourse on faith and discipleship, I choose to read this pericope through the lens of the Beatitudes, as a means of liberation for the household that is the African American church tradition at large. The purpose of a liberation interpretation is to liberate members of the African American church tradition from their bondage to ideological sins rooted in idolatry that hinder them from their ethical duty of loving neighbor. A liberative reading is done by or about a member of a marginalized group, undercuts the status quo, and refuses to allow marginal persons or groups to be placed in either a superior or an inferior subject position (Tolbert 1995: 268). Using the above qualifiers, I with single African American moms need to produce a liberative reading of Matthew's account of the Canaanite woman that will attack the sin of idolatry employed by the African American church at large, which engenders oppression for single moms.

Using Victor Turner's ideas of liminality and *communitas*, I see this theory as an added means of liberating the African American church tradition from the cultural construct of the patriarchal, male-ruled family model as absolute. Following in the steps of Arnold Van Gennep, Turner suggests that any culturally recognized, stable, or recurrent condition may be changed through the liminal phase of the rites of passage (Turner 1969: 94). The theory of liminality delineates three stages or transitions. The first phase, called separation, describes the subject's detachment from earlier fixed states or social positions. Here, an example would be the catechumen or a person going through the process of new-member classes in a Protestant church. Catechesis and other modes of study help to detach the person from lived states prior to entering the world of church. In the second phase of liminality, the subject passes through a cultural realm that has few or none of the attributes of the past or coming state (Turner 1969: 94). Again, using the catechumen as an example, this person is in a state whereby she or he is separated from the prior state not related to the church but not yet incorporated into full church membership. The final stage of liminality is called reincorporation, whereby the subject has rights and is obligated to observe the norms and standards of the community of which he or she has entered.

The liminal space is a blend of dualities such as strong/weak, male/female, educated/uneducated, and married mother/single mother that often cause schism within communities. Turner argues that the liminal space is at first like two models of human interrelatedness that are juxtaposed but are at the same time alternating between a differentiated and hierarchal society and one emerging into a relatively undifferentiated society or communion of equal individuals (Turner 1969: 96). Liminal entities are neither here nor there; rather, they are betwixt and between the positions assigned or set in place by law, custom, or convention (Turner 1969: 96). Thus members within African American church traditions along with single mothers may experience liberation and new ways of being in the undifferentiated relatedness to one another that occurs in liminal stages, a condition that Turner calls communitas.[11] Liminality further suggests that the "high" could not be the high unless the "low" existed, and those who are high must experience what it is like to be low (Turner 1969: 97). Thus communitas effects conversions and inversions that promulgate a more balanced space. Critiques of Turner's theory of liminality have argued that liminal spaces do not necessarily enhance the lives of women (Bynum 1996: 71–86).[12] However, I argue that both single mothers and other persons within African American church traditions, with a new vision of community established from the Beatitudes (5:3-12) and accounts of the Canaanite woman (15:22-28) and the church discourse (18:1-9) may be able in liminal space to forge a community in which single mothers are viewed as whole and not fractured.

MATTHEW 15:22-28: THE CANAANITE WOMAN

Matthew's account of the Canaanite woman begins with a focus on Jesus, the ecclesial authority who has left a certain place after conflict with Pharisees and scribes, regarding what does and does not defile a person (15:1). As the writer details that Jesus has gone toward the region of Tyre and Sidon (15:21), the focus immediately shifts (15:22) toward the gendered marginal person who "came out from" the region of Tyre and Sidon. I define a marginalized person as one who does not have control over his or her life situation. While the literary analysis does not provide any clues to the woman's social background, family, or socioeconomic status, the Matthean writer has constructed a relationship of subordination (Dube 2000: 129). The Canaanite is at the mercy of Jesus' authority. The healing of the Canaanite woman's daughter hinges on Jesus' response to the mother's pleas. Reading the text in this way highlights a member of a marginalized group.

A liberative reading notes that the text undercuts the status quo, according to which marginalized persons cannot and should not speak. The Matthean status quo, accordingly, posits that marginalized females do not speak in public. Peter's mother-in-law (8:14-15), the daughter of the ruler of the synagogue (9:18), and the woman who suffered from hemorrhages (9:20-25) are all silent. Someone speaks on their behalf, or there is an inner dialogue. The Canaanite woman undercuts the Matthean status quo because, despite being a gendered, marginalized person, she speaks directly to Jesus. Moreover, she speaks on behalf of her sick daughter, as did the ruler of the synagogue (9:18), when she calls out to Jesus (15:22) after identifying the plight of her daughter as her own. Here, in the grand narrative of Matthew, the Canaanite woman is not subordinated but granted an equal hearing before Jesus. The Canaanite woman falls down praising Jesus while again requesting help (15:25); and, by proclaiming that even the dogs eat the crumbs that fall from their master's table, she verbally spars with Jesus after he has likened her to the dogs (15:27). The fact that the marginalized has a voice is an important means for changing consciousness and transforming society through acts of liberation. Reading the Bible for liberation is ultimately grounded in the acknowledgment of those whose otherness is silenced and marginalized by those in power and in showing respect for their otherness by giving them voice (Weems 2006: 29). Moreover, the disciples (15:23), although for selfish reasons, help to undercut the status quo by asking Jesus to grant the request of the Canaanite woman. Liberation for a marginalized group begins to happen when, for whatever reasons, people speak against the status quo; in so doing, these people become unwitting advocates for the marginalized.

Another characteristic of a liberative reading is the disruption of the status quo that takes the form of a refusal to be definitively placed in either a superior or an inferior subject position. The question becomes: Did the Canaanite woman refuse to be categorized or accept categorization? Elaine Wainwright, in *Shall We Look For Another: A Feminist Rereading of the Matthean Jesus* (1998: 87), asserts that the Canaanite woman's acceptance of Jesus' insult produces a new space for her within the house of Israel. I believe the text can be read in the other way; the Canaanite woman refuses to be categorized. The woman's notice that both "master" and "dogs" eat the same food provides a means by which social hierarchies, which ultimately lead to marginalization, can be broken down (Levine 2001: 40). While Jesus reminds the reader that his mission is to the lost sheep of the house of Israel, the Canaanite woman sees herself as already a member of the house of Israel. She is thus positioned to receive that which the house members are entitled, including healing for her daughter.

MATTHEW 5:3-12: THE BEATITUDES PROVIDE A DIFFERENT PERSPECTIVE

Although Jesus announces that he came only for the lost sheep of the house of Israel (15:24), the Beatitudes affirm the Canaanite woman's place in the *ekklesia* of God. When Jesus speaks the Beatitudes, he speaks to the crowds (5:1), who are the poor in spirit. The crowds are not a select group of people but persons in need of the presence of God along with the promises and hopes from the lips of Jesus—as are, beyond the Sermon on the Mount, the leper (8:2), the servant of the centurion (8:6), Simon Peter's mother-in-law (8:14), and many others. Thus the Canaanite woman is not different from those in the crowds. The words of Jesus to the crowds are also words for the Canaanite woman. She is one of those who are poor in spirit. Her daughter is sick and in need of healing. The Canaanite woman cannot go to her own to receive what she needs. She is indulging another community to supply an important need. The Canaanite is also one who hungers and thirsts for righteousness/justice (5:6), as she comes seeking the power of healing for her daughter from the authority of Jesus. Likewise, the Beatitudes affirm the place of single mothers within the African American church by showing that single mothers are not different than other members of the church. The words of Jesus to the crowds are also words to other members within African American churches. All are poor in spirit and need the presence of God (5:3). Single mothers and African American church members hunger and thirst for righteousness/justice, are merciful, pure in heart, and are peacemakers (5:6-9). Both single mothers and the African American church tradition are persecuted for righteousness sake (5:11) and are blessed when all kinds of evil are uttered against them (5:12). The Beatitudes disavow dominance and subordination in the household. They function to challenge the church to be countercultural by rejecting the standards of the dominant culture that seek to create insider/outsider dichotomies. For those in African American church communities, an understanding of the Beatitudes can shift the vision of those members at large to see that they stand in the same shoes as those of single mothers. The ecclesial leader Jesus was changed from his insistence on operating within the boundaries of his community to including the gentile woman in his power to bless and heal. The account of the Canaanite woman in light of the Beatitudes is important for African American churches, which must shift from their limited vision of understanding family as only hierarchal and male-ruled to accepting more diverse forms of family.

THE CHURCH DISCOURSE: MATTHEW 18:1-9

Matthew 18 explicates how members of the church should share life with each other. This chapter suggests a paradigm shift in terms of living in community: It calls for persons to accept a radically different vision of status within a community, abandon status seeking, live in community without causing a stumbling block to others, abandon the desire to dominate others, and refrain from showing disdain to other members in the community. Matthew 18:1-9, specifically, is a block of moral teaching that has special bearing on relations among church members. Verses 1-5 demand humility, and verses 6-9 demand the elimination of all stumbling blocks (Davies and Allison 1991: 753).

Jesus announces to the disciples that, to enter the kingdom, one must become like children (18:3). The nature of a child is that of vulnerability and helplessness, because children in that social context had no social status or political significance (Harrington 1991a: 264). The child is a symbol for persons who are dependent on God. The idea of vulnerability is not only that of being open and unguarded, but also that of showing oneself as not confined to status and power. For the church, vulnerability suggests that those in the church must be vulnerable to God and to each other. Jesus' symbolic action in placing the child in the disciples' midst was an appropriate way to undercut the disciples' speculations about status in the kingdom (Harrington 1991a: 264). The idea here for some African American church traditions is that since the focus on social status based on married or single within the community of God is not a laudable marker for community life; rather, all community members must recognize their own vulnerability and helplessness if they are going to recognize the vulnerability and helplessness of others. Therefore, deference to each other based on humility grounds the community in a form of egalitarianism that demonstrates single mothers and married persons as equals within the community.

While some scholars make a distinction between Matthew's use of *paidion* ("children," 18:1-5) and *mikron* ("little ones," 18:6-9), the main concern is that Jesus assesses those viewed with lesser status as model recipients of the kingdom.[13] Moreover, the children or little ones are more than the disciples who doctrinally believe in Jesus but are the people in need of his help—the sick, the relatives or friends of sick people (Patte 1987: 249). The Canaanite woman is vulnerable and helpless due to the illness of her daughter. She is a little one, who is possibly marginalized because she is not of the house of Israel and should be regarded as a model recipient of God's kingdom. Although Jesus tells her that he has come only for the lost sheep of the house of Israel, his prior action and speech (8:5-10) projects that he will extend his mission to a little one of the kingdom.[14]

Matthew 18:6-9 details Jesus' speech concerning right action in the community.[15] It is better that a millstone be tied around a person's neck and that they be drowned in the depths of the sea than for a stumbling block to be placed in the path of a little one who believes (18:6-9). For Matthew, the concern about stumbling blocks is about realizing that causing harm to other believers also causes harm to oneself. Therefore, a stumbling block is not only that which misleads or causes one to fall away from the community and God but is also that which impedes one who is seeking the help of Jesus. The Canaanite is not officially in the community of Israel, but she recognizes the divine and healing power of Jesus. A little one such as the Canaanite, who believes in the healing restoration of Jesus, should be given every chance to flourish, whether or not she is a member of the community. Likewise, the stumbling blocks for single mothers are the constant reminders that their family is fractured or that they are not as worthy as married mothers. These reminders cause harm to the single mother and the community, in that they may cause single mothers to fall away from their religious communities. The right action that Jesus is calling for is a *salvation* for the entire African American church tradition, where there cannot be thoughtlessness toward others. For members of the African American church tradition, our life is with our neighbor; if we gain our single mothers, we have gained God. If we scandalize our single mothers, we have sinned against Christ (Davies and Allison 1991: 763).[16]

Matthew 18 suggests a paradigm shift in terms of living in community: it calls for persons to accept different visions of community by abandoning ideas of hierarchy based on domination, status seeking, and the creation of insider/

outsider dichotomies. This new vision of community posits that all are equal and viable in the community.

The Solution in Motion

The solution I have suggested is that those within African American faith communities must be liberated from the idolatry of viewing the cultural construct of the patriarchal family model as absolute, which is the root of an ideological sin that marginalizes single mothers. Instructive for providing a new vision of family are the Canaanite woman (15:21-28), the Beatitudes (5:3-12), and the church discourse (18:1-9).

Textual analysis of the Canaanite woman evinces liberative notions as she undercuts and disrupts the Matthean status quo by speaking in public and refusing to be categorized as an outsider. She speaks directly to Jesus and makes space for herself within the household of Israel. The Canaanite's bravado in using her voice is important for transformation and liberation. The Beatitudes function to challenge the church to be countercultural by rejecting the standards of the insider/outsider dichotomies of the dominant culture by disavowing dominance and subordination in the household. The absence of dominance within the household necessarily helps the African American faith community at large and single mothers to recognize that they all stand in the same shoes. We all need the presence of God in our lives. Through the Beatitudes, Jesus has put forward an ecclesiology that envisions an *ekklesia* of women and men honoring and accepting all persons as equals in the community. The church discourse in Matthew 18 calls the community to live into a new paradigm that recognizes the vulnerability of all community members, that realizes harm done to one community member causes harm to the entire community, and that understands that to receive a person is to perceive Christ in that person (Davies and Allison 1991: 760). Thus to receive a single mom into the faith community is to perceive Christ in the single mom.

Moreover, I have also suggested that, along with the new vision received from the biblical text, the perspective of Victor Turner's theory of liminality will bolster the shift in vision and engender a move toward the liberation of African American church communities from absolute family models. This idea of liminal space can be best viewed through the lens of ministries within churches. A significant number of churches have both marriage and singles ministries, each designed to enhance the lives of the participants through Bible study, discussion, and fellowship. However, these ministries, though designed to be helpful to the faith community, create two problems. First, the ministries as envisioned inevitably create separation between married and single members. Marriage is promulgated as the primary concern for church members so that they will be "whole," while the status of single is viewed as incomplete. By extension, singles ministries are often viewed as the breeding ground for marriages within the church. Second, a greater concern may be the structure of singles ministries, which most often do not differentiate between types of singles. A single mom of any variety (widow, divorcee, or unwed) is very different from the single woman never married or without children. Yet these singles (and women mainly) are grouped as one. Thus I suggest that single moms and other persons within African American faith communities enter liminal space to create an added paradigm called "family ministry" so that single mothers are not isolated from the spaces that really offer more enhancement to their lives.[17] This ministry creation from liminal space allows single mothers and members of African American faith communities to be somewhat detached from prior types of ministries, on their way to the full implementation of the concepts of family ministry.

While couples ministry is a space for couples to discuss marriage experiences, family ministries can be developed in service to the challenges of daily family life (e.g., children and teenagers, school, college education, divorce, remarriage, to name a few). This added ministry would provide enhancement to the lives of single mothers in three important ways. First, a ministry blending those who lead households will engender the formation of engaging male and female adult relationships. Single mothers can benefit by gaining other ideas about household management. Second, a family ministry has the potential to build extended family networks within the church that undergird family and household management not realized by biological family members. Third, the children of single mothers will gain extended networks of friends. As married couples invest in marriage and family life, single moms invest the same or even more time and energy, face the same struggles, and meet similar challenges as two-parent families do (Ziegler 1995: 80–93). If African American churches will play a role in discharging the stigma of single moms, I believe the new paradigm of family ministry can be the pathway to that success. Forged in liminal space, family ministry will create a community more willing to live into the unstructured and undifferentiated communitas.

Notes

1. I am using the definition of African American church outlined by Marcia Riggs (2003: 17): those congregational settings where African American Christians predominate.

2. This idea of "double marginalization" is similar to Dube's "double colonization" whereby women are doubly colonized by imperialism and patriarchy but are encouraged to view their situation from a "first-things-first" approach by privileging patriarchy over imperialism. The double colonization is evident in the feminist movement when white, middle-class feminism makes patriarchy a universal problem for all women. Women of two-thirds-world countries are oftentimes faced with more pressing problems from imperialism. Therefore, women of two-thirds-world countries are doubly colonized by imperialism and white feminists who only recognize patriarchy as an issue for women. Similarly, single mothers in the African American church are oftentimes doubly marginalized by the patriarchal church in general and by nonsingle women in particular due to family structure. For single mothers, the first-things-first approach normally takes the form of finding a husband to complete the family.

3. I am not negating the positive effects of the male presence. I am proposing that one should not make the assumption that because a child does not have a father or male figure that comes to church with them on Sundays that there is not a male presence in the child's life. A grandfather or uncle could have a strong presence in the child's life but attend a different church on Sundays. Bette J. Dickerson (1995: xv) asserts that father-absent, single-mother families are erroneously assumed to be male absent, meaning that there are no supportive males present.

4. Despite the great diversity of models of Christian families found in Christianity around the world. See Patte 2010: 408.

5. Oftentimes African American women are blamed for the fractured families because they appear strong, emotionally callous, and physically invulnerable.

6. Interhousehold exchange networks are the systems of reciprocity in which families provide mutual aid for one another. It is based on trust within an extended family that consists of a network of blood and fictive kin and friends who are included in the network more than blood relatives.

7. The most oppressive form of the use of ideals occurs when norms derived from concrete realities are applied by people in power as if they were ideals to judge situations in which people cannot possibly attain the ideal because their situation is so different.

8. In the early twentieth century, single mothers were categorized as deserted, illegitimate, or widowed. Deserted mothers were those married women whose spouses were not in the home. Many of the deserted wives of the early twentieth century did not get legal divorces because they did not approve of divorce. Marriage was an institution of God and the church, and to break a marriage covenant was a sin. Illegitimate mothers were those who had never married, such as young girls who became pregnant or older mothers who were married but whose husbands were classified as having deserted the family. The third category of single women with children was that of the widow. *Widow* had become synonymous with *virtuous mother*, while any woman whose marriage had failed was suspect. The widow discourse intensified the stigmatization of other single mothers.

9. Societal problems that influence African American single motherhood, by way of endangering the African American male, include the high levels of unemployment and underemployment, incarceration, drug abuse and distribution, incarceration, and the HIV/AIDS epidemic. See also, Jesse Washington, "Blacks Struggle with 72 percent Unwed Mothers Rate," *Women's Health on NBCNews.com*, Nov. 7, 2010, http://www.msnbc.msn.com/id/39993685/ns/health-womens_health/t/blacks-struggle-percent-unwed-mothers-rate/#.UJf9LoXhFWM. Washington suggests that the legacy of segregation, welfare laws that provide incentive for single mothers to remain single, and the drug epidemic all influence African American single motherhood.

10. Crosby asserts that doing good or acts of justice is doing the will of the Father. Doing good to single moms will then take the form of justice acts that seek to offer full inclusion to single moms in the church. This way of justice characterizes the ethical stance in the house of disciples who do their heavenly father's will (Crosby 2005: 6).

11. Turner distinguishes community (area of common dwelling) from communitas (unstructured and undifferentiated gathering of individuals). "Unstructured" does not mean a lack

of coherence or organization but a lack of fixed entities that prohibit persons from experiencing different modes of being (Turner 1969: 96).

12. Bynum argues that while liminality should necessarily effect conversions and inversions of the subject's present state, women alone in liminality do not experience reversal or elevation but continuation of their present state. My point of departure is that single mothers must not go through the liminal space alone but must be accompanied by those within their communities.

13. Davies and Allison (1991: 754) argue that Jesus begins Matthew 18 by referring to literal children but then employs the term "little one" as a designation for believers. In their judgment, 18:1-5 concerns literal children, and 18:6-9 and 10-14 has to do with believers.

14. The account of the Canaanite woman is reminiscent of the account of the healing of the centurion's servant. Both are gentiles; Jesus performs the healing from a distance; and they are commended for their faith.

15. Davies and Allison (1991: 763) suggest that on the lips of Jesus, Matthew 18:6 could have been about literal children, the disciples, or "the poor" of the Beatitudes.

16. Davies and Allison's phrasing is that if we gain our brother, then we have gained God, but if we scandalize our brother, then we have sinned against Christ.

17. I am not advocating that churches abolish marriage or singles ministries; rather, they should add a different type of ministry to their ministry offerings if new community spaces will be created.

5

When Mommy Goes to Work

A Contemporary Analysis of the Canaanite Mother

Stephanie Buckhanon Crowder

INTRODUCTION

Julia.[1] Florida Evans. Ms. Thomas. Louise Jefferson or "Weezie." Claire Huxtable. Nikki Parker. These are television images of mothers, black mothers, who worked in order to support the family. They are women who worked to put a roof over their children's heads and put food on the table. There are other images: Hattie McDaniel's "Mammy," Ethel Waters in Pinkie, Beah Richards as the "Mother Preacher" in Beloved. Time will not forget the plethora of nameless mammies and matriarchs who during slavery and the Reconstruction nursed not only their children but massah's children as well. These were hard-working, burden-bearing, heavy-load-carrying foremothers who from sunup to sundown worked in the fields only to go home and provide for their own sons and daughters.

The African American community cannot forget about unwed mothers, "other" mothers or "neighborhood" mothers, who took responsibility for any and every child in the community long before daycare became a business. Our community must tell the story of hot mommas and hoochie mommas alongside our narrating the contributions of church mothers. These are all historical and yet vibrant images of black women, black mothers. These sisters represent the reality of black mothers who have a history of working and a foundation of hard work. For some, it is a need to work in order to survive. For others, it is a matter of choice, personal fulfillment. Yet common to all is the belief that our identity, my identity as a black woman, a black mother, and a black working mother is interrelated and in many cases one and the same.

This essay, an exegetical exercise based on Matthew's portrayal of the Canaanite woman pleading for Jesus to intervene on behalf of her demon-possessed daughter (Matt. 15:21-28 // Mark 7:24-30), explores the dynamics of black mothering and work as that of advocacy as well as commitment to family. I chose Matthew's version because of the negative "Canaanite" descriptive the author applies to the mother and the way in which the disciples reject her by urging Jesus to send her away. I also found intriguing the concept of faith as evident in Matthew and lacking in Mark. For Matthew, the Canaanite woman's faith is expressed through her mediating on behalf of another—in this case, her daughter. Thus work is rooted in and is the fruit of one's faith.

I will engage in a womanist maternal theological framework. This mode of interpretation speaks to my own social location as an African American working mother. According to Stephanie Mitchem, womanism starts with an analysis of roles assigned to *black* (my addition) or African American women by their families and the dominant culture, the persistent stereotypes about black women, the combination of race with gender and *class* (my addition) and the recognition of diversity among women (Mitchem 2002: 23). Delores Williams asserts that a womanist theology challenges all oppressive forces impeding black women's struggle for survival and for the development of a positive, productive quality of life conducive to the women's and the family's freedom and well-being. As a means of differentiating itself from other approaches to feminist hermeneutics, womanist theology branches off in its own direction, introducing new issues and constructing new analytical categories needed to simultaneously interpret black women's and the black community's experience in the context of theology or *God-talk* (my addition) (Williams 1993: xiv).

Bonnie Miller-McLemore constructs a feminist maternal theology that seeks to make the flourishing of mothers and children within a feminist framework a possibility (Miller-McLemore 2002: 104). For Miller-McLemore, there is a dialogue between the procreative aspects of mothers and the creative dimension of mothers who work, particularly outside of the home. The author situates this partnership under the heading of a feminist interpretive approach that honors both "the mother" in some women and the desire for some of these mothers to work.

Since feminism primarily focuses on gender construction and not on issues of race and class, I find womanist thinking a better location for this work at the present time. Therefore, I branch off and propose a womanist maternal theological method that particularly brings to the surface the voices of mothers within this African diaspora context, whether the mothers are biological or women who took responsibility for and helped to care for another's child. It must be noted that womanist authors like Teresa Fry Brown (2000), Barbara Essex (1997), and Renita Weems (2002) to name a few have addressed mother/motherhood, but none under the auspices of a womanist maternal theology. Brown talks at length of the importance of African American grandmothers, mothers, and other mothers in handing on spiritual values or moral wisdom across generations of African American families, churches, and communities through their use of biblical mandates, precepts, and examples. Essex discusses the role of her grandmother and mother in her childhood and adult life, while Weems highlights her relationship with her mother and its impact on her relationship with her own daughter. My own approach is broader, and in some ways can envelop some of the ideas presented in the aforementioned works, but at the same time takes into consideration women of the African diaspora who represent various class and social standings. Womanist maternal theology provides the nomenclature for what Fry Brown, Essex, Weems, and perhaps some others have described.

This paper proceeds along three axes. First, I explore racial/ethnic concepts as a means of establishing the Canaanite mother, an ethnic outsider, as a typology for black mothers in the United States. Although Jesus comes to her non-Jewish territory, where technically she is the racial majority, the Gospel writer reverses the power dynamic. Thus the woman's gender relegates her to a person of minority status who needs resources from someone in power. Even in her own geographical location, the Canaanite mother takes on the role as one decentered and displaced.

Second, this exercise seeks to construct a definition of "work" to ascertain how the work of the Canaanite mother correlates with current ideas of work among African American mothers. A definition of work as activity bringing children wholeness and health emerges as Matthew portrays the woman seeking her daughter's healing outside of the home. This paper questions whether such a definition aligns or contrasts with present-day mothers who may define work in more materialistic, concrete terms.

Last, I examine whether such work compromises family structure and family well-being. As the Canaanite woman, an ethnic outsider, addresses and implores Jesus, of Jewish descent, to provide her a service, and as she publicly addresses Jesus amid a male-dominated society, she dares to cross racial and gender boundaries. I wish to ascertain whether these actions compromise not only her well-being and status but also that of her child. I also seek to determine whether this Canaanite woman is a prototype for black mothers in the United States who, while working various and odd hours, simultaneously tear down walls of racism and sexism for the sake of their children. Yet such work may endanger family construction. In other words, does a biblical mother or a black working mother become a biblical mother or black mother who wrecks, destroys, disrupts, or dismantles mother-to-child bonds and relationships in the name of work?

On Being a Racial/Ethnic Outsider

Matthew establishes Jesus as leaving the land of Gennesaret and traveling to parts of Phoenicia in the province of Syria. More specifically, Jesus enters the northern districts of Tyre and Sidon, which at that time was under Roman rule. It is in this predominately gentile territory that he encounters one labeled a "Canaanite." Unlike Mark, who identifies the mother as Syrophoenician, Matthew wants the audience to associate this Canaanite with the people who struggled with the Hebrews for the promised land. For Matthew's reader, this Canaanite is a reminder of the people God had to drive out in order for Abraham's seed to receive the promise. She is a reminder of an idolatrous people, a remnant of a people who did not honor the God of Abraham, Isaac, and Jacob. The author's mention of "Canaanite" also recalls the Matthean genealogy, which lists other Canaanite women, notably mothers: Tamar (1:3) and Rahab (1:5). Both Tamar and Rahab are also types of outsiders in that they are associated with prostitution and sexual deviance. All three women achieve their goals through skillful speech and deed while acknowledging Israel's precedence in salvation history. Whereas Amy-Jill Levine maintains that Jesus is only on the outskirts of the area, I aver he physically goes into the city (see Levine 1998: 346; Meyers 2002: 412). Jesus, a Jew, dares not only to enter into this gentile district but also to enter into conversation with a woman of this district.

After Herodias, who tells her daughter to request the head of John the Baptist (14:1-2), this Canaanite woman is the first woman to speak in the Gospel of Matthew, and she is the first woman to speak to Jesus in this Gospel. Yes, the woman with the issue of blood encounters Jesus, but she talks to herself and never responds to him (9:18-26). Matthew mentions mothers (1:18-25), a mother-in-law (8:14-15), and motherhood (10:35-37; 12:46-50). However, until this literary pause, no woman speaks to Jesus other than this ethnic outsider. The work she has to do on behalf of her daughter no longer warrants silence and does not leave place for marginalization or low self-esteem.

Whereas Jesus is an area where he is now the racial minority, Matthew employs language that depicts him otherwise. Jesus has power; the Canaanite woman desires to access it. Using a rhetoric of marginalization, the Canaanite woman's language indicates powerlessness, even in her own hometown. She refers to Jesus as "Lord" three times (15:22, 25, 27). He is the "Son of David," an acknowledgment of the magnificence of Hebrew history (15:22). Jesus initially ignores the woman's presence and does not answer her at all (15:23). His disciples try to convince him to send her away because she is making too much noise (15:24). Jesus calls her a "dog" (15:26), a derogatory term the Canaanite woman uses in turn to refer to herself (15:27). Perhaps Matthew repeats the reference as a play on the Greek words for dog (*kynaria*) and Canaanite (*Chananaia*). This "dog" only wishes for crumbs from the master's table (15:27). Finally, the Canaanite woman does not have a name. She is merely a woman who comes out and starts shouting at Jesus or a loose street dog who does not stop barking. Musa Dube substantiates this point: "To characterize a foreign woman as a 'Canaanite' is to mark her as one who must be invaded, conquered, annihilated. . . . She must survive only as a colonized mind, a subjugated and domesticated subject" (Dube 2000: 147).

Assertive, strong-willed African American women also have to contend with being called a dog, the "b" word, or just plain "bitch." Black women who seem to have it all together and who really do it have it together must fight and engage in verbal combat to get the healing they and their children deserve. Even in places or locales where African American women are the majority or are running the show as managers, supervisors, leaders, teachers, doctors, lawyers, or just being the heads of households, it is not unusual for someone to come into their home, their territory, their abode, and try to reverse the power dynamic.

Black women get challenged by both men and women who question our authority. "Who does she think she is?" "She is not the boss of me." "I didn't ask to be born anyway." Students will say one thing to an African American female professor and yet remain silent and dumbfounded at the words of her white counterpart. Like this Canaanite woman, we black women know what it is like to have the tables turned and the roles reversed.

Outsider language or society's rhetoric of submission says that "yes, you are the doctor with a medical degree from Harvard, Vanderbilt, or Yale, but I want a second and third opinion." "Are you sure about this diagnosis?" Such language says, "Yes, you are the professor, but I am going to send the dean an email discreetly or just behind your back. I am going over your head." Outsider language is the government's welfare system penalizing our inner-city moms if the baby's daddy lives with them; yet persons with privilege get welfare called tax breaks, bailouts, or subsidies. This behavior is acceptable. Outsider language says, "What does a black mother mean when she says she is a stay-at-home mother homeschooling her children? Don't you work?" Outsider language says to black mothers who work, "Why don't you stay at home? Daycares are not the place for children. Don't you miss out on their development when you work? Doesn't your husband make enough? Do you have a husband?" Such language precludes the one on the outside, the one on the margins, from ever advancing or winning. Nothing this person does is or ever will be the right thing to do. Even on our own grounds, in our native land, minding our own business, we African American women, like this Canaanite woman, can speak to reversals of power. Although her comments relate specifically to African American women professors, Nancy Lynne Westfield's words are still apropos: "The national, racial, and historical hallucinations of Jezebel, Mammy and Sapphire are embedded and deeply rooted perceptions of Black women that are in the conscience of the United States since slavery. . . . Stereotypes of Black women relegate us to a body with no mind whatsoever. . . . Heretofore, a Black woman with a mind and with sanctioned authority was inconceivable and unimaginable" (Westfield 2008: 67).

Trying to "Work" It Out

The Canaanite woman shouts at Jesus and pleads for mercy. She does not ask for anything nonessential. Her request involves life and death. She does not desire to kill a man like Herodias, the mother before her (14:1-2), nor does she desire a place in the kingdom of God like the mother of the sons of Zebedee after her (20:20-28). Her daughter is demon-possessed and needs deliverance. Her baby is not herself, and momma has done all she knows to do. So the Canaanite woman goes to work.

Matthew does not use the word *work* at all in this pericope. He does not describe the mother as working. I do. Yet interestingly enough, the writer employs the word *ergo*, meaning "work, labor, or deed" eleven times throughout this Gospel (5:16; 7:22; 11:2, 20, 21, 23; 13:54, 58; 14:2; 23:3, 5). Only once is work as "praxis," meaning "function, deed, or office," utilized (16:27). I believe *ergo*, the source or root for "energy" and "energize," delineates much physical, social, mental, and emotional effort. It is exhausting while at the same time exhilarating. Thus there is within the Gospel an idea of "work" as force of movement and not a stagnant state of being. This correlates with my own understanding of the "work" of the Canaanite mother.

So what do I mean by "work"? I mean the consistent, conscientious act of pursuing those in power and challenging authority for survival, healing, health and wholeness, and future security. To work, with or without financial remuneration, is not only to seek my welfare but also to seek the well-being of persons in my family, my community, my race, and people of the world at large. Work is active, not passive. Work is what I/we do, not what is done to me/us. Such work requires the engagement and cooperation of mind, body, and spirit. The definition of work does not maintain that stay-at-home mothers do not engage in such pursuit, challenge, or advocacy. I believe another definition of "work" needs to be developed for the important work of such mothers, particularly since society tends to attach a negative connotation to the work of mothers who choose not to "go to work" outside of the home.

The Canaanite woman works. She actively pursues Jesus because she believes that, as "Lord" and "Son of David," he has power. She works in that she does not stop shouting or pleading with Jesus to use his power to enhance her situation, although the disciples urge him to send her away. Recognizing the authority of Jesus, this nameless woman works because she challenges his hesitance to use this power to help such a powerless one such as herself. This mother works so that her demon-possessed daughter may be set free and thus survive, be healed, and be made whole. This mother works her faith and secures not only a present healing but also a future promise initially reserved for the house of Israel.

The Canaanite mother sacrifices her body in that she dares, in a patriarchal society, to speak so boldly to a man in public. After all, Matthew does not say she is under anyone's authority, and thus someone in authority could reprimand her for engaging in "out-of-place" actions. Her lack of covering could make her social prey to an abusive predator. As the author does not mention a husband, perhaps the Canaanite is a single mom. Nonetheless, she puts her mental acumen and emotions on the table in that she engages in a verbal contest with Jesus and yields to his language of marginalization for the sake of her daughter. Her work is a sacrifice of her physical, emotional, and mental self. Yet, in the end, she also reaps spiritual benefits.

Patricia Hill Collins states that understandings of work, like understandings of family, vary greatly depending on who controls the definitions. Quoting May Madison she maintains: "One very important difference between white people and black people is that white people think you are your work . . . Now a black person thinks that my work is just what I have to do to get what I want" (Collins 2000: 48). Instead of conceptualizing work by typology, perhaps the motivation and the range of the work is a better grasp of value and worth. Too often, those who earn better salaries with excessive fringe benefits and stock options easily attach self-worth with self-work. Thus using Collins—and from a broader African American context—the work of mothers who clean the academic halls to survive, heal, and become whole is just as valuable as the work of mothers who teach in these same academic halls for survival, healing, and wholeness.

Work as alienated labor can be economically exploitative, physically demanding, and intellectually deadening—that is, the type of work long associated with black women's status as "mule." Yet work can also be empowering and creative, even if it is physically challenging and appears to be demeaning. Exploitative wages that black women were allowed to keep and use for their own benefit or labor done out of love for members of one's own family can represent such work (Collins 2000: 48). Although Collins frames her definition of work particularly in black feminist thinking, aspects of survival and wholeness as apparent in the pericope surrounding the Canaanite mother are present. Work is thus more than a reluctant, "I've got to go to work." It is an intense, focused, determined, "I've got work to do!" because life and soul are at stake. There is a spiritual element of the work mothers do on behalf of their children (see Brown 2000: 59). This holistic work benefits mothers who are able to provide for their children and benefits the children as recipients of their mother's efforts. The Canaanite woman's faith spurs action, and her action also brings healing to her child.

To Wreck or Not to Wreck

I mentioned earlier the idea of whether a black mother who works or this biblical mother who works in the end wrecks or dismantles the home. "Wrecking" is the pursuit of persons, the conscientious engagement in activity, the challenging of authority that endangers a child's life. This action stunts a child's mental, emotional, physical, social, or spiritual growth. It refers to a mother's "work" that is detrimental to her child or family in general. It means that the family suffers from this work. Does a black mother who works wreak havoc and wreck a child's life? Before answering the question, there are some other issues to address.

First, we must bring to the surface the plethora of roles of mothers. Miller-McLemore maintains that the dilemma facing working mothers is the struggle between the procreative and the creative (Miller-McLemore 2002: 91). It is the tension between wanting to and needing to be mother and yet wanting to and needing to be someone else, and being both/and all the time. It is the desire to be at home, at school events, at dance lessons or athletic events and the desire to write scholarly articles, teach classes, and attend professional meetings. It is a rope that pulls in at least two ways. It is "I am also a mother" language (Miller-

McLemore 2002: 91). In addition to who I am as professor, dean, lawyer, maid, clerk, wife, sister, I am also a mother.

Therefore, second, the history of black working mothers cannot be overlooked. "Also a mother" were the slave women who nursed master's children and picked and chopped in his fields and then went to make a home for their own families. These mothers took care of their own quarters after bearing their burden in the heat of the day. "Also a mother" includes two million Reconstruction women who were the earliest housewives or stay-at-home moms. Yet, like the experience of the Canaanite woman, they represent a reversal of power. Reconstruction laws or Black Codes forced many of these postslavery mothers from their homes back into the fields. Black mothers who migrated to northern factories, those who took in laundry and took in children before there was an official cleaning business or KinderKare—yes each of these women was "also a mother."

One cannot forget the triple consciousness of family, work, and community exemplified by clubwomen like Ida B. Wells and Mary Church Terrell. As black women and black mothers, they did not relinquish their public duty. Wells "nursed her two sons, taking them on trains on the way to her lectures" (Parker 2005: 33). However, according to sociologists LaFrances Rogers Rose and Joyce Ladner, the story of African American motherhood did not begin here in the United States, but has its roots in Africa. The close bond between black women and children did not lose its importance when African women were brought to America and enslaved (Williams 1993: 34).

Consequently, African American women, African American mothers, have a history of work. Yet now the relevance of such work—and perhaps in some ways this history—is being challenged by the so-called mommy wars. This is a third element that influences the possible work-as-wrecking line of thinking. There is a conflict between mothers who stay at home with their children and mothers who work. Of course, there are benefits to both sides. There are exceptions to both sides. Stay-at-home moms are the primary soother and cuddler and are there for those benchmark moments. Children do not necessarily have the separation anxiety experienced in daycare transition. Children of working moms benefit in that they have a broader social circle with daycare workers, other children, or babysitters. Working mothers also stay in their projected career paths ("Working VS Stay At Home" 2006).

There are also drawbacks to each argument. Working mothers may experience guilt over missing a first walk or first word. For children, even the most sanitized daycares breed germs. Children are likely to attract colds and other illnesses from each other. Stay-at-home mothers deal with professional isolation, and the children obviously tend to be more attached to the mothers ("Working VS Stay At Home" 2006). Again, there are exceptions to both sides.

Does this mean that mothers who stay at home with their children are completely happy with their lives? Some are. Some are not. Does this mean that children of stay-at-home mothers are healthier or have a greater maternal-child bond? There are some cases of yes and some of no. Are children of working moms more socially developed? Are these working mothers climbing the corporate ladder with family in tow? I think the answers lie in each of our own lives and what "works" best in our own family situations. There are no absolutes, though perpetrators of these mommy wars would have us believe otherwise. What is evident is that in both cases, both sets of mothers do what they do in their children's best interests.

Most black women and black mothers have always worked and will continue to work. Some of the children who come from such homes are the most articulate, independent, socially adept, intellectually sound, and spiritually grounded persons. Yet some children struggle. I cannot say what the defining line or determining factor is. I do not think that work in the sense that I have defined wrecks the lives of children. Yes, they may miss their mommy, and yes, mommy may miss an event or two. However, quantity of times present or absent cannot be judged against quality time. I believe to each his or her own, to each mother, her own. She must use whatever "works" for her. It will work, if you work it.

The Canaanite mother went to work. Apparently, she left the child either at home alone or with relatives or neighbors, because the text does not record the daughter as being present. It is not apparent that the child suffered because of her mother's work. She was demon-possessed and already in harm's way. Her mother went to work to alleviate the torment. What is evident is that the daughter did benefit from her mother's labor. Matthew concludes this pericope with "and the daughter was healed instantly."

The Canaanite mother also gains from this work in that she is persistent and unrelenting. She pursues the power source and becomes a beneficiary of that power. She profits in that she changes Jesus' mind. She is no longer an ethnic outsider screaming after Jesus, but she engages him in an intense intellectual conversation. This encounter with Jesus, this work, affirms her gender and her faith. Jesus replies, "Woman, great is your faith. Let it be done as you wish" (Matt. 15:28).

Black mothers who work benefit themselves in that they are allowed to pursue career goals that for some are divine callings. There is a spiritual connection to this work. Such women benefit because they are able to provide for themselves and their children. We benefit since we can engage in other forms of intellectual stimulus. We gain personal fulfillment. At the same time, such work is healing to our children. They get to see their mothers in another light, not as some demeaning object projected in music videos. In addition, simple material accoutrements as food, clothing, health care, and shelter are also rewards of such work for both mothers and children. Love for their children drives most black working mothers to do what they do, just as it was the love of her daughter that drove the Canaanite woman to do what she had to do.

CONCLUSION

I began with a general portrait of media images of black working mothers and a history of black working mothers. Such a history includes black women as church mothers or the Mother Jones type. This portrait is broad enough to cover even mothers who specialize in tough love, perhaps lending themselves to the "mean mommy" nomenclature. Yet readers are perhaps more comfortable with the nurturing, caring, doting type of mommy. Regardless, one can see that the continuum of black mothering is wide indeed.

Throughout this paper, I integrated my own personal thoughts on working and black mothering; yet I did not reveal my own social location. Thus, whereas I began in broad strokes, I end with a more refined brush.

My own identity has informed my approach to this topic. As an African American mother of two sons and whose vocation it is to be both an ordained minister and a professor, I have found myself grappling with the procreative and the creative in myself. The day after I submitted the final draft of my dissertation, my first son was born. I commuted five hundred miles with my second son in utero to yield to the creative calling in me. Three months after delivering him, I sat inattentively in faculty orientation wondering, "What in the world am I doing here? I just gave birth." I have missed football games, a growth milestone here or there, and have experienced guilt for working. Yet at the same time, the loud voice that propels me beyond motherhood also confirms my work and affirms that everything is all right. The many hugs and smiles I get from my sons coming and going affirm this as well.

Where do we go from here? I think this contemporary analysis of the work of the Canaanite mother as a prototype of black working mothers leads to many places. First, in the academy, we must talk more about family and family issues as an integral aspect of who we are as scholars. Many of us bring our families to professional meetings; however, there is limited discussion on the intersection of family and career. We cannot overlook the "off-the-record" questions at job interviews about family or plans for children. Many pretenure females hear a "hint" or outright warning to wait to have children until after they have completed this matriculation process. Issues of maternity leave, timing, and class coverage are the elephant in the academic room.

Second, I maintain that, whereas womanist methods take up the mantle of class and race not addressed in feminism, more must be done to highlight internal class issues between black women who teach in the academy and black women who cook in and clean the academy. We must look for ways in which our work gives voice to black mothers on welfare, black mothers who are the working poor, and black mothers who work for other black mothers.

Last, we must address the children. If one surmises that the Canaanite mother leaves her child home alone, then the daughter is a latchkey child, a child who in our modern time has a key to the house and enters an empty home to fend for herself until Mother arrives. Our academic work must advocate for afterschool networks, faith-based initiatives, and community programs to fill in the gap. We must send a clarion call to strengthen existing programs where surrogate mothers and neighborhood grandmothers step in until momma gets off work.

Notes

1. This article is used by permission of the Society of Biblical Literature.

6

Matthean "Mothers" and Disenfranchised Hong Kong Working Mothers

Tsui-yuk Louise Liu

INTRODUCTION

This paper is a rediscovery of the Matthean "mothers" from the perspective of Hong Kong working mothers. Both mothers experience disenfranchisement of mother-child intimacy. The term *disenfranchisement* here does not refer to its political sense of removal of political privileges or voting rights. Rather, it emphasizes the reality that some kinds of losses are perceived as "less likely to be acknowledged or socially supported" (Doka 2002: 83).

It is a truism that working mothers always feel torn between their families and their careers, wherever they are in the world. The provision of such a developed international city as Hong Kong, however, is very unsupportive of working mothers. Working mothers in Hong Kong have long been suffering from the disenfranchisement of mother-child intimacy. In order to show the seriousness of the problem, some significant data will be listed out and analyzed. These important data are threefold: (1) the lowest total fertility rate, (2) the ever-increasing labor-force-participation rate of women and the ever-increasing demand for foreign domestic helpers, and (3) the failure in breast-feeding. Throughout the discussion, we are not only aiming to increase the awareness of the risky situation of Hong Kong working mothers or women but also to awaken the concern of the church and Christian organization about this issue. Disappointingly, Hong Kong churches not only fail to criticize the problem of disenfranchisement but also disenfranchise their own female employees. Due to prolonged negligence of such an important biblical theme—namely, mother-child intimacy—Hong Kong churches have unsurprisingly become oppressive patriarchal agents, wherein Hong Kong working mothers have been persistently disenfranchised. As a part of the church, I, being a typical Hong Kong working mother, am here to challenge the church to be a family-friendly model for other employers by means of a contextual reading of the Gospel of Matthew.

In the light of the contextual reading of Hong Kong working mothers, we will try to uncover the Matthean theme of "mothers," particularly "mother-child intimacy." Before entering into a discussion of the specific passages, there will be an overall presentation of the Gospel of Matthew related to specific contextual questions. Among all the twenty-six appearances of the Greek term *mētēr* for "mother" in the Gospel of Matthew, nine are specifically Matthean (i.e., Matt. 1:18; 2:11, 13, 14, 20, 21; 20:20; 27:56 [×2]). It is these nine passages, therefore, that we will analyze, expounding the theological significance of mother-child intimacy in the plot of Matthew.

The discussion will end with some reflections on the contextual problem of the disenfranchisement of mother-child intimacy experienced by (Hong Kong) working mothers and what and how the church, in the light of the newly discovered Matthean theme, should respond to their contextual lamentations, wherever they are in the world.

THE DISENFRANCHISEMENT OF MOTHER-CHILD INTIMACY IN HONG KONG

Working mothers in Hong Kong have long been suffering the disenfranchisement of mother-child intimacy. Not only is social support in Hong Kong insufficient for working mothers of young children, but the church and Christian organizations also have not realized the seriousness of the problem. As mentioned above, three significant data are particularly helpful in uncovering the problem; namely, (1) the lowest total fertility rate, (2) the ever-increasing labor-force-participation rate of women and the ever-increasing demand for foreign domestic helpers, and (3) the failure in breast-feeding. By means of the analysis of the three relevant data, we will try to point out the risky situation of Hong Kong working mothers. Following this analysis, we will raise some reflective questions about the disenfranchisement of mother-child intimacy in the Gospel of Matthew from the perspective of Hong Kong working mothers.

THE LOWEST TOTAL FERTILITY RATE

The first type of lamentation among Hong Kong females is the fertility rate. Hong Kong has the lowest fertility rate in the world.[1] According to the 2007–2008 annual report of the Family Planning Association of Hong Kong, our fertility rate is 1,024 per 1,000 females in 2007. The average parity of married couples dropped from 1.6 in 2002 to 1.5 in 2007.[2] Approximately 80 percent of fertile couples opt to have no children. Seventy percent were practicing family planning at the time of the survey; in other words, they are not preparing to have a child at the moment.

In 2011, the estimated total fertility rate of Hong Kong by the Central Intelligence Agency (CIA) was 1.07 children born per woman, which ranks the second lowest in the world (U.S. Central Intelligence Agency). However, this does not mean that the actual total fertility rate is increasing. In fact, the estimated rate is somehow misleading. In the past decade, the proportion of mainland mothers delivering babies in Hong Kong hospitals has grown steadily. In 2010, 47 percent (that is, 41,000 out of 88,000) of newborn babies in Hong Kong were born to mainland women (Fei 2011). Therefore, the actual total fertility rate of Hong Kong should be lower than the data shown.

Three factors relating to the low fertility rate must not be neglected. First, there has been an increase in the number of unmarried women in the past decade; the proportion of unmarried women among the female population of age fifteen and over increased from 28.9 percent in 1996 to 30.7 percent in 2006 (HKSAR 2006). Second, Hong Kong couples tend to delay marriage and childbearing, which in turn often causes sexual dysfunction and fertility problems (HKSAR 2007–2008). Delayed marriage has long been a problem. The median age of the first marriage for males and females was 27.0 and 23.9 respectively in 1981, but had risen to 31.0 and 28.5 by 2009 (HKSAR 2010a: 27). On the one hand, the increase in the number of unmarried women shows a tendency of more and more Hong Kong females to choose a single life, whether temporarily or for their lifetime. On the other hand, the phenomenon of delayed marriage indicates that an extended single life is preferable. Third, the stressful working and living conditions today hinder a couple's ability and willingness to raise a child. A responsible mother definitely cares for the future of her children. The particularly low total fertility rate does not mean that Hong Kong couples would not like to have their own children. Rather, it reflects that Hong Kong working couples really care for the future of the next generation, but with a pessimistic view. Hence, quite a number of Hong Kong working females are not ready or are unwilling to have a baby before they have enough preparation (for instance, a better economic condition as well as time to secure the proper environment for their children). In this way, we have fewer and fewer mothers and children in Hong Kong. This is in fact an unnoticed kind of disenfranchisement of mother-child intimacy of the entire society. Does the Jesus of Matthew understand a (potential) mother's anxiety about her child's future?

The investigation should not be stopped here. We should continue to ask: Why does Hong Kong have such a low fertility rate? Why do Hong Kong women prefer single life to married life? How is the low fertility rate related to the working conditions of Hong Kong women? Can foreign domestic helpers really outsource household production or in turn alleviate the problem of disenfranchisement of mother-child intimacy?

PROBLEM OF FOREIGN DOMESTIC HELPERS AS "SURROGATE MOTHERS"

While the labor-force-participation rate of males decreased from 80.5 percent of the total male population in 1986 to 69.4 percent in 2009, that of females increased from 48.9 percent of the total female population in 1986 to 53.1 percent in 2009 (HKSAR 2010a: 68). There is an increasing trend of more and more women sharing the role of family breadwinner. A comparative study of the labor-force-participation rate for single women and women who have been or are currently married shows a contrast. In 2009, the labor-force-participation rate for never-married women was 67.5 percent, versus 46.8 for women who had been or were married (HKSAR 2010a: 69). This great contrast reflects that a significant portion of married women might quit their career, whether temporarily or permanently, after marriage (HKSAR 2010a: 69). This in turns implies that the working conditions in Hong Kong are unfavorable to family life.

In a survey of sharing of housework, the majority of women claim that they are willing to quit their career to maintain the family order (HKSAR 2009c). Hong Kong women generally show an altruistic attitude to their families. When the working conditions are unfavorable to family life, working women, particularly working mothers, experience a great amount of tension between work and family.

How can a working mother lessen such tension? When she does not want to give up her career, the only way she can choose is to employ a domestic helper to relieve her load in domestic work. The *Hong Kong Yearbook 2009* reported a steadily increasing demand for foreign domestic helpers in HKSAR over the past three decades (HKSAR 2009b: 133). The number of foreign domestic helpers increased from 256,597 in 2008 to 267,778 at the end of 2009

(HKSAR 2009b: 133). The increase is about 4.4 percent within one year's time (HKSAR 2009b: 133). The majority of them were Filipinos and Indonesians, constituting 48.5 percent and 48.7 percent respectively (HKSAR 2009b: 133).

In 2010, the proportion of female Overseas Filipino Workers (OFWs) in relation to all OFWs was 47.7 percent (Philippine Commission on Women 2012: 6). Within these 968,000 female OFWs, Hong Kong (with third-highest demand) accounted for 11.4 percent, around 110,000 female OFWs (Philippine Commission on Women 2012: 7).

The unwanted results of employing foreign domestic helpers are as follows: Hong Kong children cannot develop a good command of Chinese in their language-developing stage, the children become little masters of the maids, and importantly, the disenfranchisement of mother–child intimacy. Many children have closer intimacy with the maids than they do with their mothers. Once the contract ends, the "surrogate mother–child intimacy" will also end. Does the Gospel of Matthew echo with lamentation the absent mother in a family?

Another unwanted result is that the ever-rising demand for foreign domestic helpers also leads to the disenfranchisement of mother–children intimacy of our foreign domestic helpers. Many foreign domestic helpers leave their own children in their mother countries and come to work in Hong Kong alone. They are also experiencing delayed marriage as well as having ever-decreasing fertility rates.[3] Their own children are forced to grow up without mothers by their side. Does Matthew address the pain of "surrogate mothers" who are suffering from their own disenfranchisement of mother–child intimacy?

Finally, we illustrate one more problem Hong Kong working mothers are facing today: nutrition for their babies.

THE FAILURE OF BREAST-FEEDING

Whether a woman breast-feeds her baby triggers anxiety among many working mothers in Hong Kong. The slightly increasing trend of breast-feeding in recent years does not reflect the reality of working women in Hong Kong. Even if one might say that the stressful working and the unfriendly living environments hinder a woman's ability to breast-feed, it still only touches the tip of the iceberg.

Breast-feeding is the best way to prevent malnutrition and mortality in the infancy stage and young childhood according to the World Health Organization (WHO) (World Health Organization 2009). Breast-feeding is also beneficial to mothers, reducing the risk of breast cancer, ovarian cancers, type 2 diabetes, and so on (HKSAR 2010b: 1–4). By means of breast-feeding, mothers generally experience enhanced mother–infant bonding (HKSAR 2010b: 1–4). The WHO therefore recommends that exclusive breast-feeding should be maintained for the first six months after birth and breast-feeding with complementary foods should follow for up to two years or beyond (World Health Organization 2009).

Following the Innocent Declaration of 1990, the Baby-Friendly Hospital Initiative (BFHI) was launched by the WHO and the United Nations Children's Fund (UNICEF) since 1991 in 152 countries including Hong Kong (HKSAR 2012). The initiative aims at protecting, promoting, and supporting breast-feeding (World Health Organization 2012).

Although the UNICEF Baby-Friendly Hospital Initiative Hong Kong Association (BFHIHKA) reported an encouraging increase of 4.9 percent breast-feeding initiation rate in 2008 (that is, the rate rose to 73.9 percent), the exclusive breast-feeding rate of 12.1 percent at four to six months is tremendously low in comparison to the corresponding breast-feeding initiation rate.[4] The report from UNICEF shows that the majority of Hong Kong mothers cannot reach the WHO breast-feeding standard—maintaining exclusive breast-feeding for the first six months after birth.

One of the reasons for the low rate of breast-feeding in Hong Kong may be due to the insufficient breast-feeding training of obstetric and pediatric doctors.[5] But insufficient breast-feeding training itself cannot explain the phenomenon. According to the data provided by the BFHIHKA, the breast-feeding rate on discharge from maternity units in Hong Kong continues to increase—from 19 percent in 1992 to 73.9 percent in 2008 (HKSAR 2009b: 4–5). The rising trend shows that the maternity units in Hong Kong have successfully encouraged breast-feeding to a certain extent.

Let us consider once again the data in 2008 provided by BFHIHKA. We need to ask why the exclusive breast-feeding rate for four to six months is only 12.1 percent, despite the relatively high breast-feeding initiation rate of 73.9 percent (HKSAR 2009a: 1). The figure indicates that something must be happening within the first three months of the baby's life.

An observable critical change is that Hong Kong working mothers are bound to resume duties in the third month after delivery. According to our labor law, working mothers are entitled to only ten weeks of maternity leave in Hong Kong, which indicates that the provision in Hong Kong is the second lowest in the world.[6]

With only ten weeks of maternity leave, are the Hong Kong government and our society really encouraging breast-feeding? The most natural way of enhancing breast-feeding is in fact very simple: let the infants stay with their mothers. In general, infants under six months need feeding for every two to three hours. When she is separated from her baby for at least eight hours of work time plus traffic time, a working mother certainly cannot breast-feed her baby for four needed feedings. Unfortunately, the human body is no machine. Lactation is a biological pattern and cannot be started, stopped, or delayed at will.

To prevent the decrease or even cessation of lactation, working mothers need to keep their lactation pattern by pumping breast milk in their working environment. It is not difficult to imagine how troublesome and inconvenient it is for a working mother to collect milk and keep the milk fresh during office hours. For instance, most workplaces have no nursery rooms; working mothers are forced to collect milk in washing rooms with unavoidable sanitary problems. With, in general, only a one-hour lunch break, how can a working mother keep her lactation pattern? Therefore, the unfavorable working conditions of mothers in Hong Kong are a crucial factor for the unsatisfactory exclusive breast-feeding rate.

Even if working mothers can tackle all these problems and continue breast-feeding after their maternity leave, it is still only possible to continue "breast-feeding" with bottles. Breast-feeding therefore often becomes just another kind of bottle-feeding. It is ridiculous to expect that this kind of "breast-feeding" can increase any mother-child intimacy.

Although the slightly increasing trend of breast-feeding in recent years seems to be good news, we still need to admit that Hong Kong mothers have failed in breast-feeding. The way of breast-feeding recommended by the WHO remains an unachievable goal for Hong Kong mothers. The failure in breast-feeding reflects the disenfranchisement of mother-child intimacy in Hong Kong.

How important is mother-child intimacy in the plot of Matthew? Does Matthew lament the disenfranchisement of mother-child intimacy?

OVERVIEW OF THE USE OF "MOTHER" IN MATTHEW

In this section, we are going to investigate whether mother-child intimacy is ever a (significant) theme in the Gospel of Matthew. Initially, I will give an overview of the use of "mother" in Matthew. Then, corresponding to the above-mentioned threefold problem of disenfranchisement of mother-child intimacy in Hong Kong, the voices of the Matthean "mother" will be analyzed in a threefold manner: (1) a comparative study of Matt. 20:20-28 with Mark 10:35-45; (2) a comparative study of Matt. 27:55-56 with Mark 15:40-41; and (3) an intertextual study of the Matthean "mother."

One of the main themes in the Gospel of Matthew is Immanuel.[7] Through the promise of Immanuel, Jesus came to the world (Matt. 1:23). The word "Immanuel" is used only once in the Gospel of Matthew, but its connotation may at least appear three times in the book. At the end of the Gospel, Jesus gives the same promise of Immanuel (see Matt. 28:20). Today, the church is a symbol of Immanuel in the world (see Matt. 18:20). But this symbol is not created by the church. The symbol of Immanuel appears first, repeatedly, as the picture of "the child and his mother" in Matthew 2 (for details see Liu 2008: 142–43). When the first Gospel chooses mother-child intimacy as the first symbol of Immanuel, the church should be aware of the problem of disenfranchisement of mother-child intimacy. As a contextual symbol of Immanuel, what is the role of the church in society and culture? If the church should take up an exemplary and pioneering role today, the church should be more gracious to working mothers and their children. Now, let us go back to the text and study in detail how "mother-child intimacy" as Immanuel is further developed in the Gospel of Matthew.

The Gospel of Matthew was no doubt written from an androcentric perspective (Anderson 2001: 29). Yet the women characters are significant; for instance, five women are deliberately mentioned in the genealogy. Other passages with women characters include the healing of the mother-in-law of Peter (Matt. 8:14-17), the healing of the woman with the hemorrhage (Matt. 9:20-22), the healing of the daughter of the ruler (Matt. 9:18-26), the mother and brothers of Jesus (Matt. 12:46-50), the Canaanite woman (Matt. 15:21-28), the woman at Bethany (Matt. 26:6-13), the women at the cross (Matt. 27:55-56), and the two Mary characters at the scene of the burial and resurrection of Jesus (Matt. 27:61; 28:1-10). Among the women characters, most are mothers.

The Gospel of Matthew represents the voices of mothers, but their voices are unfortunately ignored in the reception history of the first canonical Gospel. The different forms of the Greek word "mother" (*mētēr*) appear eighty-three times in the New Testament, approximately one-third of which belongs to the Gospel of Matthew (that is, twenty-six times). Within these twenty-six times, nine are found to be specifically Matthean (Matt. 1:18; 2:11, 13, 14, 20, 21; 20:20; 27:56 [×2]), and there is no parallel usage in the other two Synoptic Gospels. Although there are already some feminist-critical works on the Gospel of Matthew (e.g., Wainwright 1991; Levine 2001), the voices of the Matthean "mother" go unheard. Through the specific Matthean use of "mother," the exegesis here will focus on the reflection of "mother-child intimacy" in the Gospel of Matthew.

In the following sections, two comparative studies will be made (that is, Matt. 20:20-28 with Mark 10:35-45 and Matt. 27:55-56 with Mark 15:40-41). Then, an intertextual study of chapters 2, 20, and 27 will seek for the meaning of the contrast of "mother-child intimacy" with the "disenfranchisement of mother-child intimacy."

THE VOICES OF THE MATTHEAN "MOTHER": MATTHEW 20:20-28 WITH MARK 10:35-45

The identity of "the mother of the sons of Zebedee" (Matt. 20:20; 27:56) is a good entry point for addressing the disenfranchised mother-child intimacy of Hong Kong working mothers. The contextual reading mentioned above allows us not only to rethink the social-historical situation but also to echo the lamentations of Hong Kong working mothers.

The first comparative study is between Matt. 20:20-28 and Mark 10:35-45. According to the two-source hypothesis, Mark was probably the source for Matthew (Theissen 1995: 409–52). The comparative study of this pericope shows six major differences between Matthew and Mark.[8] One of the most significant changes is that "the mother of the sons of Zebedee" in Matthew has taken up the petitionary roles of James and John in Mark (Luz 1997: 160).

Why "the mother of the sons of Zebedee" makes the request instead of James and John in the parallel pericope has long puzzled scholars. The customary explanation is that Matthew, by having someone else make the request, wants to put the apostles James and John "in a better light" (Davies and Allison 1997: 86).[9] However, this explanation does not really solve the problem, for Jesus answers directly to the two apostles from Matt. 20:22 onward.[10] Furthermore, their mother might still be their instrument to make the request for themselves (Luz 1997: 161). In this way, not only are the apostles not cast in a better light, but their conspiracy against the other apostles could be more deliberate in the plot of Matthew (Davies and Allison 1997: 87).[11]

Another customary explanation for the replacement of characters is to imply that the two apostles in the plot are "sufficiently young" so that they still need care from their mother (see Davies and Allison 1997: 86).[12] Whether the two apostles are "sufficiently young" is neither obvious in Matt. 20:20-28 nor in the rest of Matthew. In fact, a person's age is not necessarily connected with who makes requests for them. The daughter of Herodias in Matt. 14:1-12 is a good example of this. In contrast to Matt. 20:20-28, Herodias prompts her daughter, despite her youth, to make the request of John's head for her.

Although both Matt. 14:1-12 and Matt. 20:20-28 describe the request of a person for another person(s), the descriptions are different. Whereas Matt. 14:8 deliberately shows the conspiracy of Herodias by the expression of "having been prompted by her mother," Matt. 20:20-28 has no comparative description of James and John. Whether they have prompted their mother to make the request for them cannot be concluded.

Another comparison is between Matt. 20:20-28 and 1 Kings 1:15-21 (Davies and Allison 1997: 87). The comparison is sound not only because of the common wording (that is, "worship" [proskyneō] [Matt. 20:20; cf. 1 Kgs. 1:16] and "sit" [kathēmai] [Matt. 20:30; cf. 1 Kgs. 1:17, 20]), but also because of the highlights of the motherhood of Bathsheba (Davies and Allison 1997: 87). First Kings 1:15 tells the reader that King David was very old and Abishag the Shunammite was ministering to the king, which in turns means that Bathsheba is portrayed as a mother rather than as a wife of David in that episode (Walsh 1996: 12). Both mothers—namely, Bathsheba and "the mother of the sons of Zebedee"—make requests to secure the future of their sons in the kingdom.

In addition, a comparison can also be made between Matt. 20:20-28 and Matt. 15:21-28, but to what extent the comparison should be made is questionable (Keener 1999: 485). At the least, both episodes clearly depict the requests of the mothers to Jesus on behalf of their child(ren). The maternal care for their child(ren) is in either case undeniable. It is difficult to draw a conclusion that the two episodes show improper and proper petitions respectively (Davies and Allison 1997: 87). One should bear in mind that Jesus does not pass a negative value judgment on either mother, even though he gives a negative answer to the petition of "the mother of the sons of Zebedee." The careful depiction of Matt. 20:20-28 does not directly turn down the petition of the mother, but indirectly shifts Jesus' dialogue with the mother to that with James and John. Just like the wise Bathsheba before King David (1 Kgs. 1:15-21), "the mother of the sons of Zebedee" falls down before Jesus and waits silently for the permission to make a request (Luz 1997: 161). The humiliation of this mother is rather clear when one compares the depiction with the opening of the parallel Markan pericope (Mark 10:35).

That Matt. 20:20-28 highlights the motherhood of the mother of the sons of Zebedee is obvious. As early as in the work of Gregory of Nazianzus, her "parental affection" and "excess of love" are well noticed (Orat. 37.14). Not only full of parental affection and excess of love, "the mother of the sons of Zebedee" presents a maternal figure full of wisdom and humiliation (cf. 1 Kgs. 1:15-21; Mark 10:35).

In short, the deliberate Matthean change of characters in making a request before Jesus (that is, the mother of the sons of Zebedee instead of the Markan characters James and John) turns the nature of the narrative from a pure power struggle among the disciples into a mother's care for the future of her sons in the kingdom of Jesus.

Deliberately, Matthew brings in this motherly care as a specific but otherwise unnoticed kind of mother-child intimacy in the first Gospel. Today, the "request" or "lament" of potential Hong Kong mothers has become implicit but still noticeable. If Jesus in Matthew ever understood the mother of the sons of Zebedee, how should the church pay attention to potential mothers' disenfranchisement of mother-child intimacy in Hong Kong or elsewhere? The voices of these disenfranchised mothers should be heard in the light of the rediscovery of the Matthean "mother."

THE VOICES OF THE MATTHEAN "MOTHER": MATTHEW 27:55-56 WITH MARK 15:40-41

The second comparative study is between Matt. 27:55-56 and Mark 15:40-41.[13] Instead of Salome in Mark, Matthew mentions "the mother of the sons of Zebedee" in the parallel pericope. Does Matthew identify the mother of the sons of Zebedee as the Markan Salome? Although the two figures appear in the same parallel pericope, there are still insufficient clues to draw a conclusion.[14] The main reason is that no other place in Matthew or Mark tells us directly the name of the mother of the sons of Zebedee. Therefore, it allows two possibilities here: the Matthean tradition is either a renaming or only a substitution.

Comparing with Matt. 20:20-28, Matthew continues to consistently call her "the mother of the sons of Zebedee" instead of any other name like Salome or the wife of Zebedee. Whether the Matthean tradition is really a renaming or only a substitution, the figure of a mother (that is, "the mother of the sons of Zebedee") is deliberately highlighted in both Matt. 20:20-28 and 27:55-56.

The figure of a mother is very meaningful in explaining Matt. 27:55-56. Mark 10:35-45 and 15:40-41 (that is, the parallel pericopes of Matt. 20:20-28 and 27:55-56) appear to be two separate, individual episodes. Through adding a maternal character in Matt. 20:20-28 and 27:55-56, the two originally individual Markan episodes are perfectly associated in the Gospel of Matthew.

In the first episode, the mother of the sons of Zebedee makes a request that her sons sit on Jesus' left and right. Instead of giving them any positive reply, Jesus points out that they do not know the meaning of their request (see Matt. 20:22). If the mother appears only in Matt. 20:20-28, then the readers may draw a conclusion that she has only made an improper, unwise petition. However, the same maternal character reappears in Matt. 27:55-56. In this second episode, this mother appears to understand "the true meaning of being on Jesus' left and right" (Davies and Allison 1997: 638) when she follows Jesus until his death.[15] Matthew remarks that there were "two robbers crucified with Jesus, one on his right and one on his left" (Matt. 27:38). Jesus' "left" and "right" becomes a literary hinge between the episode of request (Matt. 20:20-28) and the passion (Matt. 27:32-56). The mother of the sons of Zebedee, together with other women, is described as one "who had followed Jesus from Galilee" (Matt. 27:55). "From Galilee" connotes the beginning of Jesus' ministry (Getty-Sullivan 2001: 166). That is to say, these women minister to Jesus from the beginning to the end of Jesus' ministry. In contrast to the absence of her sons and other disciples, she demonstrates true discipleship to all disciples (Hagner 1995b: 855).

Among the women in the scene of the death of Jesus, three are mentioned particularly. Other than the mother of the sons of Zebedee, there is another mother, Mary the mother of James and Joseph (Matt. 27:56). The description "the mother of James and Joseph" is obviously used to differentiate this Mary from another Mary bearing the same name, namely, Mary Magdalene. The identity of this Mary is, however, still unclear, although the description "the mother of James and Joseph" has been added. It is possible, when one compares the text with John 19:25, that this Mary was Mary the wife of Clopas, the sister of Mary the mother of Jesus (Hagner 1995b: 855). It is also possible that this Mary is Mary the mother of Jesus, since the brothers of Jesus also bear the same names (Matt. 13:55) (see Davies and Allison 1997: 638). Nevertheless, it would be quite odd if she were not directly named as Mary the mother of Jesus in the scene of Jesus' death. Moreover, "Mary," "James," and "Joseph" were common names in the first century (Davies and Allison 1997: 638). So "Mary the mother of James and Joseph" and Mary the mother of Jesus might just incidentally share some common superficial characteristics.

However, if "Mary the mother of James and Joseph" is a deliberate Matthean change from the Markan "Mary the mother of James the younger and of Joses" (Mark 15:40), then Matthew might have Mary the mother of Jesus in his mind when he depicts the scene of Jesus' death. Then the death of Jesus would be grieved as if by his own mother in the presence of Mary the mother of James and Joseph.

Not only does the character of Mary the mother of James and Joseph recall the readers' memory of Mary the mother of Jesus, but the description of the three women together also has a similar effect. In the description, it is not difficult to see Matthew's alliteration of the letter *m*: "Mary Magdalene . . . Mary . . . mother . . . mother . . ." (Matt. 27:56). Through the rhetorical force of Matthew's alliteration, the image of "Mary the mother" is underlined.

Such a metaphorical understanding of Jesus' mother is allowed in the text of Matthew, for Matt. 12:50 redefines a spiritual family relationship as well as a spiritual mother-child relationship (see Sri 2005: 158). It is especially meaningful when the metaphorical image of Mary the mother is mentioned right after the confession of the centurion and those who were with him (see Matt. 27:54)—that is, Jesus as the Son of God. The death of "the Son" is now grieved by a corporate image of "Mary the mother."

Paradoxically, Mary the real mother of Jesus does not really appear in the scene of grieving the separation (Matt. 27:55-56; cf. John 19:25-27). Because of her absence, the three women at the cross appear to be a kind of surrogate mother to "the Son." The grief is even deeper when the real mother cannot stand by her son and accompany him in person to pass through his greatest hardship. The scene of grieving the death of "the Son" by "surrogate mothers" laments on the one hand the postwar children who had been adopted or placed into the care of surrogate caretakers after 70 CE and on the other hand the disenfranchisement of mother-child intimacy today. As analyzed before, mother-child intimacy of Hong Kong working mothers is disenfranchised by stressful working environments as well as employing more and more foreign domestic helpers, who are essentially surrogate mothers to Hong Kong children. At the same time, foreign domestic helpers suffer from the disenfranchisement of mother-child intimacy.

AN INTERTEXTUAL STUDY OF THE MATTHEAN "MOTHER"

Mother-child intimacy is particularly clear in the birth narrative (Matthew 1–2). Although Mary has double identities (as the wife of Joseph [Matt. 1:18-24] and the mother of Jesus), Matthew deliberately highlights her identity as a mother. In Matthew 1, we still see her double identity (e.g., Matt. 1:16, 18, 20). But in Matthew 2, she is only depicted as "his mother" (*tēn mētera autou*) (Matt. 2:13, 14, 20, 21), that is, the mother of Jesus. But even more eye-catching is that whenever he mentions "his mother" in Matthew 2, Matthew keeps constantly using the expression "the child and his mother" (*to paidion kai tēn mētera autou*) (Matt. 2:13, 14, 20, 21).

The intimacy between Jesus and his mother is not only shown by the wording "the child and his mother" but also by the togetherness of Jesus and his mother. Right after the genealogy of Jesus, we find his birth narrative (Matt. 1:18b-23). The birth narrative can be divided into five episodes, in which two main characters (Joseph and Herod) take turns appearing. For simplicity, I call the five episodes the "J-H-J-H-J Structure."[16] Within the five episodes, the togetherness of Jesus and his mother can be found in all J episodes and the first H episode. The intimate mother-child relationship becomes even more obvious when Joseph is missed in the first H episode (Matt. 2:1-12), which in turn leaves the mother-child picture in the sight of the readers.

Why is the mother-child picture repeatedly highlighted in Matthew 1 and 2? Is there any theological meaning of the intimate mother-child relationship? In fact, the picture of "mother-child" serves well as a symbol of Immanuel (Liu 2008: 142–43). The name of Immanuel is in the context of the promise that a virgin shall conceive and bear a son (Matt. 1:23). That's why the mother-child picture is being repeated again and again.

The most significant mother-child intimacy is even stronger in the second H episode (Matt. 2:16-18). The intimate mother-child picture disappears here. In contrast with the other four episodes, this episode depicts the massacre of boys as well as the grief of mothers (Matt. 2:16-18). The disenfranchisement of mother-child intimacy is deeply grieved through the weeping and great mourning of Rachel (Matt. 2:18). The contrast shows how important a child is to his or her mother.

Under the light of this intertextual study, the request of "the mother of the sons of Zebedee" (Matt. 20:20-28) should be understood as maternal protection. It also shows how important a mother is to her children. In a similar way, the death of "the Son" (Matt. 27:45-56) is depicted as a repetition of the massacre of boys (Matt. 2:16-18). Once again, the disenfranchisement of mother-child intimacy is the deepest grief of the Gospel.

In the light of this grief, the contextual problem of disenfranchisement of mother-child intimacy in Hong Kong should not be neglected. To a certain extent, the lowest fertility rate and the problem of foreign domestic helpers as "surrogate mothers" could be perceived as modernized and secularized forms of Matthean disenfranchisement of mother-child intimacy, as we have already discussed above. Last, if breast-feeding could be experienced as the most intimate physical form of mother-child relationship in the infancy stage, the failure in breast-feeding would thus mean the deepest grief of Hong Kong working mothers.

REFLECTION AND CONCLUDING REMARKS

The contextual reading of the Matthean "mother" calls for the maintenance of mother-child intimacy. The church, instead of preventing children from disturbing the order of worship in the church, should rethink how it can support working mothers today.

Working mothers face the problem of disenfranchisement of mother-children intimacy not only in society at large, but also in the church and in Christian organizations. Here, we will try to compare some significant figures in our society with those in the church.

According to *Women and Men in Hong Kong: Key Statistics 2010 Edition*, 31.4 percent of the directorate officers in the civil service in 2009 were female (HKSAR 2010a: xxv). Comparing with the figures in 1996, there was a 16 percent increase in female officers. A similar rising trend appears in nongovernmental occupations; 19.6 percent and 29.8 percent of women worked as managers and administrators in 1993 and 2009 respectively, although the proportion was still less than that of men (41.1 percent in 2009) (HKSAR 2010a: 70).

Some comparable figures of female ministers that comprise ordained and nonordained pastors in the church can be found in a survey carried out in 2009, the "Hong Kong Church Female Minister Questionnaire 2009" (see Teng-Cheung 2009). Although the survey did not cover all the female ministers in Hong Kong, 47.9 percent of female ministers have completed the questionnaire (Teng-Cheung 2009: 1), which is a relatively high completion rate. In 2009, ordained female pastors constituted 8.9 percent of total female ministers, while 10.3 percent of female ministers served as a church director or head of a local church (Teng-Cheung 2009: 5–6). Noteworthy is the percentage of female church directors higher than that of ordained female pastors, which means nonordained female ministers, who take up the leading administrative position, could have been underpaid. The low percentage of ordained female pastors is very possibly due to the rejection of ordaining female pastors in many churches. Forty percent of the female ministers declared that no ordination is allowed for female ministers in their churches(Teng-Cheung 2009: 9). The comparison between Hong Kong society and the church shows that the awareness of equal opportunity for men and women in the church still lags far behind our society. The low awareness often results in policies skewed toward men in the church.

Among 1,148 female ministers surveyed, 532 were married (Teng-Cheung 2009: 4, 41). The proportion of female ministers who have never married is 53.7 percent, which is much higher than the proportion of women who have never married in Hong Kong, which was 30.5 percent in 2009 (HKSAR 2010a:

xxiii). The high proportion of female ministers who have never married does not necessarily mean that they prefer single life. Rather, 15.7 percent are eager for marriage, while 36 percent do not reject marriage (Teng-Cheung 2009: 49). Although female ministers generally have high self-esteem and positive thinking (Teng-Cheung 2009: 50), we must still admit that female ministers experience difficulty getting married in the Hong Kong church setting.

Another figure to be noted is the extremely low fertility rate of female ministers, which is only 0.5.[17] It is much lower than the estimated total fertility rate of 1.07 in Hong Kong in 2011 (U. S. Central Intelligence Agency). Both the low marriage rate and the low fertility rate of female ministers should be understood as an unnoticed kind of disenfranchisement of mother–child intimacy.

Not only do female ministers experience the disenfranchisement of mother–child intimacy, but also our congregations. In most churches, children's ministry or mother–child ministry is very low in priority, especially those churches following in the footsteps of Rick Warren's Saddleback Church. In his renowned book *The Purpose Driven Church: Growth without Compromising Your Message and Mission*, Warren shares the success of Saddleback: "When Saddleback began, we focused on only one target: young, unchurched, white-collar couples" (Warren 1995: 160).

In Hong Kong, many churches, under the influence of Saddleback, set up the same target: young, unchurched, "white-collar couples." With this target, children's ministry often becomes secondary or even a lower priority. The group's enjoyment of the worship, children's Sunday school, and other children's activities is only a by-product. The hidden agenda is to prevent any disturbance from children and maintain a good order in the adults' programs. The best way to achieve the goal is to keep the children away and keep them busy. The result is that working mothers and their children not only suffer from the disenfranchisement of mother–child intimacy in their working life but also in the church.

Is the church aware of the seriousness of the problems Hong Kong working mothers are facing? Should there be any difference in attitude between the church and the world toward working mothers? Could the church do anything to change the situation?

We have analyzed the hopeless situation of working mothers through three significant phenomena: (1) the lowest total fertility rate in the world; (2) the increasing labor-force-participation rate of women and the ever-increasing demand for foreign domestic helpers; and (3) the failure in breast-feeding. These data show that Hong Kong working mothers are experiencing an intolerable tension between family and work. There is no indication that any social support is able to lessen the tension. Unfortunately, the church also gives too little support to working mothers. The importance of mother-child intimacy is totally neglected.

The ignorance of mother-child intimacy contrasts one of the main themes in the Gospel of Matthew—Immanuel. In the third section, we have already discussed how Immanuel is reflected by the intimate mother-child relationship. God chooses to be with his people through the promise of the coming of Jesus, which is fulfilled by a virgin bearing a child—a symbol of mother-child intimacy. The church, as a contextual symbol of Immanuel, should be aware of the seriousness of the disenfranchisement of mother-child intimacy.

In 2011, the Family Council launched a "Family Friendly Company Award Scheme" to give recognition for the efforts of companies implementing family-friendly measures.[18] By definition, no churches in Hong Kong are qualified to be a family-friendly company. In fact, family friendliness is not a new concept in the United States of America.[19] The website *Working Mother* has promoted the concept by listing the one hundred best companies every year since 1986. If even secular companies can notice the importance of the balance of work and family, how can the church disregard the importance?

Throughout the study in this paper, the church is called to take up a leading or modeling role in the society and culture. To be loyal to the Immanuel symbol, the church should be more gracious to female ministers and their children. Could the church have a better provision for female ministers, like longer maternity leave and special leave for family needs? Could the church have more flexible work arrangements like flexible working hours? Could the church think of providing child-care services?

It is a tragedy that working mothers not only face the problem of disenfranchisement of mother-child intimacy in their working environments, but also in the church and Christian organizations. The low fertility rate in Hong Kong reflects another kind of massacre of children. The church and the society need to hear the weeping and mourning of Rachel.

If there is no Immanuel in the church, how could we expect the coming of Immanuel in our society?

Notes

1. The statistics in this paragraph are drawn from Hong Kong Special Administrative Region (HKSAR) 2007–2008.

2. The "average parity of married couples" refers to the average number of children a married couple has.

3. The total fertility rate in Philippine keeps decreasing from 6.0 children per woman in 1973 to 3.3 in 2008. See Philippine Commission on Women 2012: 4.

4. The findings were released as the results of BFHIHKA's Annual Breastfeeding Survey and analysis of hotline calls at the press conference inaugurating World Breastfeeding Week 2009 (August 1–7). See HKSAR 2009a. The breastfeeding initiation rate is the percentage of live born babies born in any Hong Kong maternity unit who had ever been breast-fed to the total number of live-born babies born in Hong Kong. The breastfeeding initiation rate includes partial, predominant, and exclusive breastfeeding a few days after birth. The exclusive breastfeeding rate is the percentage of infants at four to six months who receive only breast milk and no other infant formula or solid food to the total number of infants at four to six months.

5. Obstetric and pediatric doctors who have received formal training on breast-feeding are only 4 and 11 percent respectively. See HKSAR 2009a.

6. The provisions in Singapore and Taiwan are lowest, where working mothers are entitled to just 8 weeks. The longest maternity leave—ninety-six weeks—is provided by Sweden. See Klass 2003. Here, we should also make a note that the provision of the United States should also be criticized. The United States is the only developed country that does not provide paid maternity leave nationally.

7. Kupp 1996: 157–75, in particular 239: "Jesus' identification as *Emmanuel*—God with us is one of four *main* theological *themes* in *Matthew* 1–2, intertwined with Davidic sonship, divine sonship and his messianic mission to 'his people.'" Before Kupp's research, H. Frankemölle had worked on the theme of "being with" thoroughly in his work *Jahwe-Bund und Kirche Christi: Studien zur Form- und Traditionsgeschichte des "Evangeliums" nach Matthäus* (1984: 7–83), in which he finds the theme as the key to both Matthew's Christology and ecclesiology.

8. Davies and Allison 1997: 84: "The major substantive differences between Mt 20.20-28 (168 words) and Mk 10.35-45 (193 words) are mostly confined to the first half of the pericope: (i) Mt 20.20-8 exhibits increased parallelism (cf. Mt 20.21 and 23 with Mk 10.37 and 40; Mt 20.26-7 and Mk 10.43-4). (ii) The mother of James and John appears only in the First Gospel. (iii) The posture of the petitioner (v. 20 *proskynousa*) is new to Matthew. (iv) The request in Mark, that Jesus do 'whatever we ask' (10.35), finds no place in our Gospel. (v) So too the references to 'baptism' (Mk 10.38, 39). (vi) Whereas Mk 10.35-40 is marked by the repetition of *de*, 10.41-5 by the repetition of *kai*, in Matthew this contrast is eliminated and stylistic unity achieved."

9. See also Senior 1998: 224: "Matthew may have the mother make the request as a way of softening the discordant note of the disciples' request"; Harrington 2007: 288: "Matthew . . . 'improves' the image of the disciples by having the mother of Zebedee's sons make the request on their behalf."

10. As noted by many scholars, such as Luz 1997: 161; Senior 1998: 224.

11. According to Chrysostom, *Homily* LXV, 2: "the request was rather theirs, and . . . being ashamed they put forward their mother." See "St. Chrysostom: Homilies on the Gospel of Saint Matthew," translated by P. Schaff, *NPNF* 1–10, 380.

12. Cf. Keener 1999: 485: "To accomplish their petition, they enlisted their mother; Jewish tradition accorded aged women a special place of respect. . . . Further, women could get away with asking requests men dare not ask, both in Jewish . . . and broader Greco-Roman culture."

13. For the differences in wordings, see Hagner 1995b: 854.

14. Origen is the first writer who identifies "the mother of the sons of Zebedee" in Matt. 27:56 as "Salome" in Mark 15:40, in his work *Commentariorum Series in Matthaeum*, 141 (GCS 38, 293). Some scholars, like Grassi (1989: 41), still hold the same standpoint, while others, like Witherington (1984: 120), leave the possibility open.

15. Brown 1994: 2:1157–58 highlights the distance of the women from the cross as an indication of their lack of faith. The problem of Brown's interpretation has been criticized by different scholars; e.g., Bruner 2004: 766; Miller 2004: 161.

16. J: Matt 1:18b-25; H: 2:1-12; J: 2:13-15; H: 2:16-18; J: 2:19-23. For details, see Liu 2008: 120. The insight of the captioned structure is partly from Brown 1993: 105n21.

17. According to Teng-Cheung (2009: 41), there are 129 female ministers who have one child, 176 female ministers who have two children, 30 female ministers who have three children, and 1 female minister who has four. The fertility rate is based on this data.

18. According to the scheme, family-friendly measures include "(1) Provision of special leave to meet employees' family needs—Marriage leave, paternity leave, compassionate leave, parental leave, special casual leave; (2) Flexible work arrangements—Five-day work week, flexible working hours, home office, job sharing; (3) Provision of living support—Child care service, counseling services on stress or emotional management for employees and their family members, medical protection; (4) Provision of programmes/activities which encourage work-life balance—family recreational activities, parent-child seminars, workplace open days for employees' family members; (5) Family-friendly corporate culture—the employers support and endorse the concept of family-friendly employment practices for gradual establishment of a family-friendly corporate culture. (6) During the planning process and prior to implementing each measure, employers communicate with their employees thoroughly to understand their genuine need." See HKSAR 2010c.

19. This does not mean, however, that the working condition in the United States is, overall, family friendly, but the awareness of family friendliness in the United States is definitely higher than that in Hong Kong.

7

The Emotive Semantics of Asian Context

What Does Jesus' Sorrow in Gethsemane (Matthew 26:36-46) Signify for a Korean Pastor's Kid?

Sung Uk Lim

INTRODUCTION

This paper aims to reexamine Jesus' feeling of sorrow in Gethsemane (Matt. 26:36-46) and the suffering of the reader as a pastor's kid (henceforth: PK) in a Korean context from the emotive semiotic perspective. In the present study, I argue that the suffering of Jesus, particularly for PKs, signifies the depth of *han*, an (Asian) Korean concept of suffering, which could and should be transformed into a cloud of *jeong*, an (Asian) Korean concept of eros, in the end. My assumption is that the Gospel of Matthew is founded on non-Western, Palestinian Jewish culture, which prioritizes the thymic or emotive category (euphoria vs. dysphoria) over the veridictory category (being vs. seeming).[1] Given that the meaning of a text is dynamically generated out of a plurality of contexts in a diachronic sense, we have good reason to first draw attention to the emotive category within the Jewish context of the Gospel of Matthew, which was unmistakably important within first-century Palestinian Judaism.

Then, we may well focus on the contexts of a reader in the process of the generation of meanings out of a text. In this sense, I shall foreground my own specific context, in which I personally read the given text of the Gethsemane scene. As a Korean PK, I myself feel compassionate with what Jesus would feel at Gethsemane in the face of his imminent death. In the Korean Christian milieu, a PK is supposed to sacrifice himself or herself in an effort to meet the needs of the congregation of the church. In this environment, many, although not all, PKs grow up emotionally hurt. Within the context of PKs in Korea, I shall explore Jesus' pathos or grief in Gethsemane.[2]

Perhaps one of the biblical texts most PKs would hate to read in Korea is the Gethsemane account, in association with the Akedah account. The reason for this is that many Korean pastors have a tendency to misuse and/or abuse those stories in such a way as to accentuate the "blind obedience" to God's will as well as to parents. In this way, the suffering of PKs would go unnoticed. Even so, the emotive semiotic encourages us to revisit the suffering of Jesus in Gethsemane, which runs parallel to that of PKs, to a certain extent. Hence, the present study will attempt to fathom the transformation of Jesus in such a way that he decides to submit to God's will by forsaking his own will, even though he undergoes the feeling of abandonment from his silent Father and the depths of helplessness from his sleeping disciples.

The Contextualization of the Reader: The Life of a PK in the Korean Church

To begin with, PKs in the setting of Korean ministry may be divided in two groups: PK as "perfect kid" and PK as "problem kid" (Lim 2008: 62). From a pastoral counseling perspective, laypeople in the Korean church setting have a prejudice toward understanding a PK as a "little pastor," or "second pastor" (Kim 2005: 22). Only a few PKs are able to reach the standards of laypeople with success. Rather, most PKs, due to extreme stress, cause trouble in school, as well as in church, and end up as problem kids. They try in vain to be as perfect as their parents are perceived to be by the congregation.

In reaction to the high expectations of the congregation, Korean pastors usually push their children to become perfect kids in the eyes of laypeople. In this light, PKs receive double pressure from both laypeople and their parents, while PKs, on their part, are forced to sacrifice themselves in order to live up to the expectations from both sides. Regrettably, PKs' sacrifice goes further, in that their parents have little time to take care of them, given the tough schedule related to the ministry. The remark of one Korean PK is striking: "Whenever I really needed my parents, they always forsook me for the sake of the ministry alone. I used to wait for them after the school as if an orphan. All the time I felt I as a PK was forced to sacrifice myself for the church of my parents" (Jong Hwan Kim 2005: 138–39).

This quote makes clear the miserable reality of a large number of PKs in the Korean Christian context. Most of them feel as if they were abandoned by parents who were mostly concerned with the ministry, with the least care for their children. No doubt, many Korean pastors put their energies into the ministry rather than the family, partly because they don't consider the latter as part of the former and partly because they consider it natural to sacrifice the family for the work of God. In the long run, the life of a PK in Korea has a tendency to be wretched.

A pastoral counseling perspective highlights the fact that PKs sacrifice much of their self-esteem and self-identity. The recent survey by Yoon Joo Lee demonstrates that PKs, in comparison to non-PKs, usually suffer from social problems such as goal-orientation, uniqueness, self-acceptance, self-insistence, and relationship with others (Lee 2001: 41–42). The most severe problems for PKs concern self-esteem and self-identity. Lee holds that the main reason for this is a dearth of communication between a pastor and a PK (Lee 2001:43). Korean pastors are often too busy with the ministry to communicate to their children in everyday life. In addition to lack of time, the other reason for lack of communication is that PKs have only rare chances to express their own will and emotion, being forced to comply with the will of their parents. Here, it should be remembered that the problems of PKs are closely connected with the family structure, which remains patriarchal and authoritarian in Korea.

Even though it ostensibly rejects traditional, Confucian values, Korean Christianity still maintains Confucian elements in terms of the patriarchal family structure. Take *hyo*, filial piety, one of the most significant Confucian tenets, for example. In general terms, *hyo* can be defined as a reverence for the parents and, by extension, for the ancestors. Simply put, the Korean term *hyo* can be referred to as the obedience of children to parents. There is no doubt that in conjunction with Confucianism, Korean Christianity has reinforced the control of parents over children with much focus on the patriarchal Judeo-Christian tradition. Under the patriarchal influence of both Confucianism and Judeo-Christianity, many pastors in Korea believe that their authority as father in the household is impregnable whatever the circumstances. Given that it is hard, if not impossible, for women to be ordained in Korean churches, most mothers are engaged in establishing the power of their husbands as pastors. In this context, Korean pastors expect their children to be completely obedient to their will. Conversely, PKs describe their parents as "dictators." Thus Korean PKs' voices are not heard at home or at church.

Up to now, we have observed the sufferings of PKs in the context of the Korean church. To summarize so far, the first point to bear in mind is that PKs are compelled to sacrifice themselves to satisfy the expectations of the congregation. Second, they suffer from the emotional aloofness and inaccessibility of their parents. Third, they have lower self-esteem and self-identity mainly because of little, if any, communication in relationship with their parents. And last, they undergo the suppression of their own emotion and will, being coerced to comply with the will of the parents.

As mentioned above, the context of a reader as a PK drives me to focus on the Gethsemane account because it discloses the poignant anguish over Jesus' sacrifice, which can run parallel to the pain of PKs over their sacrifices, at least to some degree. Furthermore, the conflicting relationship between God the Father and Jesus the Son is quite similar to that between the pastor as the parent and PKs.[3] In this vein, it is still puzzling that Jesus is finally transformed to a son obedient to a father's will who nevertheless abandons him. I believe that the suffering and transformation of Jesus in Gethsemane will eventually shed fresh light on the pain-ridden life of PKs, which will help them transform their relationship with their parents.

METHOD FOR ANALYSIS OF EMOTION: GREIMAS'S SEMIO-STRUCTURAL EXEGESIS

The goal of this section is to establish a method for the analysis of Jesus' emotion in the Gethsemane scene (Matt. 26:36-46). For this purpose, I take the structural semiotic model of Algirdas Greimas, which he termed the "generative trajectory of meaning" (Patte 1990: 31–32),[4] constituted by the following basic components: fundamental semantics, fundamental syntax, narrative semantics, narrative syntax, discursive semantics (thematization, figurativization), discursive syntax (actorialization, temporalization, spatialization).[5] Hence, the generative trajectory can be diagramed as shown in figure 1.

	Syntactic Components		Semantic Components
Semiotic and Narrative Structure	Deep Level	Fundamental Syntax	Fundamental Semantics
	Surface Level	Narrative Syntax	Narrative Semantics
Discursive Structure	Discursive Syntax: Actorialization Temporalization Spatialization		Discursive Semantics: Thematization Figurativization

Figure 1. Generative Trajectory[6]

Along the lines of Greimas, we can explore the Gospel of Matthew as a religious text, of which the meaning-generating dimension is closely concerned with an aspect of believing. As Daniel Patte aptly describes it, the generative trajectory touches on faith as religious phenomenon embracing human experience (Patte 1990: 218). Above all, Patte defines believing on the three levels: (1) the certainty of the existence or truth of anything; (2) the acceptance of it as true by means of witness or authority; (3) the conviction based on reasoning. For Patte, the first definition applies to the convictional dimension of faith corresponding to the fundamental and narrative semantics of the generative theory. The second applies to the discursive dimension of faith corresponding to discursive semantics. The last applies to the syntactic dimension of faith (including theology, ethics, and ideology) corresponding to the fundamental, narrative, and discursive syntactic structure.

In terms of Greimas's semiotic theory and corresponding aspect of religious phenomenon of belief as proposed by Patte, I will first reexamine as a test case the biblical scholarship of Donald Senior's typology in the structure of the discursive semantics. Second, I shall perform my own emotive semiotic exegesis of the text in the structure of fundamental, narrative, and discursive semantics, focused on the non-Western or Palestinian Jewish context.

ISAAC-JESUS TYPOLOGY IN THE STRUCTURE
OF THE DISCURSIVE SEMANTICS: A CASE STUDY
OF DONALD SENIOR'S COMMENTARY ON MATTHEW

In the view of Greimas's semiotics, Donald Senior in his commentary scrutinizes the structure of discursive semantics with particular attention to an Isaac-Jesus typology. Patte regards the "discursive semantic dimension of believing" as "believing a truth on authority" (Patte 1990: 129–72). In the discursive structure, the enunciator aims to convince the enunciatee of the authority of the enunciator, as well as the trustworthiness of the message (Patte 1990: 13).[7] At the same time, this persuasion strives to transform a reader into an enunciatee-believer who is keen to adopt the message as true on the basis of the trustworthiness of the enunciator, especially in the religious realm (Patte 1990: 132). It is through a process of figurativization, or an establishment of a new figurative world, which is structured by the root metaphor (an image), that a reader is transformed into an enunciatee-believer willing to receive the message based on the authority of the enunciator (Patte 1990: 136–37). As Patte states, "The transformation of a person into an enunciatee-believer involves the transformation of the figurative world that defines the identity of that person" (Patte 1990: 137). More precisely, a reader can become an enunciatee-believer in such a way as to synthesize his or her figurative world (symbolism) with that of the enunciator (Patte 1990: 137). This suggests that a figure (metaphor or metonym) can be polysemic, since it can convey both older and newer values (Patte 1990: 138). In a word, figurativization entails an integration of two different semantic universes—the semantic universe of the enunciator and that of the enunciatee. From a semiotic perspective, Senior makes explicit the way figurativization operates with an Isaac-Jesus typology.

In this Isaac-Jesus typology, Senior envisions Jesus as embodying "both the faith of Abraham and the sacrificial spirit of Isaac," on the grounds that the wording of Matt. 26:36-37 subtly alludes to Gen. 22:5 (Senior 1998: 303). It is worthwhile to remember Senior's words: "The Akedah Isaac or 'binding of Isaac' was a favored motif in rabbinic Judaism that stressed the exemplary faith of Abraham and the willing sacrifice of Isaac" (Senior 1998: 303). As Robert S. Barbour notes, Abraham's "blind faith" and Isaac's voluntary offering lead a reader to make a strong connection between the Akedah story and the Gethsemane story (Barbour 1970: 238).[8] In particular, both Isaac and Jesus evoke the image of the son obedient to God calling for sacrifice. At the typological level, the sacrifice of Isaac was seen in early Christianity as foreshadowing the passion of Christ (Jensen 2000). Especially striking is a sermon of Bishop Melito of Sardis in the second century, in which he underscores the importance of the sacrifice of the Lamb both in the Akedah and the Passion:

> For as a ram he was bound and a lamb he was shorn,
>   And as a sheep he was led to slaughter, and as a lamb he was crucified;
>   And he carried the wood upon his shoulders
>   And he was led up to be slain like Isaac by his father.
>   But Christ suffered, whereas Isaac did not suffer;
>   For he was a model of the Christ who was going to suffer.
> (Melito 1979: 75–77)

Such Isaac-Jesus typology encourages readers to transform themselves into enunciatee-believers by synthesizing their semantic universes with the enunciator's semantic universe (see Patte 1990: 149–52).[9]

Thus Senior analyzes the structure of discursive semantics in terms of typology: he articulates an Isaac-like-Jesus typology, through discursive semantics. He envisions Jesus as embodying the faith of Abraham and the sacrificial spirit of Isaac on the basis of the intertextuality between Matthew's Gospel and Genesis. Senior argues that Isaac and Jesus evoke the image of the son obedient to God, who calls for sacrifice. Yet this exegesis fails to make a strong case for my own context, by making little or no room for the emotion of Jesus and Isaac. The reason for this is that Senior's reading is a veridictory interpretation based on the category true/false rather than an emotive one, which is correlated with a value in the category euphoria/dysphoria in technical terms (or pleasure/displeasure in nontechnical terms). This provides a good reason for me to go further by performing an emotive semiotic. Let me describe in more detail what is at stake in my own exegesis.

AN EMOTIVE SEMIOTIC EXEGESIS IN THE STRUCTURE OF THE FUNDAMENTAL, NARRATIVE, AND DISCURSIVE SEMANTICS

Contrary to the veridictory category (being vs. seeming) in fundamental semantics, which is deeply rooted in Western culture, I assume in this essay that the Gospel of Matthew, as Timothy B. Cargal succinctly suggests, takes on the emotive category (euphoria vs. dysphoria) leaning toward emotional values, emerging from non-Western, or more precisely, Palestinian Jewish culture (Cargal 1990). There is no doubt that the meanings of a text are dynamically created out of a multitude of contexts and in a diachronic, not a synchronic sense.[10] For this reason, it is important to pinpoint the emotive category within the Jewish context in the exegesis of the Gospel of Matthew, which was clearly connected to first-century Palestinian Judaism.

In this regard, the purpose of this part is to find the meanings of the Gethsemane story from an emotive semiotic perspective. At this point, let us focus on what Jesus feels in Gethsemane. In the Gethsemane story, Jesus expresses his emotion of sorrow or grief twice as follows: "He began to be grieved and agitated" (*ērxato lupeisthai kai adēmonein*, Matt. 26:37); "I am deeply grieved" (*perilupos estin ē psuchē mou eōs thanatou*, Matt. 26:38). Before explicating Jesus' feeling, one can first construct the structure of the fundamental semantics from an emotive semiotic. The emotive category creates the "semiotic square" (Patte 1990: 121–22)[11] on the basis of the contrary opposition "euphoric" (what is felt to be good for me) versus "dysphoric" (what is felt to be bad for me).[12] The emotive square can be diagramed as shown in figure 2.

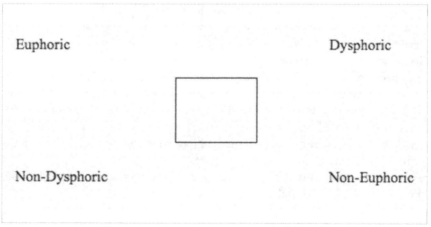

Figure 2. Virtual Valuative Modalities[13]

Then, this emotive taxonomy can be applied to what Jesus feels in Gethsemane in the structure of the narrative semantics: euphoric (what is felt to be pleasing for Jesus) versus dysphoric (what is felt to be grieving for Jesus). To take a step further, one can apply the fundamental semantic category such as life/death to the emotive taxonomy as in figure 3.

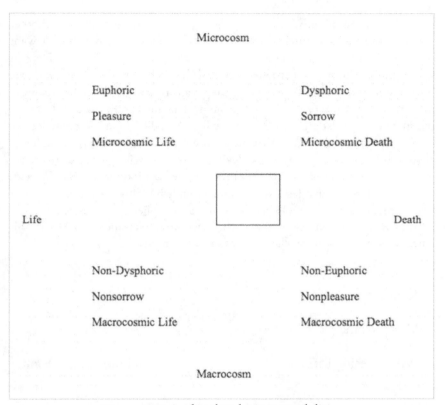

Figure 3. Actualized Valuative Modalities

In narrative semantics, Jesus' life and death can be analyzed at the microcosmic/noncosmological and macrocosmic/cosmological level. In the square, the microcosmic life and death are noncosmological life and death, while the macrocosmic life and death are cosmological life (nondeath) and death (nonlife). In the figure, I have also demonstrated the second-generation terms of the semiotic square, a second semiotic square based on meta-terms.[14] To illustrate, the contrary opposition of life and death occurs in the microcosmic realm and the subcontrary opposition of nondeath and nonlife in the macrocosmic realm. The two deixes (positive and negative implications) entail life (relative life on the microcosmic level; absolute life on the macrocosmic level) and death (relative death on the microcosmic level; absolute death on the macrocosmic level). Remember that I conventionally put the positive deixis of euphoric connotations (life and nondeath) on the left and the negative deixis of dysphoric connotations (death and nonlife) on the right.

With this in mind, we can apply the above narrative semantics to another narrative semantics as implied by the words of Jesus: "Yet not what I want but what you want" (*plēn ouch ōs egō thelō all ōs su*, Matt. 26:39b). Here, it should be kept in mind that Jesus' will and the Father's will take place in the microcosmical realm in the sense that they concern the noncosmological level. Moreover, the contrary relationship of Jesus' will and the Father's will implies the subcontrary relationship of Satan's will and God's will at the cosmological level. It is worthwhile to note that the Gethsemane scene implicitly or explicitly alludes to Jesus' temptation by the devil in Matt. 4:1, with particular reference to the temptation (*peirasmon*) motif of Jesus as well as his three disciples in Matt. 26:41. This is to say that Jesus wants his life, while his Father wants his death, at the microcosmic/noncosmological level. It is also implied that Satan wants Jesus' death, while God wants Jesus' life, in the macrocosmic/cosmological level. This narrative semantics can be illustrated as shown in figure 4.

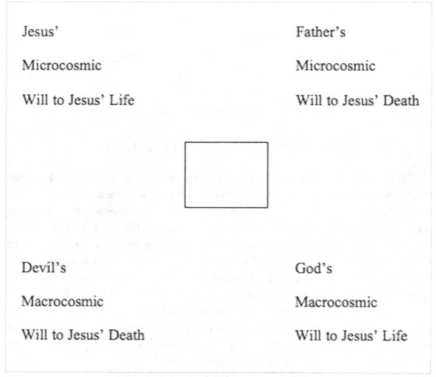

Figure 4. Actualized Valuative Modalities

It is striking that as suggested in verse 39, Jesus sets out to convert between the euphoric and dysphoric deixes by saying that he will follow the Father's will, not his own will. This means that the dysphoric deixis of the Father's microcosmic will to Jesus' death and God's macrocosmic will to Jesus' life shifts into the euphoric deixis; to the contrary, the euphoric deixis of Jesus' microcosmic will to Jesus' life and the devil's macrocosmic will to Jesus' death moves into the dysphoric deixis. This means that Jesus complies with the Father's will to his death at the microcosmic/noncosmological level, while at the same time implying that he obeys his will to his death at the macrocosmic/cosmological level. We can illustrate this new semiotic square as shown in figure 5.

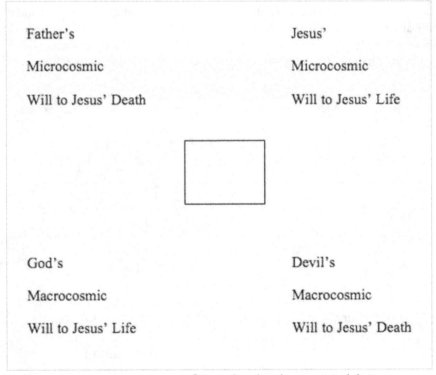

Father's

Microcosmic

Will to Jesus' Death

Jesus'

Microcosmic

Will to Jesus' Life

God's

Macrocosmic

Will to Jesus' Life

Devil's

Macrocosmic

Will to Jesus' Death

Figure 5. Conversion of Actualized Valuative Modalities

Finally, I argue that this conversion of the narrative semantics can be construed only in the discursive semantics as mentioned earlier in the figurativization. As is the case with Senior's interpretation of Isaac-Jesus typology, the Gethsemane scene, to begin with, would remind a reader of Isaac's sacrifice in Genesis 22. Figuratively speaking, Isaac plays a role as a type for Jesus, by way of symbol. The correspondences between Isaac and Jesus with respect to their death and resurrection are striking; both Isaac and Jesus are the only sons of their fathers; they are obedient to their fathers' will to sacrifice them to the point of death; they come back to life by God's hand. Thus Isaac's resurrection functions as a type for Jesus' resurrection.

When all is said and done, the figurativization in process leads the reader to become transformed into an enunciatee-believer so as to take on the message of enunciation in the structure of discursive semantics. In this case, we can reconstruct the realized valuative modalities in the discursive structure. One can generate the contrary relationship of the resurrected life and the nonresurrected death and, as a consequence, the subcontrary relationship of the permanent life and the impermanent death. Hence, the euphoric deixis of the resurrected/permanent life and the dysphoric deixis of the nonresurrected/permanent death come into being. We can diagram this semiotic square as shown in figure 6.

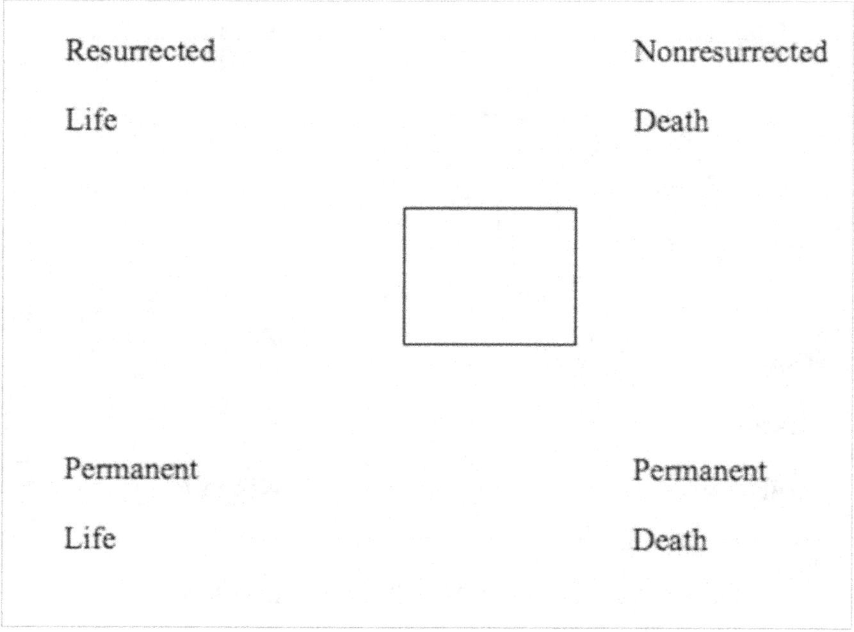

Figure 6. Realized Valuative Modalities

For a reader, especially in the fundamental and narrative semantics, it would be nonsensical for Jesus to transform himself by taking the Father's will and at the same time by forsaking his will on the assumption that death may be valued as negative. In the structure of the discursive semantics, however, the transformation of Jesus can be made plausible to the reader. The reason is that a reader can be transformed into an enunciatee-believer in the discursive semantics. As Patte notes, "Since a religious discourse aims at transforming the addressee into a believer-enunciatee, the structure of the enunciator-enunciatee relationship is always a process of transformation" (Patte 1990: 158). Through the discursive process, an enunciatee, who has a different semantic universe at the beginning, turns out to share the enunciator's semantic universe in the end. This means that a believer-enunciatee without the knowledge of Jesus' resurrection after his or her death is transformed into a believer-enunciatee with that knowledge, through the figurativization of Jesus with Isaac. Therefore, the system of figures has the power to realize the valuative modalities in the structure of the discursive semantics.

As such, the emotive semiotic sets out to reconstruct Jesus' feeling of sorrow at Gethsemane in the structure of the fundamental and narrative semantics, insofar as it comes to grips with emotional values. But the important point is that the structure of the discursive semantics enables a reader to become transformed into a believer-enunciatee by espousing the semantic universe of the enunciator through figurativization. In my own context of being a PK, I believe that I myself need to be changed into a believer-enunciatee in order to understand Jesus' transformation in Gethsemane, from which new meaning can be generated.

CONCLUDING REMARKS: FROM *HAN* TO *JEONG*

Admittedly, the emotive semiotic contributes to more deeply understanding the suffering of Jesus in the text. By the same token, it also pushes the reader as a believer-enunciatee to enter into the suffering of PKs from within the Korean Christian context, at the discursive level. I believe that most PKs would not enjoy reading the Gethsemane account alongside the Akedah account, mainly because many pastors in Korea misread both of them by stressing the "blind obedience" to God's will and, by extension, the parents'. Seen in this light, the suffering of Jesus and the suffering of PKs tend to fade into oblivion and be forgotten. Nevertheless, the emotive semiotic gives us a chance to take a closer look at the suffering of Jesus in Gethsemane and, by implication, the suffering of PKs.

Given that the transformation of the reader into an enunciatee-believer entails the integration between his or her figurative world and that of enunciator at the discursive level, we must remember that the context of the reader indeed makes a difference in the interpretation of the Gethsemane story. In this connection, Jesus' suffering can be construed as *han*, an Asian—especially Korean—concept of human suffering in the reader's context. The overwhelming experience of deep hopelessness and resentful bitterness can be termed *han* in Korean culture (Park 1993: 10). Andrew Sung Park further demonstrates *han* by stating:

> *Han* can be defined as the critical wound of the heart generated by unjust psychosomatic repression, as well as by social, political, economic, and cultural oppression. It is entrenched in the hearts of the victims of sin and violence, and is expressed through such diverse reactions as sadness, helplessness, hopelessness, resentment, hatred, and the will to revenge. Han reverberates in the souls of survivors of the Holocaust, Palestinians in the occupied territories, victims of racial discrimination, battered wives, children involved in divorces, the victims of child-molestation, laid-off workers, the unemployed, and exploited workers. (Park 1993: 10)

Thus *han* can be understood as the "wounded heart" or brokenheartedness (Park 1993: 20). In other words, the woundedness of the heart comes as the "abysmal experience of pain" (Park 1993: 15). In addition, *han* involves the complexity of ineffable feelings such as sadness, resentment, bitterness, aggression, abandonment, hopelessness, and helplessness. In the Korean context, Jesus' grief (Matt. 26:37-38) over his imminent death could be decoded as *han* for the following reasons: first, because he, more implicitly, experiences the feeling of abandonment from his silent Father (Matt. 26:39, 42, 44); second, because he, more explicitly, goes through the depth of helplessness from his sleeping disciples (Matt. 26:40, 43, 45); third, because he suffers from overwhelming sorrow to the point of death (*perilypos estin ē psychē mou eōs thanatou*, Matt. 26:38).

In spite of all this, it is remarkable that Jesus can overcome his *han* through a Korean concept of *jeong*, a "power of eros that forges its presence in the interval between the Self and the Other" (Joh 2004: 152–53). The hidden *jeong* of God the Father toward Jesus the Son is revealed in the discursive structure, with a semiotic point of view. Prior to analyzing the discursive semantics, we must keep in mind that it is not until the reader is transformed into an enunciatee-believer familiar with the Akedah story that she or he can begin to understand Jesus' *han* in the fullest sense. That is to say, we can see Jesus' suffering anew only with the knowledge of Jesus' resurrection after his death via his figurativization with Isaac.

In light of resurrection, we discover a momentum whereby Jesus can reconcile himself with God, despite his *han* over his imminent death. Even though God keeps silent in Gethsemane, we have no choice but to admit that God conceals the plan from his beloved son, just as he does for Isaac in the Akedah story. In comparison to Isaac on Moriah, it is implied that God the Father's willing the death of Jesus the Son is ultimately oriented toward his resurrected and permanent life at the discursive level. With this observation, it can be said that there God's *jeong* (or more precisely, *bu-jeong*, which means "father's *jeong*" in Korean) toward his Son Jesus is implicit. We can go further and say that Jesus can overcome his *han* through the discovery of *bu-jeong*, his Father's *jeong* toward his Son.

As Wonhee Anne Joh observes, *jeong* hints at the relationality or interconnectedness involving fundamental mutuality between the self and the other (Joh 2004: 152). The reason is that *jeong* can swing between self and other like a pendulum; *jeong* is an in-between, indeterminate, and ambiguous space between self and other, between hatred and love, and between oppressor and oppressed (Joh 2004: 153). *Jeong* and *han*, as Jung Young Lee argues, go hand in hand; they are two sides of a coin (Lee 1999). This is to say that while crossing over a diversity of boundaries and borders, *jeong* exists even within chasms, and in particular, painful interspaces (e.g., between oppressor and oppressed) (Joh 2004: 154).

What is interesting is that *jeong* can be construed to have the power to challenge and end a perpetuating chain of *han*, eventually healing the "wounded heart." Most importantly, *jeong* can dissolve the deeply rooted *han* by calling for vulnerability, wherein we can recognize the self in those parts perceived to be the other (Joh 2004: 155). Consequently, *jeong* allows us to perceive and accept the "negativized and shadowed parts of ourselves," eventually breaking off a chain of *han* in the abundance of *jeong* (Joh 2004: 155).

Likewise, it is the hidden God's *bu-jeong* as implied by the Akedah account that puts an end to Jesus' perpetuating *han* over his Father on the part of the reader. For the reader as an enunciatee-believer conversant with the Akedah account, it is obvious that Jesus in Gethsemane goes through both *han* and *jeong*, just as Isaac does. But at the same time, the readers can anticipate that God's, albeit tacit, *bu-jeong* can heal the deeply wounded heart of Jesus by calling to memory God's rescue of Isaac. Thus, Jesus' *han* can be dissolved into *jeong* at the discursive level.

Now the time has come for us to discuss the suffering of PKs as well as that of Jesus. PKs' suffering can also be seen as *han* in relationship with their parents as pastors. As noted above, we can reread the Gethsemane story along the Akedah story in the hopes that PKs, on the part of the reader, can overcome *han* through *jeong*, just as Jesus does. As is the case with the relationship between God the Father and Jesus the Son, it can be suggested that in spite of little communication between PKs and parents, there exists the hidden *jeong* of the latter toward the former. From this it follows that PKs can be empowered to trespass the rift with their parents. Undoubtedly, PKs are the beloved children of their parents. In conclusion, the suffering of Jesus, in particular for PKs, signifies the depth of *han*, which could and should be transformed into a cloud of *jeong* in the end.

Notes

1. Through a semiotic lens, Algirdas Julien Greimas and Joseph Courtès distinguish veridictory analysis and thymic or emotive analysis. On the one hand, veridictory analysis is made up of the conjunction of being and seeming in that both at all times go hand in hand. On the other hand, thymic analysis involves values operating with the category euphoria/dysphoria, to be more specific, pleasure/displeasure or positive/negative. In the present study, I prefer to employ the term *emotive semiotic* rather than the term *thymic semiotic*, with emphasis on emotional evaluations.

2. On the pathos of Jesus in Gethsemane, see Davies and Allison (1988: 502–3), who portray Jesus as a "solitary figure" separated from his disciples and even worse, from his Father God. Cf. Greimas 1987. In this article, Greimas sheds light on how to analyze such human feelings as anger.

3. Note that Korean pastors are predominantly male, given the fact that women's ordination in Korean churches is restricted to only a few denominations.

4. For Greimas, the meaning of a text is produced as a meaning-effect in which the diverse facets of a text are interrelated and perceived in a different light. One should not forget that a text itself is a mystery of meanings with multifaceted features of its own. The result is that meaning as a meaning-effect produces a multiplicity of meanings, and one of its dimensions is relational to the others. As such, Greimas's model sees meaning as a "multidimensional and relational meaning-effect" (Patte 1990: 74).

5. Each component involves a corresponding structure. One can identify these components with a threefold feature. First, the entire semiotic structures are applied to either a syntactic or a semantic component, which matches syntax and semantics in linguistics. The syntactic component concerns the syntagmatic construction of the narrative or discourse, whereas the semantic component concerns the paradigmatic construction of them in conjunction with value systems. Second, there exist two different types of relations: the one governs semio-narrative structures; the other governs discursive structures in relation to enunciation. Third, the semio-narrative structure is divided between the fundamental (deep) level and the surface structures.

6. On this, see Greimas and Courtès 1982: 134.

7. It is to be noted that the structure of enunciation consists of the domain of enunciator and enunciatee. According to Greimas and Courtès, enunciator and enunciatee can be defined as the implicit sender and receiver of enunciation or communication, respectively. Also notice that

enunciator and enunciatee are different form narrator and narratee in that the first unit involves the level of discourse but the second involves the level of narrative. Greimas and Courtès 1982: 85.

8. On the relationship between the Akedah story and the passion narrative, see Vermès 1961: 193–227; Wood 1968.

9. From a semiotic perspective, Senior in the commentary demonstrates an Isaac-Jesus typology in the structure of the discursive semantics. Transformed into a believer-enunciatee, a reader is supposed to integrate his or her figurative world with the enunciator's through a process of figurativization. One should remember that even the same figure brings about polysemic meaning-effects according to the specificity of discourse. As Greimas and Courtès note, figurativization is featured by the particularization of the intangible discourse. As Patte exemplifies, one can differently construe the same metaphor, say, "Sabbath is a palace," once it is differently specified and particularized; the metaphor can be understood in terms of "building process" or in terms of "source of power/strength." This implies that the same typology, "Jesus is like Isaac," as proposed by Senior, can be understood differently by setting it in different squares of figurative terms.

10. On the matter of the relationship between the text/art and its contexts, see Bal 1994: 144–50. Bal stands in support of the view of poststructuralism that the simiosis is to be unfolded in the specific context of time and place. She takes a step further by adding that "they (sings) are constituted by different viewers in different ways at different times and places" (149). In this view, it indeed matters what contexts constitute the reader/viewer as well as a text/art in the sense that different contexts influence interpretation in a different fashion.

11. The semiotic square, also known as Greimas's semiotic square, is defined as the visual representation of the conceptual structure of an opposition, which can be illustrated in the shape of a square. As basic structure of meaning, the semiotic square is meant to make clear the binary oppositions composed of four terms: term A; term B; term ~B; term ~A. Such a semiotic square is initially formed by the first two contrary terms. And it goes on to obtain the other two contrary terms in a way that negates of each of the first two contrary terms. As a result, the semiotic square has three different types of relationships: contrary (e.g., the relationship between A and B, and the relationship between ~B and ~A); contradictory (e.g., the relationship between A and ~A, and the relationship between B and ~B); implication (e.g., the relationship between A and ~B, and the relationship between B and ~A).

12. Undoubtedly, this emotive category (in terms of euphoria and dysphoria) interrelates to the veridictory category (in terms of reality and illusion). It is by the application of the veridictory category that the emotive category is transformed into an emotive axiologized (patternized) taxonomy. It is noteworthy that the hierarchical relationship between the emotive and veridictory categories consequently turns upside down.

13. The valuative modalities of the emotive semiotics can be divided in three ways: virtual, actualized, realized. Now we need to be alert to the meanings of each term: first, the term *virtual* means that there exists an idea of the action; second, the term *actualized* means that the action is in progress; third, the term *realized* means that the action is accomplished. The important point to be acknowledged is that virtual, actualized, and realized valuative modalities come into play at the fundamental, narrative, and discursive levels, respectively.

14. Most importantly, the semiotic square can create a second semiotic square composed of the meta-terms such as the complex term, neutral term, positive deixis, and negative deixis. Such meta-terms are molded from the four basic terms: term A; term B; term ~A; term ~B. To be more precise, term A and term B constitute the complex term; term ~B and term ~A constitute the neutral term.; term A and term ~B constitute the positive deixis; term B and term ~ A constitute the negative deixis.

PART III

Disability and Culture

8

Reading Matthew's Healing Narratives from the Perspectives of the Caregiver and the Disabled

James A. Metzger and James P. Grimshaw

INTRODUCTION

In this essay, the two authors provide a contextual analysis of healing narratives in the Gospel of Matthew (8:5-13; 9:2-8; 12:9-14; 17:14-20) that deploy a hermeneutic of disability informed by literature from disability and cultural studies as well as by personal experience with rheumatologic illness. One presenter is the spouse of a person with rheumatoid arthritis (RA); the other has ankylosing spondylitis (AS). Neither disease is curable, and both minimally involve chronic pain, loss of mobility, and fatigue.

We have selected these passages because all include: (1) a silenced ill or disabled character whose impairment (or impairments) bears some similarity to those associated with RA or AS (for example, the lame, paralytics, epileptics, the maimed, persons enduring chronic pain); (2) family or community members (for example, a Roman centurion, a parent, other companions or friends) who are (a) acknowledged over against a disparaged group (for example, Israelites, scribes, disciples) and (b) awarded agency simultaneously withheld from the disabled character they are supporting; and (3) an ideology of similitude in which all differently abled bodies are reformed in accordance with a Matthean ideal of wholeness/health (that is, an ideology rooted in Levitical health care and prophetic and apocalyptic eschatology).

Foregrounding life contexts informed by rheumatologic illness, the two authors will address representations of the disabled, Jesus, and family/ community members as well as implications for an understanding of disability today.[1]

Perspective of the Disabled (Metzger)

Before analyzing four healing texts from Matthew, I will relate my personal context of living with ankylosing spondylitis and then briefly outline my methodological assumptions. I will conclude with some brief reflections.

Context

Ankylosing spondylitis (AS) is a rheumatic disease that minimally involves inflammation of the spine and sacroiliac joints. Very often, joints and ligaments in other areas of the body such as the shoulders, hips, ribs, knees, hands, and feet are affected as well. On occasion, the disease extends its reach beyond the musculoskeletal system to the bowel, eyes, lungs, or heart. Common symptoms include pain, stiffness, and fatigue. AS is chronic and incurable. Treatment typically involves an individualized cocktail of traditional immune suppressants, TNF blockers (biologic agents), and NSAIDS, although some have found antidepressants, physical therapy, dietary changes, and holistic treatments to be beneficial as well.

The mission of the Spondylitis Association of America, the largest nonprofit organization dedicated to persons with spondylitis and their families, is "to be a leader in the quest to cure ankylosing spondylitis and related diseases, and to empower those affected to live life to the fullest."[2] Tellingly, the desire for a cure is placed first. A majority of those with the illness presumably long for a return to somatic equilibrium; this is the not the sort of disability that most are able to celebrate as distinction or reframe as mere variation. Living with AS is painful and extraordinarily tiring, and unless one harbors masochistic tendencies, one quite naturally wishes to be free of the disease.

I have had AS for five years. Although the disease manifests itself differently in different people, for me chronic pain and loss of mobility constitute its most undesirable symptoms. In addition to giving up activities (and even relationships) that once brought enjoyment, there are new financial burdens and anxieties sustained by living in a society that has elected to entrust the distribution of health care largely to private corporations, whose chief concern is maximizing profit. Fortunately, perhaps, AS most often results in what is sometimes called "hidden disability"; that is, our challenges are due not to society's disabling gaze but primarily to somatic and psychic distress. While stigma and discrimination may attend severe or advanced cases, most of us are able to "pass" as able-bodied.

Before turning to the Gospel, a few remarks on the overall impact of the illness on my outlook are in order. Importantly, like Reynolds Price, I have been able to claim the insight that the damage is done and the illness is here to stay. Chronic pain, that "unending stream of neural alarm," is no longer endowed with the significance it once was; because its central function of drawing attention to the disorder has been fulfilled, notes Price, "the mind's outrage is simply misplaced." Indeed, after a while, the only sane thing to do is "to shut down the frantic circuits and look elsewhere for ease and continuance" (Price 1994: 159). Still unclaimed, however, is the decisive attitudinal shift toward capacious acceptance of one's altered physiology that so many disabled people are eventually able to adopt (Callahan 1989: 131). Unfortunately, I cannot affirm with Sharon Betcher that I am "the picture of health" (Betcher 2001: 347), nor can I effortlessly reframe this illness as mere somatic variation purged of negative valences, as Rosemarie Garland Thomson seemingly is able to do (Thomson 1997a: 131–34, 137). Rather, the disease has disclosed at best an indifferent cosmos, more often "a dark and malefic sacred" (Bataille 1992: 73), and uprooted trust in corporeality as such (Améry 1980: 40). Full acquiescence to losses sustained by AS has not been forthcoming, nor do I expect or even wish it to be. Yet, with Leonard Kriegel, I do admittedly savor a certain satisfaction in what I am able to achieve in spite of the body's insurrection (Kriegel 1991: 55–71). And, although it now may seem to me as if we have been hurled into an unforgiving "heartless immensity" (Melville 1999: 415) or laid bare before "the fire of God's wild breath" (Dillard 1992: 334), I, like Melville's Ahab, still feel that "the queenly personality lives in me, and feels her royal rights" (Melville 1999: 498). Prayer, then, should it ever arise, would not be characterized by reverent, humble obeisance but by unrepentant "defiance" (Melville 1999: 498).

METHODOLOGICAL ASSUMPTIONS

I assume a social or minority-group model of disability chastened by what Rosemarie Garland Thomson has called "strategic essentialism," which insists on real physical difference, on the singularity or particularity of the flesh (Thomson 1997a: 23–25). Put simply, the social model asserts that "all bodies are socially constructed—that social attitudes and institutions determine far greater than biological fact the representation of the body's reality" (Siebers 2006: 173). While the medical model situates disability in individual bodies and aspires to rehabilitate them in accordance with norms defined largely by statistical science (Davis 2006), biomedicine, and late capitalism's need for a productive and efficient workforce (Betcher 2007: 1–67; Bishop 2007: 217–20), the social model locates disability in oppressive institutional structures, policies, and attitudes, all of which are anthropogenic and therefore "might be otherwise." The medical model sees dysfunctional and undesirable bodies in need of repair or cure; the social model merely presumes human variation, which most Western societies subject to punitive binaries such as "normal/ abnormal," "healthy/unhealthy," "whole/broken," even "able-bodied/disabled." The problem, then, according to the social model, does not lie in individual broken or diseased bodies but in society—in a whole array of discursive practices and exclusionary social arrangements that disable differently abled persons.[3] What is required is accommodation rather than compensation, access and justice rather than cure or erasure (Thomson 1997a: 49–51).

FOUR HEALING STORIES: 8:5-13; 9:2-8; 12:9-14; 17:14-20

Most attractive in Jesus' encounters with characters subject to pain and/or loss of mobility is a sensitivity and responsiveness to aversive experience of chronic illness. The centurion's son, for instance, is said to be "paralyzed" (*paralytikos*) as well as "tormented terribly" (*deinōs basanizomenos*, 8:6);[4] the state of mind of the man with limited function in one hand is likened to that of a distressed animal trapped in a pit (12:11); and the boy with epilepsy (*selēniazetai*) who "falls into fire and oftentimes into water" is believed to be "suffering badly" (*kakōs paschei*, 17:15). It is true that in each case the disabled person's experience of chronic illness is focalized by another and therefore may not cohere with his own perception. Disabled readers understandably may be suspicious of able-bodied constructions of illness and even question these characters' motives for rendering disability as aversive experience. What is important for me, however, is that Jesus appears to believe that each of these individuals is suffering. While it would be desirable to hear directly from the disabled themselves, it is nevertheless safe to assume that Jesus' decision to heal is based on a conviction that the ill find aspects of their illness unpleasant and wish for reprieve or even comprehensive remediation. Admittedly, Jesus' assumption that limited functionality in one hand is comparable to the distress of a trapped sheep (12:9-14) may prove especially problematic, not only because mobility loss does not necessarily entail anguish but also because empathic identification with sheep sentience is not within our grasp.[5] Nonetheless, persons with AS whose primary symptoms are pain and loss of mobility *and* who experience these symptoms as disagreeable may find Jesus' responsiveness in these narratives attractive.

For many, however, Jesus' encounters with the disabled may prove overwhelmingly and irredeemably problematic. Most glaring is that all four narratives are really about something else other than disability or even healing. Each enlists the anonymous, voiceless disabled figure to set the stage for Jesus' authoritative pronouncements, and once these one-dimensional plot functionaries have served their purpose, they vanish without a trace (in two cases, they do not even appear). At no point is the experience of disability explored in its own right. In 8:5-13, for instance, the exemplary faith of the Roman centurion foreshadows for readers the inclusion of gentile Christians ("many from east and west") in God's kingdom (vv. 11-12); in 9:2-8, the verifiable healing of the paralytic merely makes plausible the unverifiable claim that Jesus has been awarded authority to forgive sin (v. 6); in 12:9-14, Jesus' rhetorical besting of the Pharisees is punctuated with a maxim for the Matthean community on Sabbath observance (v. 12); and in 17:14-20, the take-home lesson is that nothing is impossible for the one who has faith (v. 20). The disabled themselves are virtually invisible and irrelevant. Throughout, it is *Jesus* who remains center stage; each episode is structured to highlight the protagonist's unsurpassed ethos as well as his divinely inspired logion.[6]

Troubling too is a strong remediatory impulse rooted in Levitical purity codes, prophetic eschatology, and early Jewish apocalyptic that may be extended to the Gospel as a whole. In Matthew, Jesus' healings are outward demonstrations that God's reign is being realized, but this new order does not tolerate human difference well: "Hard-pressed to resolve corporeal crisis in any other way," write David Mitchell and Sharon Snyder, Jesus habitually revises disabled bodies "into less cumbersome experiences" (Mitchell and Snyder 2007: 178–79). In so doing, he reinscribes rather than contests Levitical purity regulations and prophetic utopian visions of a new order purged of somatic deviance. Disabled people are to be included in the kingdom, to be sure, but presumably only subsequent to remediation.[7] Indeed, as Sharon Betcher observes when commenting on Marcus Borg's and John Dominic Crossan's reconstructions of Jesus' healing ministry: "Inclusion does not undo the hegemony of normalcy, nor does it participate in transvaluation. Rather, such politics can preserve a normative, if nominally multicultural community as a dominant base within which the different are paternalistically accommodated" (Betcher 2007: 87). What is implied, of course, by Matthew's remediatory impulse is that impairment is not mere variation but a deficit that has no place in a divinely inaugurated utopia. Deviance elicits discipline rather than accommodation. This thoroughgoing "eschatological imaginary" (Betcher 2007: 53), present in all four Gospels, "cheapen[s] commitments to the value of bodily life in general" and tragically has been enlisted to underwrite eugenicist discourses aimed at expunging somatic aberrance from the gene pool (Mitchell and Snyder 2007: 180, 182).

Yet, even more troubling still, in order to obtain this requisite remediation, the disabled and their representatives must ingratiate themselves to Jesus or first prove that they believe in his supernatural curative abilities. Healing is rarely dispensed gratis. For instance, in 8:5-13, rehabilitation follows upon the centurion's public confession of unworthiness before so illustrious a personage as well as an acknowledgment of Jesus' power over illness and the malevolent spirits that are so often its cause (vv. 8-9). The cure, readers are reminded at the end of the episode, was ultimately contingent on the man's "faith" (v. 13). In 9:2-8 too, Jesus is responsive not to the paralytic's suffering or supplication for healing but to his representatives' "faith" (v. 2); it is their belief in the protagonist's curative powers that wins Jesus' favor. In 17:14-20, Jesus casts the demon out of the epileptic boy only after his father kneels before the itinerant healer (*gonypetōn*; v. 14) and addresses him with the honorific "Lord" (*kyrie*; vv. 14-15). Admittedly, in 12:9-14 neither ingratiation nor faith in the healer's abilities are evident, but Jesus restores the man's atrophied hand to wholeness (*hygiēs hōs hē allē*; v. 13) presumably not from an irrepressible urge to curb gratuitous suffering or even in response to a stated request but to defy Pharisaic hegemony and model the Matthean maxim, "It is appropriate to do good on the Sabbath" (v. 12). Indeed, as Daniel Harrington has observed, "The healing of the withered hand comes almost as an afterthought, since Matthew has placed the debate about Sabbath observances at the center of attention" (Harrington 1991a: 173).

In healing narratives other than those selected for this study, ingratiation and/or faith play a central role as well. For example, in 9:27-31 Jesus tests two blind men to see if they really are persuaded that he is capable of restoring sight (or, as the case may be, granting the ability to see for the first time). He asks, "Do you believe that I am able to do this?" (v. 28). At the men's affirmative response, Jesus heals them, adding that their newfound ocular abilities were contingent on their "faith" (v. 29). Perhaps the most disturbing case of sycophantism is found in 15:21-28, where a Canaanite woman must first assent to Jesus' analogy of Jews to (God's) children and non-Jews to "little dogs" (*kynariois*) in order to obtain an exorcism for her daughter (v. 26). In fact, she shrewdly alters his original analogy so that Jews are promoted from "children" to "masters," even further enhancing Jesus' honor. Jesus responds with enthusiasm: "Woman, great is your faith! Let it occur for you as you wish!" (v. 28).[8] More often than not, then, healing is viewed not as a right or as a free gift but as a commodity disbursed only upon satisfactory ingratiation and/or public confession of Jesus' extraordinary curative abilities. "You must first endear yourself to the cosmic Benefactor," the Gospel seems to suggest, "through flattery and obeisance, and only then will health care be disbursed—health care, mind you, that is required for full inclusion in God's coming kingdom."[9]

Finally, problematic are the Gospel's mystification of biologic illness as demonic possession, perpetuation of the causal link between sin and disability, and promotion of a fantasy of cure. In 8:5-13, both the centurion and Jesus appear to assume that malevolent spirits are behind the daughter's illness, and in 17:14-20 a demon is held responsible for the boy's seizures. One potential advantage of framing illness as a product of demonic malfeasance is to shift responsibility for it to forces outside one's immediate control. That is, for a community to suggest that a demon might be the cause of a particular illness is to acknowledge, "It's not her fault." On the other hand, demonic influence bears a negative stigma that very often serves to isolate "the possessed" from the social body (see, e.g., 8:28-34), and subscription to a worldview in which illness is attributed to demons ultimately impedes our attempt to determine its biologic or physiologic origin. Should an individual wish to find at least some relief from the symptoms of her illness, entreaties to a shaman or exorcist are apt to be far less effective than consulting a reputable physician—true, it appears, even in the first-century Mediterranean world. In 9:2-8, Jesus assumes the insidious causal relation between disability and sin, but perhaps even more troubling here is that he intended merely to forgive the paralyzed man's sins; healing is dispensed not primarily as a compassionate response to suffering but in response to a challenge to his authority as the "Son of Humanity." The Gospel's promotion of a fantasy of cure is evident not only in the four episodes examined here but in all of its healing stories. In each, it is suggested that healing is immediate, complete, and lasting. Historically, nothing could have been farther from the truth; the stories were written as they are to enhance Jesus' honor and to legitimize the claim that he hails from the heavenly realm. As a folk healer, Jesus may have cured conversion disorders (Capps 2008) or helped reintegrate the disabled into their communities and even find meaning in illness (Pilch 2000: 96, 113), but he would not have had any significant effect on underlying biologic causes, except perhaps to alter physical well being to such an extent as to stimulate the body's own innate healing powers.[10] Many who are ill and/or disabled today cannot expect an immediate, complete, and permanent cure, even should they desire one; it is unrealistic, and faith communities that perpetuate this fantasy are doing far more harm than good.

CONCLUDING REFLECTIONS

One would be hard-pressed to enlist Matthew's healing narratives to underwrite a strong disability rights agenda, which aims to expose institutional structures, policies, and attitudes that have contributed to disabled people's disenfranchisement, create positive disabled subjectivities that contest deprecating stereotypes, and increase access to the temporarily able-bodied world. These stories, in fact, seem to thwart such an agenda at nearly every turn. Perhaps most concerning are the potentially deleterious effects for disabled persons in faith communities that hold this text to be divinely inspired. For congregations committed to advancing the interests of the disabled, the Gospel's strong remediatory impulse, infantilization of the disabled, promotion of a fantasy of cure, reinscription of the causal relation between sin and disability, and conscription of the anonymous (and voiceless) disabled figure to enhance Jesus' honor must candidly be acknowledged and either denounced outright or reread resistively.

I do not, however, share the intensely negative reaction to the Gospel's curative impulse that many disabled scholars understandably have. In fact, I find attractive Jesus' responsiveness to illness *aversively experienced*. Unless inclined to masochism, persons with AS generally wish to be relieved of the disease because of the abiding presence of pain. Chronic pain is difficult to celebrate or reframe as mere somatic variation. Its sheer aversiveness, notes Elaine Scarry, divides the subject, who discovers an alien, inimical companion at war with one's "true self"—a "not me" that one earnestly wishes to subdue or expel; its fundamental unshareability isolates and, though "indisputably real to the sufferer," often appears unreal to others, only compounding one's suffering. Resistant to verbal expression, it becomes "the single broad and omnipresent fact of existence," obliterating "the contents of consciousness" and destroying the capacity for speech (Scarry 1985: 51–56). Scarry finds a fitting (and compelling) comparison in torture: "Perhaps only in the prolonged and searing pain caused by accident or by disease or by the breakdown of the pain pathway itself is there the same brutal senselessness as in torture" (Scarry 1985: 35). Indeed, it seems that illness and/or disability accompanied by chronic pain (pain of the sort described by Scarry) is not something to which we should acquiesce; it ought rather to be contested.

Although I find little that is laudable in Matthew's healing narratives other than Jesus' sensitivity to aversively experienced illness, one episode not treated in this study does hold promise for a liberative reading. In 20:29-34, two blind men sitting alongside the road outside Jericho call out to Jesus, presumably hopeful that he can grant (or restore) sight. The crowd has little tolerance for these unproductive social outcasts and tries to silence the men, but Jesus refuses to capitulate to the crowd's wishes and asks them what precisely they are seeking. "Let our eyes be opened," they reply (v. 33). "Moved with compassion" (*splanchnistheis*), Jesus fulfills their request, and the men follow him along the road to Jerusalem (v. 34).

Importantly, these two men are not represented by others but approach and address Jesus of their own volition, and when the able-bodied try to consign them to irrelevance, they shout out even more loudly (*meizon ekraxan*; v. 31). Also, Jesus *asks* them what they want, and when their desires are made known, the narrator informs us that Jesus is moved to heal by "compassion": there are no religious authorities nearby for whom a lesson is drawn, and he offers no morsel of divinely inspired wisdom afterward to his followers. These disabled men, in other words, are not *used* to achieve some other (often paraenetic) purpose. Finally, Jesus neither tests the men by asking if they really believe that he possesses curative powers nor informs them that their healing was contingent on their faith. Admittedly, the men do ingratiate themselves to Jesus by extending the honorific titles "Lord" and "Son of David," but it seems we are closer here to a helpful contemporary model, an episode with true liberatory potential.

Perspective of the Caregiver (Grimshaw)

The healing stories in Matthew include male caregivers bringing their sons or fellow community members to Jesus for healing. Today in the United States, caregiving provided by men is more and more common, and my role as a husband and father has included some additional care for my spouse, who has a disability, and for our children. Drawing from the study of masculinity in the ancient Mediterranean world and from disability studies, I see in the healing stories determined male caregivers and a hypermasculine Jesus who abruptly transforms disabled bodies into abled bodies as a way to maintain a patriarchal community.

Context

Women as caregivers is the norm in the United States. In the mid-nineteenth century, the cult of true womanhood set the pattern that a woman's natural sphere of work is in the home, where, unpaid, she raises the children, takes care of the home, and may care for elderly parents as well.[11] Women were thought to be naturally suited for this role because of their compassion and ability to develop and nurture close relationships. For men to take on caregiving work, according to this tradition, is considered valiant, heroic, and perhaps deviant (Thompson 2002: 25).

Yet today male caregivers in the United States are quite common. In 2009, according to the National Alliance for Caregiving, men spent 17.5 hours a week as caregivers (National Alliance for Caregiving 2009). This weekly average has gone up since 1997, when men spent 15.5 hours per week (Thompson 2002: 26). While women continue to spend more hours per week than men, this is a considerable amount of time spent by men in caring for the elderly, children with special needs, and young adults. Not only do men care for different types of people, but they also exhibit different masculinities and caring styles. Men might provide caregiving in a more traditional male role: They continue to keep their jobs but provide caregiving around their schedules; they keep a safe emotional distance from care recipients; and they resist asking for outside support. Men, however, also do caregiving in ways women typically provide it: They work part-time and are at home much of the day; they are emotionally invested; they provide hands-on personal care with bathing and feeding. And the same man might take on these different styles. As Thompson argues, "One man, the same man, in one day can easily participate in different masculinities when he dresses and feeds his infant daughter her breakfast, oversees an afternoon-long meeting, plays racquetball, and prepares and feeds his stroke-handicapped father his dinner" (Thompson 2002: 28).

I am also a male caregiver. I am married to a woman who has rheumatoid arthritis, and we are raising two children. On the one hand, her illness is a very small part of who she is as a human being. She works full time and is fully involved in caring for our children, cooking, cleaning, and other housework. On the other hand, the arthritis is always present through daily pain and limitations. She has challenges in some physical activities and has been through multiple surgeries and procedures in the last twenty-five years.

I am still sorting through my own experience as a caregiver. While my wife has managed the illness very well, I have seen her struggle with rheumatologists and their attempt to use strong, toxic, violent drugs that might wipe away the effects of the illness but damage other parts of the body. I have sat next to her as we listened to orthopedic surgeons—often trained to work with athletes and their sports injuries—strongly recommend full-court surgeries to quickly move in, clean out, and repair the damaged site like a surgical strike. I have watched her spend long hours dealing with insurance companies and fighting over benefits. I have witnessed her amazing ability to accommodate as she worked inside and outside the home and raised children, but also her limitations when it comes to daily activities such as opening jars, carrying heavy bags, or walking long distances.

And I have tried to compensate, to open jars and carry bags and grocery shop. As a man, I feel needed and useful and strong and mobile, all things I was taught were important for men to be. Not particularly interested in watching football with the other men in my extended family during Thanksgiving, not particularly drawn to going out with the guys on the weekend, doing manly things for my wife was one of the more masculine activities I could engage in. In some ways, my role as caregiver has been quite similar to traditional models of masculinity. I see my role in continuity with that of a male provider for the household, I do active things, I complete tasks, and I maintain my professional life (Thompson 2002: 33). But in other ways, I have participated in more traditional women's roles: shopping for groceries, participating in child care, cooking, cleaning, and laundry. In this way, I have expressed different masculinities through my daily work.

My experience as a husband and father and male caregiver influences my reading of Matthew's healing passages. I interpret as a man, socialized in a patriarchal society, but also in some ways resisting the model of the "ideal man" as defined by my own culture. I especially notice the roles of caregivers in the passages. They are men, resolute in their tasks, possibly exhibiting mixed masculinities. The way other men are portrayed also surprises me. I am struck by the hypermasculinity in the passages, the masculine characters who take the stage, the masculine positioning and sparring, the need to completely (surgically, violently) wipe away the disability, the overcompensation to fix the problem.

METHODOLOGICAL ASSUMPTIONS

I draw from masculinity studies in the ancient world and disability studies. The study of masculinity in the ancient Mediterranean world demonstrates that men and women were not two different kinds of humans with different anatomy but rather humans who were more or less developed on a vertical continuum. Men were higher up on the scale because they were more complete, perfect, and developed (Anderson and Moore 2003: 68–69; Conway 2003: 164–65). Women were lower on this gradient because something had gone wrong in their development in the womb and they came out unfinished.

Masculinity was not determined solely by biological development, however, but also by one's social place in society, which involved mastery over self and others. This mastery could be seen through one's intellect and virtues (Conway 2003: 166–68; Anderson and Moore 2003: 69).[12] Piety, too, was a measure of masculinity, as men were thought to be more divine than women. Both Aristotle and Philo discuss the male as more godlike or pious than the female (Conway 2003: 168). The *Gospel of Thomas* suggests this as well when Jesus says, "I myself will lead [Mary] in order to make her male, so that she too may become a living spirit resembling you males. For every woman who will make herself male will enter the kingdom of heaven (logion 114)" (Conway 2003: 168). These characteristics of intellect, virtues, and piety partly determined one's status in society and therefore one's position regarding masculinity. This position, again, was on a continuum in which there were different levels of masculinities. At the high end of the scale were "supreme exemplars of hegemonic masculinity" that would include adult males with high social standing (Anderson and Moore 2003: 68). At the other end were those who "might best be labeled *unmen*: females, boys, slaves (of either sex), sexually passive or 'effeminate' males, eunuchs, 'barbarians,' and so on" (Anderson and Moore 2003: 69). Those who did not have perfect adult male bodies and did not have power in society were unmen. The abled body, then, was an adult male body with high social standing.

If masculinity was determined by an abled body and high social standing, then femininity was linked to a disabled body and lower social standing. A disabled body, then, was a female body with less social standing. In the ancient world, a connection was made between the disabled and female bodies. The female body and the disabled male were both deviant forms. Aristotle, in his fourth book of *Generation of Animals*, describes the female as a deformed or mutilated male; the female body was less developed or imperfect and therefore deformed (Thomson 1997b: 279–80). Galen of Pergamum, a Greek physician in the second century CE had similar views in that the male body was the ideal human body in the natural order of the world and the female body was an unfinished, underdeveloped male body.

The status of one's masculinity or femininity, however, was not static, and one's position on this continuum of masculinities was not stable. As Conway explains it, "Stories of corporeal instability—female bodies sprouting penises or male bodies becoming effeminate—reveal a genuine trepidation about the possible slippage from one gender to another" (Conway 2003: 165; see also Laqueur 1990: 122–34). Pliny the Elder, a first-century-CE Roman author and philosopher, cites stories of females changing into males (Conway 2003: 165).

Because of this view of gender, the world of men in the first century was a public world, a world of competition where masculinity was "won and kept" and where honor was at stake in every interaction (Liew 2003: 96). Men moved far away from their mother and home and entered this public world of men. It was the world of war and athletic competition, two activities often associated with masculinity (Liew 2003: 97). In this world, men must achieve and maintain their status. In his discussion of masculinity in Gospel of Mark, Liew comments on Gilmore's view of masculinity as a social achievement: "A social achievement requires interaction with other people, whether in terms of contest (competing with others for masculinity), contrast (defining one's own masculinity in light of others' femininity), and/or consent (acknowledgement from others that one is indeed a 'real' man)" (Liew 2003: 112).

This was a world of embattlement among men but also one of bonding as men won over, yet also submitted to, other men, like that of the centurion in Matthew 8 (Liew 2003: 132). As a world of combat, masculinity was about control over self and control over others. Real men, then, were seen as strong, active, mobile, aggressive, and persistent; they generated heirs and had physically whole bodies. Women were viewed as weak, immobile, passive; they did not generate heirs, and had deformed bodies (Thomson 1997b: 279, 287; Anderson and Moore 2003: 69–75; Conway 2003: 166). Yet this contested interaction between men involved submission. Men submitted to other men and acknowledged the winner's masculinity. For masculinity and the patriarchal system to survive, men both claimed victory and acknowledged winners . . . until the next battle came (Liew 2003: 131).

In light of this public male sparring, what happens when a healing takes place? As Jesus encounters other men in the public arena and is requested to heal, the context is a world of honor, patriarchy, and masculinity. More is going on than simply healing a sick person. Competition and consent ensues with all those men who are present at the healing: caregivers who have brought the one who is ill, those with Jesus and those looking on who might be critical of Jesus, and even those men not present who might be alluded to. As for the one who needs healing, his masculine status is at stake. In order to maintain or improve his level of masculinity, the disabled body must be changed. As Malina and Rohrbaugh argue, illness (as with masculinity) is a social problem, not a biological or medical problem. Those who are ill are not in right relationship within the social network; they are deviants in the cultural system. To heal them is to restore them to their social places, to put them in right relationship with the overall belief system in that culture (Malina and Rohrbaugh 1993: 70–71).

Interpreting these healing passages in Matthew from the perspective of masculinity and disability studies, I see a real concern in the narrative to maintain a system of patriarchy when faced with a disabled boy or man.

Matthew is constructing a community where masculinity is primary, a masculinity that includes a striving toward piety, a kind of manly faith. The caregivers and those looking on are being sized up and evaluated. The disabled boys are deviant and do not fit the patriarchal system. They must be immediately restored/transformed into abled-bodied boys. Jesus is the ideal man, and healing is one of the most manly of tasks, the power over the human body (Liew 2003: 113–14).[13] Jesus approaches healing in a particularly striking way—using immediate and complete surgery to bring these disabled bodies back into the proper relationship with the patriarchal system. This dramatic healing brings to mind two references. Moore, in *God's Gym*, describes a hypermasculinity of the bodies of both God and Jesus in the biblical narrative as well as the violence that takes place against bodies (Moore 1996). This might be juxtaposed with the work of Mitchell and Snyder in disability studies when they acknowledge the many attempts to normalize, or eradicate, disabilities in history (that is, the eugenics period) with the use of social engineering programs (Mitchell and Snyder 2007: 173–74, 178–83). How might these healing passages be an example of this hypermasculinity and eradication?

With this context and these methodological thoughts, I now turn to the healing passages in Matthew.

THREE HEALING STORIES: 8:5-13, 9:2-8, 17:14-20

I focus on three of the passages that Metzger and I are interpreting together. In these three, I see a common pattern with three different kinds of "men" highlighted along the masculine continuum. The caregivers function as the ideal men who bond with Jesus and fit within Matthew's patriarchal system, a separate group of men (heirs of the kingdom, scribes, disciples) serve as failed men, poor examples, who are criticized for their lack of masculinity, and the third type are the disabled boys or men, classified as unmen, who must be immediately and totally transformed by Jesus from girls to men in order to be repositioned up the scale for a better masculinity.[14] The passages highlight the emphasis on masculinity, the concern for the levels of masculinity and the realities of slippage along the gradient, and the need to maintain a patriarchal system.

In Matt. 8:5-13, the centurion is the caregiver, providing for his paralyzed son at home, and he knows how to be a man in patriarchal system.[15] He is almost the perfect man, if there is one—he is in the familiar masculine realm of the military, has fathered a child, is active by moving toward Jesus and away from him, and shows his persistence with Jesus.[16] Just as important, he demonstrates both mastery yet compliance within the patriarchal system (Liew 2003: 131). He comes to Jesus and appeals to Jesus as "Lord," humbly, as one who is properly under authority (v. 5). In responding to the centurion, Jesus resists the centurion with a question: "Will I come and cure him?"[17] The public sparring has begun. The centurion responds according to proper patriarchal script, showing his submissive position ("Lord, I am not worthy to have you come under my roof"). He knows his proper place in the hierarchy—he is both a man under authority ("I also am a man under authority") and one who has authority over men ("with soldiers under me").

The back-and-forth battle is over and Jesus and the centurion bond. Men contest one another in the public realm but also acknowledge the other as manly when appropriate (Liew 2003: 132). Jesus wins, but recognizes the centurion for his faith and claims many other active, mobile men will come from east and west to eat with Abraham, Isaac, and Jacob.[18] Notice these patriarchal dinner partners are also men who have fathered children.

The ideal men, however, must be contrasted with failed manhood. Jesus refers to the heirs of the kingdom. They will be thrown into the outer darkness and will weep and gnash their teeth. As heirs, they have not fathered children. They are not active and mobile but passive and thrown about. They do not have mastery over themselves (weeping) or their anger (gnashing of teeth).[19]

Now Jesus is about to heal the son. The son is a paralytic, an unman. He is weak, passive, unable to move, the deformed male. He is "lying at home paralyzed, in terrible distress." He literally has no control over himself or others. He is a boy, which emphasizes his lower status on the masculine continuum. This state of being will not promote the patriarchal system. So Jesus tells the centurion, "Let it be done *for you* according to *your* faith," focusing on the centurion. Piety is a sign of masculinity. So, faith here might be equivalent to or understood as an integral part of masculinity. The verse might be read: "Let it be done for you, to maintain your and your son's masculine place in the patriarchal system, according to your masculinity."

The son is then healed "in that hour," or better translated "at that moment" or "immediately" (France 2007: 304). Healing is a manly task, overcoming the natural world, and Jesus does it here from a distance. This immediate and total transformation is violent. The unman is changed from female to male, from disabled to able-bodied. Jesus' hypermasculinity violently eradicates the lack of masculinity and transforms the boy's paralytic body to what now has the potential to grow into an able-bodied man.

The pattern continues in Matt. 9:2-8 as the caregivers with faith (the ideal men) carry a paralytic (the unman) who is violently transformed by Jesus. The scribes (failed men) are conquered.

The caregivers are the strong ones who carry the disabled (another paralytic) around on a bed, showing their athletic ability (the other traditional arena of masculinity besides the military). The verb is "were carrying" (*prosepheron*, v. 2), which is an imperfect that can be translated in many ways (Brooks and Winbery 1979: 91–93). One possible interpretation is as a protracted action; that is, they have been carrying him for a long time in order to get to Jesus. The imperfect might also be interpreted as a repetitive action: they repeatedly carried him. In this case, it may be a regular activity that they carry him on a daily basis. In this passage, they carry him to get to Jesus, but perhaps on other days they carried him for other reasons. In either reading, these caregivers are strong, active, persistent, and mobile.

There is no extended public sparring between the ideal men and Jesus as there is with the centurion. The men do bring him to Jesus, as the father will bring his son to Jesus in Matthew 17 (see also Matt. 4:24; 15:30). So there is an initial submission to Jesus. The caregivers, then, show mastery over themselves and others as they carry the disabled man and they also demonstrate proper submission to Jesus, demonstrating their fitness in the religious patriarchal system just as the centurion does. Bonding does follow, as Jesus acknowledges "their" faith, presumably speaking to those carrying the bed. Like the centurion's faith, the caregivers' faith might be seen as appropriate masculinity in Matthew's patriarchal system—that is, they are good religious men by exhibiting manly faith.

The caregivers are then contrasted with the failed religious men, the scribes. The religious leaders are not manly enough. They speak "to themselves" instead of engaging in proper, honorable public debate with Jesus (v. 3). Their minds are filled with evil things. Jesus must perceive their thoughts and initiate the battle with them. Like the heirs of the kingdom in 8:5-13, they are associated with evil and they do not respond. Nor do the scribes show any signs of mobility, action, or persistence, all characteristics of those who are higher up on the masculine scale.

As in 8:5-13, the paralytic is radically changed from unman to man. The paralytic is immobile and passive. The deformed boy (effectively a girl) is violently transformed into a strong, active, mobile man—he stands up, takes his own bed to carry (like the athletic men at the beginning of the passage), and goes to his home. The crowd's response may confirm this manly demonstration and violent transformation. The narrator states, "They were filled with fear [*ephobēthēsan*]," which could mean they were afraid or they had reverence or respect; in either case, it is probably more than simply amazement.[20] The crowds then glorify God. The word "authority," referring to Jesus' authority, is used twice as well, to reinforce Jesus' command of the situation. The whole scene suggests a shocking reception, as Jesus now wields this "superhuman" power to transform women into men, the disabled into the abled, a demonstration of violent hypermasculinity (France 2007: 348).

The third passage, Matt. 17:14-20, also follows this pattern: the father (ideal man) shows the proper patriarchal form; the disciples (failed men) are conquered by Jesus; and Jesus violently transforms the son (unman).

The father comes to Jesus (as the centurion comes to Jesus), kneels before him (with appropriate manly control, not being thrown about), and addresses Jesus as Lord, showing the proper patriarchal submission. Also like the centurion, the father has brought forth a son and is active and mobile. The father takes the son first to the disciples, perhaps following the proper pecking order. This shows his persistence, like the centurion and the athletic men who carry the bed. Stamina is a manly quality. In the parallel story in Mark 9:24, the father has a failure in faith; but here he is the ideal man.

There is no discernible bonding between Jesus and the father, as there was with the centurion and those who carry the bed. Perhaps because Jesus is so upset, he quickly turns to the disciples. As Jesus contested the heirs and then the scribes, now Jesus turns on the disciples. Their failure provokes Jesus' references to a faithless and perverse generation, which might refer to a younger generation who has not brought forth children.[21] Like the scribes, the disciples decline to spar with Jesus in public, but in private after the healing the disciples debrief with Jesus. They, too, had little faith, little masculinity. The disciples are failed men.

Jesus then turns to the disabled son, previously described as an epileptic who suffers terribly and often falls into the fire and into the water. The word "epileptic" comes from the Greek verb *seleniazomai*, which means one that is affected by the moon (that is, moonstruck; see also the KJV, "lunatick"). He is controlled by something else, the moon. Ancient Greek literature associated males with the sun, but females with the moon (Liew 2003: 99). This disabled boy is like a girl, who has no control over himself, as his history of falling into fire and water demonstrates. With hypermasculinity, Jesus again violently transforms the disabled boy into an able-bodied man. He is cured instantly (the same way the disabled are cured in 8:5-13 and 9:2-8).

RETURNING TO THE CONTEMPORARY CONTEXT

I find the hypermasculinity in these passages quite suffocating, but also familiar. It seems to predominate in the medical contexts my wife and I are familiar with. Potent drugs and mighty surgeons are available to wipe out disease. Combative insurance companies must be conquered (or bonded with) in order to financially survive. My wife cannot receive insurance for physical therapy to manage chronic pain, but only for harsh chemicals and invasive procedures to swiftly wipe away acute pain. Unmen abound and must be dramatically transformed into real men: effeminate men need to be converted, undocumented workers should go home, and men with thinning hair need a treatment. My wife was treated this way in the orthopedic surgeon's office as he tried to turn her shoulder into an athletic pitching arm.

I can appreciate, however, much about the caregivers in these passages. First, most of them seem to be male caregivers. Two are fathers advocating for their sons, and the other group, which may be men but also may be women, is carrying a paralytic. Second, they are persistent and intent on caring for their children or fellow community members in perhaps the only ways they know how. Third, while they may be ideal men in this first-century patriarchal system, they also seem to be exhibiting what caregivers today would call a matrix of masculinities—they express some traditional male traits by being active and mobile and public, but they are also submitting and requesting and perhaps doing hands-on caregiving with those they are providing for.[22] This all relates to my own experience with my wife and children. As a man, I am intent on providing care for them and often express different masculinities, or should I say simply different gender roles. But this does not always seem appreciated or acknowledged in U.S. mainstream culture, where male and female gender roles are still quite sharply distinguished in many ways. I do not always feel man enough when placing parsley in the grocery cart. I often feel a need to ratchet up my masculinity by working harder and carrying heavier loads.

I ran across an alternative reading of 9:2-8 that may be a mistranslation, but it points to an interpretation that makes more sense for my context and perhaps others who care for those with disabilities.[23] The NRSV translates Matt. 9:2, "And just then some people were carrying a paralyzed man lying on a bed." They leave out the phrase "bringing to him," so it is not clear that the people are carrying the man to Jesus, just that they are carrying the man. When I first read the NRSV, and before I checked the Greek and other English translations, my mind began to wander. Perhaps they were not carrying the man to Jesus to be violently transformed from disabled to abled. Perhaps they were simply carrying him, like they did every day, to the neighbor's house for a visit or to the market to pick out food or to any of a number of places he might have gone in the village. Perhaps it just wasn't a spouse or one family member who was doing all the carrying every day. Perhaps many others helped out. Perhaps the paralyzed man is not the utterly helpless man the Jesus films make him out to be—absolutely immobile, unable to function in any way, bereft of agency. Perhaps the paralyzed man managed a fairly "normal" life, told stories to children, shared wisdom with other adults, and relied on family and community for help. Perhaps his disability did not need to be eradicated and did not prevent him from functioning as a valued community member. Perhaps he was willingly accommodated by the larger community, without the need for public sparring or concern for a high ranking on the masculinity scale. For me, this scenario would make more sense today.

RESPONSES FROM THE TWO PERSPECTIVES

Both coauthors wrote the contextual interpretations above without consulting one another. After reading each other's interpretations, we now respond briefly to each other's readings. Jim Metzger begins with his response.

METZGER'S RESPONSE

Jim's analysis of hypermasculinity and the feminization of the disabled male body in the first-century Circum-Mediterranean world is certainly resonant today. Western medicine is still suffused by a hypermasculine ethos that generally aims to "fix" or to eradicate difference rather than to accommodate or to celebrate it. And the disabled male is still so often seen as "less than" he ought to be—as deficient, incomplete, enervated.

On the one hand, Jim aligns Jesus and Matthew's disabled caregivers with the hypermasculine character of modern medicine. For those who happen to read the stories in this way, it would seem that they can neither be enlisted to underwrite a disability rights agenda nor be used to model a Christian ethic of compassion. In fact, the whole tenor of this reading goes against what disability rights advocates are trying to achieve. The most these episodes can do for Christian communities today is to serve as a kind of "antimodel"—offer a vivid reminder of what not to do, how not to proceed. On the other hand, Jim also sees in them the "persistence" of family members and friends who truly care. For Christians who choose to move in this direction, these stories at least may be rendered "safe" for disabled people and even offer inspiration or moral guidance to caregivers.

On the other hand, I find the second option to be a tough sell, and I sense that Jim might as well. Hypermasculinity and intolerance of somatic variation so saturate these stories as almost to preclude more agreeable hermeneutical possibilities: they just seem to model values too far afield from the core values of the disability rights movement. Although I would like to see ecclesial communities acknowledge this incongruity and even to go so far as to declare these stories "unsafe," the Gospels' healing narratives still command wide appeal and understandably remain important for those who wish to claim Jesus as a *moral exemplar.* Indeed, there are more pressing candidates for desacralization, such as the exodus and conquest narratives or the household codes. Eventually, though, I suspect that ecclesial communities are going to have to concede the incongruity if they are to make disabled persons feel truly welcome.

GRIMSHAW'S RESPONSE

My response will focus mostly on how we approached the passages differently, which is what I found most intriguing after reading our different interpretations. Our contexts are clearly different. Jim spent more time describing his illness and his own experience of chronic pain. I spent very little time describing my wife's illness or her experience but focused on male caregiving today and my own experience of caregiving as a man. I'm curious what Jim would say about the experience of his illness as a man.

Regarding Matthew's Jesus, Jim appreciated Jesus's sensitivity and responsiveness to those with chronic pain, but he also found problematic the disabled's need to ingratiate themselves to Jesus. I did not notice either of these. Both of these make sense from the perspective of one who is ill and seeking healing. I did not focus on an affirming quality of Jesus as healer; instead, I resonated more with the caregivers and their tenacity. Regarding the disabled characters, Jim saw them as invisible and irrelevant, while I saw them as unmen awaiting to be made men. We both concluded that the healing passages were primarily about something other than healing. For Jim it was about various authoritative pronouncements, and for me healing was about promoting a patriarchal community.

Perhaps due to our similar type of graduate education, and also life experience with disabilities, we were both resisting readers for most of our interpretations. But we also tried to find a constructive message from the interpretation, quite possibly because we both grew up in the church and have an investment in how the Bible is used in the local congregation. In addition to his view of Jesus' responsiveness, Jim found the story of the two blind men in 20:29-34 to be promising for a liberative reading. Beyond my view of the caregivers, I discovered a (mis)translation in 9:2 that provided a possible vision for readers today.

The reality of biblical interpretation is that you focus on some textual features but overlook others. One of the benefits from interpreting contextually and collaborating with another reader is that you can see the richness and depth in the text and interpretive process because of the different cultural experiences and choices that shaped the interpretations (Patte 2004: xxi–xxxii). I consider this process a healing experience compared to the fractured ways in which many communities read the Bible in their isolated silos today.

Notes

1. A brief word about our approach to this project as coauthors. Both of us briefly discussed the project initially only to decide that these would be contextual readings and to identify which passages to interpret. We then wrote our interpretations separately without consulting one another to preserve as much as possible our own contextual approaches. After completing the interpretations, we read each other's work and then wrote our brief responses.

2. Spondylitis Association of America, http://www.spondylitis.org/saa_update.aspx (accessed June 13, 2012).

3. The model has traditionally been predicated on a distinction between impairment, a bodily defect or deficit, and disability, the disadvantage imposed on top of impairment by exclusionary, oppressive social arrangements (Shakespeare 2006: 198–99). Recent theorists, however, who hold that no materiality exists independently of our language games, have begun to challenge this distinction. Impairment, it is argued, is not an essential biological characteristic, a "value-neutral" or "merely descriptive" term, but a historically contingent effect of modern biopower (Tremain 2002: 32–34, 42). Impairment, like disability, does not precede discourse but is its effect.

4. Although *pais* may be translated as "servant," *huios* and *pais* are interchangeable later on in 17:14-20 as well as in the Johannine parallel (4:46-54). Perhaps translators who render *pais* here as "servant" are following the Lukan version of the story (7:1-10), where it is explicitly stated that a "slave [*doulos*] was very sick and about to die" (v. 2).

5. In Luke, Jesus' comparing an experience of disability to the distress of a thirsty animal (13:15) or to a child/animal trapped at the bottom of a well (14:5) is more compelling because in each case chronic pain is assumed. The woman unable to straighten her back likely suffers from a form of spondylitis or advanced osteoarthritis, both of which are painful disorders, especially in the absence of modern pharmaceuticals (13:10-17). In 14:1-6, the excessive accumulation of serous fluid in connective tissues or serous cavities associated with "dropsy" (i.e., edema) might today suggest kidney disease, congestive heart failure, or cirrhosis of the liver (see also Fitzmyer 1985: 1041; Green 1997: 546). The sometimes severe swelling of edema would cause pain and stiffness and put one at increased risk for ulceration and infection. Moreover, during the first century, "dropsy" was associated in the popular mind with an unquenchable thirst: the more one drinks, the thirstier one grows (Malina and Rohrbaugh 1993: 284–85). Again, chronic pain (or chronic discomfort at a minimum) is assumed. Because of the added element of pain, it is difficult to imagine either figure celebrating their extraordinary bodies; more likely, their bodies were experienced as foe rather than friend, an additional source of anguish on top of the stigmatization to which they would have been subjected in a culture that so highly prized the unblemished body.

6. Compare Jack Dean Kingsbury's argument that Matthew's "miracle stories" function "paraenetically" to present Jesus as the exalted and authoritative Son of God as well as to encourage Christians "to offer to him their petitions for help in the sure knowledge that he desires to hear them and will employ his divine power to aid them in time of trial and need" (1978: 572–73). The corpus, for him, serves primarily christological and pastoral ends; disability and healing as subjects in their own right are not a Matthean focus.

7. Particularly striking is the imperialistic feel to the narrator's claim that "Jesus went around *all* the cities and villages, teaching in their synagogues and proclaiming the good news of the kingdom and healing *every* disease and *every* illness" (9:35). Moments later, Jesus commissions his disciples to go out and do likewise, "to heal *every* disease and *every* illness" (10:1).

8. There is no reason why readers should feel compelled to interpret her response as a reflection of her core beliefs; she may capitulate to Jesus' ethnocentrism in word only, as a clever way to obtain what she wants.

9. I find myself unable to resist a parallel to the GOP's recent health care proposals, which are structured to allocate the best care only to the "worthy" (those who are employed full-time, without "preexisting conditions," and so on), and I fear that this Matthean emphasis might too easily be conscripted to underwrite such invidious proposals.

10. Otherwise known as the placebo effect. See, e.g., Gaztambide 2008: 94–113.

11. On the cult of true womanhood, see Welter 1966; Roberts 2002.

12. One example of mastery of one's self would be the ability to control one's anger.

13. Liew argues that Jesus dominates the Romans, part of his mastery over foreigners, through his healing of the Gerasene demoniac. Healing can be about domination and control.

14. I want to thank Cheryl Strimple (colleague and Ph.D. candidate at Southern Methodist University who has worked a great deal in disability studies and the Hebrew Bible) for reading a draft of my paper and offering many helpful suggestions about methodology and interpretation, including the use of "unmen" and "girls."

15. Many scholars debate whether this is his servant or son. I follow my coauthor's argument and conclusion and use "son." See footnote 4.

16. For masculinity as linked to the military, see Liew 2003: 96. For the importance of procreation for masculinity, see Anderson and Moore 2003: 72.

17. I am arguing that this is a question ("will I come and cure him?"), not a statement ("I will come and cure him"). See Levine 1988: 111–13.

18. See especially Levine 1988: 7–8 for a discussion of the faithful in Matthew as those who are, among other characteristics, active and mobile.

19. The phrase "gnashing of teeth" can refer to anger. See Davies and Allison 1991: 31; Carter 2000: 204; Ps. 112:10. One of the signs of masculinity is the control of passions, including anger. See Conway 2003: 166.

20. The Greek word for fear, *ephobēthēsan*, is used here, not the word for amazement. See France 2007: 333, 348; BDAG 862–63.

21. See Deut. 32:5, 20, where Moses refers to the Israelites as degenerate children; France 2007: 661.

22. The phrase "matrix of masculinities" comes from Thompson 2002: 28.

23. Kathleen O'Connor might call this a retelling or reinterpretation of the story for a particular community today. See O'Connor 1998: 330–31, 333–34.

9

Reading Matthew's Gospel with Deaf Culture

L. J. Lawrence

*"It is a non-deaf world which has created
deafness as a subject of discourse."*
——Gregory and Hartley 1991: 5

Contextual biblical interpretation seeks to redress the marginalization sustained by dominant readings by voicing alternative views.[1] Here interaction will be initiated with a long-overlooked marginal perspective, Deaf culture.[2] Sally Sainsbury maintains that "the historical neglect of deaf people is as disgraceful as it is perplexing" (Sainsbury 1986: vii) and demands urgent remedy. This paper constitutes one small response to her challenge. It is worth stating at the outset that I am a hearing academic, who is a foreigner in Deaf-World. I have previously worked among Deaf groups and charted their responses to biblical stories (Lawrence 2009: 91–104); however, here I am engaged in a different sort of exercise, namely, utilizing insights from Deaf culture and creatively bringing them to bear on aspects of Matthew's Gospel and interpretation. First, labels of ability and disability with regard to the Deaf will be exposed as social constructions promoted by the (dominant) hearing world. As a result, the Deaf will be defined not through their sensory impairment but rather as a (sign) language minority culture. In light of these insights, and utilizing perspectives from postcolonial theory, I will then approach Matthew's Gospel to see whether it is a hearing-dominated text that associates sense-impairment with stigma. Following this largely resistant reading, I will move on to the more positive task of exploring aspects of Deaf culture, including emphasis on the significance of vision, sight and light, use of sign language and minority cultural status, collective ethos of communities, and use of storytelling to consider how, if at all, these Deaf cultural aspects could in fact be recovered in readings of the Gospel of Matthew.

Defining Deaf: "(Sense-)Ability" Not "Disability"

Imagine the experience of a hearing man who accidentally falls into a valley populated by the congenitally deaf. He falsely believes that in a nonhearing world, the hearing man is king; however, he soon finds out that if a culture is specifically designed around deafness, then the hearing person is in effect disabled from social interaction within it. Since he is inept and incompetent within his new context, the deaf valley-dwellers decide the only solution is to gouge out the hearing man's dis-eased ear canal so he can fully participate within their society.[3]

Cultures that challenge dominant ideas of the abled and disabled make us aware of the social construction of our categories. Martha's Vineyard, an island situated off the coast of Cape Cod, Massachusetts, is frequently mentioned in discussion of deafness, given that there is an inordinately high instance of genetically inherited deafness within the community (McDermott and Varenne 1995). Hearing and nonhearing alike were socialized into a world where sign language was the norm for communication. As a result, the deaf were not excluded or underprivileged in that context at all. Indeed, often when anthropologists asked hearing members of the community to identify d/Deaf members, they could only name a couple, despite knowing many more. This illustrates that, for this community, deafness was "so integral a part of life on the Vineyard that it attract[ed] neither attention nor moral evaluation" (Gregory and Hartley 1991: 5). Robert Johnson similarly describes the universal use of sign language (for hearing and deaf) in a Yucatec-Mayan village and reveals how the d/Deaf had full access to both the social and political life of the community in that context (Johnson 1991).

What all these examples show us is that "being able or unable to hear does not emerge as significant in itself; instead it takes on significance in the context of other sets of meaning to which . . . [one is] exposed" (Padden and Humphries 1988: 22). In short, while in both Martha's Vineyard and the Yucatec-Mayan village it was normal to be deaf, these sorts of environments are very rare exceptions. For the most part, dominant hearing discourses constitute what is normal and deafness constitutes a deviation from that norm, a dis-ability. Lennard Davis goes further in underlining the binary nature of the labels of normalcy and disability when he states:

Disability is not an object—a woman with a cane—but a social process that intimately involves everyone who has a body and lives in the world of the senses. Just as the conceptualisation of race, class, and gender shapes the lives of those who are not black, poor, or female, so the conception of disability regulates the bodies of those who are "normal." In fact, the very concept of normalcy by which most people (by definition) shape their existence is in fact tied inexorably to the concept of disability, or rather the concept of disability is a function of a concept of normalcy. Normalcy and disability are part of the same system. (Davis 1995: 2)

Often the hearing world seeks to normalize the deaf within a hearing framework through oralism (oral methods of education in which lip-reading is central, though this has been identified as a contributory factor in poor language acquisition among deaf children) or the insertion of cochlear implants. In Tony Booth's terms, "The purpose of normalization is seen not only as giving deaf and partially deaf young people access to the hearing world but also as *making them more acceptable to it*" (Booth 1991: 157, italics mine).

In contrast to the medical model of disability, which defines deafness as a biological hearing impairment, or the social-situation model, which sees disability less as an essential categorization than as a product of different environments that are abling or dis-abling for individuals, the cultural model of Deafness (with a capital *D*) sees the Deaf community as an ethnic group, with their own cultural mores and language. J. G. Kyle and B. Woll's definition of the Deaf community in their study of *Sign Language* illustrates these traits: "It involves a shared language . . . it involves social interaction and politics . . . but all of these interrelate and interact with attitudes towards other Deaf people. The choice to communicate and share information with other people must be seen as a primary feature, and because of the language used by members of the community this communication will generally be restricted to other Deaf people" (Kyle and Woll 1988: 5). Coming from a Deaf-advocacy perspective, Harlan Lane believes that the Deaf community should be understood as an ethnic group, for then "they would have the protections offered to such groups," including the fostering of linguistic minorities and ensuring "that children and adults have adequate opportunities to learn the minority language." For, in Lane's opinion, "Like all members of other ethnic minorities, Deaf people are generally not disturbed by their identity, despite the need to struggle for their rights. Culturally Deaf people have always thought and think today that being Deaf is a perfectly good way to be, as good as hearing, perhaps better" (Lane 2005: 302). Conceiving of the Deaf as a cultural minority, akin to an ethnic group, has also allowed interpreters to utilize insights from postcolonial theory to reflect on oppression suffered under the imperialistic hearing world. Hannah Lewis reveals that historical instances of the disempowerment of the Deaf (particularly in reference to their own language) are analogous to political colonization defined as "a process of physical subjugation, imprisonment of an alien language . . . and the regulation of education on behalf of colonial goals" (Lewis 2007: 32). The "colonization" of the Deaf community by the hearing in educational, religious, and academic contexts in many ways parallels ethnic colonization, for "if an *ethnos* is defined as a culturally similar group sharing a common language, then the Deaf conceivably fit that category" (Davis 1995: 77). Davis has likewise drawn comparisons between racial stigmatization and Deaf stigmatization as outsiders (Davis 1995: 78). The accessibility (or rather, inaccessibility) of texts in sign language has undoubtedly perpetuated this outsider status. With these thoughts in mind, we approach Matthew to see what definition of "normal" is operative within the Gospel and whether the Deaf are stigmatized as a result.

Sense and Stigma: Matthew as a Hearing-Dominated Text

For Erving Goffman, stigma is emblematic of how certain individuals are discredited and dis-identified from dominant maps of the normal held within societies. As such, stigma involves "perception of a negative attribute" and "devaluation of a person with such an attribute" (Yong 2007: 84). It is a concept manifested in social exchanges, rather than a static condition dependent on biomedical factors. As Thomas Reynolds explains, "Stigma is not the property of an individual body but rather the result of complex social projections that represent bodies, lumping them into general stereotypes insofar as they display undesired qualities" (Reynolds 2008: 63).

Reading strategies of resistance are suspicious of the oppressive power structures sustained by particular authors. The central concern here is to gauge whether Matthew's conception of the normal is audiocentric and as a result whether d/Deaf experience is stigmatized. At the outset, it is important to note that the faculty of hearing is of course fundamental in oral cultures, and Matthew reflects this assumption. Moreover, he has produced a written text, a medium that belies a certain word-centricity. Wayne Morris has recently challenged the utility of texts such as the Gospel of Matthew from a Deaf perspective, given that "for Deaf people, words—spoken or written—are thought to be a peculiarly hearing phenomenon" (Morris 2008: xiii). Because sign languages' primary mediums are visual and spatial, sounds and texts are not part of their communicative repertoire. Morris also notes that metaphors, as understood by hearing cultures, literally "fall on d/Deaf ears" within the Deaf community. In Morris's words, they are "linguistic characteristics . . . peculiar to hearing people" (Morris 2008: 98). In this respect, many of Jesus' parables within Matthew's gospel, which convey two levels of meaning, would be hard for Deaf communities to comprehend. Morris reveals in his study that the parable of the sower, for example, is viewed in Deaf reception to have "more to do with farming techniques than the eschatological significance which Jesus attaches to it" (Morris 2008: 92).

If the form of the Gospel itself seems to marginalize Deaf encounters with it, what of its actual substance? Even a cursory look at the Gospel in reference to sonic themes reveals a cacophony of aural imagery and thus a suspicion that the text disables the full participation of the Deaf community within its discourses. The term *akouō* features nineteen times within the Gospel. God's revelations are heard, as at the baptism (3:17) and transfiguration (17:5). Moreover, testimonies regarding Jesus' activities are heard (11:4), and Jesus' primary mode of communication is speaking to others in parables and extended discourses (e.g., 15:10; 21:33). The faculty of hearing and the organ of the ear also becomes a synecdoche for cognition and discernment: "He who has ears to hear let him hear" (11:15; see also 13:9). For Matthew, "True hearing involves listening and understanding"; thus "to have deaf, heavy, or uncircumcised ears is to reject what is heard" (Ryken et al. 1998: 223). As Matthew's Jesus declares, "This is why I speak to them in parables, because . . . hearing they do not hear, nor do they understand" (13:13).

When encountering Matthew from a Deaf perspective, one is immediately struck by the general disinterest in the agency of deaf characters. (They are portrayed as passive sites of divine healing.) Often Matthew lists the deaf and mute among other defective individuals, including lepers, the blind, the lame, and the maimed (11:5; 15:30-31), indicating a specific conception of deficiencies that will be rectified in the kingdom. Worse still, however, deaf characters are themselves made largely invisible within Matthew's Gospel, its translations, and its receptions. We encounter *kophos*, a term that can encompass muteness or deafness, only twice within Matthew's account, in 9:32-34 and 12:22. In redacting Mark, Matthew has deliberately downplayed deaf references: in a parallel account in Mark 7:32-37, the mute is defined as deaf, and Jesus inserts his fingers into the man's ears to graphically illustrate this. However, modern translations and commentators of Matthew's account (9:32–34) view the characters as mute rather than deaf (e.g., NRSV, NIV).

Daniel Harrington, for example, notes in reference to 9:32 that "*kophos* can have several meanings: unable to speak, unable to hear or both. Since the sign of the healing is the fact that the man could speak the translation 'mute' seems most appropriate" (Harrington 1991a: 132). Similarly, in reference to the 12:22 account, Harrington submits that the supplicant was "blind and mute" (not deaf): "The result of Jesus' healing him is that he both speaks and sees, that is, both conditions are healed" (Harrington 1991a: 182).

Even those exceptions among commentators who offer the possibility of these respective characters being deaf still understand them as functioning within the plot to illustrate Matthew's more central interests in prophetic fulfillment and the kingdom of God, rather than the social agency of the deaf character. Warren Carter, for example, notes in reference to 9:32-34 that "deaf mutes are promised to hear and speak (Isa. 29:18-20)" in messianic hopes (Carter 2000: 229). Similarly, Donald Hagner confirms that "the direct, unmediated healing of the man's inability to speak symbolizes the fulfillment and joy of the kingdom announced by Jesus" (Hagner 1995a: 258).

The bit parts of the sensory-impaired characters within these two stories are illustrated further by the way in which the narrative stereotypes their respective identities (the demon possession featured in the 9:32-34 account is a typical deviance label and stigmatizing strategy) and accordingly swiftly narrates their healings. Harrington notes in reference to 9:32-34 that "the healing of the mute demoniac is told so quickly that one gets the impression that Matthew's real interest lay in contrasting the reactions of the crowd and the Pharisees" (Harrington 1991a: 133). Likewise, given the startling brevity of the 12:22 account, in which the complaint and healing are accomplished in just one verse, one is forced to admit that the account serves to highlight the "focus on the accusation of the Pharisees and Jesus' response" rather than any sustained reflection on the transformed position of the healed individual (Harrington 1991a: 341). Matthew seems to assume the social marginality of the characters within these stories. They are silent, and they exhibit no social agency within the narrative whatsoever. In common with many caricatures of disability within literature, here these individuals are "not real people who happen to be deaf, but deaf characters that on the whole appear not to be real people" (Gregory 1991: 294). Rather, they stand as static props in the plot to exhibit the restoration of wholeness and illustrations of the nature of the kingdom of God.

One aspect of Matthew's account, however, that could possibly be used to disrupt the hegemony of hearing is silence. Jesus, for example, exhibits silence in the trial narrative, in his resistant response to the questioning of the high priest (26:63). The narrator also quotes Isaiah to the effect that "he will not wrangle or cry aloud, nor will any one hear his voice in the streets" (12:19; Isa. 42:2), linking silence to Jesus' servanthood role, which flies in the face of a culture that values prestige and honor-precedence. Developing this trajectory, one could also consider how silent characters within the Gospel could in effect be conceived as resistant characters that challenge what Stanley Hauerwas has termed the "tyranny of normality" (Hauerwas 2004a: 37).

To take just one example, the Canaanite woman in chapter 15 pleads on behalf of her daughter, who Matthew tells us is "tormented by a demon" (15:22). The daughter is offstage, inactive and silent throughout the whole account. Donald Senior has recognized exorcisms as specific instances where the clash between the "cult of normality" and deviations from this are most explicit (Senior 1995: 12–13). Deaf resistant readers could protest that the woman and her daughter are normalized within the exchange—the daughter is cured of her possession; the mother starts to speak like a (proselyte?) Jew: "Have mercy on me, Lord, Son of David" (15:23). Developing such resistant lines, Laura Donaldson names the daughter as a silent figure who is characterized as overcome by the demonic possession that has seized her. Donaldson, however, deconstructs this reading and pictures the daughter's plight quite differently from transgression of cultural rules about what bodies should be like. She warns that the passivity of the daughter's silent witness "insistently calls the able to investigate rigorously their own complicity in oppressively naturalized ideologies of health" (Donaldson 2005: 101). Donaldson chastises the history of interpretation for robbing this daughter of her indigenous power. Rather creatively, she probes the idea that "rather than evoking the illness pejoratively identified in the Christian text as demon possession, the daughter might instead signify a trace of the indigenous [spirituality] . . . and rather than manifesting a deviance subject to the regimes of coercive (Christian) curing, she might be experiencing the initial stages of a vocation known to indigenous people for millennia as shamanism" (Donaldson 2005: 105).

One could also creatively probe the daughter's status from a Deaf perspective; she is silent and absent from public communication, but that which is labeled as demonic by the power structures operative in the text could instead be her use of sign language as a major channel of communication. Such musings produce counter-memories, or hidden transcripts and "interrupt the hegemonic through hallucinatory confrontations with other histories" (Donaldson 2005: 98). Davis likewise, from a Deaf perspective, has noted the violations through silence that can be effected within narratives. In his words, "Deafness in effect is a reminder of the 'hearingness' of narrative. It is the aporetic black hole that leads to a new kind of deconstruction of narrativity" (Davis 1995: 115).

If multiple features of Matthew's Gospel do sustain the stigmatization of d/Deaf perspectives and promote the cult of the hearing as normal, then any method of recovery will need to access "the social-symbolic world of persons with disabilities, such that the disabling framework of the normal becomes questionable" (Reynolds 2008: 15). My next task, therefore, is to sketch some general features of Deaf culture and then see if the Gospel text itself can be sensitized along those lines.

DEAF CULTURE AND MATTHEW'S GOSPEL

If the Deaf are not to be understood primarily through their hearing impairment, but rather, as suggested previously, as a specific cultural group akin to an ethnic minority with its own language and values, then attention in recovery readings must also move beyond a sole focus on physical deafness to what Carol Padden and Tom Humphries have termed the "far more interesting facets of Deaf people's lives" (Padden and Humphries 1988: 1). Within studies and ethnographies of Deaf culture, particular characteristics and models are repeatedly identified. This is not to essentialize Deaf culture as static or monolithic. There are of course different national Deaf cultures and also variations within cultures according to differentials of race, gender, age, and geography, among other factors. The purpose, rather, is only to define general contours that unite Deaf experience and are frequently represented within the literature. Paddy Ladd has identified the "culture concept" as central in movements of resistance and change. In his opinion, "Culture is the key held in common with other colonized peoples and linguistic minorities. Political and economic power may or may not be the driving forces behind language oppression. But both the key and the lock in which it turns is culture" (Ladd 2003: 8).

Deaf cultural traits and values that will be explored here are as follows: (1) significance of vision, sight, and light; (2) use of sign language and minority cultural status; (3) the collective ethos of communities; and (4) use of storytelling. Each one of these Deaf cultural features will be read alongside selected features of the Gospel of Matthew. Hannah Lewis in her construction of Deaf liberation theology recognizes that for the Bible to have relevance to the Deaf community it must be "read in a way that affirms the distinctive language and culture of Deaf people" (Lewis 2007: 112). The imaginative and creative touchpoints offered here between Matthew's text and Deaf culture will, I hope, be a step in the right direction to producing the sorts of interpretations Lewis campaigns for.

SIGNIFICANCE OF VISION, SIGHT AND LIGHT

Those cultures that communicate without sound often put far greater emphasis on visual perception. Illustrating this, George Veditz speaks of the Deaf as "first, last and for all time a people of the eye" (cited in Padden and Humphries 1988: 2). Knowing the world through sight and communicating through visual performances also demands appropriate use of light. My previous work with Deaf communities taught me that a room needs to be brightly lit, without shadows, in order for sign communication to ensue (Lawrence 2009: 91–104). Others speak of the special resonance that images of light and darkness have within visual cultures. Many witness that the image of darkness to light is frequently used to denote "lostness in the [dark] world" and subsequent enlightenment in "finding one's people and one's home in the Deaf community." Deaf cultural stories likewise often include references to a so-called lamppost trope, where stories involving the imagery of a light, under which people are able to communicate in sign, are told (Ladd 2003: 257).

Reading Matthew with sensitivities attuned to sight and vision, one encounters a text in which forms of *oraō* occur over forty times. Statistically, therefore, it would seem Matthew is a visiocentric text and thus, at least in part, open to Deaf perception. Moreover, if d/Deaf experience is largely filtered out by Matthew, stories of the healing of the blind occur quite frequently and are even exaggerated by redacting Mark's account so that two blind characters as opposed to one feature in Matthew's narrative (9:27; 20:30). Blindness is reserved as a synecdoche for the hypocrisy and misconceptions of Jesus' bitterest enemies, the scribes and Pharisees. In chapter 23, Matthew's great diatribe against the religious establishment, Jesus' opponents are over and again characterized as blind guides (23:16-17, 19, 24, 26) despite their supposed professional command of the written Scriptures. These features would seem to indicate that blindness is conceived both physically and spiritually as a far graver sense-impairment than deafness within Matthew's world.

Continuing to trace ocular themes, and in line with Roger Hitching's estimation of Deaf theology, Matthew seems to "move away from a purely wordy God to one [conceived] in terms of vision and touch" (Hitching 2003: 21). The wise men from the East are led by heavenly portents (2:10) and warned in a dream to not go back via Herod's palace (2:12); Joseph in visionary dreams is given reassurance about the source of Mary's pregnancy (1:20) and about the family's flight to Egypt (2:19-20). Pilate's wife is the only voice of truth in the passion narrative, when she narrates her troubling dream and urges her husband to "have nothing to do with that innocent man" (27:19). God, for Matthew it seems, communicates through visions and, as a result, often usurps those whose authority is based on hearing or written words alone. It is no accident that Herod, while quizzing scribal authorities about written prophecy (2:3-5), still remains, unlike the magi, unenlightened regarding Jesus' true identity and role. Visions also play a central role in Jesus' career: A public vision of "the Spirit of God descending like a dove" (3:16) accompanies the baptism; the transfiguration likewise features Jesus' face "shining like the sun" (17:2); extraordinary cosmic signs accompany Jesus' death (27:51–53); and the close of the Gospel features the disciples witnessing a vision of the resurrected Christ on a mountain (28:17).

The imagery of darkness and light, featured within studies of Deaf culture, likewise are attested in Matthew's Gospel. Darkness is used to symbolize religious, social, and political realities, and Jesus' coming is pictured as part of God's prophetic enlightenment project: "The people who sat in darkness have seen a great light, and for those who sat in the region and shadow of death light has dawned" (4:16; Isa. 9:2). Akin to the lamppost trope so prevalent in Deaf culture, Jesus and the community he founds are likewise shown to be a "light of the world" (5:14), a lamp giving light to the whole house (5:15), and a moral example to be shone before others so that they also may also "see your good works and give glory to your Father in heaven" (5:16). According to ancient conceptions, the eye, rather than letting light in, actually emitted light to touch objects, a conception that also stands behind the graphic visual image of the eye as a lamp of the body (6:22), regulating moral disposition. In reference to mission, likewise, Matthew's Jesus states that what is told in the dark his disciples are to "utter in the light" and "proclaim on the housetops," significantly one of the most visible places from which to deliver a message. Lewis notes that "so much communication in the Deaf world starts with LOOK-AT-ME . . . that it seems the Deaf Preachers [likewise frequently] perceived Jesus as beginning his teaching in the same way" (Lewis 2007: 141).

In short, Matthew's Gospel is vision-orientated, and in this respect is open to access by Deaf culture. Indeed, the God of visions and dreams in Matthew's Gospel often subverts the power of those scribal classes who are masters of the written word and exercise hegemony over knowledge. Light and vision are positively featured and are evocative for sign-language users, for whom face-to-face performance is central and cannot be seen in the dark.

USE OF SIGN LANGUAGE AND MINORITY CULTURAL STATUS

One of the most significant factors uniting Deaf culture is of course the use of sign language. Harlan Lane speaks of "the mother tongue" as an "aspect of the soul of a people" and a visible mark of ethnicity within a specific culture (Lane 2005: 293). Accordingly, "A language not based on sound is the primary element that sharply demarcates the Deaf-World from the engulfing hearing society" (Lane 2005: 293). The respective mediums by which spoken and signed languages are communicated are very different. The former is based on sounds and words, the latter on three dimensional uses of hand and body movements and facial expressions. Of course, the visible presence of God witnessed in Matthew's "Emmanuel" (1:23-24) is itself one that fits more neatly with Deaf culture than a physically absent deity who can only be heard. Morris talks of the "idea of God being seen in human form, present among us" as having weighty significance within Deaf culture (Morris 2008: 101). For, in sign language, one must be able to see face-to-face the person one is communicating with. Accordingly, Morris cites Mary Weir's description of "Christ as a sign" allowing Deaf people's communication with God. Likewise, unlike Mark's absent Christ at the close of his Gospel (Mark 16:1-8), Matthew's Jesus appears on a mountaintop and assures his followers that he will be with them always, "to the end of the age" (28:20).

Matthew's Gospel of course does not feature sign language as such, but it does feature nonlinguistic gestures. Although these gestures are significantly different from sign language and lacking linguistic traits such as grammatical agreement inherent in sign communication, these too can nevertheless be viewed positively within Deaf culture (Senghas and Monaghan 2002: 75). Morris cites the example of a Deaf interpretation of healing narratives that use physical and visual gestures to illustrate some degree of understanding, on the part of Jesus, of communicating in ways beyond speech and words (Morris 2008: 103). For example, touch is seen within Matthew's Gospel, and forms of *haptō* occur eight times. Jesus stretches out his hand to heal a leper (8:3) and through touch cures Peter's mother-in-law (8:15), blind men (9:29; 20:34), and an epileptic (17:7). A bleeding woman famously touches the hem of Jesus' garment to be healed (9:21) and is accordingly, without words, made whole. Likewise, hands and body parts within the Gospel are not only instruments of movement but also tools of communication. Matthew frequently speaks of the right hand as a place of honor (20:21-23; 22:44; 25:33; 26:64). The gestures central to the passion narrative in Matthew are also hugely evocative signs readily received by Deaf receivers of the Gospel. The dipping of the bread in the dish symbolizes the one who will hand Jesus over (26:63), and the subsequent kiss of betrayal (26:49) visually enacts deception; the words of institution at the Last Supper act as a sign of Jesus' material presence in the ritual life of the community (26:26); Pilate's symbolic washing of hands in the trial narrative denotes disassociation from the capital-punishment sentence he delivers (27:24); the crown of thorns and the reed placed in the right hand of Jesus (27:29) are visible illustrations of the ironic mocking of his kingly power. The crucifixion itself has also been interpreted, in relation to Deaf culture, as the graphic pinning of Jesus' hands to the cross so he cannot sign or communicate; this acts as the most arresting and iconic sign of the total disability that torturous powers have inflicted on him. While there can be no simple or naive equivalence drawn between sign and gesture, nevertheless from a Deaf cultural perspective the exhibition of bodily means of communication beyond speech can function as important re-membered practices in Deaf recovery readings. Paddy Ladd likewise submits that Deaf culture "embrace[s] the planet by communicating through those very parts of our own bodies which we ourselves are afraid to utilise. Through the unique plasticity of sign languages, they move in and out of each other's very different cultures like shoals of fish, eagerly seeking out new information about different ways of living in this world of ours" (Ladd 2003: 25).

Another defining feature of sign-language use is of course occupying a minority status within a hearing culture. Ladd states, "Sign language users know that they cannot find 'home' within a majority society until the day when that society is able to use their language" (Ladd 2003: 16). They must endure the daily struggle of coexistence "alongside majority culture members who do not understand them" (Ladd 2003: 16). Deaf clubs and schools are accordingly often pictured as safe houses in which sign language is the norm and in which there is a "general disassociation from speech" (Padden 1991: 42–43). One of the most explicit ideological clashes between signed and spoken languages has occurred in the promotion of oralism within educational practice, with oralism defined as "an ideology that privileges spoken (and written) languages over signed ones, often denying the validity or linguistic nature of signing altogether" (Senghas and Monaghan 2002: 83).

While Matthew is undoubtedly a speech-dominated text (forms of *legō*, occur over two hundred times in the Gospel), and citations of spoken and written prophecies (1:22; 2:5, 15, 17, 23; 3:3; 8:17; 12:17; 13:35; 27:9) and law codes (5:27, 31, 33, 38, 43; 12:2-3; 15:3-5; 19:4-5) occur throughout, as outlined earlier, there is a certain ambivalence surrounding the authority of those who presume to be professional readers of Scripture. Likewise, one of the traits Matthew often uses to show Jesus' subversion of his opponents' authority is that he is able to understand what they are thinking (12:25). Morris understands such interceptions as a signer's adaptation to an oral culture (through lip and gesture comprehension), which actually subverts that word-centric culture. In Morris's words, "Jesus knows what the scribes are saying about him without being able to hear them . . . [for he has] been watching their lip patterns and demeanour in order to get this information" (Morris 2008: 149).

While Matthew's textual world may not be one in which the battle between sign and speech is extensively played out, Deaf marginal perspectives can no doubt find resonance with the depiction of Matthew's marginal community. Warren Carter has posited Matthew's Gospel as a counter-narrative, representative of a "minority community of disciples" who "resist the dominant Roman imperial and synagogal control" (Carter 2000: xvii). It is no accident that Matthew celebrates the revelation of God to vulnerable infants, people without speech or words, in contrast to the wise and understanding literate class (11:25). Likewise, the marginal child, unvalued and disposable, becomes the icon of true discipleship (18:3; 19:14; 21:16). Children demonstrate the "social location of powerlessness" and thus function as powerful signifiers for all those who struggle at the margins of society, including minority sign-language users (Carter 2000: 362). In Carter's terms: "All disciples are called children. Parents have no place in the alternative households. Their absence indicates a basic rejection of a hierarchical and patriarchal structure in which power is exercised over others and the creation of a different social order . . . in which all are equal" (Carter 2000: 386). For Matthew, marginality is at the heart of the Christian community's identity, ritual, and practice. And as such, as Sathianathan Clarke reminds us, it stands at one with those cultures whose social location demands that reflection and practice be unified: "It is pertinent to register the point that communities that work with their hands and are intimately related to the products they create do not have a need to separate reflective activity from the material activity they are involved with. Thus production, reflection and communication are connected and integrated into a human way of living. Praxis is a way of life" (Clarke 2002: 264).

Although Matthew's Gospel may display hegemonic textual discourses that have kept the Deaf and their language on the margins, through its subtle critiques of authority based on words and mastery of written traditions, it does nevertheless indirectly acknowledge the great contribution that cultures that speak with their hands, rather than with words, can offer. Matthew's ethos also resonates firmly with a context that is on the margins, for following Matthew's Christ inevitably leads to experiencing paralyzing rejection outside a city's walls.

THE COLLECTIVE ETHOS OF COMMUNITIES

Ladd voices a consensus when he states that "Deaf cultures are not cultures of individualism, but of collectivism, a trait which they share with 70% of the global population" (Ladd 2003: 16). One of the most significant features of collective communities is of course the explicit demonstration and performance of communal identity. Lane likewise considers that "self-recognition and recognition by others is a central feature of ethnicity" (Lane 2005: 292). It is not incidental that Deaf advocates have accordingly adopted labels like Deaf-World and Deaf-Way to illustrate their communal identity and belonging. Richard Senghas and Leila Monaghan see the spatial elements of Deaf-World being particularly evocative in relation to Deaf identity. They submit that the "DEAF-WORLD is seen as transcending national borders and invokes the experiences of d/Deaf individuals and groups as unifying events" (Senghas and Monaghan 2002: 80). Both Lane and Ladd have plotted the global and universal potential of Deaf-World. Lane reveals how Deaf people from two different cultures can nonetheless still communicate at least in part with one another and as such function like other "Diaspora ethnic minorities worldwide" who are subject to "prejudice and discrimination in the host society" (Lane 2005: 293). Ladd also points to the adaptability of sign language, which he defines as a mode of global communication that cultivates "citizens of the entire planet" (Ladd 2003: 14). In Ladd's opinion, "Such a powerful experience cannot continue to be constrained by the feeble diminutive of 'deafness'; hence the concept of Deaf seeks to encompass those larger dimensions" (Ladd 2003: 14).

In picturing Deaf culture as akin to ethnic minority cultures united by experience across geographical limits, many commentators focus on the strong emphasis on social and family ties operative within them (Padden 1991: 42–43). Ladd concurs that "tropes such as family and home are widely used and might well be drawn into a coherent symbol system" within Deaf cultural experience (Ladd 2003: 257). Similarly, the protection of the in-group through endogamous marriage, consensual decision-making, and positive identification with the language and values of the culture also serve to protect and propagate the interests of the minority collective (Lane 2005: 292).

While the substance of the collective identity in Matthew's Gospel may be substantially different from Deaf culture, the broad structure of communal identity featured there nevertheless does find resonance with Deaf experience. (Indeed, sign language as a mode of communication in a collective culture may be far nearer the earliest Palestinian oral modes of transmission of Gospel traditions than our texts would imply.) Matthew offers a number of communal identity labels by which his community can understand itself. These include *ekklēsia*, infants, and little ones. Such labels, as Carter recognizes, serve, like Deaf-World, to "secure separation from other communities [and] reinforce group identity" (Carter 2000: 9). Likewise, fictive kin and households are dominant tropes within Matthew's world. Jesus provocatively asks, "Who is my mother and my brothers?" (12:48) only to conclude that his mother and brothers are those with whom he shares faith and experience (12:49). Claims of exclusive revelation—"To you it has been given to know the secrets of the kingdom of heaven, but to them it has not been given" (13:11)—also serve to underline the different bases of authority operative within the new collective identity of the *ekklēsia*. Particular signs of that community identity are also materially and visually performed: baptism (28:19), worship (5:23-24), governance (18:15-20), eucharistic meals (26:26-29), and prayer (6:9-13) to name just a few. Such rituals serve to "create order, sustain a community in an alternative way of living and effect transformation" (Carter 2000: 9).

The global potential of Deaf-World and communication is also discerned in the way in which Matthew's Gospel plots a mission that is at first limited to "the lost sheep of the house of Israel" (10:6) but careers toward a universal mission (ethnically and racially diverse), articulated in the great commission at the climax of the account: "Go therefore and make disciples of all nations, baptizing them in the name of the Father, Son and Holy Spirit" (28:19). Like Deaf-World, Matthew exhibits a strong collective identity that he wishes to promote and through which he hopes to transcend barriers of race, class, nationality, and geography.

USE OF STORYTELLING

A frequently cited feature of Deaf culture is storytelling. Roger Hitching shows how the Deaf not only convey information through stories but also use them as a coping strategy: "In their stories, they include self-mocking elements and make fun of interactions with hearing people. Storytelling also influences how they conceptualise reality and create their worldview. In Deaf culture the storytelling mode, the dialectical nature of encounter and the greater experience of immediacy create differences in the backdrop against which reality is interpreted" (Hitching 2003: 69). Paddy Ladd has hypothesized that this feature may find its genesis in the fact that "thirst for information is a major theme in a culture . . . denied access to broadcast media and public communication . . . [and] because of the additional oralist restrictions and exclusions from parental and educational information" (Ladd 2003: 309). Of course, the fact that Matthew's Gospel was itself delivered in a culture where estimated literacy rates were only 10 percent has some resonance with this situation. Matthew likewise needs to adopt vivid storytelling elements for a nonliterate audience. From the comic-strip jibe of taking a speck from a neighbor's eye while a log sits in one's own (7:5) to the figurative storytelling marking episodes like the cursing of the fig tree (21:18–22), Matthew draws his audience imaginatively into his narrative world.

Making texts relevant to particular contemporary situations is of course the hallmark of midrashic modes of interpretation (Lawrence 2009: 91–104). Matthew has, in various ways, been understood to contain midrashic elements. To give just one example, the birth narrative is often read as midrashic haggadah. Midrashic because scriptural prophecies are woven into the entire complex, and haggadah because "the story is not told for the sake of facts alone, but in order to illustrate their deeper meaning, that is, the theological significance of Jesus as the fulfillment of OT prophecies" (Hagner 1995a: 16). Likewise, in Deaf culture, "storytelling is a form of oral transmission of text . . . and in the hands of a skilled practitioner accurately transmits what is seen as the essence of the narrative" (Hitching 2003: 70).

Moreover, the characterizations and attitudes operative within the Gospel (for example, of the Pharisees and scribes, as opposed to Jesus) likewise form an important part of the telling. In stories told in sign language, often the performer will physically change position, posture, and facial expression to denote a change of character and illustrate the outlooks of respective individuals. In such telling, aspects, manner, and mood become central parts of the storytelling endeavor. In Hitching's terms, such interpretations do not merely give the meaning "but also the speaker's attitude to his listeners and to what he is saying" within the performance (Hitching 2003: 70).

MATTHEW AND DEAF-WORLD: IDENTIFYING COMMON TOUCHSTONES

Notions of ability, disability, normality, and abnormality are socially constructed and often largely dependent on the environment in which they are used, and by whom they are advanced. In contrast to a medical model of deafness, the cultural model, which conceives of the Deaf as a linguistic or ethnic minority group, challenges us to disrupt our classifications surrounding what is normal and interpret d/Deafness as "difference not defect." For, as Deborah Creamer reminds us, every individual is limited in some respect, and as such, binary categories of us and them in reference to disability are very hard to sustain. Encountering Matthew with Deaf sensitivities on first sight seemed a predominantly audiocentric document that stigmatized, even stifled, d/Deaf presence within it. While the exposure of and resistance to oppression by a hearing "cult of normalcy" is an important part of Deaf readings, so is finding positive touchstones that allow the "meaning of the text [to] shift" in view of contemporary liberation agendas. By elucidating key features of Deaf culture and allowing them to reverberate and echo within Matthew's world, a dynamic exchange with the text in light of contemporary experience was initiated, albeit by a hearing academic. Harlan Lane, Robert Hoffmeister, and Ben Bahan warn of the "inevitable collision with the values of DEAF-WORLD, whose goal is to promote the unique heritage of Deaf language and culture" that will occur when a hearing person undertakes a journey such as the one attempted here, for "the disparity in decision-making power between the hearing world and DEAF-WORLD renders this collision frightening for Deaf people" (Lane 1996: 371). Heeding this warning, this paper does not claim to be the last sign on this topic, but rather poses an open invitation for Deaf people themselves to partake in creative interactions with texts such as the Gospel of Matthew and as such curb the perpetuation of Deaf absence from biblical texts and interpretation.

Notes

1. Used by permission of Wipf and Stock Publishers. www.wipfandstock.com

2. On language: "Deaf with capital D refers to culturally deaf people" (Lewis 2007), x. Hereafter I will capitalize *Deaf* to denote the cultural model of deafness; namely, a community united by their use of sign language and social identity through Deaf clubs, etc. Where I cite other authors, however, I have retained their original capitalization.

3. This is a creative adaptation of H. G. Wells's short story "The Country of the Blind" (1904), but here made to reference d/Deaf experience. Wells is cited and discussed in McDermott and Varenne 1995.

PART IV

Laborers and Empire

10

"Why Are You Sitting There?"

Reading Matthew 20:1-16 in the Context of Casual Workers in Pietermaritzburg, South Africa

Gerald West and Sithembiso Zwane

INTRODUCTION

Every day, groups of men, some South Africans and others from the southern African region, sit on the side of the street in downtown Pietermaritzburg waiting for work. Some have the tools of their trade with them, such as shovels and trowels, while others hold only their meager lunch in their hands. The Theology and Economic Justice Programme of the Ujamaa Centre for Community Development and Research, in the School of Religion and Theology at the University of KwaZulu-Natal, has noticed these men and has begun to work with them. On a regular basis, we have "hired" them for the day, paying an agreed wage to spend time with us reflecting on the role that biblical and theological resources play in their lives and collaborating together to find more secure work. At first apprehensive about the ideo-theological "work" we offer them, they now eagerly embrace this opportunity to "do theology." While the larger project to which they contribute is a project to construct a workers' theology with them and other casual workers, one of the building blocks of the project is contextual Bible study, a form of contextual reading in which the resources of socially engaged biblical scholars and these casual workers are shared. Among the texts we have read together is Matt. 20:1-16. We have also worked with this text in other communities of readers, approaching the text in a number of different ways, offering both "capitalist" and "socialist" ways of reading the text.

GENERAL DISTINCTIVE CONTEXTUAL FEATURES

In every South African city, there are areas where men sit on the side of the street waiting for work for the day. They are our day laborers. Most of them have some trade or work experience, but some have few formal skills, offering nothing more than their willingness to work. All of them are the flotsam of capitalism's relentless pursuit of profit, whether in the guise of the racial capitalism of apartheid or the more recent globalized form of neoliberal capitalism. They are among the products of systemic forms of economic exploitation going back more than three centuries.

In his economic analysis of this period, South African economist Sampie Terreblanche provides a detailed history and analysis of the systemic relationship between power, land, and labor. He identifies a number of successive systemic periods in South African history, beginning with "the mercantilistic and feudal system institutionalised by Dutch colonialism during the second half of the seventeenth and most of the eighteenth century (1652–1795)" (Terreblanche 2002: 14). This was followed by the system of British colonial and racial capitalism (1795–1890) and a related system of British colonial and mineral capitalism (1890–1948) (Terreblanche 2002: 15). Unfree labor patterns were intensified when the Afrikaner-oriented National Party won the general election of 1948. Although the party "did not drastically transform the economic system of racial capitalism institutionalised by the English establishment, it used its political and ideological power to institutionalise a new version of it" (Terreblanche 2002: 15). "Since 1990," continues Terreblanche, "we have experienced a transition from the politico-economic system of white political domination and racial capitalism to a new system of democratic capitalism" (Terreblanche 2002: 15). South Africa's economic system has moved, Terreblanche argues, "over the past 30 years from one of colonial and racial capitalism to a neo-liberal, first-world, capitalist enclave that is disengaging itself from a large part of the black labor force" (Terreblanche 2002: 422). This transformation, though it has "coincided with the introduction of a system of representative democracy which is effectively controlled by a black, predominantly African, elite," still exhibits "an ominous systemic character" (Terreblanche 2002: 422–23).

> In the new politico-economic system, individual members of the upper classes (comprising one third of the population) profit handsomely from mainstream economic activity, while the mainly black lumpenproletariat (comprising 50 per cent of the population) is increasingly pauperised. Ironically, individual members of the black

and white upper class in the new system seem as unconcerned about its dysfunctionality as individual members of the white elite were about that of the old. The common denominator between the old and the new systems is that part of society was/is systemically and undeservedly enriched, while the majority of the population were/ are systemically and undeservedly impoverished—in the old system through *systemic exploitation*, and in the new system through *systemic neglect*. (Terreblanche 2002: 423)

This is the macroeconomic context in which the work reflected on in this essay is located. The microeconomic and more human context of this essay, the day laborers waiting for work on the streets of Pietermaritzburg, is less clearly documented and analyzed, but is the subject of ongoing research by colleagues from the Ujamaa Centre for Community Development and Research. Economic justice has been the focus of the Ujamaa Centre's work since its establishment in 1989. The biblical studies work of the founder of one of the institutional strands that makes up the Ujamaa Centre, the Institute for the Study of the Bible (ISB), Gunther Wittenberg, was strongly informed by social scientific biblical criticism (Wittenberg 1993; 2007). Based to a substantial extent on elements of the community-based Bible movement within Latin American liberation theology, the Centro de Estudos Bíblicos (CEBI), the ISB provided an interface in which the socioeconomic dimensions of our South African realities was brought into dialogue with the (less apparent) socioeconomic dimensions of biblical texts in an attempt to take up the Bible as a weapon of systemic socioeconomic struggle (Mofokeng 1988: 40).

This strand of the ISB's work was strengthened when the House of Studies for Worker Ministry (HSWM), a sister organization, established in 1994, merged with the ISB in 1996. The HSWM was established to give an institutional form to an engagement between prophetic theology, as understood by the *Kairos Document* (Kairos 1986), and the trade union movement in South Africa (Cochrane 1991). Shaped extensively by the "worker priest" movement championed by Fr. Joseph Cardijn in the 1930s in Belgium, and embodied in South Africa by the Young Christian Workers movement (West 1995: 188–93), the HSWM used the see-judge-act methodology. This methodological process was used to do socioeconomic analysis (see), to bring this analysis into dialogue with a socioeconomic reading of God's project of liberation in the Bible (judge), and to engage in particular acts of socioeconomic transformation (act) (West 2006a).

The primary vehicle for working within the see-judge-act framework within the Ujamaa Centre is contextual Bible study methodology. Developed within the praxis cycle of action-reflection over the past two decades, this methodology provides a site for collaboration between the interpretive resources of the local community and the interpretive resources of the biblical studies academy (West 2006a). In addition to bringing potentially analogous local contexts and biblical texts into dialogue, this methodology includes an analogy of method whereby a structured and systematic analysis of the local context is brought into dialogue with a structured and systematic analysis of the biblical text (in its sociohistorical and literary contexts) (West 1995). In other words, in the tradition of Latin American Liberation Theology and the second phase of South African Black Theology (Assmann 1976; Mosala 1989), all of life, both present and past, must be subject to a socioeconomic systemic analysis.

In addition to our commitment to a critical reading of reality and biblical text, we acknowledge an overarching ideo-theological orientation that we bring to the collaborative interpretive process. In any interpretive act that brings text and context into conversation, there is a mediating realm or pole that enables the to-and-fro movement between text and context, which we might call an ideo-theological orientation (West 2009). Within the Ujamaa Centre, as our name indicates, our ideo-theological orientation is a form of prophetic African socialism. There is no self-evident ideologically or theologically neutral engagement between biblical text and social context; there is always a mediating moment, as the work of Justin Ukpong (2000), Jonathan Draper (1991; 2001), and Cristina Grenholm and Daniel Patte have demonstrated (2000). While many hide or elide their ideo-theological orientation, we foreground ours.

Specific Macroeconomic Context

We have therefore watched with dismay as our liberation government, a tripartite alliance between the South African Communist Party (SACP), the Confederation of South African Trade Unions (COSATU), and, in a leadership role, the African National Congress (ANC), has moved away from African socialism to embrace neoliberal capitalism. This need not have happened, for the macroeconomic policy with which the ANC and its alliance partners came to power was indelibly inscribed with African socialist elements. Given the ways in which the Bible had been used to support racial capitalism under apartheid, it was fitting that after more than a century and a half of racial capitalism, the first macroeconomic policy of a liberated South Africa, the Reconstruction and Development Programme (RDP), should be declared to have an "almost biblical character" by then Deputy President Thabo Mbeki (Mbeki 1995).

The RDP stated that "the democratic government must play a leading and enabling role in guiding the economy and the market towards reconstruction and development," and warned that policies concentrating primarily on promoting economic growth "would accentuate existing inequalities, perpetuate mass poverty, and soon stifle economic growth" (cited in Terreblanche 2002: 108). Thus the government was tasked with actively integrating economic growth with economic reconstruction and social development, being ever mindful of the distortions and injustices that had become endemic during racial capitalism and white political domination (Terreblanche 2002: 108–9).

Swept to power in the 1994 election, with the RDP as its election manifesto, the ANC and now national President Nelson Mandela declared the RDP to be "the cornerstone on which the . . . GNU (Government of National Unity) is based," and "the centerpiece of its socio-economic policy" (cited in Terreblanche 2002: 109). Driven to a considerable degree by the trade unions and civic organizations, the RDP emphasized that central to the new government's planning process must be "both the meeting of the populace's basic needs and the active empowerment of that populace in driving its own development process" (Saul 2005: 206). In macroeconomic terms, the RDP put forward nonmarket mechanisms for the provision of basic goods and services, advocated a process of decommodification by turning exchange-values back into use-values, and set about democratizing access to economic resources (Legassik 2007: 456–57). And even though its central chapters were compromised "in the direction of free-market premises" (Saul 2005: 206), it was hailed by left intellectuals as posing "challenges to the commanding heights of capitalism, racism and patriarchy," by proposing "structural reforms" that would start the building of socialism under capitalism and lead inexorably to a socialist transition (Legassik 2007: 457). Notwithstanding its weaknesses, the RDP was, wrote John Saul at the time, "less what it is, than what it might become" in the context of further class struggles (Saul 2005: 206–7).

Within two years of its adoption, the RDP was replaced, with almost no consultation—the hallmark of alliance liberation politics up to this point—by a new, procapitalist, macroeconomic policy, GEAR (Growth, Employment and Redistribution). Indeed, writes Martin Legassik, though the name of the RDP continued to be invoked by the ANC up to the 1999 election campaign and even later, "the economic leadership of the ANC had from the start no intention of implementing the RDP where it clashed with their pro-business aims of export-orientation, trade liberalisation, fiscal austerity or privatisation" (Legassik 2007: 457). Brought to power under the flag of the RDP, the ANC government began, within days, to dismantle the RDP's African socialist potential (Legassik 2007: 458). The iconic status of Nelson Mandela and the power of the office of the presidency were used by the ANC to enforce "acceptance" of GEAR, even though Mandela later regretted the way in which it was done (SACP 2006: 21), for there had been no discussion of the shift away from the RDP even within the ANC National Executive Committee, nor had there been any consultation with the Tripartite Alliance partners, COSATU and the SACP (Legassik 2007: 458).

In the analysis of the SACP, "the GEAR process needs essentially to be understood as the first decisive step in the launching of a new state/presidential project under the effective direction not of Mandela, but of his successor, then deputy president, Thabo Mbeki" (SACP 2006: 21). Clearly global and national realities impose real constraints, but "national realities would have allowed (and still do allow) different, much more transformative outcomes" (SACP 2006: 22). The constraints of the global economy have become more marked in the short time since Jacob Zuma's ascendancy to the presidency following our 2009 general election. But there are signs that a reinvigorated SACP and COSATU are having some impact as alliance partners on macroeconomic policy under Zuma's presidency, having been marginalized during the Mbeki presidency.

Toward a Socialist Reading of Matthew

During all this time, from before liberation through to the present, the Ujamaa Centre has been working with Matt. 20:1-16 in our Economic Justice Programme and Theology of Work Programme (recently conflated into one Theology and Economic Justice Programme). Led by the late Mzwandile R. Nunes, who was schooled by the Young Christian Workers movement, this program pioneered collaborative readings of Matt. 20:1-16 with the unemployed. As the research of Nunes's colleague Sibusiso Gwala has shown, there is considerable stigma associated with being unemployed (Gwala 2007). Unable to discern the systemic dimensions of unemployment, families and communities often blame the individual for their failure to find work. So to some extent, those sitting on the sides of the downtown street waiting for work have been driven there by shame as much as by economic necessity. Noticing these casual workers and seeking to understand their struggle more clearly, two of our young colleagues within the Ujamaa Centre's Theology and Economic Justice Programme, Skhumbuzo Zuma and Mbuyiseni Gwamanda, together with the coordinator of the program, Sithembiso Zwane, have drawn these casual workers into the work of the program, reflecting together on the systemic dimensions of unemployment.

These colleagues have respectfully approached the casual workers who are waiting for work, inviting them to join us in reflection and contextual Bible study around issues of work, unemployment, and casualization of work. Whenever we organize these workers for a contextual Bible study workshop, we endeavor to demonstrate our commitment to socioeconomic justice by compensating them for a full day's work, and we make sure that it is a decent[1] payment. This is not charity or wasteful expenditure; they work with us, engaging with a biblical text in relation to their context, to discover the true meaning of economic justice. Unfortunately, the work we offer is not permanent, but only occasional work, due to our own limited resources. But we do use our networks, among a range of faith-based and nongovernmental organizations, to assist them with finding decent work.

As indicated, contextual Bible study is our primary resource for collaborative work like this, and much of the work of Gerald West, a socially engaged biblical scholar, is to work with colleagues in the Ujamaa Centre to design particular Bible studies that are potentially appropriate to the contextual realities we are working within. We activate the Bible as a weapon of struggle for economic liberation, wresting it from the hands of those who use it to stigmatize and blame the unemployed for what is a systemic predicament. A text we have wrestled with through the years has been Matt. 20:1-16. Initially, this text was used to explore a socialist vision of society. In this collaborative reading, we focus on the recognition the parable gives to the reality of day laborers and the equitable payment to each according to their need. However, our longing for such a socialist vision was not enough to silence the features of the biblical text that stood over against such a reading. For while we overtly take up the Bible as a resource for economic survival, liberation, and life, and while we discern a prophetic socioeconomic trajectory weaving its way through the literary and sociohistorical contexts of the Bible, we are committed to respect the detail of particular biblical texts, recognizing that just as socioeconomic contestation is central to our own South African context, it is also central to the sociohistorical sites of production of biblical texts.

In this case, we were regularly troubled in our readings by the class identity of the "landowner" (*oikodespotēs*), and his autocratic manner in hiring, paying, and dealing with the complaints of the day laborers. We also worried about his payment of the minimum wage and his delegation of the task of payment to "his manager" (*epitropos*). Most of all, we were disturbed by the landowner's capitalist-sounding rhetorical question, "Am I not allowed to do what I choose with what belongs to me?" The detail of this text aroused our hermeneutic of suspicion, and we wondered if this parable should be read in a liberative manner. Clearly, it could be read as supporting aspects of socialism, but only if we ignored some of its detail. Was there a way, responsible to the detail of the text, to read this text within our socialist ideo-theological orientation?

Our determination to read this text economically was frustrated by the refusal of much of biblical scholarship to even engage with this dimension of the text. The "virtual agreement among interpreters" to interpret this parable allegorically, whether they focused their attention on Matthew's literary framing or tried to reconstruct the parable in the context of the historical ministry of Jesus, offered us scant assistance (Herzog 1994: 79–82). Fortunately, however, the Ujamaa Centre has been formed by the socioeconomic readings of and personal interaction with socially engaged biblical scholars like Gunther Wittenberg (see, e.g., 1993), Norman Gottwald (see, e.g., 1993), Itumeleng Mosala (see, e.g., 1989), Herman Waetjen (see, e.g., 1989), and Richard Horsley (see, e.g., 2009), among others. Their work has enabled us to reconstruct a socioeconomic reading of the biblical story, beginning with the God who is invoked by the cry of slaves, who try to construct an alternative socioeconomic society. However, under internal and external pressures, this emerging alternative society imitates and implements, ironically, the very tributary mode of production that subjugated their ancestors. The relentless logic of the tributary mode of production gradually and deliberately coerced peasant subsistence farmers into debt, then foreclosed on their land, forcing them to become, at best, tenant farmers on the very land they previously owned or, at worst, day laborers, such as we find in this parable (For a more detailed and referenced account of this trajectory, see West 2006b.)

We were drawn, therefore, to William Herzog's reading of this parable, identifying with his notion of Jesus as "pedagogue of the oppressed," and his location of this parable within the realities of the conflictual interface between "agrarian societies and traditional aristocratic empires." (See the subtitle and chapter headings of Herzog 1994.) Read from such a perspective, the contours of the parable are clearer. The owner of the vineyard is likely an absentee landowner, a member of the economic urban elite, employing a manager to handle the daily affairs of the vineyard, and engaged in a form of agriculture that produced "a crop that can be converted into a luxury item (wine), monetized, and exported" (Herzog 1994: 85). Unable to calculate how many laborers he will need, such is the extent of his landholdings, the owner must make a number of trips to the agora to hire workers (Herzog 1994: 89–90). Regular assessment of the number of workers he needs also enables the landowner to keep his workers to the minimum necessary to harvest the crop within the designated time period. Furthermore, by hiring small numbers of laborers during the day, the landowner exercises his "unilateral power," negotiating only with those hired at the beginning of the day for the minimum daily wage (Herzog 1994: 89–90), but leaving the wage for those hired later in the day indeterminate (vv. 4, 7) (Herzog 1994: 86). For in a context of chronic systemic unemployment and underemployment, the day laborer is in no position to insist on a just wage. "Far from being generous, then, the householder is taking advantage of an unemployed work force to meet his harvesting needs by offering them work without a wage agreement" (Herzog 1994: 86). By telling a story in which the landowner is actively involved in the economic process, Jesus foregrounds the socioeconomic contestation of his time, making the usually invisible absentee landlord visible and so setting up a direct encounter between "the elites and the expendables" (Herzog 1994: 87).

The arbitrary power of the landowner is evident in the payment process. His power is signaled in the delegation of his manager to make the payments, but is fully manifest in his deliberate flaunting of protocol by refusing to pay the first-hired laborers first; by making the first-hired wait until last, he flaunts his power and shames them. The dignity of those who have worked all day demands a response, and so they risk a protest (vv. 11-12), speaking back to power, invoking the principle of equal pay for equal work (Herzog 1994: 91–92). Singling out their spokesperson (v. 13a), the landowner condescendingly reminds the resisting workers of their contractual agreement, knowing fully well that the day laborers were never in a position to negotiate anything other than the minimum wage, and then goes on to dismiss their complaints, reiterating his right to do what he pleases with his power (v. 14), and concluding by blasphemously asserting that the land that has systemically been coerced from the very peasant farmers who are now day laborers belongs to him (v. 15) (Herzog 1994: 92–94). At this point, the systemic violence beneath this text becomes palpable (Herzog 1994: 94).

As persuasive as Herzog's reading of this parable is, we have wanted to honor that tradition in the Young Christian Workers that has read this parable as advocating aspects of socialism, so we have offered our collaborators a dialogical choice. Here is the contextual Bible study:

The facilitator shows the participants a picture of day-laborers sitting on the side of the street in Pietermaritzburg waiting for work.
Question: What do you see in this picture?
Group discussion of question.

Once the group has discussed their responses to this picture together in plenary, the Contextual Bible Study consider the following two questions together in plenary:

1. What is the text about? [All responses are recorded in an affirming manner on newsprint in front of the participants.]
2. Who are the characters in this text and what is their relationship to each other? [The plenary group is asked to form small groups of 2–3 and to discuss this question; when the process is complete, the responses are again reported and recorded on newsprint, publicly.]

The following short input is then offered to the plenary of all participants:

In the time of Jesus, many peasant farmers had been forced off their land through the tributary mode of production, and its debt trap. Those who lost their land became day-laborers. Within this socio-economic context there are two very different ways of reading this text:

1. This text can be read as presenting the egalitarian socialist vision of Jesus and the early Jesus movement (Acts 4:32-35). From this perspective, we might read the parable as a utopian vision of a socialist society.

2. This text can also be read as a critique by Jesus of the arbitrary and discriminating practices of "capitalist" landowners, who hire when they like and pay what they like. From this perspective, the workers do not receive a just wage, they receive the exact exploitative daily rate, and no more.

After some discussion of this input, the plenary is divided into two groups. Each group then engages with its own respective set of questions:

Group 1	Group 2
3. If this parable represents the egalitarian socialist vision of Jesus and the kingdom of God, what is the relationship between the landowner and the workers in this text?	3. If this parable represents the exploitative practices of the ruling elite in the first century, what is the relationship between the landowner and the workers in this text?
4. What details of the text does this position not take account of?	4. What details of the text does this position not take account of?
5. In what ways does this interpretation of the parable speak to the context of unemployment in South Africa?	5. In what ways does this interpretation of the parable speak to the context of unemployment in South Africa?

After the groups have completed the process of working through these questions, the "scribe" from each group shares their responses to each of the questions, having summarised them on newsprint.

When the reportback is complete, the following three questions are discussed in plenary:

5. What have you learned from the reading of the other group?
6. What do each of these two different readings say to our context?
7. How will you use the resources of this Contextual Bible Study to enable the church or faith community to become more engaged with the issue of unemployment?

This contextual Bible study generates considerable excitement and discussion. Most participants are unfamiliar with multiple ways of reading the same text; and most are unfamiliar with an overtly socioeconomic reading of the Bible. The discussions within each group are usually animated and intense, for we as participants have much at stake in our reading. And there is enough in the text for each reading to find a foothold, notwithstanding those details in the text that do not fit.

Matthew's framing of the parable, noted by some of the participants in group 1, seems to support an interpretation of the text that leans in the direction of a socialist project, with each and every person receiving the same wage, based on their need rather than on their contribution. Lively discussions would often ensue, as participants debated whether it was feasible to base an economic system on need. Most accepted that wages must be related to both the type of work done and the duration of work.

Group 2 participants struggled initially to adopt a "hermeneutic of suspicion," both because of their general attitude of trust toward the Bible and because of the way this parable had been preached on in their churches. They wanted more detailed information from the facilitator about "the time of Jesus," and it was only as the economic realities of the ancient world became clearer that they were able to question the biblical text. But once they began to probe the text, drawing on the resonances between their own economic contexts and what they had learned of the biblical context, they found plenty of evidence of exploitation.

But the most creative and transformative moment in the contextual Bible study are questions 5–7, where we bring the two different readings into dialogue. As we share our group's responses, we are persuaded that our reading has textual and contextual support; but when we hear the other group's reading, our own reading is destabilized. This creates space not only to interrogate our own reading of the text but also our "reading" of our context.

Having done this contextual Bible study a number of times, we have noted that there is a general tendency among most groups to move toward the reading that is critical of the power of the landowner. Though we long for the reading in which Jesus and/or Matthew offers us a socialist vision, we cannot ignore the detail of the text and our own experiences of the systemic dimensions of socioeconomic inequalities in our own country. But the transformative potential of this contextual Bible study does not reside in settling for one reading over against another, but in exploring the contestation between them, for each reading offers us ways of imagining and resources for planning for transformation.

Toward a Socialist Theology of Work

As we have indicated, one of the actions that has emerged from our see-judge-act process is to engage directly with those who sit on the sides of our streets in Pietermaritzburg, drawing them into a project on constructing a theology of casual work. As Albert Nolan argued many years ago, a theology of work can only be done by and with workers (Nolan 1996). The trained theologian has a role to play, but it is only a facilitating role, offering our resources—including our biblical and theological resources, as well as our time—to enable workers themselves to bring their inchoate and partially formed "lived" theologies of work to articulation. This is a long and slow process, but an important one.

As important, perhaps, is the next step. For having collaboratively constructed theologies of work with various sectors of workers, we are then committed to bring these local theologies of work into the public realm, "incorporating" them into the public theologies of our churches, where they can both transform and resource the church (West 2005). This component of the project is important because, as our colleague Sibusiso Gwala has argued, the dominant theology of the church stigmatizes those who cannot find work (Gwala 2007).

Our work with casual workers in Pietermaritzburg, which has now expanded to include those casual workers who clean our university offices, is a "care-ful" and ongoing process. We have had to overcome their understandable suspicions and to build real relationships of solidarity. We pay a just wage for their work, not the minimal denarius; we also provide nutritious food and a comfortable place in which to work together. We listen more than we speak, and we use our networks to try to secure more substantive employment as we discover their skills. We have found that those sitting waiting for work include those from outside the borders of South Africa, including, for example, those who have fled the economic collapse in Zimbabwe. Their presence is a significant feature of our context, for the presence of "foreigners" looking for work has fuelled xenophobic violence in South Africa in the past couple of years; so it is important for us to recognize where and how the unemployed build coalitions and solidarity, even if these are fragile and susceptible to the pressures of ethnic as well as economic agendas.

CONCLUSION

What distinguishes our readings of Matt. 20:1-16 from the bulk of the readings within biblical studies is that both of ours are resolutely systemic socioeconomic readings, with the contours of African socialism as key components of our guiding ideo-theological orientation. We resist an allegorical reading of this parable, though we do employ analogy, both an analogy of contexts (biblical and South African) and method (socioeconomic analysis of both text and context). Yet our readings are not overdetermined by our socialist ideo-theological orientation. We respect the detail of the text, recognizing that "struggle" (Mosala 1986: 196; 1989: 9; Nolan 1988) and contestation are as present there as they are in our own contexts.

And though contextual Bible study is an intervention of sorts, bringing as it does structured and systematic biblical resources (in the guise of the questions) into the collaborative interpretive process, we respect the voices of the many and various people we work with, granting their voices the same kind of weight we grant the detail of the biblical text.

Notes

1. This term is used deliberately to recall the term "decent work," which is derived from the work of the International Labour Organization; see ILO, Director General 1999.

11

Reading the Matthean Apocalypse (Matthew 24–25) in the Glocalization Context of Hong Kong's Bourgeois Society and Middle-Class Churches

Lung-pun Common Chan

INTRODUCTION

"Glocalization," a blend of globalization and localization, emphasizes a tension between the two popular concepts (Robertson 1992: 173–74; Mazlish 2005).[1] In light of glocalization, this paper adopts a glocal public approach to interpreting the Bible (Chia 2009: 75–108). It aims at recontextualizing the so-called Matthean apocalypse (Matthew 24–25) in the globalized Hong Kong. As highlighted by its governmental brand line—"Asia's world city"—Hong Kong is an international financial center, a regional hub for connecting mainland China and Southeast Asia as well as a cosmopolitan city of China, wherein the local, regional, and global interplay (HKSAR 2012b; cf. Chu 2011; Aminian, Fung, and Lin 2008: 207). The brand line, which can be seen as a typical social-semiotic sign, crystallizes Hongkongers' global consciousness.[2] Thus, from a Hongkonger's point of view, the context embedded in Matthew 24–25 could be economic globalization,[3] or precisely, glocalization, rather than *Pax Romana*. Such a recontextualization invites Hong Kong's bourgeois society (middle-class churches in particular) to a mutual dialogue with the ancient but decontextualized episode of Matthew 24–25.

On the one hand, the concept of "middle class" basically did not exist in the ancient Roman Empire (see Scheidel and Friesen 2009: 88), and hence we who belong to this class may ask the text from our own contemporary context: What is the relevance of the apocalyptic vision of an alternative world order for us, who are neither those lamented in the front line nor those being harshly criticized behind the text? We, particularly middle-class citizens of Hong Kong, are definitely neither the most serious global victims,[4] nor the greediest global predators, but simply successful survivors in a globalized economy. As middle-class Christians, we conjecture that we have already learned some survival tactics, like our numerous contemporaries in Hong Kong. Consequently, Hong Kong middle-class Christians, including me, tend to be indifferent, or even averse, to any alternative future![5]

The apocalyptic message goes unheard today: What was the social-historical function of the Matthean text for the Christian groups amid the political economy of the Roman Empire? What kind of alternative voice could be heard from Matthew 24–25 when the Matthean community was facing an imperial ideology? Was the apocalyptic text merely an unfulfilled eschatological aspiration? In other words, what did the text of an ancient context mainly concern: eschatology or futurology?[6] Contemplating the End, or searching for alternatives here and now?

Mutual dialogue can revitalize the Matthean apocalypse. It can be perceived as a recurring yearning for change. Despite both the marginalization of the Matthean community and our powerlessness in global governance, the Matthean apocalypse still generates hope for a "risk society" with the aid of apocalyptic scenarios, in which God himself will make the impossible possible.[7] Apocalyptic readers can thus be empowered as agents of social change, irrespective of the actual mode of fulfillment. Now, due to the aforesaid mutual dialogue, I, who am one of the middle-class Christians suffering from Hong Kong as a "risk society," have to change my own reading of Matthew 24–25.

ANALYZING THE LIFE-CONTEXT

In the following, the life-context in Hong Kong will first be analyzed, and afterward the biblical text in this new context. The glocal public approach adopted in this paper belongs to ideological criticism, or so-called critical theory.[8]

THE ECONOMIC GLOBALIZATION IDEOLOGY IN HONG KONG

Now let us begin our analysis of the life-context in Hong Kong. Like thousands of cities and billions of people under globalization, Hongkongers struggled unavoidably with global crises.[9] However, the societal problems of Hong Kong must be viewed in light of not only a globalizing context but also a glocalizing economy. Concerning problems of glocalization, this paper does not refer to specific global marketing of transnational firms with a local vision (see Hollensen 2011: 20–21; Kotabe and Helsen 2008: 584),[10] but emphasizes both the global impact on Hong Kong's societal issues and our socially conditioned, local features. In other words, Hong Kong's glocalization problems are not cast in the same mold as other parts of the global village. With the course of time, the bourgeois society and middle-class churches of Hong Kong became not only uncritical but even proud of our form of capitalism (Lau 2003: 385–86). According to Nobel Prize–winning economist Milton Friedman, the economic policy in Hong Kong sets the best example of the benefits of laissez-faire capitalism (Friedman and Friedman 1990: 54–55; cf. Baofu 2002: 167). The present HKSAR chief executive Donald Tsang was the first governmental voice to claim that the policy of Hong Kong was "big market, small government."[11] The underlying premise is that economic development is supported and promoted only within the limits of a small government. Aiming at sustaining the private sector on its own, the government makes no attempt to intervene in the market (Cheung 2000). Consequently, Hongkongers are co-creating numerous problems of capitalist globalization,[12] particularly glocalization. Indeed, capitalist globalization is notorious among global victims all over the world and is sometimes stereotyped as "evangelical capitalism."[13] Ideologically, capitalism should not be taken for granted (see Gilbert 2008). However, unfortunately, we are still suffering from having no dream of alternative futures.[14]

SUFFERING IN A RISK SOCIETY BUT TOO FEW REFLECTIONS ON THE "HONG KONG LEHMAN BROTHERS CRISIS"

After highlighting the ideological problem of glocalization, next comes a concrete illustration—namely, the "Hong Kong Lehman Brothers crisis." If Hongkongers ever made any success in global competitions, we remain as vulnerable survivors in a risk society. The recent "financial tsunami," and particularly the Hong Kong Lehman Brothers crisis, is a costly lesson in our collective memory (see Lee and Law 2010). The bankruptcy of Lehman Brothers started in the United States on September 15, 2008, and it had effects all over the world.[15] With "guaranteed mini-bonds" (valued HKD 15.7 billion) from Lehman, more than 43,700 Hong Kong citizens have been affected (Man 2008: 1; Liu 2008). According to the *Hong Kong Yearbook 2008*, the Hong Kong Monetary Authority (HKMA) had received nearly 20,000 complaints about "guaranteed mini-bonds" at the end of 2008. Over 4,500 cases had been investigated, including the referral of 238 cases to the Securities and Futures Commission (SFC) for follow-up action (HKSAR 2008: ch. 4). Furthermore, Hongkongers suffered from the most severe economic recession since 1954, amid cooling global demand and its knock-on effect on world trade (HKSAR 2009b: 38).[16] There has been no critical reflection from the Hong Kong government. For instance, our former chief executive of the HKMA Mr. Joseph Yam's speech "Reflections Relevant to the Banking Profession in Hong Kong"—a "prophecy" of developing Hong Kong as the offshore renminbi market—had only a few words mentioning Lehman Brothers crisis (Yam 2009).[17] How our *Yearbook 2009* posits is even more uncritical. The lasting shock from the global crisis in the Hong Kong economy is downplayed as "exceptional gyrations" (HKSAR 2009b: 38).

Unfortunately, Hongkongers have not learned the lesson. A significant change in the philosophy of governance from traditional capitalism to alternative futures is still not our dominant public discourse.[18] On the local level, not only those ruling elites but also middle-class citizens are not ready to reorient our opportunistic lifestyle and social values. Without any surprise, we scarcely resonate with those who have persistently suffered under world capitalism, who are struggling anonymously in other parts of the global village. Even after the nightmare experience of the global financial tsunami, Hong Kong's middle class still welcomes the next speculative bubbles.

Not a Joke: Work Overload but Numerous Underemployed or Unemployed as one of Hong Kong's Glocalization Problems

Apart from the Lehman Brothers crisis, Hong Kong has been facing other glocalization problems, such as ridiculous working hours. Overtime (OT) and work overload are extraordinarily common in Hong Kong, but numerous people are still underemployed or even unemployed. According to the *Hong Kong Yearbook 2009*, there was a significant increase in the overall unemployment rate from 3.6 percent in 2008 to 5.4 percent in 2009 (HKSAR 2009b: 122). The underemployment rate rose from 1.9 percent in 2008 to 2.3 percent in 2009 (HKSAR 2009b: 122).[19] The total employment decreased from 3,518,800 in 2008 to a new low of 3,479,800 in 2009. At the same time, the yearbook reports seemingly "good" news on the rise of the median monthly employment earnings from HKD 10,100 in 2007 to HKD 10,500 in both 2008 and 2009. The employment earnings, however, were not as positive as reported in the yearbook. In 2009, one year after the financial tsunami, 14.4 percent of employed Hongkongers were earning less than HKD 5,000 (HKSAR 2009b:

122). In Hong Kong, unemployed, underemployed, and underpaid are one side of the coin.

The other side of the coin: we Hongkongers who work among the longest hours in the world, devote more than 48 hours weekly to our career (Lai 2008). The Hong Kong Confederation of Trade Unions (HKCTU) successfully aroused public concern regarding Hongkongers' long working hours (Lai 2008),[20] which can be defined in three ways: (1) hours exceeding the statutory normal hours; (2) hours exceeding work-life-balance beyond which workers experience negative affects; and (3) hours exceeding workers' expected working time (Sangheon, McCann, and Messenger 2007: 37). Discouragingly, Hong Kong meets all three criteria. First, since the first decade of the twentieth century, the Hours of Work (Industry) Convention, 1919 (No. 1) was enacted as the first global standard on working time, which upheld the principle of "8 hours a day and 48 hours a week" (Sangheon, McCann, and Messenger 2007: 1).[21] A recent study by the International Labour Organisation (ILO) documents the worldwide evidence from 2005 that the forty-hour limit is now statutory normal working time in a large number of countries (Sangheon, McCann, and Messenger 2007: 2, 20). As declared in the 1933 Working Time Directive, the EU clarifies that "the average working time for each seven-day period, including overtime, does not exceed 48 hours" (article 6).[22] In other words, the forty-eight-hour limit is enunciated as the maximum weekly working time. Furthermore, the Universal Declaration of Human Rights, article 24, states that "everyone has the right to rest and leisure, including reasonable limitation of working hours and periodic holidays with pay."[23] Despite all the aforesaid standards, no provision is set to govern the maximum working time for an employee in Hong Kong's employment legislation. In Hong Kong, it is merely a matter of agreement between the employer and the employee (Chan 2004). As a consequence, Hongkongers' actual working hours generally exceed the standard upheld by the ILO (precisely, by 21.8 percent in 2010). Based on the *State of Work-Life Balance in Hong Kong 2010 Survey* conducted by the Community Business, the report reveals that, on average, Hongkongers work 48.7 hours per week. The actual working hours are still climbing (cf. the 48.4 hours Hongkongers worked per week in 2009), despite the increase in the number of companies offering a five-day work week (from 35.0 percent in 2007 to 45.7 percent in 2010) (Ng 2011: 6; cf. Ng and Bernier 2009: 4). Second, numerous Hongkongers experience poor work-life-balance; three problems topped the list: (1) prolonged fatigue level; (2) lack of family time; and (3) work pressures with insomnia and poor diet (Ng 2011: 13, fig. 1). Third, Hongkongers' actual work-life ratio was 83:17 in 2010 in contrast to a preferred work-life ratio 61:39 (Ng 2011: 13, fig. 1). Professor Winton Au of the Chinese University of Hong Kong conducted a survey confirming that the median expected hours per week of Hongkongers is 44 hours—a long-lasting social norm in Hong Kong. In fact, Hong Kong employees work frequently up to 54 hours (Au 2011). A single illustration will suffice. A recent survey conducted by Frontline Doctors' Union, found that physicians were working, on average, 65 hours per week. More than one-tenth of them serve up to an 80- or even 100-hour week (Lee 2008; Ho 2011). But according to a Eurofound project published in 2008, the average weekly hours worked amounted to 37.8 hours in most EU countries, 38.8 hours in the US, and 41.7 hours in Japan (Demetriades and Pedersini 2008: 35).

In short, the global financial tsunami resulted in underemployment or unemployment, with thousands of people standing idle in the labor market. Paradoxically, other Hongkongers are persistently suffering from work overload and poor work-life balance.

GLOBAL STRUCTURAL POVERTY BUT NONE OF HONGKONGERS' BUSINESS?

Last, global structural poverty will be discussed in the Hong Kong context. As revealed in the *Human Development Report 2009*, the Gini Index of Hong Kong had already reached 43.4, having the most serious disparity between the rich and the poor among the thirty-eight most developed economies (see Panel on Welfare Services 2011).[24] This information has aroused public concern in Hong Kong. However, established international standards for defining poverty in context(s) must be locally qualified. Hong Kong should therefore adopt a benchmark tailor-made to our specific contexts. Apart from the Gini Index, Hong Kong's glocalized poverty can be viewed according to other measures. Traditionally, poverty is defined as "income poverty," using either an international standard (the USD 1.25-a-day poverty line) or a local one (UNDP 2010: 96). Thus, in the Hong Kong context, working-poor households refer to "those households with a monthly income below 50% of the median income of households of the same size and with at least one member working" (Panel on Welfare Services 2011: 1). For instance, in 2009, half of the median income of a one-person household was HKD 3,300, two-person HKD 6,750, three-person HKD 9,150, and four-person HKD 12,650. Today, this definition of "working-poor households" is still the most widely used measure of income poverty in Hong Kong. The Hong Kong Council of Social Service (HKCSS), using the same measure plus the size of unemployment, posited that the poverty rate kept increasing. According to the press release of HKCSS on September

27, 2009, it was 17.9% in the first half of 2009. In other words, about 1.236 million people are living under the Hong Kong poverty line.[25] Comparing with the 1.21 million under the poverty line in 2008, there was an increase of twenty thousand within only half a year's time (HKCSS 2009).[26] The poverty rate reached a new high in this "Asia's world city."

In addition to the Gini Index and the income poverty, the multidimensional measure of poverty becomes the new trend. In the *Human Development Report 2010*, the Multidimensional Poverty Index (MPI) is first introduced, aiming at identifying "overlapping deprivations suffered by households in health, education and living standards" (UNDP 2010: 86). Likewise, a set of twenty-four multidimensional poverty indicators, including eighteen life-cycle-based and six community-based poverty indicators, has been newly compiled in Hong Kong. Originally, the set aims at enabling "the public to better understand the extent of poverty in different age groups," and assessing "the effectiveness of measures in alleviation and preventing poverty" (Panel on Welfare Services 2011: 2). Discouragingly, this new, glocal set is covering up the size and the location of the neediest in Hong Kong. The "six indicators showed improvements [in 2009] in comparison with 2008" (Labour and Welfare Bureau 2009), which could alleviate our poverty problems, but the indicators do not reflect the actual severity of the poverty problems and have in fact just scratched the surface. The "effectiveness" in poverty alleviation provides an excuse for those ruling elites not handling the most acute problems. Most noticeably, our Hong Kong government has shown less satisfactory performance on alleviating elderly poverty in 2009 (Labour and Welfare Bureau 2009: 8–9). The middle class seems to be indifferent to poverty. The global multidimensionality of poverty revelation becomes a glocalizing excuse on urban poverty in Hong Kong.

The *Human Development Report 2010* reveals that about one-third of the population in the global village—that is, almost 1.75 billion people—experience multidimensional poverty. In addition, 1.44 billion people are suffering from less than USD 1.25 a day for their livelihood. Fifty-one percent of the multidimensional poor are Hongkongers' neighbors whose home is South Asia (UNDP 2010: 96–98). As UN Secretary-General Ban Ki-moon's saying goes, "We must not fail the billions who look to the international community to fulfill the promise of the Millennium Declaration for a better world. . . . Let us keep the promise" (UNDESA 2010: 78). Who cares about the promise? Is Hong Kong not better off taking an unsympathetic attitude toward global structural poverty? Indeed, only a few middle-class Hongkongers hear about or remember the Millennium Declaration (2000) (United Nations General Assembly 2000).

In a nutshell, all aforesaid aspects—globalization, the financial tsunami, long working hours, and structural poverty—have shown features of glocalization in the Hong Kong context. Before reading the chosen text (namely, Matthew 24–25) glocally in the Hong Kong context, this text will be briefly introduced in an ancient Roman imperial context.

ANALYSIS OF THE TEXT 1: TEXT IN ANCIENT ROMANIZATION CONTEXT

The Matthean apocalypse (Matthew 24–25) was not only a reception but also a contextual reading of the Markan apocalypse (Mark 13).[27] This enlarged discourse directly criticizes the uncritical attitude of the Matthean community toward the Roman imperial "gospel" and indirectly criticizes the Roman socioeconomic ideology.[28]

Starting at Matthew 24, the author begins building the fifth discourse in the Gospel.[29] This is Jesus' so-called eschatological discourse (Wenham 1984: 1).[30] According to the two-source theory, Matt. 24:1-44 basically adopts a Markan structure (Klostermann and Gressmann 1909: 319–33),[31] that is, Mark 13:1-37. Matthew 24:1-35 aligns with its Markan source. The unit announces an eschatological message, which the Roman Empire would not agree with. There was no way the empire could claim her fate according to the Matthean depiction. Thus the episode serves not only as a critique but also as a deconstruction of the Roman imperial discourse.

However, the author of Matthew has not entirely adopted the Markan apocalypse, altering the Markan content while preserving the basic idea of Mark 13:32-37. He modifies the content by three similes—the simile of the flood (Matt. 24:36-39), the simile of the rapture (Matt. 24:40-42), and the simile of the burglary (Matt. 24:43-44). The first two were most likely extracted from the Q source (Luke 17:26-27 and 17:34-35) (Luz 1997: 446. Also cf. Smith 2009: 99–116). Noticeably, Matt. 24:42 is a Matthean supplement to the Q material (cf. Luke 17:34-35). This supplement has reframed the rapture, which had been represented in a simile in the Q source, to a simile itself (Matt. 24:40-41). In other words, the parousia is the signified in all three cases, while the flood, the rapture, and the burglary are all similes. In addition to Matt. 24:43-44, the three similes call for building up risk consciousness. This calling is insightful, especially when the audience was living in such a strong empire.

Afterward, the author expanded the Markan apocalypse with three additional parables. Two of them—the parable of the faithful or the unfaithful slave (Matt. 24:45-51) and the parable of the three servants (Matt. 25:14-30)—parallel Luke 12:41-48 and Luke 19:11-27 respectively, and so are considered Q material.[32] In between these, the editor adds his unique material, the parable of the ten bridesmaids (Matt. 25:1-13). By means of the aforesaid three parables, the Markan eschatological scenario is enriched by Matthean decision-making alternatives in each parable. The focus is shifted from the End back to here and now. These three demand the audience's preparedness, for they are alerted to the return of Jesus. They should prepare themselves, as the empire was at risk.

At the last part of the entire discourse, the author concludes with another peculiar passage, the story of the sheep and the goats (Matt. 25:31-46). Taking this story alone into consideration, the readers could not have known whether any wicked person would be punished or not. What the text proclaimed to the intended readers was the sin of indifference. People were not called to prepare themselves alone. Instead, they had responsibilities for taking care of the needy in a "risk society."[33]

After the prolonged discourse, the passion narrative begins in Matthew 26. Jesus is on the way toward his chosen destiny. Thus Matthew 24–25 recalls Jesus' forecast of his own leave of absence. The theme—the awaiting of the lord's return—recurs throughout the entire Matthean discourse. In other words, the text aspires not to the sustained prosperity (or sustainability) of the Roman Empire, but to an alternative future.

This overview of the Matthean apocalypse is illustrated in table 1.[34]

Table 1: The Overview of the Matthean Apocalypse (Matthew 24–25)		
Scenario of Eschatological Signs 24:1–35		
Changeability: ideology critique		

Simile (I) 24:36–39 Flood	Simile (II) 24:40–42 Rapture	Simile (III) 24:43–44 Burglary
The Son of Man's arrival at unexpected hour	The Lord's arrival at unknown hour	The Son of Man's arrival at unexpected hour
Immediacy: necessity for building risk consciousness		
Social activities: daily or occasional	Social responsibility: male or female	
Living in a Risk Society: Everywhere at Risk		

	Risk negligence in daytime activities	Risk management in nighttime crimes
	Living in a Risk Society: 24-Hour At-Risk	
The Flood came	Left behind	(Property loss)
Risk consequence(s)		

Parable (1) 24:45–51 The Faithful or the Unfaithful Slave	Parable (2) 25:1–13 The Ten Bridesmaids	Parable (3) 25:14–30 The Three Servants
Absence of the master	Absence of the bridegroom	Absence of the master
Unpredictability: Necessity of Preparedness		
Early arrival of the master	Later arrival of the bridegroom	
Risk due to unpredictability of the arrival time (unpredictable duration of preparation)		
	Underestimation of the degree of preparedness	Overestimation of the degree of preparedness
	Risk due to unpredictability of the degree of preparedness	
Weeping and gnashing of teeth	The door is shut	Weeping and gnashing of teeth
Consequence of unpreparedness		

Story of the Sheep and the Goats at the Last Judgment 25:31–46
Sin of omission/sin of indifference in a risk society

Today, however, the Matthean apocalypse is filtered by those beneficiaries from global capitalism and has therefore mutated into a capitalistic form of Christian stewardship. Recently, in Hong Kong dozens of ad hoc books and articles have been published by Christian financial experts due to the global financial crisis. They all quote Matt. 25:14–30 in support of the stewardship principle at the heart of Western capitalism. Hong Kong middle-class churches' prevalent contextual reading of the Matthean apocalypse might have made ourselves one day subject to criticism from the suffering third world. Hong Kong's bourgeois society urgently needs an alternative contextual reading of Matthew 24–25, whether we are still amid the financial tsunami or in a post-financial-tsunami world or facing the coming of the so-called financial tsunami II.[35]

ANALYSIS OF THE TEXT 2: TEXT IN MODERN GLOCALIZATION CONTEXT

In this section, the alternative contextual reading of the Matthean apocalypse will be illustrated in accordance with its structural plot (see table 1). The entire illustration will be divided into four main subsections: (1) the scenario of eschatological signs (Matt. 24:1-35); (2) the three similes (Matt. 24:36-44); (3) the three parables (Matt. 24:45 – 25:30); and (4) the story of the sheep and the goats at the last judgment (Matt. 25:31-46). The four subsections will be discussed in an orderly manner, which correspond to the four aforementioned glocalization problems, namely, (1) globalization, (2) the financial tsunami, (3) long working hours, and (4) structural poverty.

CONTEXTUAL READING OF MATTHEW 24:1-35: CRITIQUE OF THE ECONOMIC GLOBALIZATION IDEOLOGY

For the post–AD 70 reader, Matt. 24:1-2 is perceived as Jesus' fulfilled prophecy (Green 2000: 249, 251; see also Hagner 1995b: 701–3).[36] He appears in the text as a prophet who can see the future (Davies and Allison 1997: 333). In some sense, the apophthegm is still valid today. Hongkongers may neither be interested in the fallen Jewish temple, nor believe in any religious, nonscientific prophecy. However, in the public domain, the entire Matthean apocalypse can be interpreted as a vision with futurological insights.[37] Undoubtedly, the ancient Jesus would not apply a quantitative approach to trend studies. Nevertheless, the Christians' reception of Jesus' prophecy was reinforced by their perception of the social trends in the imperial Roman history. From a futurological perspective, the ancient text might still be insightful in our glocalized economy.

Unlike those Markan readers, the Matthean disciples' concern was not only the fall of Jerusalem, but also the sign(s) of the parousia and the End (Gaston 1970).[38] Today, this latter concern is secularized and transformed into a quest for global sustainability.[39] In a modern context, both antiglobalists and alternative thinkers criticize globalization as an ideology harmful to sustainability.[40] In a similar way, Matt. 24:3 by implication criticizes Roman ideology. Thus the fall of Jerusalem indicates the problem of local sustainability within the Roman political economic system.

Noteworthy is the "gospel of the kingdom" in Matt. 24:14.[41] It depicts a catastrophic picture contrary to the ideological propaganda of the ruling authority. People should not uncritically trust Rome's "messianic" claims. The ruling ideology was denied because it resulted in military ambitions (Matt. 24:6), interethnic conflicts (Matt. 24:7a), international chaos (Matt. 24:7b), human-induced calamities (Matt. 24:7c), natural disasters (Matt. 24:7d), persecution of minorities (Matt. 24:9), interpersonal hatred (Matt. 24:10), higher crime rate (Matt. 24:12a), undermining universal value (Matt. 24:12b), cultural heritage damage (Matt. 24:15), and loss of homeland (Matt. 24:16-22).[42] Thus the "gospel" has an unmasking power. It could thus function as an antithesis to the Roman ideology at that time and to any other ideology in history.[43] In our case, globalization comes to the fore. This does not mean that all antiglobalization movements deserve the title of the "gospel." As in the past, some messianic movements should not be counted as "messianic" (Matt. 24:4-5, 23-26) (Davies and Allison 1997: 338–39; Senior 1998: 267). What the "gospel" really means is "critical" in nature—a critique to other critiques, an antithesis to other antitheses.

At the end of Matt. 24:1-35, the changeability of a political economy (in this case, *Imperium Romanum*) comes into question (see table 1). The text depicts an ultimate scenario of the sudden, dramatic coming of the Son of Man. Up to now, the literal fulfillment of the scenario has not yet come true. But it has already served as a social-historical relief for the Matthean community. Being kept in their collective memory, the (western) ruling power was so super that those (eastern) revolutionaries had become corpses (Carter 2003).[44] The memory was visualized in the text: the eagles will gather wherever the corpse is (Matt. 24:28).[45] The scene may refer to the destruction of the temple or Jerusalem in 70 CE (Green 2000: 252–53. Cf. Reicke 1972: 121–34; Davies and Allison 1997: 338–39).[46] Nonetheless, the message is that no superpower is too super. The Son of Man, who also comes from the East (Matt. 24:27), is even more powerful, and consequently, the worldwide Roman political economy cannot resist the divine change (Matt. 24:27, 29-31). Hope of change gives reason for endurance under the evil superpower (Matt. 24:32-35). Is such a guarantee applicable to our modern case of world capitalism? The Son of Man has not yet returned, and hence it is legitimate for any global loser to identify himself or herself with the "generation" (Matt. 24:34) who hopes for the arrival and those corresponding changes. Every generation should indeed believe that no existing political economic system is unchangeable. Is the transcendental vision just a utopia or "opium" for the losers? At least, the vision declares the ethical standpoint of transcendence and thus marks a judgmental standard for Hongkongers, who may not be direct losers in the unfair global competitions.

In light of the foregoing discussion, Hong Kong middle-class churches should not uncritically conform ourselves to the economic globalization ideology. We should rediscover our unmasking power and revive our critical nature. In a few words, Matt. 24:1-35 serves as an ideological critique (see table 1).

CONTEXTUAL READING OF MATTHEW 24:36-44: ECHO OF THE FINANCIAL TSUNAMI IN A RISK SOCIETY AND AWAKENING OF THE MIDDLE CLASS

Apart from the unmasking power, we should regain our risk consciousness during a modernization (or postmodernization) process. The three similes—the simile of the flood (Matt. 24:36-39), the simile of the rapture (Matt. 24:40-42), and the simile of the burglary (Matt. 24:43-44)—have a common theme: the immediacy of the parousia (Matt. 24:36, 39, 42, 44). People seem to have no readiness for any change in life. They engage in daily social activities (for example, meals) as usual (Matt. 24:38a). They are also accustom to any occasional social gathering (for example, the wedding in Matt. 24:38b). Each gender has been socialized to take up his or her social responsibility in a society (Matt. 24:40-41). Life is so ordinary. The "eschatological" event of the three similes says the opposite: stability is not the true picture of Roman society. The society is at risk, for the Son of Man or the Lord can end it unexpectedly. In this sense, everywhere (Matt. 24:36-39, 40-42) and at every time (Matt. 24:40-42, 43-44), there are hidden "risks" if people would like to pursue a stable life in the Roman world. Risk consciousness should be built up. The discussion above has already been summarized in table 1. Now let us go further. Is modern society safer than the ancient one? Hongkongers hope so. Two core values—stability and prosperity—serve as standards of our Hong Kong bourgeois society and middle-class churches. Actually, as Niklas Luhmann tells us, aiming at complexity reduction, system differentiation becomes characteristic of modern society (Luhmann 1977: 9–71). Modernity does not equal risk minimization. As Ulrich Beck's saying goes, we are now living in a risk society. His *Weltrisikogesellschaft* differentiates several types of global risks, including ecological risk, financial risk, terrorism risk, and biographical risk (Beck 2007: 37). Hong Kong is by no means exceptional.

In accordance with the three similes, risk in the mind of Matthew's audience has at least three forms: (1) natural catastrophe, for example, flood

(Matt. 24:39); (2) divine intervention, for example, rapture (Matt. 24:40, 41); and (3) human-induced calamities or loss, for example, burglary (Matt. 24:43). In other words, risk is either caused by nature, by God, or by human beings. The Hong Kong public may not accept divine intervention as a universal explanation for risk. In addition, severe natural catastrophes hardly occur in Hong Kong. Human-induced loss is our main concern. Due to the relatively low crime rate in Hong Kong, her citizens generally have no great fear of personal evil, for example, burglary, robbery, and so on. But structural evil endangers us. Our economy relies too much on the financial sector. Under the recent financial crisis all over the world, we feel our vulnerability in the global village. Our economy cannot be listed among those most seriously damaged. However, the crisis has an impact on us collectively at a social-psychological level. Our relatively higher frequency of naming the global crisis as a "financial tsunami" reflects the impact. Hongkongers have a great fear of this economic flooding, so that the text echoes our glocal anxiety.

Does the text only function as an echo? While Matt. 24:40-42 illustrates risk negligence, Matt. 24:43-44 may put an emphasis on risk management (see table 1). Normally, risk management means loss avoidance or damage control. At first glance, loss or damage refers to flood, separation, or burglary in the text. Then the problem arises: Why does the text make an analogy of the Son of Man's arrival (a positive event, at least from the Christians' point of view) with these destructive images? Whoever belongs to one of the beneficiaries from the Roman political economic system, he or she may conform to the dominant ideology uncritically for the sake of risk management. Finally, he or she will experience loss at the time of the Lord's arrival. Unless he or she stayed awake for the awaiting of the Son of Man, the antithesis to the Roman imperial ideology, he or she will be the loser at the final stage. For Hongkongers, risk management means keeping alert to one's own properties and investments. However, the text (Matt. 24:43-44) alerts us: the Son of Man can act as if a thief against our possessions (See Stanley 2002; Fletcher-Louis 1998). To avoid this, now we need to discern who the "thief" is in the world of capitalism (Nielsen 1992). The suggested answer is this: whoever plays the capitalistic game unfairly, he or she is the "thief" against others' possessions. Furthermore, is the game's structure itself a "thief" in the third world?

In brief, Hong Kong middle-class churches exist in a risk society, together with other Hongkongers. The global financial tsunami, especially the glocal "Hong Kong Lehman Brothers crisis," brings worries to numerous Hongkongers. We should echo our neighbors' anxiety. Even more important, we need to reflect on how economic globalization takes the act of burglary against millions and millions of third world neighbors.

CONTEXTUAL READING OF MATTHEW 24:45—25:30:
ACTIONS AND REACTIONS TO GLOCALIZATION PROBLEMS

Similar to the three similes, the three parables—the parable of the faithful (Matt. 24:45-51), the parable of the ten bridesmaids (Matt. 25:1-13), and the parable of the three servants (Matt. 25:14-30)—also have their own coherencies: absence of the host (Harrington 1991b). All of them show the necessity of preparedness during the awaiting of the master or the bridegroom (see table 1). The text calls for human actions in the interim period. Alternative life philosophies are juxtaposed for the comparison of their destinies. In aid of implicit speech-act force, all three parables urge every audience or reader to opt for his or her own mode of living. In the Roman society, most Matthean community members belonged to the lower class such as slaves and maids. Even so, the text reminds them their freedom despite the limitation, either faithful or wicked (Matt. 24:45 vs. 24:48), wise or foolish (Matt. 25:2b vs. 25:2a), trustworthy or lazy (Matt. 25:21, 23 vs. 25:26). At last, their final appraisals will be given by the coming Lord rather than their earthly hosts. The modern middle class in Hong Kong can definitely enjoy far greater freedom than those ancient slaves. In a pluralistic Hong Kong society, everyone can pursue his or her own lifestyle. Nonetheless, the text speaks to us: we must lead a responsible life in a glocalized society.

Comparing the first parable, the faithful or unfaithful slave, with the second parable, the ten bridesmaids, both (wicked) slaves and (foolish) bridesmaids encounter risk due to unpredictability of the host's arrival time (see table 1). On the one hand, the texts dealt with a problem of the earliest Christian communities, that is, the uncertain time of parousia. On the other hand, they handled a dilemma between freedom and responsibility. Ancient slaves pursued or even fought for their freedom (Bradley 1989; Strauss 2009). Frequently, they experienced no freedom to do (or not to do) whatever they liked. The life of Roman slavery or of the lower class was neither calculable beforehand nor fully controllable by oneself (Joshel 2010; Ulrike Roth 2010). In spite of the lack of freedom, the two texts warned them that they should keep in their mind a persistent responsibility, which was accountable not only to their earthly host but also to the divine one (see Matt. 25:13). Unlike those ancient slaves, Hongkongers enjoy our own autonomy. Regardless of autonomy, we still generally lack persistent commitment. One-off economic behavior (for instance, using disposable utensils, upgrading electronic devices in a very short period, and so on) characterizes Hong Kong culture. Are we aware how ecologically unfriendly our one-off glocal behavior is? Responsible commitment in terms of earth sustainability should not be one-off, but persistent.

Next, let us compare the second parable with the third one. Both (foolish) bridesmaids and (lazy) servants are under risk because of the unpredictability of the degree of preparedness (see table 1). As a result, both parties have too few in preparations. Undoubtedly, Roman slaves were very vulnerable to punishment, due to the inestimable demand of their earthly hosts. In spite of this, they had no right of excusing their own inactiveness. In fact, the text deals with how the earliest Christian communities prepared for the parousia. The Matthean community should be very enthusiastic for preparing the coming of the divine host. Nowadays, do Hongkongers also show essential zealousness in preserving earth sustainability?

The discussions above illustrate how the three parables challenge Hongkongers—that is, persistent responsibility and essential zealousness for the benefits of earth sustainability. Now we turn our questioning to the texts.

In the third parable, the *talanta* can be interpreted in association with economic activities. The association is obvious when the master queries why the slave did not invest his money with the bankers for the purpose of earning interest (Matt. 25:27). In this parable, the unbalanced distribution and reward (that is, five, two, and one talents) is intended to motivate the reader to be faithful to the master. The apparent result is: the rich become richer and the poor become poorer (Folarin 2008), which in turn supports prosperity theology. Literally speaking, this parable seems to justify wealth accumulation or to reinforce the mechanism of economic globalization. This kind of capitalistic interpretation, however, covers up the dark side of glocalization.

In fact, the parable is not really attractive to modern readers, particularly Hongkongers, for there are no true rewards; the master is the only one who gains capital and interest. What the first two servants get after their faithful work is just more and more obligations without gaining more payment. In a contextual reading, the case would be quite similar to the experience of Hongkongers: the workers become more overloaded or need to work overtime, but their wages keep decreasing. Hongkongers do not experience any incentives for recognizing our contributions, but just an excuse for structural exploitation by wealthy entrepreneurs. The rules of the capitalistic game legitimate such exploitations. In contrast, a contextual reading sympathizes with the third servant, that is, the servant with one talent. He is like a Hongkonger who is not as competitive as other workers and is then fired for poor performance.

In the first parable, rewarding the faithful slave with more obligations may be perceived as more evidence of exploitation (Matt. 24:47). Furthermore, in Matt. 24:49, Hongkongers see the wicked slave beating his fellow slaves. The parable does not provide enough information for further interpretation. But the slave's awareness of the delay of his master seems to be a crucial point (Matt. 24:48). We cannot explain his psychological change, but he definitely has no right to commit this act. Only his master does. In other words, he performs the role of the master. If such an interpretation is feasible, it also reflects one of our glocalization problems. Middle-class employers subconsciously abuse their foreign domestic helpers in Hong Kong when they perform the role of an employer. News about foreign domestic helpers being emotionally, physically, or even sexually abused can sometimes be heard.

Last, the master of the last parable is never concerned about where the other two servants got their interest, or more precisely, who would be the debtors of the bankers. We could imagine the debtors should be those who were in need of money, and most probably, they were the peasants. Originally, the peasants hoped to get rid of their poverty, and so they became debtors. But the social-historical vicious cycle was that the peasants often could not escape the poverty merely because of their debt. From this perspective, we may construct a critique of the structural evil of the political economy.

CONTEXTUAL READING OF MATTHEW 25:31-46: FROM GLOCALIZATION PROBLEMS TO GLOBALIZATION CARE

Sin(s) of omission (or so-called sins of indifference) in a risk society equates to the keynote of "the story of the sheep and the goats at the last judgment" (Matt. 25:31-46; see table 1). However, in the *Wirkungsgeschichte* ("history of effects") of the story, Leo Tolstoy (1828–1910) rewrote a short novel, *Where Love Is, God Is* (1885) based on it. The short novel cites the passages, "I was an hungered, and ye gave Me meat: I was thirsty, and ye gave Me drink: I was a stranger, and ye took Me in"[47] (Matt. 25:35) and "inasmuch as ye have done it unto one of the least of these My brethren, ye have done it unto Me"[48] (Matt. 25:40), without its counterpart, that is, Matt. 25:41-45.[49] Though the author successfully highlights the imminent presence of Jesus as reward to the righteous, the sin of omission was unfortunately lost sight of during the history of reception. If the sin of omission was not the keynote, it would be redundant in the Matthean passage. Furthermore, Tolstoy's imminent presence of Jesus can be understood as a positive reinforcement to the righteous, while the Matthean separation of the sheep from the goats in the last judgment condemns those who show apathy toward others. Noteworthy is that those being condemned are not the evildoers, but are merely indifferent to the needy.

As global villagers, Hongkongers may learn from the story to beware of the sin of omission toward our neighbors all over the world. We cannot presume that every Hongkonger will be encouraged to do charity by seeing the fate of the sheep or the punishment of the goats. The awareness of the sin of omission summons our moral conscience toward the glocal losers and the global victims.

Conclusion and Contextual Reflections

To summarize, in Matt. 24:1-35, Jesus criticizes the materialistic temple in light of obvious, eschatological signs. Does the canonical text not criticize Hong Kong middle-class churches from paying too much attention to our "temple" (for example, church buildings, church growth, and so on) but too little concern to global trends? Today, the traditional apocalyptic discourses should be upgraded to empirical, scientific forecasts, with religious concerns always in sight. If Hongkongers may have any standpoint in world capitalism, let us stand by those global victims! For their good sake, we should keep earth sustainability in mind. It is a secularized concept of the parousia. The parousia has not occurred yet. Is the disciples' ideologically critical question concerning the End also meaningful for Hong Kong middle-class churches? If our answer is no, does it mean that we are ideologically blind? Should global sustainability not be discussed as a higher priority of our church agenda?[50] Should the dark side of the economic globalization not be unmasked among us?

It is noteworthy that Matt. 24:36-44 is not talking about the poor, but those who have properties (Matt. 24:43) and lead a stable life (Matt. 24:38, 40, 41). In the modern case, they are more or less equated with the middle class. Like those figures in the text, the middle class lives in a society with hidden risks everywhere and at all times. Like other Hongkongers, Hong Kong middle-class churches have the same fear of financial tsunami (that is, the modern flood). That's why we play the game of risk management (that is, being alert to "burglary") like the first world. Our end justifies our means: we need to maintain our churches' financial sources. Throughout the past, we have already learned well the survival tactics of playing the global investment game. When we have no reflection on the dark side of world capitalism, the Son of Man will come to us, as if he were a thief. In the modern world, the metaphor can proclaim an ironic warning to those who plunder the third world as if an act of burglary of another's homeland.

How do Hong Kong middle-class churches act and react to the problems of glocalization? Traditionally, we prefer the teaching of stewardship (Matt. 25:14-30), which in turn makes us submissive to the rules of the capitalistic game (Sirico 2000). Other Christian financial experts may take an aggressive approach to the interpretation of the text. This approach legitimates the investment activities of our churches or of individual Christians. However, we seldom recognize the structural evil resulting from workload and overtime problems. Academic institutions should be subsidized and professionals should team up to do critical research on and against the dark sides of world capitalism. But churches show very little interest in reflecting on the existing political economy. Undoubtedly, churches, like the world, sometimes exploit our employees too.

To a certain extent, Hong Kong middle-class churches can be proud of our involvements in numerous local, regional, and worldwide social welfare programs. These contributions should not be neglected, but Matt. 25:31-46 reminds us from another perspective. Are there any shadows in our glocalized Hong Kong or in other parts of the global village to which our churches have seldom paid attention? If we do not reach out to those glocal losers or global victims, are we committing the sin of omission? If we neglect their needs or marginalize them, does it mean that our social contribution serves only as a window dressing for the ideology of economic globalization?

With the alternative contextual teaching of the Matthean apocalypse, Hong Kong middle-class churches can be revitalized as one of the proactive forces of social change in this glocalized society and even her motherland—China—which is economically growing but still in a societal mess. Indeed, this apocalypse as a whole echoes the felt needs and emotional insecurity of Hong Kong's bourgeois society and middle-class churches. We are suffering from economic globalization and glocalization. Unfortunately, we are also "left," "evil," "foolish," "lazy," and "cursed," but not because we are intrinsically so. Instead, we will be labeled in this way if we are still uncritical toward world capitalism, unprepared for any reformation or even revolution and immobilized to act as an ideologically critical force in the glocalized context. Finally, if we stay unchanged before the "eschaton," we will experience "double sufferings"—financially, under glocalization, and from our conscience, by being accused by the suffering third world.

Notes

1. "Glocalization" can also be defined as "internal globalization" (see Roudometof 2005).

2. In this paper, "Hongkonger" and "Hongkongese" are synonyms. To a certain extent, Hongkongers' "global consciousness" can be categorized in the so-called third wave of globalization (Robertson 2003: 169–270).

3. "(Economic) globalization" has been a buzzword since the 1990s. It is defined "as a process of widening, deepening, and speeding up of worldwide interconnectedness, particularly in the economic sphere" (Held et al. 1999: 2). "While definitions of globalization vary, at the most abstract level it can be defined as the aggregate of historical changes that cut across the boundaries of the states, societies, cities, and regions. These include the world-wide supply of standardized images, cultural icons. . . . Connections of all sorts across the planet not only become increasingly dense but, in the extreme, instantaneous. In this sense, satellite communication and financial transactions are the most advanced representatives of accomplished globalization. In short, flows count, boundaries recede" (Immerfall and von Hagen 1998: 1–2).

4. Global victims refer to those anonymous losers in globalization; see Anspach, , Blanc, and Bessieres 2001.

5. Concerning "alternative future(s)" one can read Stiglitz 2006.

6. The history of interpretation of the Matthean apocalypse is briefly summarized in Luz 1997: 411–18. Up to now, the eschatological approach has been very common. Just recently, however, futurology (the study of projecting probable, possible, and preferable futures) can be perceived as a new religious movement (see Amarasingam 2008: 1–16). This paper suggests that futurology can also shed light on ancient apocalyptic literature.

7. The term *governance* "is used increasingly by both analysts and practitioners to denote the intentional pursuit of shared goals by any group of actors, which may or may not include governments, whereas 'international' or 'global' governance is used to describe the pursuit of such shared goals by actors across national boundaries" (Pollack and Shaffer 2001: 287). In ancient societies, "risk" mainly referred to natural disasters; while modern societies are exposed to insecurities due to the consequence of modernization, such as financial crisis, pollution, etc. See Beck 2007: 6–9.

8. For similar methodology, see Chia 2009: 75–108; cf. Leveque 2009.

9. Concerning global crises, one can read, for instance, Spoor 2004.

10. Global marketing with a local vision can be termed as "glocal marketing."

11. HKSAR is the abbreviated form of "Hong Kong Special Administrative Region." "Big market, small government" was announced in the Economic Summit on "China's 11th Five-Year Plan and the Development of Hong Kong," which was held on September 11, 2006 (Monday), in Hong Kong (see Tsang 2011).

12. Tony Smith argues against "capitalist globalisation," but for a Marxian model of "socialist globalisation" (Smith 2006: 15–163, 296–344). Despite Smith's insights, socialist globalization is not the stance of this paper.

13. "Evangelical capitalism," which was coined by Abbas J. Ali, refers to "a form of capitalism that celebrates unfettered freedom of corporations in the national economy and is zealously promoted to other nations as the Savior of humanity, with complete disregard for the desires of people in developing countries and their lawful insights over their resources and properties" (Ali 2009: 133).

14. Methodologically, scenario planning or mapping can be used to anticipate futures and generate scenarios, which is what is meant by "alternative futures" in this paper (see Sumner, Ballantyne, and Curry 2010).

15. Alan Greenspan, the former chairman of the U.S. Federal Reserve, said that the global financial crisis (2008–2009) had "turned out to be much broader than anything that [he] could have imagined," and he called it a "once-in-a-century credit tsunami." See David Nason, "'I Made a Mistake,' Admits Alan Greenspan," *The Australian*, 25 October 2008.

http://www.theaustralian.com.au/business/opinion/i-made-a-mistake-says-greenspan/story-e6frg9mf-1111117848644.

16. The Hong Kong unemployment rate returned to 3.6 percent in December 2010–February 2011 (HKSAR 2011).

17. Regarding "offshore renminbi market," it refers to a platform for building up demand for China's official currency as an international currency for trade settlement and investment purposes (see Chan 2011).

18. Two noticeable types of social activists have tried to enact alternative public discourses in Hong Kong recently. One is the so-called Post-80s phenomenon, while the other comes from Hong Kong social enterprises. Both are still gaining momentum. See Chang, Ng, and Chan 2010; Ng 2010).

19. Hong Kong underemployment rate fell to 1.7 percent in December 2010–February 2011 (see HKSAR 2011).

20. Gloria Lai, "HK Staff Work Some of Longest Hours In World"; also cf. Agnes Lam, "HK Fifth Worst on Global Work-hours Scale," in *South China Morning Post*, 18 July 2008. http://www.scmp.com/article/645727/hk-fifth-worst-global-work-hours-scale. HKCTU's so-called "5th Ranking in Weekly Working Hours" seems inaccurate. Anyway, "[Hongkongers] work some of longest hours in world" is still a valid claim.

21. Since 1930, the scope was "extended to cover all but agricultural workers by the adoption of the Hours of Work (Commerce and Offices) Convention, 1930 (No. 30)," (Sangheon, McCann, and Messenger 2007: 8). Concerning "eight-hours per day," the classic monograph is Rae 1894.

22. Available from http://www.eu-working-directive.co.uk/directives/2003-working-time-directive.htm.

23. Available from http://www.un.org/en/documents/udhr/index.shtml#a24.

24. Concerning the thirty-eight very high human development economies, particularly the Gini Index of Hong Kong, see UNDP 2009: 195.

25. Including 714,000 persons living in households with income below the average Comprehensive Social Security Assistance (CSSA) payments (see Panel on Welfare Services 2011: 3).

26. Detailed report is available from http://www.hkcss.org.hk/cm/cc/press/documents/2009poverty.doc.

27. This paper does not investigate whether there was a pre-Synoptic tradition of Matthew 24–25 (see Wenham 1984: 373). What this paper concerns is a "contextual" reading of any pre-Matthean tradition of the Matthean apocalypse.

28. Concerning the Matthean community, the first Gospel alters Mark's audience of Jesus' apocalyptic discourse from a single disciple (Mark 1:1) and afterward four disciples (Mark 1:3) to the entire community of the "disciples" (Matt. 24:1) (see Senior 1998: 266). The Matthean apocalypse is an expanded form of Mark 13 (Hare 2009: 273).

29. The discourse is characterized by the customary concluding formula of Matt. 26:1. See Bacon 1930.

30. Matthew 24–25 are also termed "the Olivet Discourse" (Boice 2001: 500) or "the Sermon on the Mount of Olives" (Boice 2001: 497).

31. Klostermann and Gressmann comment verse by verse on Matthean sources.

32. Whether Matt. 25:14-30 came from a Q source is disputable. See the discussion of Weiser 1971: 227–58. However, whether the passage belongs to Q does not affect the interpretation here overall.

33. Regarding "risk society," see n7.

34. Table 1 shows its own originality of structural analysis. Concerning traditional analysis, see, e.g., Sibinga 1975.

35. Both "post-financial tsunami" and "financial tsunami II" are common internet terms. "Financial tsunami II" refers to the so-called second wave of the financial tsunami 2008–2009; for instance, see Chang 2011.

36. Hagner argues against the stance of *vaticinium ex eventu*. However, neither the futurist nor the preterist interpretation is the concern of this paper. If the Gospel of Matthew was ever circulated in the post-70 era, the reader could understand the text as Jesus' fulfilled prophecy, regardless of the date of composition.

37. Traditionally, the Matthean apocalypse can be understood ethically in light of "utopia" imagination (see Gnilka 1989: 464–81). However, "futurological" here refers to social trends rather than mere imagination.

38. However, the interaction between the fall of Jerusalem and the Matthean apocalypse is not Gaston's focus of research. Cf. Luz 1997: 420.

39. Concerning "global sustainability," one can read Schellnhuber et al. 2010; Schweickart 2009.

40. This paper does not stand absolutely with antiglobalists. In other words, the Matthean apocalypse could also be interpreted from the perspective of alternative globalization(s) (see Hosseini 2010).

41. Scholars normally concern the global nature of missional audience of this verse (see Ulrich 2007: 64–83).

42. "Human-induced calamities" refers to "famine," while "undermining universal value" corresponds to "most people's love will grow cold." "Cultural heritage damage" points to the destruction of the Jewish temple in this case. "The abomination that causes desolation" (NIV) may refer to "the attempted desecration by Caligula (40 c.e.), to the destruction of the Temple itself . . . or to a future 'eschatological defilement' associated with the anti-Christ" (Gurtner 2008: 147).

43. Warren Carter posits that the Gospel of Matthew comprises numerous counter narratives against the "Roman Imperial Theology" (Carter 2000: 466–97; 2001: 2–3, 20–53 in particular). Cf. Chan 2007: 109–214.

44. I do agree with Carter's findings that "the eagles in Matt. 24:28 refer to Rome and its military power" (Carter 2003: 477). His question—"What is the relationship of these eagles to the 'corpse'?" (Carter 2003: 477)—sounds great, but his answer is imprecise (Carter 2003: 468: Carter argues "that the scene depicts the Roman army, symbolized by the eagles . . . , destroyed in the final eschatological battle when Jesus, Son of Man, returns to judge the Roman imperial order."). Hence, I try to verbalize here the underlying presupposition of the text.

45. Undoubtedly, the eagle was a visual symbol of Roman imperial power, in spite of the common translation of the noun as "vultures." Hence, "eagles" is a preferable translation in this case. See Carter 2001: 87.

46. Reicke rejects any Matthean reference to the fall of Jerusalem in 70 ce.

47. Leo Tolstoy, *The Forged Coupon & Other Stories by Leo Tolstoy* (Rockville, MD: Arc Manor, 2008), 75.

48. Ibid.

49. Despite the long history of interpretation of Matt. 25:31-46, Matt. 25:41-45 is seldom discussed. As a consequence, "sin of omission" is downplayed in comparison with other ethical challenges of the story. See Donahue 1986. Even Donahue does not discuss "sin of omission" in his article.

50. For recent discussion on public theology about sustainability, see Jenkins 2008.

12

Resist No Evil and Save No Money

*Reading the Sermon on the Mount for a Christian Social-
Economic Ethics in China*

John Yieh

The Sermon on the Mount (Matthew 5–7) contains Jesus' major teachings on varied spheres of human life, including social relations and economic behavior. Consequently, it is sometimes considered "the Magna Carta of the Kingdom of God," presenting the way of God in direct opposition to the way of the world, especially as manifested in mammonism, violence, and power (Ragaz 1945: 7–9, 78–85, 132–49). As a new powerhouse in the global economy, the flourishing nation of China is facing the same challenges of greed, corruption, exploitation, and inequality that accompany economic success in industrialized nations and capitalist societies. Reading the Sermon on the Mount vis-à-vis China's social challenges in a booming economy, several questions on text, context, and their interactions can be raised for hermeneutical reflection. Is Jesus' teaching conditioned by and therefore limited to the peasant society in first-century Palestine? Can his provocative ideals be applied to a Chinese socialist society and a transitioning market economy? Can his Jewish apocalyptic worldview be understood in an atheist nation thriving in a postmodern world? If yes, how can a contextual reading of Jesus' teaching be properly interpreted to address China's social dilemma? What impact can such a cross-cultural appropriation have?

To answer these application questions, this paper attempts to launch a dialectical reading of the Sermon on the Mount and China's social-economic issues, allowing Matthew's text and China's context to converse, enlighten, interrogate, and challenge each other. Such a dialectical reading, I believe, may shed light on some overlooked meanings of the Sermon on the Mount and demonstrate how Jesus' ancient wisdom may address modern issues in transforming ways. To enable a deep-level dialogue, both the ancient biblical text and the Chinese social contexts need to be carefully examined. Because the Sermon on the Mount has been interpreted in multiple ways in the West, a "history-of-effects" (*Wirkungsgeschichte*) examination of this influential text, focusing on Matt. 5:38-48 and 6:19-34, will be executed to show how the rich and broad implications of Jesus' kingdom ethics have fared in the West and how they may or may not serve as useful spiritual resources for ethical reflection on the social-economic issues confronting China today. Because the Chinese ethos is shaped by a confluence of Confucian culture, the Chinese style of socialism, the market-oriented economy, and nationally planned programs, a brief analytical description of the current Chinese society is also in order before the cross-examination of the text and the context can be started. My goal is to see how Jesus' radical teaching on loving enemies and trusting God, both of which are fundamental in Christian moral vision, may contribute to China's effort to construct new social norms for the economic order. Last, it is hoped that this contextual reading of the Sermon on the Mount may yield valuable insights and raise new questions for the Christian West to engage in honest theological self-reflection on social ethics and economic justice in capitalist societies.

DIALECTICAL READING: ONE TEXT AND MANY CONTEXTS

Contextual biblical interpretation presupposes that a biblical text makes sense only in context. As I see it, in order to understand and interpret a biblical text properly, three distinguishable contexts need to be taken into account. First is the original context, in which and for which the text was written. In the case of the Sermon on the Mount (SM), this first context involves the reasons and purposes of Matthew the Evangelist who compiled Jesus' sayings and the capacities and conditions of his intended readers in late first century. New Testament scholars have developed several critical methods, such as historical criticism, rhetorical criticism, and sociological approaches, in seeking to recover this first context.

Second is the new context, in which new readers at later times try to understand, explain, and appropriate a biblical text for their own purposes that may be different from those of the author's. In the case of the SM, this new context involves the preachers, theologians, or any interested readers today who want to see how Jesus' radical ideas may counsel or challenge their views and their lives in the twenty-first century. Many recent ideological criticisms, such as liberation-theological, feminist, and postcolonial critiques of the Bible focus precisely on the new readers and their experiences in specific contexts. With these two distinctive contexts in mind, biblical scholars often assume that once a sound exegetical study of the biblical text in its first context is honestly and competently done, one can readily transplant the meanings they have methodically excavated from the text into the "here and now" for theological, spiritual, and moral applications or ideological critiques. The original and the new contexts are so different from each other that scholars have tried to bridge the two with such ideas as the "fusion of horizons" (Gadamer 1989: 300–307) or the "hermeneutical circle" (Schleiermacher 1997: 112–13). All these credible efforts notwithstanding, there is one problem; namely, biblical scholars and hermeneuticians seem to assume that nothing significant has happened in the vast gaps of time and culture in the past millennia between the biblical text and today's readers.

What has often been overlooked is the third context, the various historic contexts in the history of interpretation. These historic contexts give rise to several influential interpretive traditions, such as Augustine in the Roman Catholic Church, John Chrysostom in the Orthodox Church, and Martin Luther in the Protestant Church. For their followers, these interpretations function as what Gadamer calls the "effective historical consciousness" (*wirkungsgeschichtliches Bewusstsein*) (Gadamer 1989: 341–79) or common tradition and collective knowledge, which enables them to understand and communicate with each other. These influential interpreters have indeed shaped the hermeneutical presuppositions of many readers today. In order to be conscious of and conscientious about one's hermeneutical prejudice as a reader and to learn from influential interpretations mindful of their historical consequences, a "history-of-effects" (*Wirkungsgeschichte*) approach, persuasively advocated by Ulrich Luz (Luz 1994; 2005: 333–69), deserves to be taken. When a reader embarks on a contextual reading of the biblical text, it would be prudent, therefore, to envision a stream of contexts in which the text is explained and a surplus of meaning exposed, beginning with the original context of the author and its intended readers, followed by a series of historic contexts in the history of interpretation, and ending in the new context in which the reader here and now tries to make sense of the text for his or her purposes.

A contextual reading should not be a one-way street, simply searching for useful meanings in biblical text to address the issues in modern context that the reader sees fit. Nor is it appropriate to simply assert the reader's ideological high ground, to critique or subvert the meaning of the biblical text, which remains a one-way street, only in the opposite direction. Rather, to engage in a contextual reading, readers should be willing to enter a tug-of-war with the text in its various contexts, so that the abundant meanings of the text and the multiple implications for the contexts can all be explored and examined as they try to understand and appropriate the meanings of the text for new contexts. A contextual reading should therefore be a dialectical process of interactions between the reader and (1) the text in its original context, (2) the text in its historic contexts, and finally (3) the text in its new context here and now. The historic contexts are particularly helpful, because they provide examples and correctives to help a present-day reader make proper interpretations of the text for his or her new context.

A History-of-Effects Review

Before attempting a contextual reading of the SM in dialogue with the social-economic contexts of China, we will review two of Jesus' most controversial sayings—resisting no evil and saving no money—to see how they have been interpreted in some historic contexts in the West (see Yieh 2007: 21–24). Having become integral parts of a rich tradition of the SM, these historic interpretations remain widely influential in Christian ethics.

"Resist no evil" (Matthew 5:39)

Jesus' saying "resist no evil" (5:39) is followed by "love your enemies" (5:44) and found at the end of the so-called antitheses of the SM. Both sayings concern personal relationship. They overturn the conventions of proportional retaliation ("an eye for an eye and a tooth for a tooth," 5:38; cf. Exod. 21:24; Lev. 24:20; Deut. 19:21) and fair reciprocity ("love your neighbor and hate your enemy," 5:43; cf. Lev 19:18 lxx; Deut 7:2). These two counterintuitive sayings have often been considered distinctive of Christian moral ideals, and have inspired Gandhi's nonresistance revolution against the British colonization and Martin Luther King's nonviolence campaign for civil rights in the United States. Even with these stunning examples, Christians often ask: "Should we not resist evildoers in defense of the innocent? Is it wise to show weakness before our enemies? Why should we love murderers or terrorists and pray for them? And if we do, what shall we pray?"

In history, resisting no evil and loving enemies have been interpreted in opposite ways as social contexts change, with far-reaching affects on church relations with the state. In the first three centuries, Christians were a minority in the Roman Empire, with no claim to legal rights. Submissive endurance and willing martyrdom were their quiet but inspiring witness to the kingdom of God, a different order than Caesar's. After the conversion of the emperor Constantine (318 ce), Christians began to find themselves in the position of political authority. Suddenly, they were responsible for public decisions. With the change of social location, the church faced a new question. How were they to reconcile the teaching of "nonresistance" and "loving enemies" (Matthew 5) with the state's responsibility for justice and the sword (Romans 13)? As one response, Augustine proposed a "just war" theory (Augustine 1972: 843–94, esp. chs. 7, 12; cf. Thomas Aquinas, *Summa Theologica* 1947: 1359; Cahill 1994: 55–80). When necessary and appropriate, force can be used, in proportion and as the last resort, to resist evildoers and to fight enemies. Vowing to take back the Holy City, however, the Crusaders did not heed Jesus' teaching of nonresistance or love of enemies. They reckoned that their war was permissible and holy. Sadly, the atrocities they committed against Muslims continue to plague the world today. During the Reformation, Luther, who was alarmed by the destructive anarchy of the Peasants' War, decided to place the authority of the state above the teaching of the SM, in order to maintain peace and order. For him, Christians, like all others, are persons-in-relation, so they should follow the law of the SM in the life of the church, but follow the law of the state in tending to the affairs of the world, following the "two kingdoms" theory (Luther 1962: 75–129; Althaus 1972: 43–82; Stephenson 1981; Malysz 2007).

Even though Catholic and Protestant churches have often worked with the secular power to maintain social order, and have regularly domesticated Jesus' kingdom ethic, some minority Christian groups, such as Waldensians, Mennonites, and Quakers, have been committed to a literal interpretation of this teaching. Their Christian pacifism stands squarely in the pre-Constantine heritage, and it testifies remarkably to the radical gospel and new life in the kingdom of God.

Evidently, Christians are divided on how to implement nonresistance. An idealistic view, on the one hand, stressing the importance of intentions in ethical decision-making, suggests that we resist no evildoers and love our enemies, as God has done for us in Christ, and take a pacifist approach in dealing with bullies, criminals, and terrorists. Revenge lies in God's hands, and love will conquer evil. A realistic view, on the other hand, stressing the importance of consequences for ethical thinking, advocates retributive justice, for God expects the state to protect the innocent and punish the wicked. On a larger scale, this latter view may also argue for a just war, when necessary and appropriate. Defending the innocent is both a practice of love and a proper task of government. Gandhi and Martin Luther King seem to have combined both views, when they took courageous actions to demand justice from evil power by adopting the principle of nonviolence.

Having seen how the two competing strands of interpretation regarding "resist no evil" have been interpreted in historic contexts, how can we deal with this teaching of Jesus today? First of all, the four specific examples in 5:39-42 suggest that a pattern of behavior imitating God's indiscriminate mercy and inclusive love is the final goal for our character formation as God's children. It is essential that we grow in Christian virtue with the community of faith and strive to be perfect in our moral life, as God is perfect (5:48). As Stanley Hauerwas eloquently argues, "We are called, therefore, to be perfect, but perfection names [means] our participation in Christ's love of his enemies. Perfection does not mean that we are sinless or that we are free of anger or lust. Rather, to be perfect is to learn to be part of a people who take the time to live without resorting to violence to sustain their existence" (Hauerwas 2006: 72). Second, both strands of interpretation try to live out the fundamental teaching of the sayings—love your neighbor as yourself. The question is which neighbor—victims or perpetrators—should be given the weight of concern in each situation. The approach to this teaching may also need to differ between an individual and a nation, because different responsibilities are involved. It is clear that not all faithful people will appreciate the rationale of nonresistance in the same way. Those who have experienced God's unconditional love in their lives may be able and willing to risk forgiving evildoers and embracing their enemies. But there will also be cases in which the powers of the state, acting as God's servant, should be exercised for the sake of the innocent and the whole community (Rom. 13:1-7). A history-of-effects perspective helps us make sense of how one text can cut in different ways at different times.

If the SM is understood not as either law or gospel, but as the "new covenant" that God has made with us in Christ the new Moses, which encompasses divine grace and human commitment, it is important to remember that, as children of the covenant, Christians should always strive to commit no violence against others and love their enemies (6:33) (Yieh 2007: 14–16). In this way, they may serve as salt and light, individually and collectively, to show to the world how even the most ferocious violence, enmity, and hurt can be dissolved by the radical love of Jesus and the cross.[1] It takes bold determination, but in Christ there is an alternative way to end conflict, violence, and war.

"SAVE NO MONEY" (MATTHEW 6:19)

Besides human relationship, Jesus also teaches on possessions and wealth. "Do not store up for yourselves treasures on earth" (6:19). "You cannot serve God and wealth" (6:24). In a capitalist society, where money talks and wealth rules, how do we respond to these two sayings? Why not store up treasure on earth? After all, we can use our resources to take care of our loved ones and do charity work. If we choose poverty, we might ourselves become burdens to others. And is there always a conflict between loyalty to God and the pursuit of wealth? Isn't wealth a form of blessing? Can wealth not be used to show God's glory and serve the needy?

In the history of interpretation, two major concerns are noteworthy. The first is a concern that total renunciation of possessions could alienate wealthy people from the gospel and reduce the church's ability to care for the needy and support its missions. This teaching became particularly challenging when Christians began to move upward socially and do well economically. Many interpreters tried to mitigate Jesus' radical demand by arguing that it was all right to own wealth, as long as one's heart was not enslaved by it. They called this position "the purity of intention" and justified it with Jesus' words: "For where your treasure is, there your heart will be" (6:21). Seeing the heart-wrenching misery of the poor in London's slums in the eighteenth century, John Wesley famously encouraged Christians to earn as much as they could, to save as much as they could, and to give as much as they could. In a sermon on Matt. 6:19-23, therefore, he explained that the saying against storing up earthly treasures did not stop a person from saving enough money to stay out of debt, to acquire the essentials of life for oneself, and to supply the basic needs of one's family (Wesley 2002a: 199–218). When people tried to gather more possessions than necessary, however, they would subject themselves to the temptation of pride, desire, and dependence on wealth rather than God. To rich people, thus, Wesley's advice was not to cling to wealth but to be rich in good works, generous, and ready to share. The second concern is that denouncing possessions could encourage idleness among Christians, as Paul once warned the church in Thessalonica: "Admonish the idlers" (1 Thess. 5:14). So, even though monks lived in voluntary poverty, most of them worked hard to prevent their ascetic and prayerful life from making them idle (Luz 2007: 346–48). The Protestant ethic, which affirms possessions as a blessing and emphasizes dedication to work as a vocation to support family and community, was another indication of the concern that denouncing wealth might lead to irresponsibility. Jesus' radical teaching is thus domesticated. Might this be one reason why capitalism reigns in the West and, for good or ill, in the global economy?

How do we interpret this teaching today? Is it practical or feasible in our capitalist culture? If taken as strict law, renunciation of possessions means that Christians should not have savings in the bank or invest in any pension fund. If taken as a counsel of gospel, this may mean that they should trust in God's providential care without worry or contingency plan. But if taken as the new covenant, it may mean that the children of God can trust fully in God's fatherly care as we plan wisely and work diligently to serve God's purposes in this world (Yieh 2007: 25). By serving God first instead of wealth, they will be able to live an alternative way of life, free from the temptation of materialism and consumerism, and indeed free to serve the needy, thus bearing witness to God's kingdom of grace and fulfilling God's righteousness in their lifestyle.

This history-of-effects review shows that every interpretation is contextual. There is a range of valid interpretations of the same text. Many are accepted as legitimate by the church, though some are considered out of bounds due to negative consequences. This review further demonstrates how interpreters in historic contexts have tried to unpack the "kernel of meaning" within the structure of Jesus' teaching and uncover its potential "directional meanings" for changing situations.[2] Their interpretations are both expositions and appropriations in nature. As I explore what the SM may say to Chinese contexts, therefore, all possible meanings of the text will be carefully considered.

SOCIAL-ECONOMIC CONTEXTS IN CHINA

As a biblical scholar, my purpose in this essay is to explore what a contextual interpretation of the SM may yield, when Jesus' radical sayings on resisting no evil and saving no money are read in the social-economic contexts of modern China. As a Chinese Christian, it is also my hope to find out what moral implications these two sayings might offer to help construct a Christian social-economic ethics in China. A brief description of the Chinese context is now in order.

The People's Republic of China was founded in 1949 by a socialist revolution led by Mao Tse-tung. The vast population of the Chinese people was extremely poor and had suffered for a long time under the oppressive Qing dynasty, corrupt Republic government, exploitative landowners, and a ruthless business class. Peasants farmed the land all year round, but their children starved to death. Miners dug for coal deep underground while their parents froze. Poor people enjoyed no human rights or dignity. Many could not survive a bad year, because there was no social support, economic justice, or charities in the feudal system. And there were so many consecutive bad years of famine, floods, colonial aggressions, and civil wars that people became hungry and desperate. The disparity between the privileged and the disfranchised became so huge, the political system so corrupt, and the social structure so unfair that the Communists' struggle against the bourgeois and their pledge to share land and wealth among all citizens eventually won the support of the proletariat and the respect of the intellectual elite. The Communists' ideals and promises to feed the hungry, cloth the naked, break the tyranny of social classes, and share the property in common sounded very similar to Jesus' announcement to the Jewish people suffering under the colonial rule of the Roman Empire concerning the good news of the kingdom of God (Matt. 5:3-11; Luke 4:18-19). It may not be far-fetched to say that the Communists promised to bring the good news to the poor and proclaim the year of the Jubilee to the underclass Chinese when they took over in 1949.

Once they had taken power, the Communists reversed the social relationship of their citizens almost immediately. The goal of the Communist Revolution was to liberate the poor people of the lower social classes from the exploitation and oppression of feudalism and classism. The new government began to redistribute land, reverse social stations, and reeducate the old ruling classes. Peasants and laborers were now called the "red five categories" (*hong wu lei*) and were given preference for new opportunities, while landowners and intelligentsia were labeled as "black five categories" (*he wu lei*) and allowed only limited access to social resources. Social relationship in the new China was redefined with the principle of justice and retribution rather than mercy or forgiveness. So tension and hostility between social classes continued to wreck social cohesion and community life. Personal relationships, even the intimate ones between parent and child or husband and wife, were marked by fear and distrust. At the international level, many Chinese held deep resentment against the colonial countries that had invaded China, especially "the little Japan" that slaughtered millions of innocent Chinese people and established the surrogate nation of Manchuria on China's soil. How could they forgive the atrocious war crimes of rape, looting, arson, and execution committed by the invading Japanese soldiers in the Nanjing Massacre of 1937 (Chang 1998; Brook 1999)? Some Japanese nationalists' rebuttal to the extent of the massacre only further offended and embittered the Chinese people. Even though the Chinese realized the importance of maintaining an amicable relationship with the developed countries for practical purposes, how could they be expected to love their enemies, those aggressive foreign powers that had sought to divide their land and conquer them? The devastation and humiliation caused by the colonial wars, the Sino-Japanese wars, and the cold war in the last one hundred years taught them a hard lesson: resist the evildoer and hate your enemies. For survival and self-defense in a fiercely competitive world, a country has to know who its sworn enemies are and fight them at all cost. It does not have the luxury of indulging evil aggressions. The well-being of its people is at stake.

On the front of economic reconstruction, it is unfortunate that power struggles among party leaders soon triggered the catastrophic "Cultural Revolution" (1966–1976), which destroyed numerous cultural traditions, social institutions, valuable properties, and human lives, and, as a result, slowed down the construction of the new China. Since the 1980s, however, Deng Xiaoping's "Chinese style of socialism" and the "Reform and Open" policies have set China on a new course, quickly moving them forward in economic development. In three decades, China rapidly grew to be a global power. By 2010, the confident and strident China had assumed an international leadership role in the UN Security Council, become an economic powerhouse second only to the United States and Japan, and hosted the Olympic Games in Beijing and a World Exposition in Shanghai. China's economic success and continuing growth are particularly remarkable in the midst of a global recession that began in 2008. The biggest factory for the world and the most promising market of the world, China is also becoming the most powerful investor around the world. New skyscrapers are rising in every city, an expanding network of superhighways is connecting different regions, and an increasing number of entrepreneurs are raking in record-high profits from foreign trade. The so-called Chinese style of socialism, which combines the socialist ideals to share wealth with the poor and the capitalist strategies to pursue profit by innovation, enables China to adjust nimbly to the ever-changing global economy. The total control of the Communist government over its human and natural resources also makes its nationally planned programs remarkably focused and effective. There are good reasons why China has become prosperous in such a short time.

With rapid success in economics, however, China has also undergone radical social changes. Children in rural areas are leaving home to study in universities and work in big cities, so family relationships have become strained and the elderly receive no support from their loved ones. Entrepreneurism is the key to success, but individualism also poisons the traditional ethos of community. While wealthy entrepreneurs become the new social elite, peasants in rural area and factory workers on mass production lines become discontented with the vast gap between the haves and the have-nots. Crimes and frauds increase at an alarming rate, while people in some sectors lag far behind and become desperate. There are also growing cases of bribery and corruption in business dealings, favoritism and nepotism in social privileges, and other problems associated with greed and power. As economic growth improves their life conditions, people also begin to ask for civil freedom and political reform. These bubbling social problems may lead to political turmoil, so the government is duly concerned.

In order to preempt potential troubles, the Chinese government has taken prominent measures in recent years to prosecute corrupted officials, suppress overheated housing prices, and promote social harmony.[3] These three measures reflect the government's deepest concerns over political, economic, and social stability and its worry about popular unrests that may set back the progress China has made so far. In order to maintain social cohesion, the Sixteenth Central Committee of the Chinese Communist Party in 2006 mandated the government to construct a "harmonious socialist society," defined as "a democratic society under the rule of law, a society based on equity and justice, an honest and caring society, a society full of vigor, and a stable and orderly society in which humans live in harmony with nature, strive to develop social services, promote social equity and justice, foster a culture of harmony."[4] Notice how equity, justice, and stability are repeatedly emphasized in this statement. In the contexts of economic boom, social changes, and political control, what would Jesus' teaching on "saving no money" mean to the Chinese people? What questions might they bring to Jesus? What can a contextual interpretation reveal about its demands? What can the SM say to some of China's major concerns today?

A Contextual and Cross-Cultural Cross-Examination

Bearing in mind the various interpretations and serious consequences of Jesus' teaching, I will now engage in a dialogue with these two biblical texts and the social-economic contexts of China to see what insights concerning ethics might be learned. Admittedly, this engagement is made with my personal experience and particular perspective in three ways: as an ethnic Chinese who is concerned about the opportunities and challenges Chinese people are facing today, as a Christian who believes the Bible has valuable and critical messages for everyone, including Chinese people, and as a scholar who appreciates multiple critical approaches to biblical interpretation and tries to understand the complexity of the rapidly changing society in China. I should acknowledge also that my interpretation of the SM has been critically informed by some insights from the history-of-effects review.

"RESIST NO EVIL" (MATTHEW 5:39)

First, on nonresistance as a principle for human relationship, it is my estimation that Chinese contexts will raise three critiques against Jesus.

1. Entrenching submission and victimization? When Jesus advises his disciples to resist no evildoer and turn the other cheek to make it convenient for attackers to strike again, by giving up their belongings to robbers without a fight, by working slavishly for their oppressors, and by serving anyone who has an unreasonable demand, isn't he encouraging a submissive attitude that perpetuates victimization? The Chinese Communists who have fought for decades to liberate peasants, laborers, and other victims from the oppression of a feudal society would without a doubt raise the first critique against this saying by asking: Why not uphold the dignity of the victims and support their right to self-defense? Does the entrenchment of submission and victimization by a teaching on nonresistance prove that Marx was right to say that religion has been used by the bourgeois class as opium for the fainthearted and a psychological tool to control the poor? In contrast to this teaching, the Chinese Communists would prefer to instill in their people an attitude of self-assertion and to pursue a human relationship based on equality, fairness, and reciprocity among all, and yes, exploiters and oppressors should be brought to justice.

2. Reinforcing cultural colonization? Why does Jesus talk about nonresistance when his compatriots and followers suffered oppression and persecution from the Romans? Does he not care about racial justice? Chinese people have suffered from colonial aggressions of European countries, America, and Japan since the nineteenth century, so they remember the suffering and humiliation that their ancestors had to bear when their country was weak. Should they continue to take the abuse of racial aggression from foreign powers? How can Jesus' saying be considered right or useful to a China that has finally become an emergent power? From a postcolonial critical point of view, should Chinese people not be encouraged to stand up for their right and dignity in resisting colonial enemies? Does this teaching of Jesus become an accomplice for the oppressive system of the imperialistic and colonial powers? Might it not reinforce cultural colonization in the form of neocolonialism in this supposedly postcolonial time period?

3. Justifying social injustice? Why should the victims be asked to forgive their enemies and forfeit their legal right to retributive justice, while perpetrators are only asked to repent? If the Jewish law is reasonable enough to use the principle of "an eye for an eye and a tooth for a tooth" to address the wrong and grievance in human relationship and maintain basic fairness with the punishment fitting the crime, why does Jesus release the perpetrators from

their responsibility so easily? Why does Jesus love the wicked assailant more than the innocent victim? How can social justice be realized? Undoubtedly, the Chinese Communists will think "loving enemies" an absurd idea out of touch with reality; that is, the reality of a class society. In his writings and speeches, Mao Tse-tung often relates the idea of love to the reality of class struggle (Whitehead 1977: xiii, 127). In his view, love of all humanity cannot exist until social classes are eliminated, because classes split the society into antagonistic groups. Everyone seeks his or her own interest, and every class takes advantage of the others. Addressing a group of writers and artists who naively think the spirit of love can transcend classes, therefore, Mao says in no uncertain terms: "We hate Japanese imperialism because Japanese imperialism oppresses us. . . . We cannot love enemies. . . . We cannot love social evils. . . . Our aim is to destroy them" (Mao Zedong 1967: 3:69–98, see esp. 73–74, 90–91). For the common Chinese people who inherit Confucian tradition, they can appreciate the self-sacrificing acts of kindness to benefit families, friends, and neighbors, but not without limit and certainly not including enemies. This is why Motze, a famous ancient Chinese philosopher who teaches "loving all humankind without discrimination" (*jian ai tian xia*), was admired but at the same time rejected as outside the mainstream of Chinese moral tradition, even as Chinese Christian scholars find his teaching compatible with Jesus' teaching on loving enemies (Wu 1940).

To these critiques, what could a Christian interpreter of the SM say? As a Chinese Christian scholar, I would respond in the following way.

1. To empower the victims. First of all, resisting no evil does not necessarily mean humble submission to one's antagonists or adversaries for the sake of appeasement. Nor does it mean that victims should simply succumb to the threat of violence on individual or national levels. It is true that one common human instinct is to avoid suffering when powerless and to seek vengeance when powerful. But Christian ethics recognizes the tragic reality of violence engendering violence, abundantly attested in human history. No person has ever lived a lifetime without encountering violence, feuds, or wars. What, then, is the best way to break the cycle of violence? As God has done to remove the bondage and power of sin with amazing love by giving up Jesus to die for sinners, Jesus' teaching on nonresistance and loving enemies is, paradoxically, to "subvert" the human desire to avenge and to disarm the human inclination to impose violence and hurt on enemies. In fact, choosing to resist no evil and to do more than what the oppressor demands is a courageous act to claim autonomy and take control over one's own body and mind, especially in the face of structural evil and oppressive systems. As Daniel Patte rightly argues,

"Those who have no control over their lives are given control over their lives. A new reality is conjured" (Patte 1999: 188). It is a sign of extreme courage, and it can be empowering to the victims and demonstrative of their spiritual superiority.

2. To liberate them from violence. Resisting no evil can also liberate people from the tyranny of anger and hatred and make it possible to reconcile with enemies and restore relationships. Quarrelling lovers do not make up because they seek revenge and continue to aggravate each other. Broken families cannot be reunited if members file lawsuits against one another. Someone needs to be willing to bear the hurt and take the initiative to stop the spiraling descent into further antagonism; otherwise, all shall become blind and lose their teeth. The Chinese may never forget the disgrace and devastation caused by the military aggression of the Japanese Empire in the last century. If the two neighboring countries wish to get along and cooperate for a better future, however, Japan needs to apologize for their war crimes and China needs to forgive Japan. This is certainly very difficult, and will require strong and wise leaders to make it happen. But it can be done. In fact, history has witnessed an unthinkable bloodless revolution in India. By adopting Jesus' nonresistant principle, Gandhi successfully disbanded the colonial rule of the British Empire, even though it had overwhelming military might, legal power, and cultural hegemony. Following Jesus' teaching, Gandhi not only won independence and liberty for his people but also demonstrated the triumph of moral power and spiritual dignity.

3. To create a harmonious society. In recent years, China has made remarkable economic progress, increasing its GDP, constructing new infrastructure, and improving its standard of living; but it has also seen crime hikes, racial riots, and growing disparity. Stressed relationships between the rich and the poor, in particular, have become a potential threat to political stability, so much so that the Chinese government has made it a priority in policy to construct a harmonious society. To maintain justice, it has also strengthened law enforcement against political and financial corruption. Legal measures may indeed accomplish some justice, but they cannot force people to live in harmony. To bring forth social cohesion, Jesus' teaching can be very helpful, because it promotes the spirit of forgiveness and acts of generosity to one another, and it nurtures moral character and motivates people to do good for others. China has a long cultural tradition that considers moral character the foundation stone to building a moral society and a harmonious world. Jesus' virtue ethics, embodied in the SM, is one of the spiritual values that Christianity may add to the Chinese government's concerted efforts to establish

a harmonious society. As Manhong Lin rightly points out, "The purpose of discussing unselfish love, embodied in both Christian message and Chinese culture, is to introduce a possibility for people to refrain from being self-centered and from selfish desires so as to live into a healthy relationship among the individual, community, and society" (Lin 2010: 183).

"SAVE NO MONEY" (MATT 6:19)

As China adopts a free-market economy to create wealth, its people are enjoying a better life and feeling pride as citizens of a strong country. In this particular economic context, what issues would Chinese readers take with Jesus on his advice to save no money?

1. Encouraging personal idleness? We live in a world where there is no free lunch, and only those who work hard will have a chance to make money and improve their lives. The initial success of the Chinese economy lies very much in the entrepreneurship and work ethic of its diligent labor force and its willingness to serve as the factory of the world. So hardworking Chinese readers will no doubt question the impact of Jesus' saying on saving no money. If there is no profit to make or money to save, why would anybody work so hard? What will be the driving force or incentive? Would this saying encourage idleness, foster laziness, create poverty and cause social problems?

2. Escaping social responsibility? According to Matthew, Jesus bases this saying on a conviction that God is a loving Father in heaven who has taken care of the birds in the sky and the lilies in the field and will certainly provide for God's children. And Jesus does not want his disciples to worry about their provisions of life such as food and clothing. But isn't there an English proverb that says, "Heaven helps those who help themselves"? If people do not make efforts or sacrifice to take care of themselves, why should God bother? If many believers withdraw from economic activities and retreat to a monastery, will it not have a negative impact on the progress of the community? Does this saying of Jesus encourage escapism from social responsibilities and the due contribution every member of the society should make for family and nation?

To such critiques, I as a Chinese Christian biblical scholar would respond in the following way.

1. To avoid idolatry of materialism. I would argue that Jesus does not mean to condone idleness but to warn his disciples that pursuing wealth may lead to the idolatry of materialism. Money is power, and it can buy so many good things in the world that people may easily fall prey to its grasp and become its slaves. In the pursuit of money, people are often tempted to forego spiritual

values or moral duties. Corruption, bribery, and nepotism become rampant in business deals. Anxiety, depression, and addiction also plague human minds. People may also think that money can guarantee a good life for them into retirement, but Jesus' teaching reminds them that the worldly wealth is not reliable because it can be consumed by moth and rust and stolen by thieves. The crash of the banking system in the United States and Europe in 2008 and the dispute over the monetary exchange rate between the United States and China in 2010 illustrate the vulnerability of the financial system that dominates the lives of individuals and nations. Jesus asserts that by not storing up treasures "for themselves" (6:19), people's minds will be free from worry.

2. To pursue spiritual values. Jesus discourages his disciples from saving treasures on earth, but he urges them to store up treasures in heaven, where God is and where their hearts are. As I see it, therefore, Jesus encourages people to work hard and make money, but then to use it as a good instrument for right purposes, helping the poor, sheltering the homeless, feeding the hungry, and releasing the captives. When they use their wealth to do charities for the vulnerable and the disfranchised in the world, they will be rewarded by God because their deeds of righteousness will be counted as done to Jesus himself (25:31-46). People who take Jesus' advice not to save money also learn to rely on God's care and in so doing experience God's presence and power. Such spiritual values are more precious than the treasures one can store up. Thus Jesus says: "Strive first for the kingdom of God and his righteousness, and all these things will be given to you as well" (6:33).

A CHRISTIAN SOCIAL-ECONOMIC ETHICS?

My contextual reading of the SM in the social-economic contexts of China shows two fundamental differences between Jesus and the Chinese readers in terms of belief system. First, Jesus' belief system is monotheistic. Jesus' two sayings are based on a monotheistic view in which the creator God is also a loving Father who cares for all humanity. It is in imitation of this perfect God who brings rain and sun to both the righteous and the wicked that believers should resist no evil and love their enemies, and it is by trusting in this God as the loving Father that they can strive for the kingdom of God and its righteousness without any worry about their material needs. It is also based on the faith in this caring God that Jesus calls for his followers to live an alternative way of life vis-à-vis the way of the world, which operates on the principle of reciprocity when it comes to human relationship (an eye for an eye and a tooth for a tooth) and on the principle of self-reliance when it concerns monetary matters (savings account and pension fund).

The other component in Jesus' belief system is the coming of the kingdom of God. Believers may find spiritual strength to resist no evil and save no money, because they believe that God will soon render justice against the wicked and will surely show mercy to God's children. For nonbelievers, Jesus' two sayings will understandably seem unreasonable and foolish. Herein lies the reason why the two ethical systems, Christian and Chinese, may collide with each other. Monotheism provides believers with a perspective above this world and promises divine justice and blessings beyond death; so it offers hope. In contrast, atheism values human efforts and seeks to render justice in this world; so its ethical system tends to be more pragmatic.

The dialogue between Jesus' two sayings and China's contexts brings to focus the issue of self-interest. Self-interest is one of the most powerful driving forces to motivate a person to work hard and earn success in economic pursuit, but it also often causes worry, anxiety, and depression and alienates a person from competitors or opponents. Indeed, self-interest is the very reason that greed and power can capture and enslave one's soul. As is the case with Christian pacifists and religious volunteers who are willing to pass over vengeance to make peace with enemies and to help the poor and the needy with all their possessions, it is Jesus' radical teaching that nurtures such a spiritual character and creates a community of faith and love. The whole society will benefit from even just a few committed disciples of Jesus, because, as light and salt, they will show the rest of the world how Jesus' radical teaching can transform lives and change the world. I think this is a point many Chinese readers with a long history of moral tradition and a great love for community can appreciate, even if they cannot agree.

It is also worthwhile noticing that, besides their functions to shape moral character in individuals, Jesus' teachings on loving enemies and trusting God may serve as ethical principles to help create a healthier society. Sometime before Communist rule, when China was in disarray because of colonial invasions, government corruption, and civil wars, some Chinese Christian scholars proposed to use Jesus' teaching as a guideline to build a new China. Wu Leichuan (1870–1944), for instance, argued that Jesus' moral teaching in the SM not only reveals the ideal vision of a Jewish kingdom of God but also serves as a blueprint for the construction of a new China. Jesus' teaching could reform moral character and turn China into an ideal society of freedom, equality, and charity (Wu 1936). As a Confucian-turned-Christian scholar, Wu advocated a program called "saving the nation with moral character" (*dao de jiu guo*), because he believed that morally reformed people can change the ethos of the society and consequently transform the life of the nation. In imitation of Jesus, one's moral character could be reformed to make an impact on the society. In this regard, Wu's idea is comparable to Stanley Hauerwas's virtue ethics (Hauerwas 1981: 111–52). Now, of course, China as a nation has stepped into a different time and condition, and its current challenges have to do with the concerns over economic equality, social justice, and political stability. Whether or not Jesus' radical teaching on relationship and money can effectively address these concerns in China's contexts remains to be seen, but I think these two sayings offer a different point of view and several ideas worthy of careful and continuous reflection. A person's belief system and value system determine the way he or she deals with others and manages wealth. It is at this root level that a contextual reading of Jesus' teaching in the SM has yielded some insights that may inform a person's social-economic ethics and influence the way he or she behaves. These insights may also help many people in the West who have recently experienced the conflict with parts of the Muslim world and the financial meltdown caused by the crooked deals and irresponsible management of bankers and investors. Jesus' radical teaching continues to demand a proper response from all of us today. Those who have ears, let them hear.

Notes

1. For bold theological articulation of these themes, see Volf 1996 and Hauerwas 2004b.

2. Ulrich Luz defines "kernel of meaning" as the meaning of a biblical text that "corresponds to the given structures of a text," and a "directional meaning" as that which "gives a present direction to the readers on their way to new lands." It is in the interaction of these two meanings that the dynamics of the biblical text can be understood (Luz 1994: 20).

3. A glance of news reports on *Xinhuanet*, the website of the Chinese government's official news agency, reveals these efforts. For example, "China's to Step Up Economic Restructuring," http://english.gov.cn/2010-02/27/content_1543777.htm); "China Turns to Risk Evaluation to Cure Corruption," news.xinhuanet.com/english2010/china/2011-01/16/c_13693291.htm; "China to Control Inflation, Property Market," news.xinhuanet.com/english2010/video/2011-02/03/c_13717942.htm.

4. "Communiqué of the Sixth Plenum of the 16th CPC Central Committee," http://news.xinhuanet.com/english/2006-10/11/content_5191071.htm.

PART V

Community and Borders

13

The Hard Sayings of Jesus in Real-World Context

Reading Matthew 5:38-48 within the Occupied Palestinian Territories

Dorothy Jean Weaver

The words of Jesus in Matt. 5:38-48 surely qualify for the proverbial list of Jesus' hard sayings. The commands "Do not resist the one who is evil" (5:39a, my translation), "Love your enemies" (5:44a), and "Pray for those who persecute you" (5:44b) are words we might wish that Jesus had never spoken or that the Gospel writers had never preserved.[1] Such commands appear illogical, counterintuitive, and even scandalous.

But within Matthew's narrative, these words are vital to Jesus' call to greater righteousness (see 5:20a) and the life of the kingdom of heaven (5:20b). Accordingly, those who follow Jesus as his disciples face these hard sayings as the ongoing call to an extraordinary life of faithfulness within a real world peopled with evil ones, enemies, and persecutors.

Such is surely the case for present-day Palestinian Christians living in the Occupied Palestinian Territories.[2] Their community has lived for more than sixty years with the aftereffects of the 1948 Nakba (catastrophe), in which they lost more than half of their ancestral lands to the state of Israel. And since 1967, they have lived under occupation by the state of Israel and under military rule by the Israeli defense forces. Accordingly, when Palestinian Christians read Matt. 5:38-48, they encounter the radical call of Jesus in a context where others (whom they might view as evil ones, enemies, and persecutors) build walls around their cities, expropriate their lands, destroy their homes, bulldoze their olive groves, put roadblocks in front of their villages, impose curfews and closures on their towns, and erect military checkpoints that restrict their freedom of movement.

This paper offers a twofold contextual reading of Matt. 5:38-48. The first reading utilizes narrative criticism to analyze the text from my own scholarly context as a student of Matthew's Gospel. This reading assesses 5:38-48 within Matthew's overall narrative, attending to narrative location, internal structure, use of vocabulary, biblical and real-world allusions, and ultimately the narrative/theological message for Matthew's first-century community.

The second reading assesses the pragmatic significance of these hard sayings of Jesus for twenty-first-century Palestinian Christians. What do these first-century words of Jesus mean to present-day Palestinian Christians living under Israeli occupation? And where does the call of Jesus become visible within the real world of the Occupied Palestinian Territories? This reading emerges from personal conversations with Palestinian Christians from the West Bank and Jerusalem, most of them long-term acquaintances whom I know from frequent sojourns in Israel/Palestine as traveler, tour leader, and sabbatical scholar. And the impetus for this reading lies in two crucial and interwoven influences on my life as a scholar. The first is my lifelong interest in questions of violence and nonviolence, an interest nurtured from childhood by the biblical teachings and the historical heritage of the North American Mennonite community, within which I grew up and which I claim as my own. The second influence, much more recent but no less profound, is my own existential encounter with the ongoing life challenges faced by the Palestinian people, Christians and Muslims alike, living under Israeli occupation.

The paper concludes with a brief comparison of these two contextual readings. How do these readings relate to each other? Where are their coherences and/or divergences? What happens to scholarly biblical interpretation as biblical text engages with the real world? How does the twenty-first-century Israeli/Palestinian context influence the interpretation of this first-century Matthean text?

MATTHEW 5:38-48: A NARRATIVE READING

To read a text within its narrative context is to encounter that text sequentially within the flow of the narrative. The text therefore "derives its significance not simply from its content as such but from its relationship to the other 'events' in the unfolding narrative" (Weaver 1990: 28). Accordingly, a narrative reading of Matt. 5:38-48 must attend first to the preceding text (1:1—5:37), second to the text itself (5:38-48), and finally to the subsequent text (6:1—28:20).

MATTHEW'S NARRATIVE PRE-INFORMATION (1:1—5:37)

As David B. Howell notes in his study of narrative rhetoric within Matthew's Gospel, "The initial information about the attitudes, characters, and narrative world which is projected [within a narrative text] plays a large part in the process of teaching readers the correct interpretive techniques for reading the text" (Howell 1990: 115). And the initial information provided by 1:1—5:37 offers multiple clues to the interpretation of 5:38-48.

One such clue is the Jewish/messianic character of Matthew's narrative. This narrative opens with a Jewish/messianic genealogy beginning with Abraham (1:1, 2, 17), the ancestor of the Jewish people (see 3:9), continuing through (King) David (1:1, 6, 17) and the deportation to Babylon (1:11, 12, 17), and rising to its climax with Jesus the Messiah (1:1, 16, 17). Accordingly, Matthew's accounts of the birth and infancy of Jesus (1:18—2:23) feature Joseph, son of David (1:20), and Jesus the Messiah (1:18; 2:4), who "has been born king of the Jews" (2:1), who "is to shepherd [God's] people Israel" (2:6) and whose messianic designation is that of "my [= God's] son" (2:15; cf. Ps. 2:7).

John the Baptist (3:1-17) is an eschatological Jewish prophet, "the Elijah who is to come" (11:7-15; cf. 17:10-13; Mal 4:5). John's water baptism (3:5-10, 11a) foreshadows the arrival of a messianic figure who is "more powerful" (3:11b) and will "baptize . . . with the Holy Spirit and with fire" (3:11d). And John's prophetic pointers toward the Messiah find prompt fulfillment.

Jesus is baptized by John (3:13-16a), endowed with the Holy Spirit (3:16b), and affirmed by the voice of God for his messianic ministry (3:17; cf. Ps. 2:7). He is then "led up by the Spirit into the wilderness to be tempted by the devil" (4:1) in a series of encounters that highlight his messianic calling (4:3, 6; cf. 4:9). Jesus resists these temptations (4:4, 7, 10), dispatches Satan (4:10-11a), and is served by angels of God (4:11b). He then relocates from Nazareth to Capernaum in messianic fulfillment of the Scriptures (4:12-16; cf. Isa 9:1-2). And from here, Jesus Messiah commences his mission, proclaiming the kingdom of heaven (4:17), calling disciples (4:18-22), and engaging in a peripatetic and charismatic ministry of teaching and healing that draws massive crowds from all directions (4:23-25).

Within this highly charged messianic context, Jesus goes up the mountain (5:1a), recasting the image of Moses at Sinai in a messianic and eschatological mode, and inaugurates his messianic ministry by teaching his disciples about the kingdom of heaven in the hearing of the crowds (5:1-7:29). In Terence Donaldson's words, "The gathering to Jesus on the mountain in Galilee . . .

should be seen in the context of the eschatological gathering of the people of God. The disciples are the foundation of the eschatological community called into being by the messianic activity of Jesus, and the crowds are being invited to join their fellowship. The Sermon, then, is the messianic interpretation of the Torah for this community—the authoritative declaration of the characteristics which this community is called to exhibit" (Donaldson 1985: 115).

Jesus opens his inaugural address with blessings on those who exhibit the characteristics of the kingdom of heaven (5:3-12; cf. 5:13-16). He then defines his coming in terms of messianic fulfillment: "Do not think that I have come to abolish the law or the prophets; I have come not to abolish but to fulfill" (5:17). Following this programmatic declaration, Jesus then illustrates his messianic fulfillment of Scripture with a sixfold litany: "You have heard that it was said . . . But I say to you . . ." (5:21-26, 27-30, 31-32, 33-37, 38-42, 43-48). The text of 5:38-48 creates the conclusion and climax of this litany.

The implications of Matthew's messianic motif for interpreting 5:38-48 are manifest. Jesus Messiah has come to carry out God's messianic agenda: To bring Jewish history to its climax (1:1, 2-16, 17); to "shepherd [God's] people Israel" (2:6) as "king of the Jews" (2:2); to "fulfill all righteousness" (3:15); to resist the temptations of Satan as the true and faithful Son of God (4:1-11; cf. 2:15; 3:17); to proclaim the arrival of God's realm (4:17); and to "fulfill . . . the law [and] the prophets" (5:17). Accordingly, Jesus' scriptural citations ("You have heard that it was said . . .") find messianic fulfillment in Jesus' exposition ("But I say to you . . ."). Conversely, Jesus' calls to action reflect messianic interpretation of Jewish scripture.

A further interpretive clue is the narrative juxtaposition of King Herod (2:1) and Jesus "who has been born king of the Jews" (2:2). As one who "seeks the life of the child" (2:13, 20) and slaughters the infants of Bethlehem to execute this scheme (2:16-18), Herod undeniably demonstrates evil character. The irony of the narrative, however, is that Herod, in spite of his worst intentions and his manifest power, cannot carry out his single goal—namely, to destroy the child. Instead, Matthew portrays Herod as utterly powerless vis-à-vis the angel of the Lord, who persistently dispatches people just in time to foil Herod's plots and save the life of the child (2:12, 13, 19-20, 22). In the end, Herod lies dead (2:15, 19, 20), while the child is alive and well in Nazareth (2:21-23). The message is clear. Evil people can create horrific human devastation (2:16-18), but they have far less power than they or others imagine. And it is God, not the powers of evil, whose agenda ultimately wins the day.

A related interpretive clue emerges from the Beatitudes of Jesus' inaugural address (5:3-12). Here Jesus pronounces kingdom blessings on the "poor in spirit" (5:3), those who "mourn" (5:4), the "meek" (5:5), those who "hunger and thirst for righteousness" (5:6), the "merciful" (5:7), the "pure in heart" (5:8), the "peacemakers" (5:9), and those "who are persecuted for righteousness' sake" (5:10; cf. 5:11-12). And with these extraordinary blessings, Jesus puts his listeners on immediate notice that the kingdom of heaven stands fundamentally at variance with "the kingdoms of the world and their splendor" (4:8) and ultimately with all human notions of power and greatness (see 16:21-23; 18:1-4; 20:24-28).

RESPONDING TO EVIL ONES AND ENEMIES (5:38-48)

The text of 5:38-48 concludes Jesus' litany on the greater righteousness. This litany deals with murder (5:21-26), adultery (5:27-30), divorce (5:31-32), swearing of oaths (5:33-37), retaliation (5:38-42), and hatred of enemies (5:43-48). Each section opens with the words, "You have heard that it was said," followed by a Jewish Scripture. And each section ends with the refrain, "But I say to you," in the authoritative voice of Jesus Messiah, followed by Jesus' messianic fulfillment of the Scripture.

In each section, Jesus' greater righteousness contrasts sharply with what his listeners have previously heard. The prohibition of murder (5:21; cf. Exod. 20:13//Deut. 5:17) now extends to mere anger (5:22-26); and adultery (5:27; cf. Exod. 20:14//Deut. 5:18) reaches beyond the physical acts of the body to the lustful thoughts of the heart (5:28-30). Jesus prohibits divorce (5:31; cf. Deut. 24:1) "except on the ground of unchastity" (5:32). And he forbids the swearing of oaths (5:33; cf. Lev. 19:12; Deut. 23:21), calling his followers to a simple "yes" or "no" response (5:34-37). The final two sections of Jesus' litany (5:38-42, 43-48) fit this same pattern, even as they depict the vivid challenges of everyday life for Jesus' disciples in a world of violence and oppression.

This is a world of physical assault and insulting behavior: "If anyone strikes you on the right cheek . . ." (5:39b). Within the honor-shame culture of Matthew's first-century Middle Eastern narrative, such a backhanded slap is considered an insult. A backhanded slap, in Warren Carter's words, "expresses the power differential of a superior who disdains an inferior: a master with a slave, a wealthy landowner with a poor farmer or artisan, a Roman with a provincial, a wise man with a fool or a child . . . , a government official with a difficult prophet (1 Kgs 22:24), the religious elite with a dangerous preacher (Matt 26:67)" (Carter 2000: 151–52). But such an insult is likewise a brutality. Accordingly, Jesus depicts a world where his followers regularly encounter both physical assault and public insult.

This is a world where lawsuits against impoverished debtors are common: "If anyone wishes to sue you and take your tunic . . ." (5:40a). Jewish law prohibits taking and keeping a person's outer garment or cloak, since this may well be their only blanket (Exod. 22:25-27; Deut. 24:10-13; cf. Amos 2:7-8). But there is no such law against taking the tunic, the undergarment worn next to the body. Accordingly, Jesus reveals a convenient legal loophole for taking an impoverished debtor to court and demanding the very shirt off his back.

This is a world where Jewish civilians live under Roman military occupation. And the Romans, even the least among them, have all the privileges associated with military conquest and occupation. Here a Roman foot soldier may compel any civilian to carry his pack for one mile (5:41a; cf. 27:32).[3] And the civilian is obliged to comply with this command, no matter how inconvenient or burdensome.

This is also a world where Jesus' disciples encounter indigents on the streets who beg money from the passersby (5:42a) and friends and neighbors who seek to borrow from them (5:42b). In this world, profoundly affected by "poverty and exploitative practices of tax and debt," desperate economic realities can create evil ones even out of poverty-stricken compatriots (Carter 2000: 153).

Finally, this is a world where Jesus' disciples encounter enemies and persecutors (5:43-44). Here one's very life is at stake. As Matthew's reader already knows, these people do such things as seek the lives of innocent children and carry out brutal massacres to destroy them (2:1-23). And throughout his public ministry, from Galilee (5:10-12) to Jerusalem (23:34-36), Jesus persistently identifies the persecution of God's faithful ones—presumably by their enemies—as the distinguishing mark of their faithfulness. The prophets have already met this fate (5:12; cf. 21:33-36; 23:29-31), as will John the Baptist shortly (4:12a; 14:1-12; 17:9-13). Jesus will likewise die at the hands of others (16:21; 17:22-23; 20:17-29; 21:33-46; 26:1-2). And he promises his disciples the same persecution (5:10-12; 23:34-36).

Here in this brutal world, Jesus' disciples have heard the scriptural calls to "eye for eye and tooth for tooth" (5:38; cf. Deut. 19:15-21) and hatred of enemies (5:43b; cf. Lev. 19:18).[4] "Eye for eye and tooth for tooth," the ancient *lex talionis*, calls for a measured but mandated response by the Israelite community to the evil in their midst. Deuteronomy 19:15-21, the closest biblical antecedent to Jesus' citation, spells out a detailed legal process that establishes but strictly delimits the liability of the offender.[5] The community must punish the offender with the identical violence that he or she has inflicted on the victim, no more and no less.[6]

But just as before (5:21-37), Jesus responds to these scriptural appeals ("You have heard . . .") with his own authoritative messianic interpretation ("But I say to you . . ."). And Jesus' responses surely scandalize his listeners.[7] Jesus' command "Do not resist" (5:39a) is an apparent affront to those who regularly suffer violence and oppression. And it resounds like a call to total capitulation to evil people and total passivity vis-à-vis evil powers.

But appearances are deceiving. Jesus immediately follows up this call to nonresistance (5:39a) with an illustrative list of nonresistant actions (5:39b, 40, 41, 42a, 42b). And each of these imperatives is an active verb: turn (5:39b); let . . . have (5:40); go (5:41); give (5:42a); do not refuse (5:42b). Even the single negative command (5:42b) clearly implies a positive action. Accordingly, Jesus' call to nonresistance is in fact a call to active response.

But Jesus' commands are not merely active. They are also unexpected. The very fact that Jesus identifies these actions as nonresistant implies that they do not fit expected norms. There is nothing natural or instinctive about these responses. Instead, they need to be thought out instantaneously, in the thick of real-world challenges. They require mental agility, creativity, and spontaneity. Accordingly, these responses cannot be anticipated in advance. Instead, they take the evil one by surprise and disrupt all instinctive patterns of action and reaction.

These responses likewise bring the evil itself into clear focus and confront the evil one with the implications of his or her actions. The one who demeans another with a backhanded slap on the right cheek must treat the other as an equal, if they now issue a front-handed slap on the left cheek. The one who sues another for his tunic and receives the cloak as well now faces public shame when the defendant leaves the courtroom stark naked. And the soldier who compels a civilian to carry his pack one mile now faces dangerous legal consequences when the civilian carries his pack two miles instead.

Further, the casuistic (if . . . then) form of Jesus' commands clearly suggests that Jesus has not offered an exhaustive list of rules. Instead, Jesus' repeated formula suggests that these illustrations serve merely as the first items in a list that extends indefinitely, as far as changing circumstances demand and creative imagination enables (Tannehill 1975: 42, 69). These imperatives are thus not rules to be rigidly applied. Rather, they point toward a moving, growing, ever-transforming pattern for nonviolent living in a violent world.

Here Jesus shatters the ancient and seemingly indestructible linkage between action and reaction reflected in the *lex talionis*. In place of obligatory retaliation, Jesus now frees his disciples to act rather than react in the face of evil and to take creative and nonviolent initiatives vis-à-vis their antagonists.

The implications are revolutionary. As Warren Carter notes, "The servile refuse to be humiliated; the subjugated take initiative by acting with dignity and humanity in the midst of and against injustice and oppression which seem permanent" (Carter 2000: 154).

Now Jesus sets forth his final commands: "You have heard that it was said, 'You shall love your neighbor and you shall hate your enemy.' But I say to you, 'Love (and keep on loving) your enemies. Pray (and keep on praying) for those who persecute you'" (5:43-44, my translation). The shock effect of these words is manifest. Jesus' call transforms instinctive hatred into unimaginable love. Enemies and persecutors, those who arrest, torture, and kill Jesus' disciples (10:16-39; 22:1-10; 23:34-36; 24:9-13), are the very people whom they must love and for whom they must pray. And these responses are not once and done. The present tense imperatives "love" (*agapate*) and "pray for" (*proseuchesthe*) imply repetitive actions. Thus loving enemies and praying for persecutors are the ongoing agenda of everyday life. The challenge of Jesus' words is immense.

But Jesus' logic is also clear. Jesus offers a motive clause (5:45-48) grounding the actions of his disciples in their identity as children of their Father in heaven (5:45a) and, by the same token, in the character of the Father, whose children they are (5:45b). Within the Hebrew thought world, to be children of another means above all to resemble that one in character and actions (cf. John 8:39, 42). Thus because God "makes his sun to rise on the evil and the good and sends rain upon the righteous and the unrighteous" (5:45b/c) and because God is their "Father in heaven" (5:45a, 48), Jesus' disciples are called to love their enemies. Since God bestows blessings with scandalous impartiality, the children of God will likewise reflect God's love for all people, even evil ones, enemies, and persecutors. In so doing, they will fulfill the greater righteousness to which Jesus has called them (5:20; cf. 5:46-47). And they will also, through God's empowering grace, exhibit God's perfection (5:48b) within their human existence (5:48a).[8]

MATTHEW'S NARRATIVE POST-INFORMATION (6:1—28:20)

Jesus has issued an extraordinary challenge. But a question persists. How are these words of Jesus reflected in the actual lives of God's faithful ones, Jesus included? Matthew's answer to this question emerges in the story lines of the prophets, John the Baptist, Jesus, and Jesus' disciples. These story lines have begun prior to 5:38-48. And the collective portrait is unmistakable. God's faithful ones consistently suffer at the hands of evil ones. And they do so without retaliating in kind. The prophets were persecuted long ago (5:12b).

John the Baptist has been arrested prior to Jesus' public ministry (4:12; cf. 4:17). Jesus' own life was threatened at birth (2:1-23); and he now faces renewed persecution (cf. 5:11). And Jesus assures his disciples that they too will one day "be persecuted . . . on [his] account" (5:11; cf. 5:10). Now these story lines play themselves out. And Matthew's endings are consistent with his beginnings.

The story line of the prophets (5:12; 23:29, 30, 31) reflects simple, nonviolent commitment to the mission to which they have been sent (21:34, 36). The parabolic slaves of the landowner go as they are sent and attempt their mission, namely, "to collect his produce" (21:34). When their mission is rejected and they themselves are brutalized and killed, there is no mention of retaliation. Their calling is to "collect the produce" of the vineyard, not to take the lives of the tenants. And the suffering of the prophets (5:12; 23:29, 30, 31) is an ongoing reality, even as God persistently sends emissaries into a brutal world to carry out God's ongoing agenda (21:34/36a; cf. 23:34a).

The story line of John the Baptist is similar. John, the one sent to prepare the way for Jesus (11:10; cf. 3:3), finds his mission ultimately rejected (14:3-4). Accordingly, John suffers the violence of the violent (11:12), and he forfeits his life in brutal fashion (14:8-11; 17:12) for the sake of righteousness (21:32a). But there is no hint that John engages in retaliatory violence vis-à-vis the violent powers of his world (11:12). John's calling as the "Elijah who is to come" (11:14b) is to "prepare the way of the Lord" (3:3) and proclaim the word of the Lord (3:2, 7-12; 14:4), not to enact the wrath of God (3:10, 12).

The story line of Jesus highlights Jesus' profound commitment to a messianic mission that is nonviolent in character. Jesus teaches, proclaims, and heals (4:23//9:35; cf. 11:1) in a strongly life-affirming ministry, where "the blind receive their sight, the lame walk, the lepers are cleansed, the deaf hear, the dead are raised, and the poor have good news brought to them" (11:5). Nevertheless, Jesus knows that his ministry, like that of John, will ultimately be rejected (17:12).

But Jesus does not retaliate (cf. 26:53). Instead, he heads deliberately toward Jerusalem, keenly aware of divine necessity (16:21-23; cf. 26:54). And he regularly predicts the brutal fate that awaits him there at the hands of his enemies (16:21-23; 17:22-23; 20:17-19; 26:1-2; cf. 21:33-46). Jesus' commitment to nonretaliation is firm and unshakable. When Peter challenges Jesus' prediction of suffering and death (16:21-22), Jesus rebukes him sharply (16:23). When Judas identifies Jesus for arrest (26:47-49), Jesus replies, "Friend, do what you are here to do" (26:50a). When a disciple wields a sword in Jesus' defense (26:51-52), Jesus issues a categorical rebuke: "Put your sword back into its place; for all who take the sword will perish by the sword" (26:52). And

Jesus flatly rejects the option of divine retaliation: "Do you think that I cannot appeal to my Father, and he will at once send me more than twelve legions of angels?" (26:53). During his trial, Jesus refuses to defend himself against the accusations of his opponents (27:11-14). And he suffers to the death (27:50b) rather than retaliating against his enemies (26:53) or responding to their taunts (27:40, 42-43).

The story line of Jesus' disciples depicts them initially as impervious to Jesus' call to nonresistance (16:21-22; 26:51). But in the world beyond the end of the narrative, the picture looks strikingly different. Here Jesus' disciples are sent by divine calling (9:38; 10:5, 16; 22:3, 4; 23:34, 37) to a mission that is life-affirming (10:7-8, 12-13), invitational (22:3a; cf. 22:2-4, 8-10), and gracious (10:8b). But this mission, like that of Jesus, will meet with rejection. In fact, Jesus knowingly sends his disciples out "like sheep into the midst of wolves" (10:16). There they will be "maligned" (10:25b), "hated" (10:22a; 24:9b, 10), "mistreated" (22:6), "seized" (22:6), "flogged" (10:17b; 23:34b), "handed over" (10:17a, 19a, 21a; 24:9a, 10), "dragged before governors and kings" (10:18a), "persecuted" (10:23a), "stoned" (23:37), "crucified" (23:34b), "killed" (10:28a; 22:6; 23:34b), and "put to death" (10:21b; 24:9a).

But Jesus calls his disciples not to retaliation but rather to a surprising range of nonviolent responses. At times, Jesus counsels prudence. The disciples must "leave" the houses where they are not welcome (10:14), "flee" from the towns where they are persecuted (10:23), "beware" of people (10:17a), and "be wise as serpents and innocent as doves" (10:16b). Elsewhere, Jesus calls his disciples to throw caution to the wind: "Do not worry" (10:19a), "Do not fear" (10:26a, 28a, 31a, my translation), "Speak in the light" (10:27a, my translation), "Proclaim from the housetops" (10:27b), "Acknowledge me before others" (cf. 10:32a). Jesus even calls his disciples to vivid prophetic actions: "Let your peace return to you" (10:13b) and "Shake off the dust from your feet" (10:14b). But more than this is not theirs to do. Their calling is to carry out the peaceable mission to whom they have been sent and, like Jesus, to suffer without retaliation when others inflict violence.

But the story lines of God's faithful ones do not end with suffering and death. Those who do not resist evil ones but instead love their enemies and pray for their persecutors ultimately "find" their life through "losing" it (10:39b) and are "saved" by "enduring to the end" (10:22b; 24:13). And Matthew's narrative ends with the same profound irony (2:1-23) and the same divine laughter (Ps. 2:4) with which it began. In the resurrection narrative (27:62-28:20), as in the birth narrative (1:18-2:23), God gets the last laugh. Here Jesus' enemies discover that God has bested them at their own game, undone their death sentence, raised Jesus from the dead, and left the well-secured tomb empty. The message is clear. God alone has ultimate power. God alone has the prerogative to right the wrongs of history. And God alone will surely and powerfully vindicate God's faithful ones for their obedience in mission, their creative nonresistance to evil ones, their persistent love of enemies, their constant prayers for persecutors, and their faithfulness in suffering and death.

MATTHEW 5:38-48: A PALESTINIAN CHRISTIAN READING

To read Matt. 5:38-48 as a twenty-first-century Palestinian Christian is to encounter the radical call of Jesus day by day within the challenging context of the Occupied Palestinian Territories. This call comes to Christians across every spectrum. The sixteen people interviewed for this paper reflect a wide range of churches: Anglican, Armenian Orthodox, Baptist, Charismatic, Greek Orthodox, Latin Catholic, Lutheran, Melkite/Greek Catholic, and Quaker. They are women and men ranging in age from their twenties to their seventies. And they represent differing professions: health care, tourism, education, organizational administration, pastoring, writing, and public speaking. But in spite of the demographic differences, the responses reflect strong similarities.

THE CHALLENGE OF MATTHEW 5:38-48

Broad consensus emerges over the challenge of Jesus' words. From Samia's perspective, "These are some of the very difficult passages that we [face] with the Occupation. It's not easy to be a Christian."[9] Nora notes the unique character of Jesus' words: "You don't find these verses in any of the other religions. For us the neighbor and the enemy are one."[10] And like Samia, Nora finds it challenging "to follow Jesus every single day under Occupation" and confesses her difficulty at times in completing the Lord's Prayer, with its call to forgive. As Imad explains, "When the enemy keeps on doing what [he or she] is doing, this is where the victim will not tolerate the oppressor. It is difficult for people oppressed on a daily basis to forgive the oppressor."[11] Alex notes that "because of our human nature . . . these teachings seem to belong to other creatures and not to us."[12] Solomon wonders, "How can Jesus tell us to do such a thing?"[13] And Cedar and Samia highlight the difficulty of explaining these words to children who witness daily the indignities and brutalities of the occupation. Palestinian Christians clearly recognize the enormous challenge of Jesus' words.[14]

JESUS THE PALESTINIAN UNDER ROMAN OCCUPATION

But even as they struggle with Jesus' words, Palestinian Christians readily identify the single most crucial factor for them in interpreting these words—namely, the identity of Jesus himself. In a 1996 conversation, Naim, when questioned about the source of his courage to proclaim good news to his Palestinian congregation, replied simply, "We take courage from the fact that Jesus was a Palestinian who lived under Occupation."[15] And this factor remains crucial for Palestinian Christians. In Rana's words, "When people think about Jesus, they don't usually think of him as living under occupation." But she adds, "Jesus brilliantly understood power structures . . . and he really understood the context that [oppressed people] live in."[16] As Fadi observes, Jesus "was born under Roman occupation [and] knew that his disciples would face problems."[17] And Alex refers to the "vicious military occupation" of Jesus' day, while Imad cites the massacre of the innocents and the crucifixion of Jesus as vivid illustrations of the violence carried out by that regime. Without question, it is their direct identification with Jesus, a first-century Palestinian Jew living under Roman occupation, that gives twenty-first-century Palestinian Christians the courage to engage these hard sayings of Jesus in their Israeli-occupied world.

JESUS AND THE LAW

Another crucial interpretive factor is Jesus' relationship to the Jewish law, the Torah. Issa notes that Jesus "is abolishing the law, even though he said he was fulfilling it," while Solomon and Samia conclude that Jesus has "turned the tables upside down [from the Old Testament]."[18] Solomon notes further that Jesus "was referring to the Sharia" and "wanted to change this concept." Mitri draws a more detailed comparison between Jewish Torah and Muslim Sharia.[19] In his perspective, both of these understandings of law lead to a "false" and "very exclusive" focus on purity laws. And out of his own twenty-first-century experience, Mitri notes that "Torah and Sharia have a very very ugly face. As a Palestinian Christian I know what it means if religious groups try to impose religious laws on women, on other religious groups, and on the society at large, claiming God for such a behavior." By contrast, Mitri observes that "the Gospel is in contradiction to Sharia. . . . Jesus talks about an inclusive community, which thinks of the enemy as a potential neighbor. [So] Jesus wanted to say that

[the] exclusion [reflected in the Torah] has nothing to do with God." And Mitri rephrases Jesus' concluding words (5:48) accordingly: "You need to be whole, because God is inclusive and not exclusive."[20] Issa, for his part, speaks of the "new Scripture" that Jesus brings to his followers, a Scripture summed up in the word *love*. Clearly, Jesus' challenge to the Jewish Scriptures is crucial to twenty-first-century Palestinian Christians.

JESUS' CALL TO RESIST EVIL, NOT EVILDOERS

Another interpretive clue relates to the definition of *nonresistance* and to the distinction between individuals and systems/structures. To begin with, Palestinian Christians are clear about what Jesus' call does not mean. In Rana's words, "No way is it about accepting injustice." Nora likewise affirms that "Jesus doesn't mean to accept being dehumanized." Nor does Jesus call his followers to be "passive" (Daoud) or "apathetic" (Fadi), but instead to be "peace*makers*" (Fadi, emphasis Fadi's).[21]

But Palestinian Christians are also clear about the need to distinguish between individuals and the systems/structures in which they participate. Mitri notes that "Jesus is not calling us to surrender to evil," but rather to "resist the system and love the people."[22] Zoughbi distinguishes carefully between "public life" and "private life," observing that Jesus' call "not to resist" applies to individuals who do evil and not to the systemic/structural evil in which they engage: "Jesus was not against the person but against the system. . . . The enemy is a friend in waiting. The system is evil, not the person."[23] Accordingly, Zoughbi recognizes "the potential of everyone to be transformed," citing Zacchaeus and Saul/Paul as biblical examples of such transformation.[24] But Zoughbi pointedly leaves the task of transformation in God's hands: "God will take care of those who are not transformed and give them time to be transformed." In the meantime, Zoughbi sees "no limits to forgiveness on the personal level."

Accordingly, there is no room for personal vengeance, but only for the justice of God. In Zoughbi's words, "God judges. We don't." But he points to the "poetic justice" reflected in Jesus' warning that "all who take the sword will perish by the sword" (26:52). And Fadi appeals to the scriptural dictum placing vengeance in God's hands: "'Vengeance is mine, I will repay,' says the Lord" (Rom. 12:19; cf. Deut. 32:35).

But with vengeance out of the picture, the "hard question" remains for Alex: "How do we love the people we are resisting?" In Solomon's view, this challenge calls Palestinians "to differentiate between Israelis and their acts," namely, to "hate the deeds and not the person." Salim has an even more nuanced perspective, noting that Israelis who engage in oppressive acts are themselves "victims" of the system they support.[25] Zoughbi likewise acknowledges this complex dynamic, referring to "the hyphenated character, the oppressed-oppressor." And both Salim and Zoughbi struggle with the challenge of defining good and evil. Zoughbi asks, "Who is righteous? Who is unrighteous?" And Salim ponders the situation of the Israeli security guard at the airport, whose aggressive actions appear evil to an innocent Palestinian traveler but who "thinks he is doing good." Accordingly, Salim concludes, "If we understand the context of the action of the oppressor, that helps us to forgive."

Ultimately, however, Palestinian Christians insist that evil systems/structures must be resisted. Salim affirms that "the whole political situation needs to change." The Kairos Document, drawn up by Palestinian Christians in 2009 and signed by heads of churches, puts the issue as follows (4.2/4.2.1):

> Love is the commandment of Christ our Lord to us and it includes both friends and enemies. This must be clear when we find ourselves in circumstances where we must resist evil of whatever kind. Love is seeing the face of God in every human being . . . . However, seeing the face of God in everyone does not mean accepting evil or aggression on their part. Rather, this love seeks to correct the evil and stop the aggression. The aggression against the Palestinian people which is the Israeli occupation is an evil that must be resisted. . . . Primary responsibility for this rests with the Palestinians themselves suffering occupation.[26]

Alex ponders accordingly, "What if the evil is a government? . . . Is Jesus ruling out all forms of resistance? . . . When the authority . . . is evil, how do we know when resisting is legitimate and when it is not?" Zoughbi's response is that "Jesus didn't ask us to succumb, but to challenge the oppressor and to weaken the structure of violence." And as evidence of Jesus' own resistance to systemic/structural evil, Zoughbi appeals to Jesus' exorcism of evil spirits ("Jesus calls us to get rid of evil.") and the cleansing of the temple ("Jesus didn't prevent us from resisting. He gave us an example when he turned over the tables."). Mitri, Rana, Jean, and Daoud likewise speak of "resistance" even as they associate this with "love" (Mitri) and "nonviolence" (Rana, Jean, Daoud). And Nora clearly implies "resistance" when she notes, "I think Jesus is saying, 'Do not resist the evil one *with evil*'" (emphasis Nora's).

JESUS' STRATEGY OF NONVIOLENT RESPONSE

To ask how Palestinian Christians interpret Jesus' strategy of nonviolent response is to engage a rich spectrum of reflections. Some people focus on the impact of nonviolent resistance on the evil person or system/structure. Zoughbi observes that to "turn the other cheek" is "humiliating" to the attacker: "Your hard strike didn't do anything. Try again!"[27] And he notes that to "give the cloak as well as the tunic" is to "[trivialize the evil person's actions] by showing that [he or she] is silly." Nora views "turning the other cheek" as "defying nonviolently," an action that serves to "[make] the [other] person ashamed of what they are trying to do." Rana speaks of "loving enemies" as "doing something beyond expectation," a response that will "stop them" in the course of their actions. In Solomon's words, "Loving the enemy is more harmful to the enemy than getting revenge. It makes the enemy think twice." And for Zoughbi, Jesus' strategy of nonviolent response serves ultimately to "expose the structure of the injustices" and, within the context of twenty-first-century Palestine, to "let the world see how the Israelis are acting."

But Palestinian Christians see far more in Jesus' strategy of nonviolent response than humiliation, shame, and the exposure of injustices. Mitri depicts Jesus' strategy as one in which the "enemy" is "a potential neighbor," or in Zoughbi's words, "a friend in waiting." For his part, Daoud notes that to adopt nonviolent resistance has the effect of "changing the other" in the process: "If you transform your enemy to be your friend, he will not shoot you." Imad affirms that "Jesus' strategy is to . . . employ love rather than hatred" and ultimately "to bring about tolerance." And Fadi asserts that "the teaching of Christ makes sense, because it encourages [Christians] to plant seeds of peace and justice rather than anger and revenge."[28]

Further, as Palestinian Christians recognize, Jesus' strategy of nonviolent response also has an impact on those who take such actions. In Mitri's perspective, Those who engage in retaliation "become victims in this spiral of violence. Jesus wants his disciples to be subjects, who act and do not just react." The issue is about "you becoming in control and not falling into the trap of reaction or revenge." In Rana's terminology, "Jesus is trying to empower [the] victim." Jesus' verbs call people "to act not react." And Jesus' words are thus "words of empowerment." As a result, Rana affirms, "You decide how you will be treated. So you will start thinking of yourself not as a victim but as empowered." Daoud notes that employing nonviolent resistance "needs strength from the inside" and requires "going deep." But such action clearly builds the same strength that it requires. When you "change the other" by "transforming your enemy to be a friend," Daoud asserts, "this is the strength that Jesus was talking about." And clearly this is strength gained through persistent practice. For her part, Nora pushes this persistent practice out into a lifelong perspective as she speaks of Jesus' call to perfection: "You retain the divine in you by reacting how you react. . . . Our whole life leads us slowly and gradually to the divine. [And] every experience we have in loving the enemy leads us closer to that image."

TWENTY-FIRST-CENTURY IMPLICATIONS: THE DYNAMICS OF VIOLENCE

Palestinian Christians reflect solid agreement on the dynamics of violence and the explicit strategies of those who engage in it. As Mitri notes, "Jesus' words are definitely for the real world." And Palestinian Christian analysis of this real world is thoughtful and penetrating.

There is strong consensus on the purpose of the violence carried out by the Israeli occupation. In Imad's words, "The enemy is trying to humiliate and intimidate you and lead you to use violent action," thus "driving you to the edge," while Amal concurs that "they want to push us to violence." Daoud asserts in general terms that "resisting evil with evil is what the evil wants," while Rana makes the principle specific: "The Israelis want us to react in a certain way."[29] Mitri notes that "the Occupation triggers things [that lead] you to react." And he illustrates this principle with the September 2000 incident on the Haram al Sharif/Temple Mount in Jerusalem that resulted in the major outbreak of hostilities now known as the Second Intifada: "[When] Sharon [came to the] Al Aqsa, he knew that he would trigger a reaction from the Muslim community." For Palestinian Christians, it is clear that violence not only engenders violence but in fact requires counterviolence in order to thrive.

Ironically, however, Palestinian Christians likewise recognize that those who employ their power to oppress others also have deep fear of those whom they oppress. Amal recounts the story of a night when soldiers invaded the Tent of Nations and forced Amal and other family members out of the house into the cold. As they did so, Amal questioned them: "Why do you come now? Why not during the day? You are afraid of me?" And Daoud notes similarly that soldiers who "jumped out of the field" to detain him and his family and search their car late one evening were "very, very afraid."

A further point of clarity relates to the debilitating impact of violence on those who employ it. Nora has a question for the security guards at the airport, who put Palestinian travelers through intensive searches widely known as "the VIP treatment": "Do you enjoy doing what you are doing?" And she concludes, "They are dehumanizing themselves when they dehumanize us." Salim would like to see a study of the people who work in airport security, noting that "the guy that checks you [at the airport] is a victim [of the system he supports]." Imad describes an Israeli television documentary featuring a remorseful Israeli, trained as an assassin to kill wanted Palestinians, who eventually reached a "moment of truth" and realized that he himself had been turned into a "killing machine." And Samia recounts the story of a Jewish man who apologized to Palestinians for his role in evicting Palestinians from their homes in 1948, because, as he realized, "this was what the Nazis did to his family."

But Palestinian Christians are likewise clear about the crucial impact of their own responses to those who are violent. Rana notes that to counter violence with violence "will only play to the prejudices that some Israelis have of Palestinians." Imad asserts that "we should avoid violence, so that they don't have any excuse [to engage in further violence against us]." And Daoud comments, "When you act differently, this confuses the other, [because you are] resisting the evil with good." Rana concurs that to live out the words of Jesus not only "empowers [you]" but also "shatters what the Israelis may think." Salim ponders the missiological impact of his airport encounters: "How I respond to [security personnel] can force them to check their conscience. Maybe I will have an opportunity to tell them about Jesus." And Fadi cites Jesus' call (Matt. 5:16) to "let your light shine before others, so that they may see your good works and give glory to your Father in heaven."

TWENTY-FIRST-CENTURY IMPLICATIONS: PALESTINIAN CHRISTIAN RESPONSES TO VIOLENCE

To inquire how Palestinian Christians respond in real life to the everyday violence they encounter is to engage with poignant and courageous stories of faithfulness under duress and, at times, with stunning accounts of transformation at the least expected times and places. These stories reflect a wide range of circumstances and strategies.

Simple strategies are crucial for Nora and Salim. They take books with them to the airport and take care not to "lose control" (Nora) or to get "triangled emotionally" by security personnel (Salim). And Nora notes, "The Occupation has brought out the best in me. Not only has it taught me self control; but it has also helped me live the teachings of Jesus Christ." Amal and her family—whose farm has repeatedly been threatened by Israeli court cases, military incursions, and settler vandalism—"refuse to be enemies." Instead, they choose to "act positively" and "stay on the land" rather than "emigrate, [resign themselves], or react violently." And they cite the story of Naboth's vineyard (1 Kings 21) to explain why they will not "sell their heritage." Similarly, Rana extends the strategic actions and attitudes of a moment or a day into a lifelong stance: "We internalize [our nonviolent resistance]. Immigration stops becoming an option. Immigration is what the oppressor wants. Nonviolent resistance means the conscious decision to stay in this land and thrive."

Fadi, Samia, Nora, and Cedar name prayer as a fundamental response to violence. When Fadi experiences "uneasiness and frustration" while waiting at checkpoints, he "[prays] for the situation, that the Lord will soften the hearts of the soldiers so that they do not yell . . . and that [they] will help the people." Samia speaks of a prayerful practice taught her by her father, who encouraged her to "evaluate the day" every evening before she goes to sleep and identify the places where reconciliation needs to happen. Nora tells of handing olive branches to Israeli soldiers at the wall with the words, "We are praying for the inner walls to fall down." And Cedar recounts a poignant story about her "Arab Jewish" neighbor in Haifa, whose only son was conscripted into the Israeli defense forces during the Six Day War in 1967: "I used to stand with her and pray with her for her son to come home. I cried with her, I prayed with her, my neighbor, my enemy. . . . You cannot *not* feel for your neighbor."

Forgiveness features significantly within Palestinian Christian responses to violence. Alex says of his mother, who lost her husband and her property in 1948: "She focused on forgiveness and moving forward rather than living in the past. For this reason, she refused to go to a refugee camp [festering] with resentments and anger." Zoughbi, who recognizes "no limits" to personal forgiveness, comments that "if the Lord has mercy because we are sinners, then we need to reconcile with brothers and sisters [and clearly enemies as well]." Salim, who needs "a day or two to undo feelings of anger" after encountering airport security, nevertheless notes that "part of the ability to forgive is to understand the context of the action of the oppressor." And he adds, "It's not only important to forgive, which is a hard process in itself, but we also have to be engaged in a process of reconciliation with the other side in order to understand and to address their grievances." Cedar cites the "miracle story" about her son, who had at one time "lost his will to live" due to the violence in Nablus, but who later told his mother, "I don't want to hate. I forgave them." And Cedar herself, who has found great help in "reading spiritual books from other cultures about rising above pain," states simply, "I have faith in God and in human beings, even the ones who are torturing. . . . I believe . . . that in everybody there is something of God . . . I can forgive. I don't have to try. I don't have enemies."[30]

Personal contact with people on all sides of the conflict is crucial for Daoud: "The issue is to listen and try to understand. When [the Israelis] come to know [you], it shows them that you are also a human being." And Daoud goes on, "Political moves [that is, high-level governmental negotiations] have no function. I cannot give you a gift I don't own. I cannot promise peace if I don't have it. It should start with [personal contact]." Amal comments, "You can't make peace without meeting people. If we don't talk, people appear to [us] like enemies. We have to be prepared to talk with people." And Daoud and Amal offer as illustration the story of a woman from a nearby settlement who was invited to a meeting one day at the Tent of Nations. As the meeting started, she sat with her arms crossed in a defiant gesture. But as Daoud described the difficulties of life on the farm without water or electricity—both forbidden by the Israeli authorities—the woman became very agitated. Daoud was certain that she was about to attack him verbally. Instead, she interrupted him to say, "You have no drinking water. But we have swimming pools! I had no idea! I was brought from America. I was offered a house in the settlement. I have been living here for nine years. I never knew that I had neighbors. You are normal people." And the woman came back to the Tent of Nations with her husband at Rosh Hashanah to wish the family Happy New Year. "This is not peace," Daoud explains. "This is the foundation for peace."

Such stories of transformation emerge in widely varying contexts. Cedar recounts the story of a soldier who was once posted to a detail on the roof of her family's house. And as he went through her home one day and saw a Bible, he commented, "You are followers of Jesus!" "Yes," Cedar replied. "And you ought to be too!" This interchange led Cedar to open the Bible to Isaiah 7 and engage in serious Bible study with an Israeli soldier. Sometime later, Cedar discovered a loaf of sliced bread in her kitchen (at a time when curfew had been on for a month and the pantry was bare). Cedar refused the loaf of bread, waiting for the soldier to "come back in civilian clothes." But, as she concludes, "We made a friendship."

For his part, Alex tells of a letter disseminated by a "prominent Messianic Jewish brother" that "viciously attacked" Bethlehem Bible College following a BBC conference titled "Christ at the Checkpoint." As conference organizer, Alex responded to this attack in a letter "that expressed a desire for healing and reconciliation," even as it acknowledged points of disagreement and causes of "offense." When the messianic Jewish community read his appeal, Alex notes, "they were astonished by the letter and said, 'The Palestinians have taken the moral high ground.'" And Alex concludes, "Consequently, we met together, we ate a meal together (both Messianic Jews and Christians), and resumed fellowship and cooperation. Had I responded to [the] letter with the same spirit that was in [the] letter, the gap between us would not have been bridged."

For Daoud, a moment of transformation began with a terrifying incident in which Israeli soldiers with faces painted "jumped out of a field" and stopped the vehicle in which he was traveling with his family late one evening. In spite of his plea that the children were sleeping, the soldiers demanded that the family leave the car, so that they could search it. So Daoud woke his children and said to them (in English that the soldiers could understand): "Don't worry. They are friendly soldiers." Half an hour later, the soldiers finished their search. But before they left, one of the soldiers said to Daoud, "Please apologize to your family. We did something wrong." And Daoud concludes, "If you transform your enemy to be a friend, he will not shoot you."

But enemies do not always become friends. At times, the only victory for the victim of violence is the shame of the aggressor and their own personal dignity. In his 1995 volume, *I Am A Palestinian Christian*, Mitri recounts an incident from the First Intifada, at a time when the residents of Beit Sahour had instigated a tax boycott to protest the fact that they were receiving no services (Raheb 1995). The Israelis then retaliated against this boycott by confiscating the furnishings of the households involved. As Mitri tells the story, one day the tax collectors entered the home of an elderly Christian woman and her family and spent hours removing their furniture and household goods, while the family watched. As the tax collectors prepared to leave the empty living room, the woman said to them, "You forgot the curtains. Please do not forget to take them down too and remove them." And in Mitri's words, "An eerie silence descended on the room. Shamed and guilty, the soldiers left. They took everything but the curtains. At that moment the old woman had achieved dignity. At that moment the triumphant Israeli army had lost the battle. An old woman had defeated them. She gave her enemy, who wanted to sue her and take her dress, her coat also. That became reality. That was resistance" (Raheb 1995: 111).

At other times, faithfulness to the call of Jesus must serve as its own and sole reward. In his 2004 volume, *Bethlehem Besieged: Stories of Hope in Times of Trouble*, Mitri recounts the day when he was held hostage in his pastor's office while Israeli soldiers vandalized the building (Raheb 2004). Mitri's words to the soldiers, remarkably gracious though they were, elicited neither shame nor kindness in response:

> [A] soldier told me, while destroying a painting, "You have here a very beautiful facility."

I said, "We love beauty. We worked so very hard to make this place beautiful. And we take daily care to keep it like this." Another soldier started making fun of me: "You sound like a very wise person." I answered, "The real wise person is he who can transform his enemy into a neighbor, and not his neighbor into an enemy." The commander obviously did not like my answer at all. He shouted at me to shut up, and he ordered his soldiers not to talk to me anymore. (Raheb 2004: 22)

In the end, however, it is hope that energizes Palestinian responses to the violence of the Israeli occupation. For Amal (whose name means "hope"), this hope is a palpable reality that not only energizes her but also powerfully influences both the friends and the enemies who encounter it. Amal credits her father with instilling in his children a resilient hope and a dream for a future built on reconciliation. "Don't give up hope," he told them. "If you give up hope, you can't stay [on the land] one day. You have to prepare people for peace. I want you to continue to fulfill my dream to bring about reconciliation." Such hope-filled action becomes, in Amal's words, "a power that you cannot resist" and a power that serves ultimately to "break the [cycle] of violence." So Amal and her extended family tend their farm tenaciously and creatively, host international work groups that volunteer on the land, organize children's camps, run computer classes in the nearby village, provide space for Israeli/Palestinian dialogue, and offer seminars about nonviolent defense of Palestinian lands. And for Amal, even enormous setbacks can be transformed into victories. As she notes with manifest joy and clear emphasis, "[Israeli settlers] uprooted 350 trees, *but we replanted 700 trees*!" And she continues, "A Jewish group came and sponsored 100 olive trees and planted them *with their own hands*!" Such hope-filled actions draw the immediate attention of both enemies and friends alike. After the olive trees were replanted, Israeli settlers came back, asking angrily, "Why did you replant the olive trees?" But a Muslim woman asked Amal, "From where do you have this patience? I want to come and learn every day."

For Palestinian Christians, the call of Jesus to nonviolence is ultimately a calling that involves all of life and creates the agenda for a lifetime. In Jean's words, "You can't preach love of the enemy in isolation. The inner and the outer go together." Rana notes, "It's everything. It's not segmented or compartmentalized. It's the whole life." And for Nora, "Our whole life leads us slowly and gradually to the divine. [And] every experience we have in loving the enemy leads us closer to that image."

Conclusion: From Scholar's Desk to Real World

To compare the narrative reading of Matt. 5:38-48 above and the Palestinian Christian reading of this text is above all to discover fundamental similarities at work. Common to both readings is a keen awareness of the harsh context of Roman occupation within which Jesus lived and in contrast to which he taught his followers about the kingdom of heaven. Common also to these readings is recognition of the extraordinary challenge of Jesus' call "not to resist the one who is evil" but instead to "love your enemies." In addition, these readings both insist that Jesus' call to nonresistance is a call not to passivity but rather to nonviolent action. And ultimately, both readings acknowledge in their own ways the divine irony that reveals that earthly powers of evil, regardless how powerful they may appear, are nevertheless powerless vis-à-vis the genuine power of God to transform death into life and enemies into friends.

But there are likewise divergences between these readings. On the one hand, such scholarly emphases as the messianic cast of the Gospel of Matthew and the Matthean motif of fulfillment of the law and the prophets (cf. 5:17-20) contract in the real-world exegesis of Palestinian Christians into a strategic emphasis on the newness Jesus has introduced. On the other hand, real-world Palestinian Christian exegesis of Matt. 5:38-48 adds a wealth of biblical parallels and allusions (Naboth to Saul/Paul, Isaiah to Romans) that reach well beyond the scholarly confines of a narrative study based in the Gospel of Matthew. But perhaps most significantly, this real-world Palestinian Christian exegesis contributes a rich panoply of real-life perspectives and experiences to illustrate and confirm the truth of even the most challenging of Jesus' hard sayings. If Jesus' words are "definitely for the real world" (Mitri), then real-world exegesis is likewise crucial to the scholarly enterprise. Let the reader understand.

Notes

1. All biblical citations reflect the New Revised Standard Version unless otherwise designated.

2. This may also apply to Palestinian Muslims. Note the response of Mohammed (not his real name), a Palestinian Muslim, when asked (in a "Life of Jesus" course for tour-guiding students) to identify the "important themes" in the Sermon on the Mount: "I can't do this assignment. Jesus is a very important prophet for us. And everything that he said is important." Mohammed eventually submitted a paper far more extensive than that of any of his colleagues.

3. As Carter notes (2000: 152–53), "The verb 'forces' (. . . *angareusei*) refers to requisitioning labor, transport (animals, ships), and lodging from subject people (called *angaria*)."

4. Note, however, that Lev. 19:18 refers only to "loving your neighbor" and does not mention "hating your enemy." For such language, see Ps. 139:21-22.

5. Of the three (Septuagintal) versions of the *lex talionis* found within the Jewish Scriptures (Exod. 21:22-25; Lev. 24:19-20; Deut. 19:15-21), only Deut. 19:15-21 includes the specific vocabulary of Matt. 5:39, namely, "resist" (*anthistēmi*: Deut. 19:16) and "evil one" (*ho ponēros*: Deut. 19:19).

6. For a detailed discussion of Deut. 19:15-21 vis-à-vis its messianic fulfillment in Matt. 5:38-48, see Weaver 1992: 32–71.

7. See 11:6, where Jesus pronounces a blessing on the one "who is not scandalized" (*mē skandalisthē*, my translation) by him or his messianic ministry (11:2-5).

8. See Jesus' promise to his disciples: "When they hand you over, do not worry about how you are to speak or what you are to say; for what you are to say will be given to you at that time; for it is not you who speak, but the Spirit of your Father speaking through you" (10:19-20).

9. Samia Khoury, board member, Sabeel Ecumenical Liberation Theology Center.

10. Nora Carmi, former coordinator of community-building and women's programs, Sabeel Ecumenical Liberation Theology Center.

11. Imad Nassar, program manager, Wi'am Palestinian Conflict Resolution Center.

12. Rev. Alex Awad, dean of students, Bethlehem Bible College and Pastor, East Jerusalem Baptist Church.

13. Solomon J. Nour, headmaster, Hope Secondary School (deceased August 5, 2011).

14. Cedar Duaybis, board member, Sabeel Ecumenical Liberation Theology Center.

15. Rev. Dr. Naim Ateek, Anglican priest and founder/director of Sabeel Ecumenical Liberation Theology Center.

16. Rana Khoury, vice president for development and outreach, Diyar Consortium.

17. Fadi Al-Zoughbi, minister, House of Bread Church.

18. Issa (not his real name) is a Bethlehem tour guide.

19. Rev. Dr. Mitri Raheb, pastor, Evangelical Lutheran Christmas Church, and founder/president, Diyar Consortium.

20. As Mitri notes, however, there is a steep price to pay for such a radical challenge: "The cross was the consequence for daring to question the Torah."

21. Daoud Nassar is the founder/director of the Tent of Nations.

22. See the words of Jean Zaru, presiding clerk of the Ramallah Friends Meeting: "We have to love the enemy, but we resist with nonviolence," and of Nora: "Jesus is saying, 'Do not resist the evil one *with evil*'" (emphasis Nora's).

23. Zoughbi Zoughbi, founder/director, Wi'am Palestinian Conflict Resolution Center.

24. Cf. Solomon's comment: "These people can be changed. . . . In every person there is something good and something bad."

25. Dr. Salim Munayer, founder/director, Musalaha, and professor of theology, Bethlehem Bible College.

26. "Kairos Palestine 2009: A Word of Faith, Hope, and Love from the Heart of Palestinian Suffering," http://www.kairospalestine.ps/?q=content/document.

27. Or, as Nora puts it, "I'm still here! I'm standing up!"

28. Conversely, Fadi notes that "revenge is not a way of life." And he invokes the words of Mahatma Gandhi that depict "the whole world as blind and toothless" if people continue to exact "eye for eye and tooth for tooth." Salim similarly notes that "at the end of the day resisting evil [violently] brings more evil than good."

29. Amal Nassar, physiotherapist, Caritas Baby Hospital, and member, Tent of Nations.

30. But forgiveness does not necessarily come easily or automatically. Samia tells of an Israeli Arab man who requested a glass of water from her as he was working for the Israeli military in closing off the street in front of her house. Samia's initial response was, "Go, let your masters give you a drink!" Samia's aunt then challenged her with the words, "That's not how you were brought up!" This caused Samia to reconsider and to give the man a glass of water. "I hated myself for that," Samia reflects, "the way I reacted."

14

Reading the Gospel of Matthew Ecologically in Oceania

Matthew 4:1-11 as Focal Text

Elaine M. Wainwright

Contextual biblical interpretation continues to challenge biblical scholars because our contexts keep shifting and changing, as does our own awareness within these changing contexts. Hence, if we claim to be contextual biblical interpreters, our scholarship will need to keep changing with our contexts. This has been the experience of my years of engagement in biblical scholarship as my feminist consciousness has shifted and changed through engagement with many women in different contexts. Awareness of my own and also global contexts of colonization expanded this feminist consciousness to include the postcolonial optic. Such a shift did not, however, mean abandoning one contextual lens for another; rather, an awareness of profound injustices in my context has meant that I have had to learn how to integrate not only changing but also multiple perspectives. It is necessary to continually permeate boundaries, both contextually and hermeneutically.

The current cry of the planet rising up in a myriad of different contexts has challenged me to negotiate yet another boundary and to shift my contextual lens yet again. Awareness of the prevailing social imaginary of mastery that became more and more evident in feminist and postcolonial analyses must now be extended beyond a focus solely on the human to include all Earth beings. And so my current project of reading the Gospel of Matthew ecologically is yet a more nuanced response to the challenge of contextual biblical interpretation to continue to negotiate new marginal spaces in critical engagement with context.

In this essay, I undertake an ecological reading of Matt. 4:1-11, using an approach that I am developing for a reading of the entire Gospel of Matthew.[1] The broad material context for such a reading is Oceania. Initially, therefore, I turn to this context, providing just a brief glimpse of some of the significant ecological imperatives that call for both a change of perspective and action in that location. In the second section of the essay, I give a brief description of both a hermeneutical and methodological approach that can facilitate an ecological reading of biblical texts, of which the Gospel of Matthew is just one example. This provides readers with an understanding of the features that guide my ecological reading of Matt. 4:1-11 as an example of a contemporary contextual biblical interpretation.

OCEANIA AS CONTEXT FOR READING

In the Melbourne daily newspaper *The Age*, on July 29, 2009, Adam Morton reported on those believed to be the first climate change refugees, the people of the Carteret Islands, seven tiny volcanic atolls belonging to Papua New Guinea and situated almost one hundred kilometers northeast of Bougainville in the South Pacific Ocean (Morton 2009). These refugees are in the process of leaving their homes, their islands, and being set up on Bougainville land acquired by the Catholic Church for their use. Scientists are aware that their situation is complex and that geological factors other than climate change may be affecting the islands, causing them to sink as well as the sea levels to rise. But those rising sea levels together with the changes in temperature, violent storms, tsunamis, and other effects on/of the ocean are some results of rising temperatures caused by human emissions of carbon dioxide into the atmosphere and its inability to escape. The lifestyle of some in our world is having a catastrophic impact on others, with the peoples of Oceania or the Pacific bearing the burden in untold ways and the ocean itself and its complex ecosystems and species being changed and destroyed. Climate change is, therefore, one of the most urgent global concerns, whose effects are devastating and urgent for the small island nations located in the Pacific (or the region of Oceania, as it is becoming known), for their ocean contexts, and for all Earth constituents of whatever life-form in the region.[2]

It is from this region, as an Australian biblical scholar currently working in New Zealand, that I seek to undertake an ecological reading of the Gospel of Matthew. I join other scholars in the region who are undertaking similar interpretive tasks from a variety of perspectives. Oceania is the place of origin of the Earth Bible project, a five-volume set of collections of essays overseen by a team of scholars located in Adelaide, Australia, and directed by Norman Habel (see Habel 2000; Habel and Wurst 2000; 2001a; 2001b; and Habel and Balabanski 2002). The Team developed six ecojustice principles to guide ecological readings of biblical texts (Habel 2000: 38–53)[3] and invited a range of international scholars to read selected texts from across the two testaments guided by these principles. Among those texts selected, only two focus specifically on Matthean Gospel texts, my own article in volume 1, "A Transformative Struggle towards the Divine Dream: An Ecofeminist Reading of Matthew 11" (Wainwright 2000b) and that of Adrian M. Leske, "Matthew 6:25-34: Human Anxiety and the Natural World" in volume 5 (Leske 2002).

The work of the Earth Bible team was continued through Norman Habel's establishing a Consultation on Ecological Hermeneutics at the annual meeting of the Society of Biblical Literature, beginning in 2004. Out of this consultation emerged *Exploring Ecological Hermeneutics*, a volume edited by Norman Habel and Peter Trudinger, the cochairs of the consultation, and published in 2008. No studies of the Matthean Gospel appeared in this volume. During this decade, however, other important ecological readings of biblical texts began to emerge in the region. Robert Barry Leal undertook a study of wilderness in the Bible with particular attention to the experience of wilderness in an Australian context (Leal 2004). He did not, however, specifically develop an ecological hermeneutic. Anne F. Elvey did undertake that task as she read selected Lukan texts from an ecological feminist perspective (Elvey 2005).[4] I also sought to integrate an ecological with a feminist and postcolonial perspective in my study of women healing in the Greco-Roman world (Wainwright 2006) and to develop ecofeminist readings of specific texts. But the explicit development of my ecological hermeneutic was limited (Wainwright 2008a; 2008b). Ecological issues have also been taken up in the region by theologians, including Ilaitia S. Tuwere (2002), Ama Tofaeono (2000), Winston Halapua (2008), Nicola Hoggard Creegan (2007), Neil Darragh (2000), and Denis Edwards (2004; 2005; 2010). It was no surprise, therefore, that the inaugural meeting of the Oceania Biblical Studies Association, held in Auckland in July 2010, in conjunction with the theological society, Waves of the Moana, chose as its theme "Climate Change in Oceania: Biblical and Theological Responses." Also at the 2010 meeting of the Society for Asian Biblical Studies, Dr. Nasili Vaka'uta delivered one of the keynote addresses with a focus on reading eco-wise in Oceania (Vaka'uta 2010).

Biblical scholars in the region are beginning to undertake ecological readings of biblical texts and traditions with particular attention to their context in Oceania, a context that is experiencing quite profoundly the effects of climate change and global warming. Indeed, in the very month in which I am finalizing this article, the two cities that I call home in southeastern Queensland have been devastated by floods, of tsunami proportions, it is said.[5] And as I initially reviewed it, Christchurch, a major city on the south island of New Zealand was devastated by a 6.3 category earthquake.[6] It is within this context of Oceania both broadly and specifically that I place my ecological reading of the Gospel of Matthew.

READING THE GOSPEL OF MATTHEW ECOLOGICALLY

Undertaking such a task has entailed developing a framework for reading that I can only outline here. I have been significantly influenced by Lorraine Code's *Ecological Thinking.* In her work, she demonstrates the need for a new social imaginary if we are to address the ecological crisis, and it is that new or emerging imaginary that she calls "ecological thinking." She envisages such thinking as working against the instituted social imaginary of mastery in all its forms—human domination of human and all other life-forms constituting Earth or the anthropocentrism that characterizes so much current thinking and practice. It therefore requires a hermeneutics of suspicion or a critical appraisal of all forms of domination that have been so prevalent in Earth's history. But such a critique will not, in itself, bring about transformation. Code herself goes on to describe the significance of what she calls "reconfiguration": "The *instituting* imaginary is a vehicle of radical social critique: it requires thinking and acting away from received conceptions of knowledge, subjectivity, responsibility, and agency, from positions located squarely within the power-infused rhetorical spaces where knowledge making and knowledge circulating occur; determining how reconfigurations might be proposed, innovative hypotheses articulated and tested in and for that climate, that place, positioned as it is in relation to other places and climates" (Code 2006: 33). As a critical and reconstructive epistemology, ecological thinking shares characteristics with other critical epistemologies such as feminism and postcolonialism, or as Code suggests: "[it] emerges from and addresses so many interwoven and sometimes contradictory issues—feminist, classist, environmental, postcolonial, racist, sexist—that its implications require multifaceted chartings" (Code 2006: 3–4). Its focus, however, is Earth and all its constituents and the function of power within the relationships among all Earth's constituents—including the human but within the broader web of relationships.

The particular lens that I have chosen to enable ecological thinking to function within a process of reading the biblical/Matthean text is habitat. For

Code, ecology is a "study of habitats both physical and social" in a way that shifts the nature/culture divide of the epistemology of mastery (Code 2006: 25).[7] She defines habitat as a "place to know" such that "social-political, cultural, and psychological elements figure alongside physical [and I would add material] and (other) environmental contributors to the 'nature' of a habitat and its inhabitants at any historical moment" (Code 2006: 37). But habitat will always be limited—limited by human perspective, human worldview/s as well as limited by Earth itself, which is always beyond, always more than our knowing.[8] This tension will characterize the use of habitat as a key interpretive category, noting that habitat is more than place but also that place will be explored in new ways in dialogue with emerging critical theory and from an ecological perspective. Habitat and in-habitants (the more-than-human, which includes the human together with all Earth's constituents) are interactive and yet inseparable, such that "habitat" can function as a key interpretive lens for reading ecologically.

Biblical studies has long been concerned with the interrelationships of text and context, but attention to context often entailed a nod toward setting as the ground in and on which human activity took place. Within an ecological reading, context will be considered in relation to "habitat" and their relationship within the complex process of text production and text interpretation or meaning-making. For an ecological reading attentive not only to the reciprocity of text and con-text[9] but also to the complex web of author/reader in/and context, habitat will be significant in order to return the reading process toward Earth. In this, Code reminds us again that habitat itself is not just place in its materiality, but place in which materiality is inextricably linked to "ethologies, genealogies, commitments, and power relations that shape the knowledge and subjectivities enacted there; the intractable locational specificities that resist homogenization or suggest novel connections; the positionings available or closed to would-be knowers; the amenability or resistance of both human and nonhuman entities to being known" (Code 2006: 100).

The biblical methodology that best facilitates an ecological reading for me is sociorhetorical. Habitat can function as an interpretive key within an analysis of the text's inner texture (its characters, plot, setting, rhetorical features, and other aspects of that inner texture). Similarly, in relation to the text's intertexture, habitat provides an important ecological lens in analyzing other texts that constitute the materiality, textuality, and rhetoricity of a given Matthean text. There is, however, a second axis of intertextuality; namely, those meanings and texts that a reader attentive to Earth engages with in the process of reading/interpretation—theories of space, time, and materiality for instance; agrarian texts, poetry, and other nature writings, to identify but some. Vernon Robbins names the third texture of his sociorhetorical model "the social and cultural texture."[10] Within an ecological reading, I am suggesting that this third texture be called the "ecological texture." It will include analysis of those social and cultural features that are generally seen to constitute the human community, as these are encoded in the text. But this analysis will be extended to recognize all Earth relationships and their dynamics, as these too are encoded in the text. The sociorhetorical reading that I am proposing, therefore, uses "habitat" as interpretive key within a reading of the inner texture, intertexture, and ecological texture of the Matthean text.

The term I use in order to highlight the complex reciprocity of author-text-reader in/and habitat as place to know and place from which to know in an ecological reading is *inter-con/textuality*. It is not only concerned with relationships between texts but also between texts and "contexts" as these are encoded within texts. It will also include the interweaving into this reciprocity of the multiple aspects of habitat and the shift in consciousness necessary to hear those aspects of Earth encoded in the text. This is necessary because these interrelationships have been silenced by previous readings so that they are almost forgotten by readers. Or, more seriously, they have been erased. An ecological reading therefore seeks to hear the erasures that the text evokes.

In an inter-con/textual reading, habitat, in all its diversity of the embodied, materially and socially related Earth beings, of social, temporal, and physical locations, of their histories and genealogies and of their power relations, functions as inter-con/text. It is woven into the texture of the text. The reader will need to listen for the re-mark Timothy Morton describes as a kind of echo in the text that makes readers aware that there is but a "hair's breadth" between foreground and background in a way that leads to "questioning the genuine existence of these categories" (Morton 2007: 54). Ecological readers will be attentive to that echo which takes us to the hair's breadth between habitat as background and foreground, which breaks down the binaries while not collapsing the categories themselves into a singularity that destroys the very diversity of ecosystems.

In concluding this theoretical section, I want to emphasize that the ecological reading I am proposing can be used in the interpretation of any text. If ecological reading is limited to texts that highlight Earth, then it will continue to be seen as peripheral. I am arguing here that reading ecologically is integral to a reading of all texts. In this regard, then, our reading and interpreting of biblical texts can contribute, in its turn, to the shaping of the new and emerging social imaginary that Code calls "ecological thinking." This, in its turn, will affect the reader's context, shifting consciousness, but also, for some, leading to ethical action or engaged "ecological citizenship," as Deane Curtin calls it (Curtin 2005: 195).

READING MATTHEW 4:1-11 ECOLOGICALLY

Matthew 4:1-11 belongs in the broader literary context of Matthew 3–4, which I have named "From Wilderness to Waterfront," as both John and Jesus move from wilderness to waterfront, with an additional waterfront to wilderness movement by Jesus. Given that the Jordan River flows through the wilderness of Judea, the boundaries between the two as they are encoded in the biblical text are somewhat porous in some parts, until Jesus moves to a new waterfront, that of Capernaum (Matt. 4:12-13). Inter-con/textually, however, both wilderness and waterfront characterize Matthew 3 and 4 as they permeate the text, constituting, as they do, con-text and habitat.

From the opening phrase of Matthew 4, especially 4:1-11, *erēmos*/"desert" pushes up into the narrative as the destination of Jesus' movement from the waterfront of the Jordan into the wilderness. Given that spatiality continues to be a significant feature not only of the text of Matthew 4 but also an ecological reading of it, I have found Edward Soja's theory of "space" and Edward Casey's theoretical reflections on "place" to be significant second-axis intertexts.

Soja recognizes three ways in which space functions (Soja 1999). For him, Firstspace is "perceived space," or that which can be mapped geographically. From this perspective, *erēmos*/"desert" functions textually in Matt. 4:1 to evoke that area extending west from the lower Jordan River and the Dead Sea into the hill country of Judea. There is nothing more precise in the text. This is one level of space encoded in the text in a way that suggests what Casey recognizes—namely, the significance of place—in that where a person is contributes significantly to who and what the person is at any given time. He goes on to name *place* as "the environing subsoil of our embodiment, the bedrock of our being-in-the-world" (Casey 1993: xv, xvii). This is to move toward Soja's notion of Secondspace, or conceived space—that is, how space is conceived metaphorically or symbolically by the human community in its relationship with the "environing subsoil" of its embodiment.

Robert Leal summarizes the intertextuality that contributes to the Secondspace or metaphorical and social understanding of *erēmos* in Matt. 4:1, conceiving wilderness as the place of divine encounter in which discipline, purification, and/or transformation take place often as a result of the harshness of the environment in relation to human habitation (Leal 2004: 135–71). Casey says in this regard that "the desolate physiogonomy of wilderness is doubtless felt most poignantly in circumstances of isolation" (Casey 1993: 197), which is the experience of Jesus narrated in the text.

Wilderness is encoded in the opening verse of Matt. 4:1-11, evoking both its materiality (Firstspace) and its metaphorical (Secondspace) character. It is a space that has its own particular ecosystems but a place that can be harsh for those of the human community who have not learned to live there.[11] Casey even speaks of the "fleshlike character" of wilderness, recognizing it as an instance of the "flesh of the world" (Casey 1993: 209), reminding me as ecological reader of Sallie McFague's metaphorical conception of Earth as the body of divinity (McFague 2003). It is a place of encounter in its many aspects.

In the Matthean narrative, Jesus is brought into the wilderness not according to his own choosing but impelled by one named "spirit"/*pneumatos*. The reader has encountered such a spirit, who has been characterized earlier as "holy" (1:18, 20; 3:11) and "of God" (3:16). This spirit was associated with the birth of Jesus as Emmanuel, the one in whom God is not just with the "us" of the human community but the "us" of the entire more-than-human community. This Earth community includes not only the human but also all other Earth constituents. To name a spirit that is holy and that is intimately caught up with Jesus, the human/material embodiment of "God with the Earth community" is to evoke the interrelationship of materiality in all its manifestations with divinity. In Matt. 3:16, this spirit is named as "of God" but manifest in the materiality of one of Earth's constituents, namely, a dove—the material, the metaphorical, and the mythical interrelate in this opening verse. Given the spirit-Jesus relationship in the narrative, the reader will not be surprised at the text's describing Jesus as being led into the wilderness by this spirit.

What is surprising in the narrative is the appearance of one named *diabolos* (4:1, 5, 8, 11; 13:39; 25:41), whose purpose is to tempt Jesus. The Matthean phraseology is so familiar to contemporary readers that we lose something of the surprise connection. While intertextually, "testing" may draw into the text the experience of the Israelites in the wilderness (Exod. 15:25; 16:4; 17:2, 7; 20:20), there it was God who was testing Israel, not the devil. The presence of the *diabolos* evokes Satan's testing of Job, but in that instance the verb *peiradzō* was not used. Habitat may indicate the emphasis: Jesus is tempted in the wilderness, as was Israel, but he is to be tempted by the *diabolos*, one of those beings in the Hellenistic worldview who existed between divinity and humanity—the mythical aspect of the narrative continues, but it is grounded in the material.

Verse 2 is framed by two verbs that describe the very grounded experience of Jesus. He fasts (for forty days and forty nights), and he is hungry. Jesus does not engage with the space that is the wilderness/desert for his sustenance, as did John (3:4). Rather, Jesus makes an alternative choice, namely, not to eat of the sustenance the desert could provide. Reading through the lens of the remark, one recognizes the "hair's breadth" between background and foreground functioning in this verse. If the reader brings a Firstspace appropriation of wilderness/desert to the foreground, this allows for an exploration of the wilderness in interaction with Jesus and he with it. It is not just background for the Jesus story, nor is it simply a symbolic or conceived Secondspace. Rather, Jesus is portrayed in relation to it in a way that is profoundly challenging; he chooses to fast forty days and forty nights. Textually, he is located in the diversity of habitat/s and Earth constituents that is desert, and his relationship with these is to fast from taking them as food.

Jesus' fast in the desert contrasts John the Baptist's response to his habitat (Matt. 3:4). Habitat can call forth different responses. Jesus' chosen and lengthy fast may alert the ecological reader to possible human ethical responses to the processes of desertification that may be the result of climate change in the twenty-first century. Such processes of desertification are affecting both Australia and the once exceedingly fertile islands of the Pacific and are in extreme contrast with the violent storms and flooding that have seemed to follow one upon the other in recent years (Nunn 1997: 3–5).[12] Not only can one live with/in and draw from habitat, but recognition of some of the violent disruption of habitat, symbolized in the text by desert wilderness, may also call for a fast within the human community.

Reading the *erēmos*/"wilderness" or desert through the lens of Soja's Thirdspace, or what he calls "lived space," it functions as a site of marginality, but not a marginality that is "imposed by oppressive structures." Rather, it is a site that "one chooses as a site of resistance," a space where boundary-crossing is possible (Soja 1999: 271).[13] It is a place where Jesus fasts for forty days and forty nights. In this way, he is characterized intertextually through the lens of the prophet and mediator of a covenant with the divine, namely, Moses and Elijah (Exod. 34:27-28; 1 Kgs. 19:8). Moses fasted for forty days and forty nights, and Exod. 34:28 goes on to say "he neither ate bread nor drank water," the sources of food and drink the Earth gives for the sustenance of the human community. Elijah journeys for forty days and nights on the strength of the food and drink that he is given in the wilderness. Thus fasting can be read inter-con/textually as a symbol of human reliance not only on divinity but also on Earth. The abstaining from food brings an awareness of this—Jesus is hungry (Matt. 4:2).[14]

The prophet of God with/in whom God is with God's people (Matt. 1:23) or the beloved in whom God is well pleased (3:17) must know this reliance, the hunger that comes from the choice not to eat nor to drink for a period of time (McVann 1993: 14–20).[15] Jesus has been lead into this marginal or liminal space not as a location imposed on him but as a space that he clearly embraces and from which resistance will be possible.[16]

This resistance becomes manifest as one reads the account of the three tests or temptations that Jesus faces (4:3-10) through the lens of Soja's Firstspace, Secondspace, and Thirdspace. The Firstspace location of the three tests differs. The wilderness or desert remains the perceived space for the first test, and in it, Jesus experiences hunger as a result of his fast. The test offered to Jesus is to change stones into bread, to intervene in Earth's processes and the delicate interrelationship between the human and other-than-human Earth elements. Jesus resists the challenge. Reading his response from a Thirdspace or resistant space and an ecological perspective, one can hear him affirming Earth interrelationships and their interconnectedness with the divine.

The *alla* ("but") in the phrase "the human one/the *anthrōpos* shall not live by bread alone, *but* by every word that proceeds from the mouth of God" (v. 4) could be interpreted as opposing the sustenance of human food with the sustenance of God's word.[17] Bauer, Arndt, Gingrich, and Danker, however, offer an alternative way of understanding the connective: "the other side of the matter, (or) but yet" (BDAG 45).[18] The human one must be in right relationship with both Earth elements and with God. Matthew 3:15 associated the unfolding of Jesus' story in terms of "fulfilling all righteousness" and such righteousness or right ordering or justice will characterize Jesus' own preaching (see 5:6, 10, 20; 6:1, 33).

Reading from an ecological perspective, such right ordering will not be seen solely as right relationships within the human community and between the human community and God, but all Earth's constituents will be included in the interconnected web/s of right or just ordering. Jesus' response to the first temptation resists the diabolic proposal to manipulate Earth's elements for one's own satisfaction or gratification, providing a challenge to contemporary readers in a world where such manipulation contributes to ecological degradation in multiple ways. The text does not speak against such manipulation but puts it into the complex of right relationships that Jesus constructs. It challenges the human community to careful ecological evaluation of the scientific and industrial processes it puts in place (see Knappett 2005; Knappett and Malafouris 2008).

The Firstspace location of the second test is the pinnacle of the temple in the city of Jerusalem. Already in Matthew's Gospel, Jerusalem has been portrayed as the center of political power, with Herod's building program providing it with the built environment of a royal city (see Wainwright 2010). It was also the religious center, given the location of the temple within the city. This temple had been reconstructed by Herod, using the massive stones that can still be seen on the site. But the temple also bears all the ambiguity of this reconstruction by Herod, whose use of power and of the material was in opposition to claims of divine presence. Some of this ambiguity is already woven into Matt. 2:1-12, where Jerusalem is contrasted with Bethlehem, the place in which Jesus was born. The devil's taking of Jesus to the "holy city" and placing him on the "pinnacle of the temple" evokes these Firstspace and Secondspace connotations inter-con/textually as Jesus is represented as having it all within his extraordinary purview. Place and power with all their political, social, cultural, and religious connotations play within the ecological texture of the text constituting habitat.

Power can be analyzed horizontally, in the web of power that constitutes the Thirdspace reading of this second temptation, in which power shifts across boundaries in the interchange constructed in the text. The power attributed to Jesus by way of the title "son of God" is being tested in this second temptation by the *diabolos* or tempter in the context of this intersecting web of power. The tempter places Jesus in a position of oversight of all the visual symbols of Herod's political and economic power that have combined to accomplish the transformation of material resources into the city below. The tempter then challenges Jesus within the framework of the challenge/riposte functioning between them. In the first such contest, Jesus bests the tempter with his citation of Deut. 8:3. The tempter now throws out the challenge of a different text to Jesus: Ps. 91:11a, 12. This is a psalm that uses a complex range of images to evoke God's assurance of protection. The cited verses of the psalm are interpreted literally by the tempter, challenging Jesus to throw himself down bodily and to expect extraordinary divine intervention to counteract his human action. Jesus interprets divine power very differently. He cites Deut. 6:16 and its prohibition against tempting God and in doing so evokes the intertext Exod. 17:1-7 and the people's "testing" of God at Massah and Meribah.[19] There the people trust neither God nor Earth to provide them with water to drink along their wilderness journey, and yet it is the intersection of the power of both God and Earth that will sustain them. This is the reliance that must not be tested, not some self-initiated challenge to God's care as put before Jesus by the tempter. In the Thirdspace of the pinnacle of the temple, where alternatives are possible from this marginal space, power has been contested, affirming the dynamic relationship between God and Earth.

Readers in Oceania will recognize that the complex web of relationships linking water, the Earth, and the divine, evoked by the intertextuality of Exod. 17:1-7, has been threatened by current climate change. At times and in some contexts, the break in the web of relationships affects the ocean, with which the peoples of Oceania are so intimately interconnected.[20] At other times, disjunction functions in relation to much-needed water on the larger islands of Australia and New Zealand when these are faced with regular droughts.[21]

Power emerges even more explicitly in the third temptation, whose location is the top of a very high mountain from which "all the kingdoms/*basileias* of the world" are visible. Intertextually and from a Secondspace perspective, the tops of high mountains are seen metaphorically as the abode of divine power. This was so in relation to the gods of those with whom Israel contested (Deut. 12:2) as it was for Israel's God (Ezek. 20:40). Both Moses and Elijah encounter God on the mountain height of Sinai or Horeb—Exodus 34; 1 Kings 19). Also, the gods of Rome "were thought to reside on Mt. Olympus," as Warren Carter demonstrates (Carter 2000: 110). From this place of divine power, the tempter shows Jesus "all the kingdoms/*basileias* of the world." In the negotiation of power, the tempter takes on the mantle of divinity. These "*basileias* of the world" are the political, economic, social, and religious centers and realms of power that are being offered to Jesus with all the "honor . . . fame, recognition, renown . . . (and) prestige" (BDAG 257) that accompanies them.

Already in the narrative, however, John the Baptist has proclaimed that there is an alternative *basileia* near at hand, that of the heavens (3:2), and that there is one coming after him who will carry on his task of eschatological prophet (3:11-12). Jesus has been intimately linked with John by way of John's baptizing of him to fulfill all righteousness or right ordering, and according to McVann's interpretation, Jesus is thereby initiated as just such a prophet by way of the ritual process McVann identifies in Matthew 3-4 (McVann 1993).

The price offered to Jesus for these *basileias* with all their political, social, economic, and religious power (their glory according to the text) is that he fall down and worship (*proskynein*) the *diabolos*. In this way, Jesus would recognize the tempter's power and would honor his claim to this power with homage, the homage given to divinity. Power plays within the ecological texture of this text with the tempter's challenge to Jesus to prostrate himself, echoing the demands of Gaius Caligula, who during his tyrannical rule demanded such prostration and, as Theissen notes, even "attempted to have himself worshiped in the temple at Jerusalem in place of the biblical God" (Theissen 1992: 215). Jesus once again speaks from the Thirdspace, the mountaintop as marginal space that allows a third word of resistance—only God shall be worshiped; only God will be given the homage of one's life. Jesus has shown himself to be "beloved Son" (3:17), to be faithful son (4:3 and 6), unlike Israel, who is also called "son" or "firstborn son" (Exod. 4:22-23; Deut. 8:5; 14:1; and Hos. 11:1, already cited in Matt. 2:15).[22]

The first two tests of the beloved challenge the web of right relationships that connect the divine, human, and the other-than-human. The third test, which purportedly challenges the power that characterizes the *basileias* of the cosmos, seems to break the web, focusing only on divine power or the divine/human interrelationship presented as cultic service.[23] Earth appears to be excluded at this climactic point in the narrative, as are divine-human relationships imaged in ways other than power. This alerts the attentive ecological reader to the necessity from time to time to read against the grain of the text or to bring to it a hermeneutics of suspicion.

Such an approach, which is indeed a Thirdspace or alternative reading site available on the margins of the text, alerts readers to the exclusion of the female from this entire narrative. Jesus, the tempter (4:3), and God (explicitly in 4:10 but implicitly throughout by way of pronouns) are all gendered male. The ecological reader will need to take up the space of resistance given to Jesus in the text and to read against the grain of this gendering, bringing into the imaging of God, at least, echoes of Sophia or of the female divine imaged as dove from 3:16-17.[24] It will also be necessary to carry the web of relationships that functions in Jesus' successful negotiation of the first two tests into that of the third. This brings a recognition that the *basileias* of the world are not just centers of power in its many manifestations. These *basileias* include the material, complex ecosystems and habitats as well as humanity with the sociopolitical, cultural, and material interrelationships woven within the term *basileia*. The restoration of right relationships is imaged in a return to the mythical: the *diabolos* departs and angels minister to Jesus.

A RETURN TO CONTEXTUALITY IN CONCLUSION

The ecological reading of the opening pericope of Matthew 4 has demonstrated that attention to the material, to habitat, and to the holy offers ways of both reading the text anew in the light of ecological thinking and of informing the emerging social imaginary that Code calls "ecological thinking" by way of such new readings. Subtle movements between inner, inter-, and ecological textures of the Matthean text using this perspective have allowed new meanings to emerge in front of the text, but always taking account of the inter-con/textuality within the text. A fine but strong web keeps them connected.

As these readings have unfolded, they have already spoken into the context of Oceania. One way in which this has occurred has been simply the raised awareness of the materiality of ecosystems, habitats, and power as these have been encoded in the text. With this awareness, readers are invited by their ecological reading to recognize that this same materiality and power is woven into the fabric of every aspect of each reader's life. This is a spiraling outcome of a committed and ethical reading of texts; namely, that such reading in fact brings about more deeply in the reader's consciousness the very perspective that initially gave impetus to the reading. This, however, is not simply to be trapped in a circle of prejudice, as the text often invites the reader into vistas of meaning potential that could never have been imagined before entering into the reading process.

This ecological reading of a small segment of the Matthean Gospel drew out potential ethical response to the ravages of climate change in Oceania, especially that of desertification. Readers were invited to be attentive to the fragile web of relationships that can constitute living with/in wilderness as exemplified in John the Baptist. An ecological reading also alerted readers to the more radical response of fasting exemplified in Jesus and the recognition of the need to discern the most appropriate response. Both approaches will be ethical and can be taken up in communities of "ecological citizenship" depending on local contexts and their issues.

Power also played within the complex web of the text of Matt. 4:1-11, and as ecological readers in Oceania are faced with the imperatives of changing climate, changing oceans, changing patterns of rain and drought, their negotiation of the play of power within the text may provide them with facilities to analyze and respond to the powers operative in their different contexts. Diabolic power was visible and active in the mythological fabric of the biblical text. Identifying and naming such power is a skill that needs to carry over to the interplay of human power in relation to Earth's resources. To whom do they belong? Who has the power to transform them and at what cost to the environment? These are some of the questions that the ecological reading of the Matthean temptation narrative raises. They can be taken up as the text encounters multiple new contexts in Oceania, where such questions are raised from the marginal Thirdspace created by the text, the place where new understandings are possible. They could be asked of the power exercised by mining companies in Papua New Guinea and elsewhere that pollute rivers with waste and tailings, destroying fish and other animals, disturbing complex ecosystems and rendering arable land a wasteland instead.[25] There will be many other contexts in which power, especially human power, will be questioned by the reading of the Matthean text, inviting readers to move to a new space, a new place, where new ways of thinking and acting can take place. This is to move to that marginal space where the anthropocentric perspective is challenged and a new social imaginary characterized as ecological begins to emerge.

The reading/s proposed in this essay are both informed by and can inform Oceania's ecological reader, aware as I am of the multivalent relationships of peoples, nations, and ecologies within the region. They open the way for the engagement of other readers from contexts different from my own to come into dialogue with these readings and to produce others that together may lead to new ecological praxis in the region as constituent of reading Matthew's Gospel ecologically in Oceania.

Notes

1. This is for the Earth Bible Commentary Series, edited by Norman Habel, and to be published by Sheffield Phoenix.

2. For a more extensive analysis of the effects of climate change in Oceania, see Sem 2006.

3. The six principles for reading biblical texts ecologically are set out and discussed as follows: the principle of intrinsic worth, the principle of interconnectedness, the principle of voice, the principle of purpose, the principle of mutual custodianship, the principle of resistance.

4. She develops her approach more fully in *The Matter of the Text: Material Engagements between Luke and the Five Senses* (2011).

5. Toowoomba and Brisbane in southeastern Queensland suffered severe flooding in the week of January, 9, 2011.

6. On Tuesday, February 22, 2011, an earthquake or a severe aftershock of the first earthquake of September 4, 2011, struck the city of Christchurch in the south island of New Zealand, killing over one hundred people. Since that time, an earthquake and tsunami have struck the eastern coast of Japan, its effects rippling out across the Pacific Ocean and its islands.

7. Hillel 2006: 278n1, defines *ecology* as "the interrelationship between living communities and their habitats," nuancing this with a further term, *cultural ecology*, which for him "describes the mutual influences of the environment and the culture of a society."

8. Rigby (2004: 436) discusses the four ways Heidegger proposes that the earth pushes up into a literary work, one being "as that which withdraws and remains hidden." The other three ways of earth becoming visible in text that Heidegger highlights and which Rigby lists are (1) as "the ground upon which we make our dwelling"; (2) as "matrix . . . which supports the relation of all natural beings in their corporeal interconnectedness with other beings"; and (3) "in its own materiality."

9. Code (2006: 5) notes that the approach suggesting that "text is best explained when it is inserted into or returned to context," fails, from an ecological perspective, because it "bypasses their reciprocally constitutive effects." Even though she is not addressing biblical studies, her insights are important for this discipline, in which text and context have been and are central.

10. I have significantly modified the approach of Robbins (1996), but his overall approach has influenced mine. I am most grateful to him for his critical comments on my approach. These have strengthened my methodological framework for a socio-rhetorical ecological reading.

11. It is important to note that the Australian indigenous peoples have lived in its interior desert(s) for forty thousand or more years prior to European invasion.

12. The following Reuters text of January 5, 2011, captures the fluctuation: "With summer floods swamping much of the northern Queensland state, the Bureau of Meteorology said the second half of 2010 was the wettest on record, with La Nina conditions firmly established by July. The switch to the intense La Nina occurred quickly, replacing the drought-causing El Nino pattern at the start of 2010" (http://www.earthwire.org/climate/default.aspx?r=2010&rn=Oceania).

13. For Soja, Thirdspace calls for a different way of thinking about space, an opening up of new possibilities of being in relation to space. It allows for the marginal to find a voice, as we have seen in postcolonialism and feminism.

14. Sawicki (1994: 136) also makes this point very explicitly, as I do in this reading.

15. McVann reads the fasting and the testing of Jesus through the lens of the ritual process constituting Jesus as a prophet. One critique I would bring to McVann's article from an ecological perspective is that he sets up a contrast between Jesus' "submission" to the devil in "nature" so that he can overcome him "in *culture*" (17). It is just such a divide that has shaped much of the oppression of both women and Earth and one that an ecological reading seeks to negotiate.

16. Halvor Moxnes (2003: 102) comes to this same conclusion from a different perspective.

17. McVann (1993: 17) represents such a reading when he claims in relation to 4:4 that "fidelity to God's word supersedes even basic necessities such as food."

18. See also Carter 2000: 109, who recognizes that "the verse does not disparage human hunger" nor is it proposing "a dualism of physical and spiritual needs."

19. The lxx of Exod. 17:2 uses the verb *peiradzō*, which is being used in Matt. 4:1-12.

20. See Halapua 2008 for a fuller exposition of this relationship.

21. As noted earlier, the irony is that as I was finalizing this essay, the Australian landscape, which is so often parched and longing for rain, was under water as a result of extreme floods, especially all down its eastern states.

22. For an analysis of this text from a feminist perspective, see Wainwright 2000a.

23. BDAG 587 gives the meaning of *latreuō*, which occurs in the text of Deut. 6:13 and is cited in Matt. 4:10, as servitude or cultic service.

24. For much more extensive analysis of this imagery, see Shroer 2000: 132–63.

25. See by way of example, see "TED Case Studies: Mining in Papua New Guinea," http://www1.american.edu/ted/papua.htm; Christine Ottery, "Papua New Guinea gives green light to deep-sea mineral mine," *The Guardian*, October 21, 2010, http://www.guardian.co.uk/environment/2010/oct/21/papua-new-guinea-mine; and *Papua New Guinea Mine Watch*, weblog, http://ramumine.wordpress.com/.

15

Matthew 6:9b-13 (The Lord's Prayer)

Explorations into a Latino/a Optic on Language and Translation

Francisco Lozada Jr.

INTRODUCTION

The overall aim of this reading is an exploration of this hermeneutical question, What does a Latino/a reading of a biblical text look like? In other words, how does the intersection of a Latino reader and biblical text affect the meaning of the text? The intent of this document is not to provide a definitive answer to this question, but rather to identify issues and questions that add to the discussions of interpreters who focus on Latino/a hermeneutics. To examine this issue, I employ the Lord's Prayer from the Gospel of Matthew as an exemplar to explore the relationship between reader and text. Why the Lord's Prayer in Matthew? First, the Lord's Prayer is a text I use at times to discuss the development of New Testament methods.[1] Second, when I discuss the issue of the translation of the Lord's Prayer, and various theoretical approaches to that translation, I find that my Latino/a optic or experience is constantly present. Thus I cannot help but consider that issues related to language and translations of the text are part of the interpretative process. Third, the Lord's Prayer is a common text that readers know and say in a variety of contexts.

This reading is divided into two parts. The first part focuses on the context of the reader, in this case myself. The second part concentrates on the context of the text.[2] My fundamental concern here is to explore the intersection of an aspect of the reader's identity—language and translation—and the text's literary identity. This reading of the Lord's Prayer is exploratory in nature in that it represents an initial examination of the association between the reader and the text in the reading process. Thus this reading is not meant to engage any academic issues raised by other scholars but rather to raise various issues evolving from my reading of the Lord's Prayer that might have liberative and ethical significance for Latino/a and other communities.

With regard to an examination of the reader's context, the focus of the first part of this discussion will center on language and translation by way of the social location of the reader. A key factor associated with translation is the element of language. Language is one identity factor that contextualizes my reading, and that is also important for other readers, whose heritage language is other than English or, more generally, whose language is other than the dominant language of their host country. Regarding the Lord's Prayer itself, the focus is on the literary or rhetorical identity of this work. To date, discussions regarding the respective identities of both the reader and the text (the Lord's Prayer) remain incomplete, because any discussion regarding the reader's historical and sociohistorical settings are always contextual and remain at a distance, particularly the text.

Context of the Reader

As a child of colonized parents who migrated to the United States from Puerto Rico, and as one who now identifies himself as a U.S. Latino of second/third generation background, both language and translation remain issues of identity for me in the United States. Latinos/as are not alone in this issue. Many other communities whose first language is not English may also resonate with language and translation issues. In my particular case, my first language is now English, yet my unconscious is still colored by Spanish. (For example, I occasionally dream in Spanish.) Even so, my occasional mispronunciation of either English or Spanish words points away from the notion of originality or "native" speech, language, and translation. Among native English speakers, my various mispronunciations of English words point to my Latino identity and identify me as one whose context was not English-speaking. Similarly, among native Spanish speakers, my pronunciation and dialect point to my being other than a "native" of Latin America. These language markers are not unique to my situation since language, vocabulary, and accents that are not considered "standard" will most often serve as cultural, ethnic, or even national location points that listeners use to place speakers. In this light, the considerations and meanings associated with language and translation can be quite complex and are usually intertwined with identity.

FROM SUBJECT TO OBJECT: LANGUAGE AND TRANSLATION

As one who learned and spoke Spanish from a very early age, but who, through assimilation, lost much of that language skill, the intersection of translation, language, and culture has always been a vital factor of my identity.[3] Specifically, as my communities (that is, the United States and Latin America) often use language as a placeholder or identifier of cultural or ethnic membership, I am often located as "other." This is true for many people who live in more than one cultural, ethnic, national, or even racial milieu. Indeed, choosing which language one speaks at home—whether it is the language of one's parents or the language of the larger society—is part of the process of translating the identity of the speaker as insider, outsider, or both.

Similarly, when I am in Latino/a or Latin American communities, whether I choose to speak Spanish has outcomes for the perceptions of my identity. In other words, as a result of my choice of language, someone is translating something about me. I have noted that this is also true if I do not speak Spanish the "right" way. I recognize this when someone of Latin American descent tells me that I speak like a *gringo*, indicating that I am different from them and from other "native" speakers.[4] Likewise, my family in Puerto Rico casts me as one who does not care about the language and now identifies me as an *Americano* (U.S. American).[5] In the past, I translated such comments as negative statements and indicators of one or more of my identities. For instance, I felt they identified me as one who was too lazy to learn my parents' language (or who had parents who were too lazy to teach me). This is no longer the case, since I have "detranslated" such comments; that is, I have refused this particular translation of my identity. Even so, I know that I am constantly and consistently transformed from a subject to an object. The transformation from subject to object may also be experienced by the non-Spanish-speaking U.S. Latino/a who goes to Latin America and finds himself or herself translated from a U.S. Latino to an Anglo or even a U.S. Latino/a with little command of Spanish who finds himself or herself identified by others in the community as not "really" a Latino/a. These are the realities of migration, globalization, empire, or colonization, and the resultant negative affects these factors have on community members. In turn, these negative affects leave many communities, from Argentina to Mexico, lost in translation. Again, this experience is not unique to Latinos. One can find this dynamic in many other communities across the United States, across the globe, and throughout various historical periods of migration into the United States. The reality is that we are always translating something or someone from subject to object—as I do myself when I translate others and when I translate a biblical text like the Lord's Prayer.

HIERARCHY OF LANGUAGE

The process of translation is associated with language, which typically has a hierarchical structure. In other words, similar to class, ethnicity/race, and nationality, language exists in a perceived hierarchy. This is evinced within the English language. For example, those who speak closest to the "proper" English of England are considered closer to the original language and people. Also, proper English is associated with the Midwestern dialect or the "Ivy League" New England dialect, which itself implies a host of social locations, including being more cultured, having a higher level of education, and being connected to the "established" northeastern families that can trace their lineage back to the colonial period (think William F. Buckley).[6] Conversely, those who speak the "nonstandard" U.S. English are likely to be associated with lower levels of education, urban or rural communities, the regionalism of the South, latter-day immigration, and less "established" or "notable" families. Likewise, in Spanish, those who speak the "prestigious" Spanish of Spain speak closest to the original language (Castilian Spanish) and people of Spain.[7]

Among U.S. Latinos/as, whose immediate roots are primarily from Latin America, those who speak closer to the "proper" Spanish language of Latin America's primary colonizer, Spain, are perceived as closer to Spain than to Latin America—even though those dialects of Spanish in Latin America are products of the historical colonization of the territory and its indigenous populations and African populations (Perissinotto 2003). In this way, the meanings of language, or the ways in which the uses of language are socially translated, become part of the domination of a subject—in turn dictating its transformation into an object. In essence, this is a method of achieving control of populations via the process of translating the language, culture, and texts of a given people, and then assigning these factors to a very low status level in the social hierarchy. The act of translation then, as with the case of geographical landscape and texts, "is an act of desacralizing"—an act akin to those found in the colonial histories of Australia, Ireland, New Zealand, Nigeria, and even the United States, where mapping became the necessary adjunct of imperialism by the English, French, and Spanish upon the indigenous and other colonized people (Young 2003; 141; Stavans 2003: 35). Similarly, language and translation in New Testament studies also exists in a perceived hierarchy, with classical or attic Greek perceived as more loftier and closer to the ancient Greek culture when compared to the Hellenistic or Koine Greek. Within the field of biblical studies, the formal-correspondence approach to translation is perceived as closer to the original text's meaning than the dynamic-equivalence approach (Kevern 2008). So, even the way in which the text is translated is based on a hierarchical system that has implications regarding the "merit" and "quality" of the translation.

TRANSLATOR

The act of a language's translation always involves a translator. The translator is always involved—consciously or unconsciously—in "false" (as some would say) or alternative translations. For instance, the most famous translator in Latin American history was La Malinche (also known as Malintzin, Malinalli, or Dona Marina), who served as a Nahua translator for Hernán Cortéz and the Spanish conquistadores. Cortéz relied on her for understanding almost everything about the native coastal gulf peoples of Mexico whom he encountered (Stavans 2003: 25). Unfortunately, at times, she has been portrayed as a traitor, hence her name La Malinche ("unpatriotic Mexican") (Stavans 2003: 168). La Malinche performed her translations of places by representing her own culture, once removed by language from the indigenous culture but nonetheless a translation and interpretation of the original. Her role is similar to the role of Sacagawea, who played the role of translator for Lewis and Clark in the eighteenth century. One can find many similar reports of translators and translations with only a cursory examination of the history of the French and the Spaniards in North America. Whether it is an act of diplomacy, treachery, or an act of resistance, translations open up the space for the appropriation of a conquering culture (Sugirtharajah 2002: 155–78).

Both of the previously mentioned women are no different from any of us who play the role of translator, whether translating the spoken word or text. We are once or twice removed from the original but nonetheless provide translations and interpretations—albeit ones filtered through the particular lenses of our own historical periods and cultural contexts. In the specific case of the Latino/a experience, translations and interpretations can vary depending on generation, ethnic background, and geographical location in the United States to name a few factors. As mentioned earlier, Latinos/as may also speak a Spanish dialect considered by the "old guard" of the language to be "improper"—one that reflects their regional home country rather than that of Latin America or Spain.[8] For better or worse, the Spanish dialect in all its formations exists in a perceived hierarchy, just as Latinos/as themselves are categorized within a perceived hierarchy within and outside their own communities.

Thus all Spanish-speaking people in the United States are engaged in several concurrent acts of translation. Each individual translates the world, while they are simultaneously being translated by their pan-Latino/a constituencies and by the dominant English-speaking constituencies. For instance, the dialects of recent immigrants from less-developed countries in Latin America are typically perceived by many Spanish teachers to be informal or incorrect Spanish (read: not the Spanish spoken in Spain). These teachers then mistakenly attempt to teach the immigrant group members as if they were Anglo-speakers and not heritage speakers. Heritage speakers are those who have a background in the language of their parents or grandparents. In the case of Latinos/as, heritage speakers are those with the Spanish language in their background (Perissinotto 2003: 177). They may leave certain letters out of their pronunciations (for example, eta for esta, which is very typical of Caribbean dialects) (Stavans 2003: 177–78) and writings (e.g., poyo for pollo, llo for yo), or use words in what is sometimes called Spanglish—the mixing of Spanish and English words in syntax in the United States (for example, *washerteria*). These individuals are frequently judged by their pronunciations and writing skills rather than their knowledge of Spanish, and so are often perceived as "weak" speakers. In other words, heritage speakers are perceived as having a lack of literacy and thus are constantly corrected for their use of nonstandard Spanish orthography in Spanish classes. As such, many Latinos/as, those who have traveled to the center from the periphery, are constantly serving as cultural translators. As cultural translators, they are translated by their use of Spanish. They also encounter other translated people and translate their own home experiences to each other to form new languages such as Spanglish.

How does all of this relate to translating the Lord's Prayer? As previously discussed, translation and language are intertwined workings in culture. Translation is not simply a one-way process. It is a two-way process in which I translate the text and the text translates me. It is a cultural interaction, and, an act of reempowerment. This activity of translation is one in which I aim to explore within contextual hermeneutics. The purpose of this particular engagement of the Lord's Prayer is to investigate this exploration. Ergo, what follows is a brief literary analysis of the Lord's Prayer through a Latino/a optic.

CONTEXT OF THE TEXT

Given this background on language and translation from a Latino/a optic, how would such a background play a role when brought to bear on the Lord's Prayer in Matthew (6:9b–13)? In this second part, I shall briefly explore the literary identity (rhetorical structure) of the Lord's Prayer, followed by a modest discussion of the effect of a Latino/a optic on the identity of the document.

LORD'S PRAYER AS A LITERARY PRODUCT

The Lord's Prayer is found in the narrative unit of the Sermon on the Mount (5:1—7:27), in which Jesus is portrayed as a teacher who reveals the identity of God. The Sermon on the Mount is the first of four other major discourses in Matthew (10:5-42; 13:1-52; 18:1-35; and 24:3—25:46), and the Lord's Prayer falls within the narrative section involving the teaching of Jesus (6:1-18). The prayer (6:9b-13) is included in the second of three subsections, and thus is found between the subsection of instruction on almsgiving (6:1-4) and the third subsection, instruction on fasting (6:16-18). The Lord's Prayer (6:9b-13) is framed with instructions by the Matthean Jesus regarding how to pray, how not to pray (6:5-9a), and what conditions must be met to attain God's forgiveness (6:14-15). Overall, the three subsections (6:1-4; 6:5-14; 6:16-18) involve the Matthean Jesus' providing instruction to the disciples (broadly understood) on how to practice their piety (giving alms, praying, and fasting) in the spirit of true worship of God, unlike the "hypocrites" (*hypokritai*)[9] in the synagogue. The Lord's Prayer, as such, serves as a central narrative division (6:9b-13) within the central narrative subsection (6:5-14), functioning in a didactic and apologetic fashion, and framed as a petition or direct response to God.

The Lord's Prayer consists of seven petitions, with a request on how to address God, "Our Father in heaven" (*Pater hēmōn ho en tous ouranous*, 6:9b). The prayer itself is launched with a direct command, through the use of the imperative mood, by the Matthean Jesus to the readers on how to pray, "You then pray like this" (*Houtōs oun proseuchesthe humeis*, 6:9a). This text is not part of the prayer itself, but it draws the reader in from the sphere of the earthly/empire realm and into the sphere of God/empire that follows (6:9b). This imperative by the Matthean Jesus, therefore, constructs two communities. One, a narrative community that prays incorrectly and falsely ("hypocrites") and within the world of the public eye, and the other, a new community that prays correctly and truthfully (disciples) and within the world of God (reign of God in the present) (Kingsbury 1986: 130).

Such a clear either/or construction of the world may not resonate for many Latinos/as, including myself, who find themselves uncomfortable with having to choose only one way to pray, or one place to worship for that matter. Once an either/or framework is established, it can compel many to choose one world over another and associate the "outsider" with the "hypocrite" and the "insider" with the "true" believer. My cultural experience with translation and language suggests that, when this type of dichotomous choice is presented as the only option, hierarchies are established. These hierarchies are analogous to the issue of superior/inferior dialects in either Spanish or English. Moreover, the prayer itself is introduced around an either/or world when it calls for a proper way to say a prayer. A Latino/a experience may challenge this either/or world as it does when challenging laws forces them to choose between languages. Yet many Latinos/as may receive the hierarchy or dichotomy, especially in establishing their identity as "insiders" in the United States, by calling for the learning of English as the gateway to the "American Dream" (Stavans 2003: 3).

NARRATIVE ANALYSIS

As indicated above, the Lord's Prayer in Matthew begins with a call to the "Father": ("Our Father in heaven") (Boring 1995: 203). This call indicates three key items. First, the "Father" belongs to everyone. This is supported by the nominative plural personal pronoun ("our," *hēmōn*), and thus establishing a universal understanding of God. Second, God is addressed as the "Father" (*Pater*), thus constructing a world governed solely by a male, and consequently, envisioned solely from a male perspective. Third, the call indicates that the spatial location of the "Father" is in heaven (*en tois ouranois*), thus constructing a hierarchical and superior world—the world of heaven to come—when compared to the current, evil world (Boring 1995: 203).

From the perspective of a Latino/a optic on language and translation, the question of hierarchy finds expression again in this call to prayer. The fundamental issue of this call is how the notions of mother and father are placed in opposition, and thus in a hierarchy. In language, the use of proper or "Castilian" Spanish or "standard" English became associated with elite membership and power, and those who do not speak in these dialects are identified as less powerful "others." Likewise, in this text, the term "Father" became associated with the notion that men should be in higher positions than women, and ultimately evolved into the notion that power was the sole property of men.[10] This notion, translated as machismo, still remains strong among many Latino/a communities, as evinced through the voices of Latinas (Isasi-Díaz 1996; Tamez et al. 1987). The language of "Father" thus creates tension in a world where Latinas remain hidden from view in ecclesiastical and cultural leadership roles.

Seven petitions to the "Father" follow this brief call to God. The first three petitions (6:9c; 6:10a; 6:10b-c) refer to God, supported by the second-person singular pronouns ("your," *sou*) in all three petitions. In the first petition, "Hallowed be your name," the imperative "hallowed" or "make holy" (*agiasthētō*) begins with honoring God's name. The petition provides reverence to God by commanding worship or veneration. The petitioner submits to the glorification of God. The second petition, also beginning with an imperative in Greek, "come" (*elthetō*), calls for the reign or kingdom (*basileia*) to be present in the here-and-now. Thus a bringing forth of the reign of God to the present world is one in which an established rule (empire) is called for now and not later (Boring 1995: 203). And finally, the third petition, initiated with another imperative, "be done" (or "be made," or "be created") (*genēthētō*), calls for the will of God to be completed as well (*genēthētō to thelēma sou*," Your will be done").[11] This is a call to bring forth God's intentions and reign to those who are not righteous in this world. In other words, it is a petition to bring into this world what is already present in heaven ("On earth as it is in heaven"), accentuated with the particle of comparison ("as," *hōs*) (6:10c). This call in the first three petitions to initiate the reign of God and the will of God in the here-and-now accentuates a world ruled by God, thus overturning or abolishing a world governed by "hypocrites." In short, it is a call for one world to prevail over another in the name of God.

In commending this particular call, the prayer leaves no room for negotiation on how to pray and what to pray for: the reign of God in the here-and-now is the appeal. For many Latinos/as, where one uses Spanish—whether it is outside the home or inside the home or both—is a serious debate. For many members of the older generations, the use of any Spanish at all is seen as a disgrace. The truth is that parents and grandparents, including my own, demanded (as in, the use of the imperative) that children speak in a particular manner as a way to improve one's family condition. Similarly, the Matthean Jesus calls for a better condition of the world via the reign of God and acceptance of the "right" way to pray.

The second set of petitions (6:11; 6:12; 6:13a; 6:13b) are all cast in the imperative, except for one (6:13a), which is in the subjunctive mood (6:13a). They all make requests on behalf of human beings as opposed to requesting conditions from God, as witnessed in the first three petitions. This is easily supported through the use of first person plural pronouns, "us" (*hēmin*), "our" (*hemōn*), "we" (*hemeis*) that return the attention to humanity.

Beginning this second set of petitions is the fourth petition (6:11, "Give us this day our daily bread"). The word "give" (*dos*) is again in the imperative, but this time softened to suggest a request rather than a demand (Brooks and Winbery 1979: 128). The request is on behalf of "us" (*hēmin*), the ones who are behind the appeal. It is a request for all those who are not included among the "hypocrites." It is a request that is not for tomorrow, but is for the present, as supported by the adverb *sēmeron* ("today" or "this day"). The request is for bread (*arton*), which actually begins the clause in Greek, thus suggesting its centrality to the petition. It is bread that signifies or calls attention to issues of hunger and nourishment as well as poverty (Boring 1995: 204). The adverb "daily" (*sēmeron*), modifying "give," points to the frequency of receiving this bread. This is bread not just for today but also for tomorrow (Boring 1995: 204). The call for bread as the first request on behalf of a community, therefore, points to the claim that bread signifies nourishment for a community that is hungry, poor, and simply trying to survive the consequences of existing as "others" within the confines of an empire (Carter 2001).

From the Latino/a optic discussed above, speaking neither Spanish nor English properly is a signifier of less education and poverty. How one speaks and what one eats are often correlated as signs of where one is located. Often, lower levels of education, poverty, and hunger are associated with the "lower" classes, where these factors are daily realities of survival. They are also realities of power in empires that neglect or are merciless toward the poor. That the prayer mentions bread as one of its requests, then, signals an expression of the "lower" classes among its narrative hearers. This petition therefore underscores the contrast between the world of the powerful and the world of the powerless that presently shapes human existence in the narrative world.

The fifth petition of the Lord's Prayer consists of two clauses: "And forgive us our debts, as we also have forgiven our debtors" (*kai aphes hēmin ta opheilēmata hēmōn, hōs kai hēmeis aphiemen toes opheiletaes hēmōn*, 6:12a and 12b). The first clause petitions on behalf of the community once again, and the second clause draws a comparison from the community's past actions.

The petition begins with a transitional conjunction, "and" (kai), continuing the pattern of requests already provided in the Lord's Prayer. What follows is an imperative of entreaty through the use of the word "forgive" (*aphes*), thus calling for a softening of the request and perhaps with the word "please" accompanying the imperative ("please forgive") (Brooks and Winbery 1979: 128). Again, the request is on behalf of a community as expressed through the use of the pronouns "us" (*hēmin*) and "our" (*hēōn*). The object of the petition is "debts" (*opheiletais*). Whereas the previous object of request was "bread" (*arton*), signifying poverty and hunger/nourishment, here the word "debt" surely implies an economic reality.

One of the identity markers from language and translation is the question of origins. For instance, how one uses a particular word, whether it is in

English or Spanish, leads to an explanation of the origins of words and identity. Similarly, one of the major issues regarding the Lord's Prayer is how to translate the Greek words *opheilēmata/tois opheiletais* ("debts"/"debtors" or "trespass"/"those who trespass"). As in any translation, a betrayal of the "original" exists.[12] As such, the quest for the "original" meaning and context is an aim for translators. This quest necessarily leads readers in the English-speaking world to decide which translation to use in Matthew's prayer. Which of the two dominant translations of the Greek does one use—"debts"/"debtors" or "trespass"/"those who trespass"? The former has prevailed in many English translations.[13] My point here is not to challenge the prevailing translation of Matt. 6:12, and thus argue for a different one than the standard "debts"/"debtors." Rather, my intention is not only to call attention to the activity of translation in order to show that language and translation are inaccurate activities, but also to demonstrate that language and translation of ancient and modern texts always involves some sort of reflection of origins and explanation of identity.

For instance, the translation of *opheilēmata/tois opheiletais* as "debts" and "debtors" has its roots in the King James Version of the Bible of 1611, which was in turn influenced by translations from the Latin Vulgate, with the words *debita* and *debitoribus*.[14] As readers have learned from Sugirtharajah's work on the KJV's reception history, these translations are part of the colonial enterprise of the British culture and empire. The British Empire imposed this translation on its colonies, and ultimately the KJV translation became the standard. Other very important English-speaking translators, such as William Tyndale (1526), preferred "trespass" and "trespassers" ("And forgeve vs oure treaspases eve as we forgeve oure trespacers"), yet Myles Coverdale (1535) in his translation of the prayer translates the Greek words as "debts" and "debtors" (And forgeue vs oure dettes, as we also forgeue oure deters). John Wycliffe in 1395 (and foryyue to vs oure dettis, as we foryyuen to oure dettouris) follows the same translation.

Clearly, the translation of Matthew's "Lord's Prayer" has varied throughout history, but the dominant tradition has been to translate *opheilēmata/tois opheiletais* in English as "debts" and "debtors." However, both are possible translations of the ancient Greek terms *opheilēmata/tois opheiletais*. With the translation of the Christian Bible into Latin in the second to third century, English translators, by the fourteenth century, took the two key Latin words that looked similar to the English "debts" and "debtors," from which they were translated and used in the prayer. Similarly, the Latin Catholic Mass, which bases the Lord's Prayer on Matthew's version, reads *Et dimitte nobis debita nostra, sicut et nos dimittimus debitoribus*. In English, this reads "and forgive us our trespasses, as we forgive those who trespass against us" (*Latin-English Booklet Missal for Praying the Traditional Mass* 2009: 38–39). My point in this is that translation of this prayer has been constantly changing based on its context.

From this modest discussion, one can observe that language and translation are challenges to understand given the intricate histories and boundaries between these factors that many Latinos/as experience as minoritized people in the United States (Bailey, Liew, and Segovia 2009). Like the history of *opheilēmata/tois opheiletais*, the language and translation approaches that Latinos/as use today throughout their daily lives are not the same ones employed by previous generations. Languages and identity are in constant evolution, just like the prayer itself.

The sixth petition is the first and only negative petition (6:13a). This petition begins with a transitional conjunction, "and" (*kai*), carrying a final but continual flow of demands already present in the Lord's Prayer. The clause "And do not bring us to the test" (*kai mē eisenenkēs hēmas eis peirasmon*) is placed in the subjunctive mood, as expressed through the plea "do not bring" (*mē eisenenkēs*), thus calling for a prohibition of leading the community ("us," *hēmas*) to the test or temptation (*eis peirasmon*).

The second clause (6:13b) is the seventh and final petition of the Lord's Prayer, and begins with a contrastive, emphatic conjunction, "but" (*alla*), thus calling for a different request from the possible consequence of the previous clause (6:13a). Returning to the imperative mood as expressed through "deliver" (*rhysai*), the petition is to "rescue" the community from the "Evil One" (*ponērou*). This time, the request is not for nourishment or economic forgiveness, but deliverance from the evil temptations that surround the community. The petition calls for a life or lived life in the present as it is lived in the world of the Father (6:13c).

The sixth petition depicts an evil world. From the Latino/a optic discussed above, language and translation may lead to a deliverance from some sort of the evil world encompassed by an either/or dichotomous sense of language. Depending on one's stance regarding the use of English and/or Spanish (and their variations) as part of a Latino/a identity, one might find coming to terms with the constant mutation of language, translation, and identity as a kind of deliverance. Not deliverance in the theological sense, but rather a social deliverance, in the sense of living between languages and translations. The "evil one" is the one who aims to teach a particular model of language as the only way, with the intent to civilize. I suspect this includes even those who teach and advocate a single "right" method of prayer and worship.

CONCLUSION: THE LORD'S PRAYER FROM A LATINO/A OPTIC

As I initially stated, this discussion has been more exploratory than definitive. In other words, my initial examination of the Lord's Prayer through the question of language and translation was not intended to follow the traditional track of searching for the right meaning and the question of truth through the traditional lines of translation theory. Rather, my focus is to provide a sample of Latino/a hermeneutics that aims to bring attention to the process of translation through a Latino/a optic. This line of questioning, I believe, has not been explored seriously in the field of Latino/a biblical hermeneutics. As such, regarding the Lord's Prayer, I aim to briefly raise three translation issues, from the context of the Latino/a reality discussed above: (1) The issue of identity determined by language only; (2) the issue of one approach or philosophy to translate texts; and (3) the experience of retranslation by the translator. The consideration of these issues has led me to ask more questions than it has provided answers.

The issue of determining one's identity on the sole basis of the language one speaks is problematic. Many people, like texts, contain a variety of identities based on a variety of social or cultural factors. Likewise, the Lord's Prayer contains multiple identities as well. What I briefly discussed above was a glimpse of the Lord's Prayer's as a literary product. My reading of the Lord's Prayer was not a closely delineated identity as produced by commentaries or along the lines of a formalistic approach. Nonetheless, it reflects a literary identity from a particular perspective. The prayer itself is cast as one made up of a variety of petitions. Drawing on the experience of language and translation discussed in the first part of this essay, what is considered a "very good" translation seems to be a continual focus in translation approaches. In some respects, this aim to provide a "very good" translation is the best path, since respecting the identity of the text is a very important component of any interpretation. However, this focus on looking for something intrinsic in the identity of a text may overlook the question of extrinsic factors that influence the identity of the text. As constructing identity based on one sole social factor eschews the construction of a total identity, so does engaging the Lord's Prayer or any ancient or foreign text or person for that matter.

The issue of one approach to or philosophy regarding the translation of texts is also a question that needs attention in the field of contextual hermeneutics, including Latino/a hermeneutics that utilizes two languages. Most scholars use the two dominant approaches to translation, namely, dynamic and formalistic approaches. The purpose of the dynamic approach is to reproduce the original idea behind a translation. Contrastingly, the purpose of the formalistic approach is to reflect the original words behind a translation. However, the selection of either of these approaches contains an inherent decision regarding which approach is better than the other, or perhaps which theory results in the translation that is closest to the original meaning of the text. Both of these approaches overlook the fact that the identity of the prayer evolves as it is influenced by the intersections of the identities of the text and the interpreter. For instance, the prayer inevitably became part of ecclesial language, and was rarely challenged. The point here is that a variety of different approaches to translation is needed and not just the traditional dynamic or formalistic approaches. The Lord's Prayer, and other ancient texts for that matter, must undergo translation ad infinitum in multiple approaches, languages, and perspectives, as well as other alternative translations; otherwise, the translations of the Lord's Prayer will only reflect a worldview that is influenced by Western translations and positions.

Finally, the experience of retranslation by the translator and its resultant effects on the translator or reader needs exploration in Latino/a hermeneutics. As mentioned above, whenever translation occurs, one translates between two cultures. The translator slowly disappears in the translation, leaving the translated text or object (or person) fixed, and the translator absorbed into the translation itself. In other words, the art of translation involves practice (Young 2003: 138). What is translated is a copy or a reproduction of the original. What changes, therefore, is not only the material identity but also the identity of the reader/translator. Contextual hermeneutics could benefit much if scholars were to begin examining the dynamics between the identity of the reader/translator and the text during the interpretative process. For instance, in my case, my identity exists on the borders of two or more worlds. In my translation of the Lord's Prayer, the identity of this reader, from the optic of his Latino identity, sees a prayer not fixed within its ancient context whose identity mainly comes from a vertical dimension of history as through one's historical background (or ancestors), but also from a horizontal dimension of the present as through one's literary background in the context of the present (or in relation to others). It is through the combination of the two dimensions that identity is changed. It changes with time and in its relationship toward others.

The relationship between reader and text is very complex and at times very challenging to explain when the context of the reader is at the forefront. However, what contextual hermeneutics, and in this specific case Latino/a hermeneutics, offers is an opportunity to reflect on the origins, meanings, and explanations of one's own interpretations. So what does a Latino/a reading look like? It takes the role of the reader and text seriously, in its attempt to understand the worlds of both the reader and the text and to derive a deeper and perhaps fuller meaning of the text via their interaction.

Notes

1. I have always found the discussion of methods, using the Lord's Prayer as the sample text in Duling and Perrin 1994 very helpful to teach the development of approaches to introductory New Testament students. Much of my analysis of the Lord's Prayer is dependent on this introductory text.

2. The assignment for this reading called for taking seriously the context of the reader and the text. I aimed, therefore, to give divided attention to both elements (reader and text) of the interpretative process.

3. In my particular case, both paternal and maternal grandparents arrived in the United States from Puerto Rico with all siblings in the 1950s, with one set of grandparents returning and another remaining. This experience is reflected among many U.S. Puerto Rican families. Language and translation surely played a role in the crossing of boundaries on a daily basis.

4. The term *gringo* refers to Anglo Americans. See Stavans 2003: 136.

5. Depending on the context, the term *Americano* in my household referred either to Anglo Americans in general or to those Anglo Americans living the "American Dream" of cultural, economic, and political power.

6. I understand that one's perception and geographical location regarding what is "proper" English is relative. I am speaking primarily from the perceptions of my socio-educational experiences in the United States. Having been raised in the Midwest (Cleveland, Ohio), the New England "dialect" was perceived to be higher in the hierarchy of languages. This may not be the case in other Midwesterners' perception or others throughout the country. For an excellent review of the development of the English language, see Bryson 1990.

7. Similarly to my perceptions of English, I realize that one's perception, experience, and geographic locations where Spanish is spoken may be different from mine in this assessment of the Spanish language.

8. The guard I am referring to is the *Real Academia Española de la Lengua Castellana* founded in 1713. See Stavans 2003: 28–35.

9. All interpretations are my own unless otherwise noted.

10. I do understand that for many Latinos/as and others, the metaphor "Father" (*Padre*) has enduring and comforting symbolism, particularly in times of need. I am not trying to take away this sense of connection, but rather suggest that for others it may mean something different.

11. This text (6:10c) is missing in Luke's version of the prayer (Luke 11:2-4).

12. The notion of "original" is problematic.

13. American Standard Version ("And forgive us our debts, as we also have forgiven our debtors"); New American Standard ("And forgive us our debts, as we also have forgiven our debtors"); New International Version ("Forgive us our debts, as we also have forgiven our debtors"); Revised Standard Version ("And forgive us our debts, as we also have forgiven our debtors"); New Revised Standard Version ("And forgive us our debts, as we also have forgiven our debtors"); New American Bible ("and forgive us our debts, as we forgive our debtors"). In Spanish, Sagrada Biblia ("como también nosotros perdonamos a los que nos ofenden"); La Biblia de las Américas ("Y perdónanos nuestras deudas, como también nosotros hemos perdonado a nuestros deudores"); La Nueva Internacional ("Perdónanos nuestras deudas, como también nosotros hemos perdonado a nuestros deudores").

14. "And forgiue vs our debts, as we forgiue our debters"—King James Version. *Et dimitte nobis debitanostra sicut et nos dimisimus debitoribus nostris*—Latin Vulgate.

16

Matthew's "Least of These" Theology and Subversion of "Us/Other" Categories

Jeannine K. Brown

The parable of the sheep and the goats, from Matthew 25, has become a central text in many circles—ecclesial and theological. In the context from which I come and to which I primarily contribute, this passage and its themes are receiving increased attention. Bethel Seminary, where I teach New Testament, is self-described as an evangelical, pietistic institution. Although we are growing in cultural diversity, our Midwest campus is largely white and middle-class in makeup. The majority of churches we serve can be similarly characterized.

I am intrigued by what seems to be the growing use of Matt. 25:31-46 in the sermons and popular writings of this religious constituency. My central question in this essay is whether the appropriation of this passage by white evangelicals tames the messages of this Matthean text and its potential for significant challenge. Specifically, how does evangelical appropriation of this passage contribute to an understanding of the other? Is there attention to the motifs of solidarity and power displacement—motifs that encourage a blurring of boundaries between us and other? To explore these questions, I concentrate on two aspects of the pericope, the identification and function of the "least of these" (25:40, 45) and the power implications of this judgment/justice story. In tandem with this textual exploration, I analyze evangelical usage of the passage to identify themes that emerge in its appropriation.[1] To focus my analysis of evangelical use, I will draw primarily on a representative homiletic example—a sermon by Haddon Robinson, professor of preaching at Gordon-Conwell Theological Seminary.[2]

Situating Reading and Context

I write from and to an evangelical ecclesial context, defined in part by its commitment to a high view of scriptural authority for faith and praxis and a hermeneutic of trust in relation to the Bible. The latter results in readings of the Bible that are "with the grain" of the text, rather than "against the grain," which openly question certain assumptions and messages of the text. This latter perspective is often referred to as a hermeneutic of suspicion.[3] I locate my reading of Matthew 25 in this essay within a hermeneutic of trust. Additionally, I presume that the biblical text, and Matthew 25 in particular, will and should speak in some way to contemporary churches and Christian faith communities.

At the same time, my own experiences as a female biblical scholar in a church tradition and a guild that have been primarily shaped and almost exclusively led by men have caused me to be suspicious of various readings of the text offered from these contexts. The application of a hermeneutic of suspicion toward the reading traditions of which I am a part has shaped my own reading values and perspective. The concerns expressed in this essay arise precisely from this juxtaposition of reading with the grain of the biblical text and against the grain of my own reading tradition. It is from this vantage point that I offer my own reading of Matthew 25 in, with, and against my own context, with the hope of offering challenge and encouragement to all within my context, including myself, to live more fully in line with Matthew's "least of these" theology.

Matthew 25:31–46: Key Issues and Narrative Context

While a thorough textual analysis of Matt. 25:31-46 is not possible for the purposes of this essay, two interpretive issues emerge as particularly relevant. The first issue is the identity of the "least" (*elachistos*, 25:40, 45): Are they the Christian poor, hungry, and underprivileged? Or do they represent the disadvantaged among all humanity? The conclusions reached by interpreters on this question contribute to the text's function in subverting or possibly confirming insider and outsider categories. The second issue addressed is a shift of power and advantage that is suggested by the passage in its literary context. This is an issue that is not often directly addressed in commentaries but which nonetheless has implications for the question at hand.

A brief look at the placement of this scene within the narrative context of Matthew highlights the importance of the text. Matthew 25:31-46 is unique to Matthew and concludes the final of five major discourses of Jesus in that

Gospel (chapters 5–7, 10, 13, 18, 24–25), making it the last teaching of Jesus in Matthew's narrative. When, in the concluding passage of Matthew, the eleven disciples are exhorted to teach all nations to obey all that Jesus has commanded (28:19), it is primarily these five discourses that come to the reader's mind, with the climactic teaching moment being Matt. 25:31-46. And, while the recipients of the five great discourses on the story level have been primarily the disciples (along with the crowds in Matthew 5–7, 13), Matthew's reader has been drawn to understand herself within the audience of the discourses on the rhetorical level. This is especially true toward the end of each discourse.[4] Thus the shape of the narrative invites the reader to understand Matt. 25:31-46 as a climactic moment in the Gospel and to embrace and obey Jesus' teaching in it.[5]

THE IDENTITY OF "THE LEAST OF THESE"

The first issue to address—the identity of the "least of these"—is vigorously debated in Matthean studies. After exploring the two primary possibilities that emerge among interpreters, we will look at recent anglo-evangelical appropriations of the text in relation to this category of "the least."

TWO READINGS AND THEIR IMPACT ON BRIDGING CATEGORIES

In the first reading, what has been called a universalistic reading, the "least" (*elachistos*) refers to the poor and destitute among all humanity. Ulrich Luz observes that this reading "has the strongest impact [today] not, to be sure, on exegesis per se but rather on theology overall" (Luz 1996: 273).[6] This observation seems to be corroborated by Gustavo Gutiérrez, who contends that "exegetes are alarmed by the way that many theologians use this text."[7]

Arguments for a universalistic position of the *elachistos* come from a number of textual facets.[8] First, evidence of a nonliteral use of *adelphos* in Matthew that goes beyond Jesus' followers (e.g., 5:21-24, 47; 7:3-5) would allow for the possibility of its use more broadly in 25:40. Second, some scholars point to the omission of *adelphos* in the parallel verse (25:45) to argue their position (Davies and Allison 1997: 429).[9] Third, the framing of 25:31-46 as portraying universal judgment argues for understanding the "least" in a universal sense as well (Gutiérrez 1973: 19; Hultgren 2000: 322; Schnackenburg 2002: 258).[10] Contextual arguments include Matthew's exhortation to love one's enemies (5:44) as a theme that needs to shape the interpretation of 25:40 and the implicit connection between 25:31-46 and the fifth of Matthew's

Beatitudes ("blessed are the merciful," 5:7), which is unqualified in its scope (Davies and Allison 1997: 429).[11]

A second major interpretation of *elachistos* (what I'll refer to as a particularistic reading) is that the "least of these" are Christians or a subset thereof (e.g., itinerant missionaries).[12] This view gains support largely from the further qualification in 25:40: *tōn adelphōn mou* ("the least of these, my brothers and sisters").[13] Given the way the evangelist has used the familial term *adelphos* to refer to Jesus' followers across his Gospel (when used nonliterally; e.g., 12:49-50; 18:15), continuity of usage is typically argued for 25:40. Followers of Jesus, on this view, are the most likely referent for *elachistos*, especially if this term is used intentionally to echo its comparative *mikros* (see below), used at 10:42 and 18:6-14 as a designation for disciples and/or members of the believing community.

My interest in these two views for the purposes of this essay relates to the contribution of either reading for defining boundaries in this judgment scene. It would appear obvious that a universalistic reading of *elachistos* blurs boundaries between insiders and outsiders—the us and the other—since in this reading Jesus himself identifies not only with his own people who are in need but also with the needy of the entire world. Gutiérrez, borrowing the language of Yves Congar, speaks of "the sacrament of our neighbor" to express the collapsing of the boundary between Lord and "least of these" (Gutiérrez 1973: 201). This language also narrows the gap between Matthew's reader and the "least." If Jesus is shown to be in solidarity with the "least" to such an extent that what is done to them is done to him, then those who act on behalf of the "least" join in that same solidarity, not just for Jesus' sake, but also for the sake of the "least." Gutiérrez continues, "The neighbor is not an occasion, an instrument for becoming closer to God. We are dealing with a real love of [humanity] for [its] own sake and not 'for the love of God'" (Gutiérrez 1973: 202).[14]

While a universalistic reading tends to blur boundaries between us and other, the obverse—that a particularistic reading highlights boundaries—is not necessarily true, at least not universally so. Some who favor or even argue for a particularistic reading of *elachistos* also admit to an obscuring of clear categories in this passage. For example, Dan Via, while acknowledging that Matthew's most explicit statements lead to a reading of "my least brothers [and sisters]" as believers, argues that "the text refuses to stay within these limits" (Via 1987: 92). He bases a wider referent for *elachistos* on the surprise of the "sheep" juxtaposed with the close connection between Christ and his disciples in Matthew more broadly: "It is difficult to see how a person could meet a disciple and not know that he has also met Christ. . . . [Since the church's ministry is modeled after that of Jesus,] to have encountered a disciple is to know that person as a disciple of Jesus" (Via 1987: 92; similarly, Hultgren 2000: 322). For Via, the surprise of the sheep over encountering Jesus in the "least" indicates the latter must include others beyond disciples.

Ulrich Luz, who argues that a universalistic interpretation of *elachistos* is unfounded on the basis of the passage, nevertheless explores ways that this text pushes at its limits (to borrow Via's language) (Luz 1996: 308). First, he notes, "Matthew has handed on this explosive text; even though for himself, as for the entire church, it is love for the members of the congregation that stands in the foreground" (Luz 1996: 309). In addition to Matthew's inclusion of "this explosive text," Luz speaks of the destabilizing effect of the text. To the extent that Matthew

> was concerned to show that the Christian church has no special privilege in the final judgment, but rather will be asked . . . only about her deeds of love.
> . . . This Matthean text carries with it a warning against every attempt at Christian or ecclesiastical self-absolutizing. The modern proponents of the "universal" interpretation have sought to take further steps in this same direction of "de-absolutizing" the Christian church. Accordingly, they do not work with the sense of the biblical text itself, but rather with the direction in which it points. (Luz 1996: 309–10)

Both Via and Luz identify a kind of blurring of boundaries—a bridging toward the other—within or via the text. Though it seems that the categories of sheep, goats, and "least of these" are clearly delineated, their edges blur as the scene unfolds. R. T. France, who argues for Christians as the referent of *elachistos*, also indicates some measure of border ambiguity. He points to the element of surprise in this regard. Both sheep and goats are surprised that their treatment of the "least" was actually action toward Jesus. "They have helped, or failed to help, not a Jesus recognized in his representatives, but a Jesus incognito. . . . They seem closer to what some modern theologians call 'anonymous Christians' than to openly declared supporters of Jesus himself" (France 2007: 959). Thus some particularistic readings of *elachistos* appear to lead (in spite of themselves) to boundary ambiguities between us/other.

CONTEXTUAL APPROPRIATIONS

A sermon by Haddon Robinson on Matt. 25:31-46, "Surprises at the Judgment," serves as a focal example of Anglo-evangelical appropriation of this passage (see note 2 above). Additionally, six sermons that draw on this passage as their primary text have been reviewed to corroborate themes identified in Robinson's message.[15]

In his sermon, Robinson refers only in passing to the identity of the "least of these" (though not using the language of "least" or an equivalent). In that brief comment, the particularistic reading is evident: the ones who didn't receive help from those on the king's left are "those who belonged to [Jesus]" (Robinson 2000: 143).[16] Interestingly, there is a similar lack of emphasis on "the least" in the other sermons reviewed. Either the emphasis is laid on the *elachistos* as *adelphos*, with the elements of status and disadvantage of the "least" left behind with the term (two of six sermons); or the language of "least" is simply missing from the sermon altogether (two of six sermons).[17]

As Robinson expands on the identity of "those who belonged to [the king]," he gives two homiletical examples: a young female student of his who had recently lost two family members and a financially struggling seminary couple. This confirms his reading of "the least" as Christians. It is significant that, although he includes these examples of persons whom he helped without realizing the importance of his actions, his focus is more on the "unremembered acts of kindness" that characterized the sheep of the story than on the "least" with whom Jesus identifies (Robinson 2000: 144–45).[18]

The subtle shift of focus from persons in need to a Christian's (sheep's) kind actions may account for Robinson's omission in addressing solidarity with the "least" in his sermon. This omission is also characteristic of the six sermons reviewed. In only a few cases do these preachers allude to concepts of solidarity or identification between Jesus and the "least" or between faithful Jesus followers and the "least." One sermon explicitly invokes the principle that whatever Christians do for others in Jesus' name they do for him. Another gives the illustration of St. Francis, who saw the face of Jesus in a leper he served. The other four sermons reviewed tend to emphasize, along with Robinson, the importance of acts of kindness (two sermons) and/or to focus on the importance of faith over works. This focus on the action of a believer over the person for whom the act is done is reminiscent of Gutiérrez's indictment of someone being "more interested in the charitable action he was performing than in the concrete person for whom it was done" (Gutiérrez 1973: 200).

Another emphasis in Robinson's sermon, which was also found in the six others, is an apologetic for faith versus works as the basis for salvation.

While this issue has been raised in Matthean commentaries on 25:31-46, the sermons reviewed gave more attention and energy to this concern. All five sermons by Baptists (see note 15) at least touched on the issue of faith and works, arguing that Matt. 25:31-46 does not teach that Christians are saved because of what they do. A few of these spend significant time responding to this issue.[19] Robinson also gives attention to this issue, assuring his hearers that this passage doesn't communicate that doing charity gets you into heaven; rather, the actions of believers are based on God's work in their lives (Robinson 2000: 143). In the end, people will "make it in" through "brokenness of spirit, throwing themselves on God's grace" (Robinson 2000: 145). This emphasis directs attention away from actions done for "the least" as a criterion of judgment.

THE POWER DYNAMICS OF MATTHEW 25:31-46

A more overarching, though implicit, issue that arises from the text and intersects with ways of appropriating it in an evangelical context is one that receives sparse attention, both in the scholarly literature and in popular usage of the passage. Often unrecognized are the power dynamics that are assumed and addressed by this passage in its Matthean context and that have implications for current reflections on the text. These dynamics and structures of power are evident in (1) the terminology used (*elachistos*, "least of these"); (2) authority themes occurring more broadly in Matthew's Gospel; and (3) a shift of power at the climactic moment of this judgment scene.

First, Matthew's use of "least"—*elachistos*—illuminates a status category. The evangelist uses a related term in two previous contexts: *mikros* ("little ones") in chapters 10 and 18. In support of understanding these words as status terms, one can look to Louw and Nida's categorization of certain usages of both *mikros* and *elachistos* under the heading "Low Status or Rank (including persons of low status)" (Louw and Nida 1988: 1:739-40). In each Matthean context, this terminology has status connotations. In Matt. 10:42, Matthew's use of *mikros* illustrates the ultimate act of welcome (to Jesus, who identifies with those sent out in his name, 10:40). As his followers are to welcome prophets and righteous people (10:41), they should even welcome the *mikros* ("little one") who is a disciple. The argument here uses a more unexpected category to stress the importance of welcome: not only should prophets or righteous people receive welcome, but even a *mikros*—one of lower status—is to be welcomed as Jesus would be. The status denotations of *mikros* are further emphasized by its use in the third and final position of the series and the action of giving to a little one "even a cup of cold water" (10:42). Actions done toward (even) this "little one" prove the depth of welcome expected by Jesus.

In chapter 18, the status implications of Matthew's use of *mikros* are even more evident. The chapter begins with the disciples asking Jesus a status question: "Who is the greatest in the kingdom of heaven?" (18:1). In response, Jesus brings a child into their midst as an answer to their question. Given that children had little status in first-century Greco-Roman society, the object lesson is about status and emulation of the person of low status (Brown 2002: 71). This is confirmed in 18:4, where Jesus speaks of becoming humble (*tapeinoō*) like children, emphasizing their relative lack of status (BDAG 990; France 2007: 678–79; Davies and Allison 1991: 757).[20] Welcoming children, those of low status, is then tied to welcoming Jesus himself (18:5; similar to 10:40). In 18:6-14, the references to children transpose into language of *mikros*. These "little ones" are not identical to children; they are a broader group within the church. Yet they too are characterized by lowly status and the vulnerability that would result from it.[21] Relevant in this regard is the injunction to Jesus' followers not to despise the little ones in their community (18:10), with the implication being that it might be easy to do so.

Turning to Matthew 25, the evangelist draws on a superlative of *mikros* to indicate a group that is marginalized and vulnerable—*elachistos*.[22] By using this term in line with the previous usages of *mikros*, the author emphasizes the lack of status and the vulnerability of "the least of these" as compared to the other groups in this scene (the king, the sheep, and the goats). By using this distinctive term (the superlative, *elachistos*, rather than *mikros*), the low status of this group is especially emphasized in Matthew 25. The status connotations of this language in 25:31-46 are explored more closely below, especially in relation to the power differentials evident in the passage.

Second, the power dynamics at play in this passage intersect with the theme of authority across the Gospel of Matthew, and more specifically with the relationship between Jesus' authority and the community of believers. While the motif of Jesus' authority is ubiquitous in Matthew, the granting of authority to Jesus' disciples (the twelve, specifically) is more circumscribed. The reader first hears of authority given to the Twelve at Matt. 10:1, where authority to participate in the ministry of Jesus in performing healing and exorcism is granted.[23] Then at the climactic scene of Peter's confession of Jesus as Messiah, authority is promised to Peter in the declaration that the keys of the kingdom will be given by Jesus to him and that his binding and loosing activity will be effectual (16:19). While the referents of these images are debated, what is clear is that Jesus promises future ecclesial authority to Peter.[24] Identical language of binding and loosing is used in Matthew 18 by Jesus to indicate the (future) authority of the twelve disciples, and Matthew's community by extension (18:18). As Matthew's Jesus looks ahead to a (postresurrection) time when his followers will carry out his mission and commands, he envisions them acting on his authority.

Yet the final scene of Matthew complicates (and clarifies) this picture. As Jesus meets the Eleven in Galilee after his resurrection, he declares: "All authority in heaven and earth has been given to me" (28:18). The astute reader, having heard the words of Jesus to his disciples at 16:19 and 18:18 might assume that in this final moment of Matthew's Gospel Jesus will hand over at least a measure of his authority to the disciples as promised. This is precisely what Jesus does not do, according to Matthew. Instead, Jesus commissions his disciples to missional living—baptizing and teaching—and promises his own presence with them "to the very end of the age" (28:20). Any authority granted to Jesus' disciples—and to the Matthean community by extension—is a derived authority. It is an authority that comes via his presence. Thus, for Matthew, the disciples and the church do not possess authority; it belongs to Jesus alone (28:18). Their access to that authority is through his presence with his people (1:23; 18:20; 28:20).

This thematic assessment of authority in Matthew sets the stage for a reading of Matt. 25:31-46 that highlights the power shift, which occurs as the scene progresses. The king (25:34; a figure of authority) has separated all humanity into two categories.[25] The scene develops as the criterion of judgment is clarified: both groups are judged on the basis of their treatment of Jesus (25:34-36, 41-43). So far, so good; all is as expected. Human response to Jesus is the crucial criterion of kingdom inclusion as throughout Matthew.

The unexpected comes when Jesus defines their response to a Jesus who was hungry, thirsty, a stranger, naked, sick, and imprisoned. This is a different Jesus from the one who uses his authority to heal the sick, to feed the hungry, to welcome the stranger (e.g., Matthew 8–9). Or so it would seem.[26] Clarification comes when, in response to the similar question from both groups, Jesus specifies, "Whatever you did for one of the least of these . . . you did for me" (25:40). Whatever we call this relationship between Jesus and the "least"—whether solidarity, identification, or substitution—what is significant is that Jesus is present with them in a way that reorients readerly expectations.[27] The scene has, up to this point, had three characters/groups: the king (Jesus), the sheep on his right, and the goats on his left. And Jesus is the one with ultimate authority. The introduction of the *elachistos*—"the least of these"—and their clear alignment with Jesus himself redistributes power in the scene. The authoritative Jesus is shown to side with the "least," a group that, by definition, lacks status and power. Thus, just as Jesus has shared the disadvantages and marginalization of the least with them (he was hungry, sick, and poor), so the least now aligned with his power and authority via his presence. We have seen that Matthew connects Jesus' authority with his presence, especially in 28:18-20 (also 18:18-20). If Jesus is especially present with "the least," then by implication Jesus' power is accessed by them as well. The reversals of the kingdom that have been highlighted by Matthew's Jesus become reality (e.g., 5:3-10; 19:20; 20:16; 23:11).

CONTEXTUAL APPROPRIATIONS

Turning to the ways in which this kind of reading intersects with evangelical appropriations of the passage, it is telling that very few sermons reviewed raised issues of power, especially related to structural or systemic issues or empowerment of those most marginalized. One sermon does accentuate Jesus' authority and power in the passage, drawing on Matt. 28:18 for his universal authority, but does not interact with the status connotations of *elachistos*. In fact, only one of the sermons surveyed attends to the status connotations of Matthew's language of "least." The preacher of that sermon speaks of the tendency to serve and help important people, since these actions often pay us back in some way.[28]

Robinson's sermon provides a fairly typical response to the features of the passage that have the most potential to address issues of power (and challenge a status quo)—namely, the status connotations of *elachistos* and Jesus' identification with this group. On the one hand, Robinson never uses the language of the "least," choosing to frame the recipients of Christian kindness as "those who belong to him" (Robinson 2000: 143; see discussion above). As a result, he does not mention the status connotations of this Matthean language, nor does he attend to the power differentials implicit with this language and its use in conjunction with the other actors of the story.

Alternately, the sheep's surprise at Jesus' identification with the "least" is highlighted. In fact, the feature of surprise accounts for about half of the sermon and its title. Key to an assessment of Robinson's interpretation of this feature is his repeated statement that "little [unknown,] unremembered acts of kindness and love" are to characterize Christians (Robinson 2000: 143; essentially repeated on 144). These unremembered acts, according to Robinson, are those "that we hardly think about but are important to the king" (Robinson

2000: 143). Interestingly, the other sermons reviewed provide additional examples of this theme. One preacher speaks of little actions of service and the importance of "little bitty choices," another of "spontaneous acts of kindness." Another cites D. L. Moody about a willingness to do little as well as great things.

An observation and an interpretation seem called for here. First, the minimization of the actions toward "the least" is thematic. The recurring use of the diminutive "little" is striking (across three sermons, including Robinson's). What might be described as significant actions of solidarity are described as "little acts" or even "little bitty" ones. While Matthew uses the diminutive "least" to speak of persons who are disadvantaged and seemingly insignificant, in the sermons this language shifts to describe seemingly insignificant actions. This language displacement may be due in part to the element of surprise in the story. Since the sheep (the righteous) have not recognized Jesus as the recipient of their actions, they are surprised by his words in 25:35-36 (e.g., "I was hungry and you gave me food"). Yet the element of surprise is not tied to the seeming insignificance of these actions but to the fact that Jesus was present for and in the action toward the "least."

Second, the shift in emphasis from marginalized person to insignificant actions assists the thematic movement from power and status categories to privatizing and individualizing motifs. The privatization of Matthew's acts of justice and mercy is communicated in the interpretation of these acts as "little unknown, unremembered acts" (Robinson 2000: 143).[29] The passage is individualized through a focus away from Jesus' identification with the *elachistos* to an emphasis on "acts of kindness and love that flow from [a person's] inner nature—which has been touched by God" (Robinson 2000: 144). According to Michael Emerson and Christian Smith, in their sociological study *Divided by Faith: Evangelical Religion and the Problem of Race in America*, individualism is a particularly tenacious trait of white evangelical Christianity. As they note, "Individualism is very American, but the type of individualism and the ferocity with which it is held distinguishes white evangelicals from others . . . for them individuals exist independent of structures and institutions" (Emerson and Smith 2000: 76).[30] This individualizing tendency may contribute to a devaluing of actions apparent in the language of "little acts" and the like, in some of the sermons reviewed. If the pull of individualism minimizes solidarity with the other, then it is not difficult to understand how actions of solidarity would be minimized in more individualistic interpretations of Matthew 25. This minimization of action, in turn, might contribute to the emphasis in most of the sermons on arguments against viewing this passage as supporting judgment by works.

Gutiérrez, in his discussion of Matt. 25:31–46, warns against an individualistic understanding of the love of neighbor and our encounter of God in the poor. For Gutiérrez, neighbor "refers to the exploited social class, the dominated people, and the marginalized race. The masses are also our neighbor. . . . Indeed, to offer food or drink in our day is a political action; it means the transformation of a society structured to benefit a few who appropriate to themselves the value of the work of others" (Gutiérrez 1973: 202). Attention to the power dynamics at play both in Matthew and in Christian actions, even "charitable" ones, provides a needed corrective to these individualizing tendencies and readings.

In fact, a recent article by Shane Claiborne offers from and to a broadly evangelical audience a compelling contrast to an individualizing focus of Matthew 25 (Claiborne 2010).[31] Claiborne speaks of the "layers separating us from others, especially those who are poor from those who are not. There are obvious layers like picket fences and SUVs, but there are also the more subtle ones like charity." He then riffs on Matthew 25:

> When we get to heaven, though, I'm not convinced Jesus is going to say, "When I was hungry, you gave a check to the United Way and they gave me something to eat," or, "When I was naked, you donated clothes to the Salvation Army and they clothed me." Jesus is not seeking distant acts of charity. He seeks concrete acts of love: "*you* gave me something to eat . . . *you* gave me something to drink . . . *you* clothed me . . . *you* invited me in . . . *you* looked after me . . . *you* came to visit me [in prison]" (Matt. 25:35-36). (Claiborne 2010: 84)

Claiborne addresses issues of us/other that may very well be embedded in practices of charity. He also goes on to note power differentials that can be maintained, while supposedly helping the least of these. "Faith-based nonprofits can tend to mirror secular organizations, maintaining the same hierarchies of power and separation between rich and poor. They can too easily merely facilitate the exchange of goods and services, putting professionals in the middle to guarantee the rich do not have to face the poor and power does not shift" (Claiborne 2010: 84).

CONCLUSION

This study has examined the intersections of scholarly and ecclesial interpretation and appropriation of Matt. 25:31-46. Particular attention was paid to the identity and function of the *elachistos*—"the least"—in the passage and in representative evangelical preaching of it. An attempt was made to assess power dynamics within the text, especially the realignment of authority that implicitly occurs in Jesus' solidarity with the "least." While the evangelical preaching reviewed has not much addressed or responded to these structural dynamics of the text, other voices, some home-grown like Claiborne, have begun filling this gap. It is my hope that this essay would spur such conversations and appropriations to offer fresh readings and hearings of this—as Luz calls it—"explosive text."

Notes

1. I am grateful for the collaborative guidance of Bethel colleagues Drs. Steven J. Sandage and Carla M. Dahl, especially related to methodological issues of my analysis of sermon samples. The qualitative method used involved analysis of selected sermons (see n15) especially for treatment of the particular issues of (1) the identity of the "least" and (2) power and status contours of the parable. Additionally, themes that emerged and were then analyzed included the element of surprise in the parable (by sheep and goats) and added discussions of faith vs. works in the sermons.

2. Choosing Haddon Robinson as representative of evangelical preaching is not difficult to justify. As Duduit (2010) puts it, "Haddon Robinson is one of the most influential persons in the homiletical world. The author of the immensely popular textbook Biblical Preaching. . . , he has influenced thousands of evangelical preachers through his writing and through his former students who now teach homiletics."

3. For a helpful discussion of these stances to the text and a bridging perspective, see 2011: xxxviii–xli. The dialectic of a hermeneutic of suspicion and a hermeneutic of trust derives from Ricoeur; these concepts are applied in hermeneutical discourse both to the text and to the reading context. For example, see Ricoeur 1974.

4. Rhoads and Michie (1982) speak of a Gospel's rhetorical level to describe a second layer of the narrative beyond the story level. It is on the narrative's rhetorical level that the (implied) author communicates with the (implied) reader. For use of these narrative categories and for an argument that the reader perceives a growing inclusion in the audience of the five Matthean discourses, see Brown 2005: 19–35.

5. According to Gutiérrez (1973: 196), this passage "seems to many to summarize the essence of the Gospel message." Gutiérrez cites Trilling (1969: 2:216) in this regard, who refers to Matt. 25:31-46 as "a summary of the whole teaching of the Gospel."

6. Both Luz and Donahue (1986: esp. 3–8) provide a helpful review of the recent history of interpretation on this issue.

7. Hultgren (2000: 318) observes that "this interpretation prevails in various studies of NT ethics."

8. Proponents of the universalistic view include Davies and Allison 1997: 429; Hultgren 2000: 320-25; Gutiérrez 1973: 197; Schnackenburg 2002: 258; Wenham 1989: 91. For a history of interpretation of Matt. 25:31-46 with a thorough catalog of commentators and their views, see Gray 1989.

9. Hultgren (2000: 321) notes that the six descriptors (hungry, thirsty, etc.), which are the antecedents of *elachistos* and *adelphos*, are very broad and should be allowed to define *elachistos* more universally.

10. Schnackenburg (2002: 258) also notes the absence of "in the name of a disciple" in 25:40, which is included in 10:42.

11. All biblical quotations are from the NRSV.

12. Held by Luz 1996: 280–84, 286; Hagner 1995b: 744–45; Senior 1998: 283–84; France 2007: 964–65; Garland 2001: 248; Carson 1984: 520; and Turner 2008: 605–6. Robert H. Gundry (1982: 514) holds that "'one of these littlest brothers of mine' refers to those who carried the gospel from place to place as they fled persecution."

13. While masculine in form, *adelphos* is used generically (inclusively) in many contexts; therefore, it is rightly rendered "brothers and sisters" here (i.e., siblings).

14. Siker (1997: 129) notes that "the single most important [Scripture] passage for Gutiérrez is clearly Matt. 25:31-46. . . . Gutiérrez refers to this passage no fewer than forty-seven times in his writings."

15. Of seven sermons from sermonsearch.com that used Matt. 25:31-46 as their primary biblical text, six were deemed to fit the relevant demographic for this paper. Five of these were from Baptist church contexts, and one was from an Assemblies of God church leader. (The seventh, which was not used, was from an Episcopal priest.) Admittedly, this is an exploratory survey of a small number of sermons by white, American males without access to ways they would define their own cultural frameworks. Future research in this area might include interviews of preachers, as well as a cross-cultural examination of preaching on this text.

16. The six sermons reviewed offered distinctive readings of the identity of the "least": one indicated that the "least" are fellow Christians; two argued that they are Jews (with one drawing from the *adelphos* term for this, not mentioning "least"); and two read the "least" concept as representing anyone in need.

17. In one of these, after a brief reference to the six actions of 25:35-36, the preacher gives significant time to the issue of faith and works; see below. In the other sermon, the preacher has a single sentence indicating that the sheep are commended for their service to the weak as well as the strong.

18. Language of "(little) . . . acts of kindness" occurs three times in the sermon (144, 145, 146).

19.

The single sermon from an Assemblies of God preacher speaks of the actions of Christians as evidence of the work of the Spirit in their lives.

20. For ongoing status concerns in this section of Matthew, see "great" language at 20:26 (also 23:11) and "first"/"last" concepts at 19:30; 20:16, 27, as well as in the parable of the workers (20:1-15).

21. Hultgren (2000: 317) refers to the *mikros* as "vulnerable disciples." Orton (2003: 499) notes the connection of the *mikroi* to sheep in both Matthew 10 and 18, defining the former as "vulnerable followers of the shepherd, at the mercy of wild animals (10:16) and apt to stray (18:12-14)."

22. Note BDAG 521; Horst and Schneider 1993: 1:426; Zerwick and Grosvenor 1981: 84; and Mounce 1993: 177; Via 1987: 92, each of which indicates that *elachistos* is used as a superlative for *mikros*. Contra Luz (1996: 302), who argues that *elachistos* should not be understood based on *mikros*. Davies and Allison (1997: 429n54) note that in manuscripts∑(sixth century) and 067 (sixth century) *mikrōn* occurs in 25:40 and in manuscript 700 (eleventh century) *mikrōn* replaces *elachistōn* in 25:45. This indicates that some scribes understood these terms to be related.

23. Although the Twelve struggle to live up to these expectations; see 17:14-20; Brown 2002: 99-101.

24. The likely referents to these images are the delegation to a steward for household management (keys of the kingdom; see France 2007: 625) and interpretation of the applicability of laws (binding and loosing). On the latter, see Powell 2003: 438.

25. The king is introduced in the passage as the Son of Man (25:31), a likely Danielic reference highlighting the vindication and authority of this figure. France (2007: 960) contends that the "judgment scene is set in language largely drawn from Dan 7:13-14 and its wider setting." Although some interpreters limit the scope of this judgment scene (either to exclude the church or Israel), there is good reason to read the scene as a universal judgment (see Luz 1996: 292–94).

26. The citation of Isa. 53:7 at Matt. 8:17 does, however, hint at a kind of substitution that Jesus brings for the sick: "He took up our infirmities and bore our diseases."

27. See Gutiérrez (1973: 201) for a list of possibilities concerning the nature of the relationship between Jesus and the "least."

28. "We didn't visit. We didn't care. We didn't love. We didn't use the gifts that we have. Oh, if it had been some important person. We were to help them. If we had thought that we could help and get something in return through the back door, ah, we would have visited then."

29. Regarding the themes of justice and mercy, see Via (1987: 84), who notes that Matt. 25:31-46 "picks up and develops the stress in chap. 23 on the weightier matters of the law—justice, mercy, and faith (23:23)."

30. They go on to explain: "Contemporary white American evangelicalism is perhaps the strongest carrier of this freewill-individualist tradition. The roots of this individualist tradition run deep, dating back to shortly after the sixteenth-century Reformation, extending to much of the Free Church tradition, flowering in America's frontier awakenings and revivals, and maturing in spiritual pietism and anti-Social Gospel fundamentalism. Although the larger American culture is itself highly individualistic, the close connection between faith and freewill individualism to the exclusion of progressive thought renders white evangelicals even more individualistic than other white Americans."

31. Self-described as "the top magazine for savvy, spiritual 20somethings," Relevant is geared toward younger evangelicals and beyond. The advertisements in Relevant demonstrate the evangelical focus of the magazine; college ads include Messiah College, Liberty University, Calvin College, Dallas Theological Seminary, and Indiana Wesleyan Seminary. Claiborne is a graduate of Eastern University; for his final part of that degree, he attended Wheaton College, a self-identified evangelical school. While at Wheaton, he completed an internship at Willow Creek Community Church, a self-identified evangelical megachurch.

Bibliography

Ali, Abbas J. 2009. "Evangelical Capitalism and Organization." In *Organizations, Markets and Imperial Formations: Towards an Anthropology of Globalization*, ed. Subhabrata Bobby Banerjee, Vanessa C. M. Chio, and Raza Mir. Cheltenham, 132–60. Northampton, MA: Edward Elgar.

Allison, Dale, Jr. 2001. "Matthew." In *The Oxford Bible Commentary*, ed. John Barton and John Muddiman, 844–86. Oxford: Oxford University Press.

———. 2005. *Studies in Matthew: Interpretations Past and Present*. Grand Rapids: Baker Academic.

Althaus, Paul. 1972. *The Ethics of Martin Luther*. Philadelphia: Fortress Press.

Amarasingam, Amarnath. 2008. "Transcending Technology: Looking at Futurology as a New Religious Movement." *Journal of Contemporary Religion* 23 (January): 1–16.

Améry, Jean. 1980. *At the Mind's Limits: Contemplations by a Survivor on Auschwitz and Its Realities*. Trans. S. R. Rosenfeld and S. P. Rosenfeld. Bloomington: Indiana University Press.

Aminian, Natalie, K. C. Fung, and Chelsea C. Lin. 2008. "Outward FDI from East Asia: The Experiences of Hong Kong and Taiwan." In *New Dimensions of Economic Globalization: Surge of Outward Foreign Direct Investment from Asia*, ed. Ramkishen S. Rajan, Rajiv Kumar, and Nicola Virgill, 171–208. Hackensack, NJ; Singapore: World Scientific.

Anderson, Janice Capel. 2001. "Matthew: Gender and Reading." In *A Feminist Companion to Matthew*, ed. Amy-Jill Levine, ed. 25–51. Sheffield: Sheffield Academic.

Anderson, Janice Capel, and Stephen D. Moore. 2003. "Matthew and Masculinity." In *New Testament Masculinities*, ed. Stephen D. Moore and Janice C. Anderson, 67–91. Atlanta: Society of Biblical Literature, 2003.

Anspach, Mark, Yannick Blanc, and Michel Bessieres. 2001. "Global Markets, Anonymous Victims." *UNESCO Courier* 54/5: 47–51.

Aquinas, Thomas. "Whether it is always sinful to wage war?" *Summa Theologica* 2-2.40. Trans. Fathers of the English Dominican Province. New York: Benziger Bros., 1947.

Assmann, Aleida. 1999. *Erinnerungsräume: Formen und Wandlungen des kulturellen Gedächtnisses*. Munich: C. H. Beck.

Assmann, Hugo. 1976. *Theology for a Nomad Church*. Maryknoll, NY: Orbis.

Assmann, Jan. 2006a. "Form as a Mnemonic Device: Cultural Texts and Cultural Memory." In *Performing the Gospel: Orality, Memory, and Mark: Essays Dedicated to Werner Kelber*, ed. Richard A. Horsley, Jonathan A. Draper, and John Miles Foley, 67–82. Minneapolis: Fortress Press.

———. 2006b. *Religion and Cultural Memory: Ten Studies*. Trans. Rodney Livingstone. Stanford: Stanford University Press.

Au, Winton. 2011. "Survey on Overtime Work in Hong Kong." Chinese University of Hong Kong press release. April 20. http://www.cuhk.edu.hk/cpr/pressrelease/051104e.htm.

Augustine. 1972. *The City of God*. Trans. Davd Knowles, Middlesex: Penguin.

Bacon, B. W. 1930. "The 'Five Books' of Matthew against the Jews." In *Studies in Matthew*. New York: Henry Holt.

Bailey, Randall C. 2010. "What Ever Happened to the Good Old White Boys?" Review of *Global Bible Commentary*, ed. Daniel Patte. Nashville: Abingdon, 2004. http://www.vanderbilt.edu/AnS/religious_studies/GBC/proscons.htm.

Bailey, Randall C., Tat-siong Benny Liew, and Fernando F. Segovia, eds. 2009. *They Were All Together in One Place? Toward Minority Biblical Criticism*. SemeiaSt. Atlanta: Society of Biblical Literature.

Bal, Mieke. *On Meaning-Making : Essays in Semiotics*. FF. Literary Facets. Sonoma, CA: Polebridge, 1994.

Balz, Horst, and Gerhard Schneider, eds. 1993. *Exegetical Dictionary of the New Testament*. 3 vols. Grand Rapids: Eerdmans.

Baofu, Peter. 2002. *The Future of Capitalism and Democracy*. Lanham, MD: University Press of America.

Barbour, Robert S. 1970. "Gethsemane in the Tradition of the Passion." *NTS* 16/3: 231–51.

Barton, Stephen C., Loren T. Stuckenbruck, and Benjamin G. Wold, eds. 2007. *Memory in the Bible and Antiquity: The Fifth Durham-Tübingen Research Symposium*. Tübingen: Mohr Siebeck.

Bataille, Georges. 1992. *Theory of Religion*. Trans. Robert Hurley. New York: Zone.

Bauckham, Richard. 1995. "Tamar's Ancestry and Rahab's Marriage: Two Problems in the Matthean Genealogy." *NovT* 37/4: 313–29.

Beck, Ulrich. 2007. *Weltrisikogesellschaft: Auf der Suche nach der verlorenen Sicherheit*. Frankfurt am Main: Suhrkamp.

Betcher, Sharon V. 2001. "Rehabilitating Religious Discourse: Bringing Disability Studies to the Theological Venue." *ResSRev* 27/4: 341–48.

———. 2007. *Spirit and the Politics of Disablement.* Minneapolis: Fortress Press.

Bishop, Jeffery P. 2007. "The Broken Body and the Disabled Body: Reflections on Disability and the Objects of Medicine." In *Theology, Disability, and the New Genetics: Why Science Needs the Church*, ed. John Swinton and Brian Brock, 214–33. New York: T&T Clark.

Booth, Tony. 1991. "Challenging Conceptions of Integration." In *Constructing Deafness*, ed. Susan Gregory and Gillian Hartley, 157–64. London: Pinter

Boice, James Montgomery. 2001. *The Gospel of Matthew.* Grand Rapids: Baker, 2001.

Boring, Eugene. 1995. "Matthew." In *New Testament Articles, Matthew, Mark.* Vol. 8, *The New Interpreter's Bible*, ed. Leander Keck. Nashville: Abingdon.

Bradley, Keith R. 1989. *Slavery and Rebellion in the Roman World.* Bloomington: Indiana University Press.

Brook, Timothy, ed. 1999. *Documents on the Rape of Nanjing.* Ann Arbor: University of Michigan Press.

Brooks, James A., and Carlton L. Winbery. 1979. *Syntax of New Testament Greek.* Lanham, MD: University Press of America.

Brown, Jeannine K. 2002. *The Disciples in Narrative Perspective: The Portrayal and Function of the Matthean Disciples.* Atlanta: Society of Biblical Literature.

———. 2005. "Direct Engagement of the Reader in Matthew's Discourses: Rhetorical Techniques and Scholarly Consensus." *NTS* 51 (January): 19–35.

Brown, Raymond E. 1982. "Rachab in Mt 1:5 Probably Is Rahab of Jericho." *Bib* 63/1: 79–80.

———. 1993. *The Birth of the Messiah: A Commentary on the Infancy Narratives in the Gospels of Matthew and Luke.* ABRL. New York: Doubleday.

———. 1994. *The Death of the Messiah: From Gethsemane to the Grave: A Commentary on the Passion Narratives in the Four Gospels.* 2 vols. ABRL. New York: Doubleday.

Brown, Teresa L. Fry. 2000. *God Don't Like Ugly: African American Women Handing on Spiritual Values.* Nashville: Abingdon.

Bruner, F. D. 2004. *Matthew: A Commentary: The Churchbook Matthew 13–28.* Grand Rapids: Eerdmans.

Bryson, Bill. 1990. *The Mother Tongue: English and How It Got That Way.* New York: William Morrow and Company,

Budak, Neven. 2004. "Post-Socialist Historiography in Croatia since 1990." In *(Re)Writing History: Historiography in Southeast Europe after Socialism*, ed. Ulf Brunnbauer, 128–64. Studies on South East Europe 4. Münster: Lit, 2004.

Bynum, Caroline Walker. "Women's Stories, Women's Symbols: A Critique of Victor Turner's Theory of Liminality." In *Readings in Ritual Studies*, ed. Ronald L. Grimes, 71–85. Upper Saddle River, NJ: Prentice Hall, 1996.

Byrskog, Samuel. 2006. "A New Quest for the Sitz im Leben: Social Memory, the Jesus Tradition and the Gospel of Matthew." *NTS* 52/3: 319–36.

Cahill, Lisa. 1994. *Love Your Enemies: Discipleship, Pacifism, and Just War Theory.* Minneapolis: Fortress Press.

Callahan, John. 1989. *Don't Worry, He Won't Get Far on Foot.* New York: William Morrow and Company.

Capps, Donald. 2008. *Jesus the Village Psychiatrist.* Louisville: Westminster John Knox.

Cargal, Timothy B. 1990. "The Generative Trajectory in Certain Non-Western Cultures." In *The Religious Dimensions of Biblical Texts: Greimas's Structural Semiotics and Biblical Exegesis*, ed. Daniel Patte, 265–75. Atlanta, GA: Scholars.

Carroll, John T. 2001. "Children in the Bible." *Int* 45: 121–35.

Carson, D. A. 1984. *Matthew.* The Expositor's Bible Commentary. Grand Rapids: Zondervan.

Carter, Warren. 2000. *Matthew and the Margins: A Sociopolitical and Religious Reading.* The Bible and Liberation. Maryknoll, NY: Orbis.

———. 2001. *Matthew and Empire: Initial Explorations.* Harrisburg, Pa.: Trinity Press International.

———. 2003. "Are There Imperial Texts in the Class? Intertextual Eagles and Matthean Eschatology as 'Lights Out' Time for Imperial Rome (Matthew 24:27-31)." *JBL* 122/3 (Fall): 467–87.

Casey, Edward S. 1993. *Getting Back into Place: Toward a Renewed Understanding of the Place-World.* Bloomington: Indiana University Press.

Chan, Bucky K. H. 2004. "Understanding Overtime." *Career Times.* June 25. http://www.wkll.com/database/artices/en/2004-06-25.pdf.

Chan, K. C. 2011. "HK Most Compelling Offshore RMB Market." *On the Record.* May 22. http://www.news.gov.hk/en/record/html/2011/05/20110520_193346.shtml.

Chan, Lung-pun Common. 2007. "Eine Sozialwissenschaftliche Untersuchung der Metaphor des Lammes in der Johannesapokalypse." Th.D. diss., University of Heidelberg.

Chang, Iris. 1998. *The Rape of Nanking: The Forgotten Holocaust of World War II.* New York: Penguin.

Chang, Matthias. 2011. "Red Alert: The Second Wave of the Financial Tsunami." *Global Research.* April 20. http://www.globalresearch.ca/red-alert-the-second-wave-of-the-financial-tsunami/16218.

Chang, Nina, Luther Ng, and Michelle Chan. 2010. "Post-80s Activist Christina Chan; Police Video Recording of Protests; Who are the post-80s generation?" Hong Kong: RTHK production. Video recording.

Charles, Ronald. 2011. "Rahab: A Righteous Whore in James." *Neot* 45/2: 206–20.

Cheung, Anthony B. L. 2000. "New Interventionism in the Making: Interpreting State Interventions in Hong Kong after the Change of Sovereignty." *Journal of Contemporary China* 9/24: 291–308.

Chia, P. P. 2009. "On Constructing a Critical Sino-Public Biblical Theology: A Glocal Public Approach." In *The Open Text: On the Relation Between Biblical Studies and Public Theology*, 75–108. Hong Kong: Verbum.

Chrysostom. Homily LXV. 2 (P. Schaff [trans.], NPNF 1-10, 380).

Chu, Stephen Yiu-wai. 2011. "Brand Hong Kong: Asia's World City as Method?" *Visual Anthropology* 24 (Jan–Apr): 46–58.

Clarke, Sathianathan. 2002. "Viewing the Bible Through the Eyes and Ears of the Subalterns in India." *BibInt* 10: 245–66.

Claiborne, Shane. 2010. "The Great Divide." *Relevant* 45 (May–June) 84–85.

Cochrane, James R. 1991. "Already, but Not Yet: Programmatic Notes for a Theology of Work." In *The Threefold Cord: Theology, Work and Labour*, ed. James R. Cochrane and Gerald O. West, 177–89. Pietermaritzburg: Cluster, 1991.

Code, Lorraine. 2006. *Ecological Thinking: The Politics of Epistemic Location*, Studies in Feminist Philosophy. Oxford: Oxford University Press.

Collins, Patricia Hill. 2000. *Black Feminist Thought.* 2nd ed. New York: Routledge.

Conway, Colleen M. 2003. "'Behold the Man!' Masculine Christology and the Fourth Gospel." In *New Testament Masculinities*, ed. Stephen D. Moore and Janice C. Anderson, 163–79. Atlanta: Society of Biblical Literature.

Cooey, Paula M. 1999. "Ordinary Mother as Oxymoron: The Collusion of Theology, Theory, and Politics in the Undermining of Mothers." In *Mother Troubles: Rethinking Contemporary Maternal Dilemmas*, ed. Julia E. Hanigsberg and Sara Ruddick, 229–49. Boston: Beacon.

Creamer, Deborah Beth. 2009. *Disability and Christian Theology.* Oxford: Oxford University Press.

Crosby, Michael. 1988. *House of Disciples: Church, Economics, and Justice in Matthew.* Maryknoll, NY: Orbis.

———. 2005. *Spirituality of the Beatitudes: Matthew's Vision for the Church in an Unjust World.* Maryknoll, NY: Orbis.

Croy, N. Clayton. 2011. *Prima Scriptura: An Introduction to New Testament Interpretation.* Grand Rapids: Baker Academic, 2011.

Curtin, Deane. 2005. *Environmental Ethics for a Postcolonial World.* Lanham, MD: Rowman & Littlefield.

Darragh, Neil. 2000. *At Home in the Earth: Seeking an Earth-Centred Spirituality.* Auckland: Accent.

Davies, W. D., and Dale C. Allison Jr. 1988. *Matthew 1–7.* ICC. London: T&T Clark.

———. 1991. *Matthew 8–18.* ICC. London: T&T Clark.

———. 1997. *Matthew 19–28.* ICC. London: T&T Clark.

———. 2004. *Matthew: A Shorter Commentary.* London: T&T Clark.

Davis, Lennard J. 1995. *Enforcing Normalcy: Disability, Deafness and the Body.* London: Verso.

———. 2006. "Constructing Normalcy: The Bell Curve, the Novel, and the Invention of the Disabled Body in the Nineteenth Century." In *The Disability Studies Reader,* ed. Lennard J. Davis, 3–15. New York: Routledge.

Decharneux, Baudouin. 2008. "Les généalogies du Nouveau Testament." *Académie Royale de Belgique: Bulletin de la Classe des Lettres* 6e série Tome XIX: 95–121.

Demetriades, Stavroula, and Roberto Pedersini. 2008. *Working Time in the EU and Other Global Economies.* Luxembourg: Office for Official Publications of the European Communities.

Dickerson, Bette J., ed. 1995. *African American Single Mothers: Understanding Their Lives and Families.* London: Sage.

Dickson, Kwesi A. 1984. *Theology in Africa.* London: Darton, Longman & Todd.

Dillard, Annie. 1992. *The Living.* New York: HarperPerennial.

Doka, Kenneth J., ed. 2002. *Disenfranchised Grief: New Directions, Challenges, and Strategies for Practice.* Champaign, IL: Research Press.

Donahue, John R. 1986. "The 'Parable' of the Sheep and the Goats: A Challenge to Christian Ethics." *TS* 47: 3–31.

Donaldson, Laura. 2005. "Gospel Hauntings: The Postcolonial Demons of New Testament Criticism." In *Postcolonial Biblical Criticism*, ed. S. Moore and F. Segovia, 97–113. London: T&T Clark.

Donaldson, Terence. 1985. *Jesus on the Mountain: A Study in Matthean Theology.* JSNTSup 8. Sheffield: JSOT Press, 1985.

Duarte, Alejandro Alberto. 2004. "Matthew." In *Global Bible Commentary*, ed. Daniel Patte, 350–60. Nashville: Abingdon.

Duling, Denise, and Norman Perrin. 1994. *The New Testament: Proclamation and Parenesis, Myth and History.* 3rd ed. Fort Worth: Harcourt Brace College Publishers.

Draper, Jonathan A. 1991. "'For the Kingdom Is inside You and It Is Outside of You': Contextual Exegesis in South Africa." In *Text and Interpretation: New Approaches in the Criticism of the New Testament*, ed. Patrick J. Hartin and Jacobus H. Petzer, 235–57. Leiden: E. J. Brill, 1991.

———. 2001. "Old Scores and New Notes: Where and What Is Contextual Exegesis in the New South Africa?" In *Towards an Agenda for Contextual Theology: Essays in Honour of Albert Nolan*, ed. McGlory T. Speckman and Larry T. Kaufmann, 148–68. Pietermaritzburg: Cluster, 2001.

———. 2002. "Reading the Bible as Conversation: A Theory and Methodology for Contextual Interpretation of the Bible in Africa." *Grace and Truth* 19/2:12–24.

———. 2008. "Biblical Hermeneutics in a Secular Age: Reflections from South Africa Twenty Years after the Kairos Document." In *The Bible in the Public Square*, ed. Cynthia Briggs Kittredge, Ellen B. Bradshaw Aitken, and Jonathan A. Draper, 39–54. Minneapolis: Fortress Press.

Dube, Musa. 1999. "Consuming a Colonial Time Bomb: Translating Badimo into 'Demons' in the Setswana Bible (Matthew 8:28-34, 15:2, 10:8)." *JSNT* 73: 33–59.

———. 2000. *Postcolonial Feminist Interpretation of the Bible.* St. Louis: Chalice.

Duduit, Michael. 2010. "Expository Preaching in a Narrative World: An Interview with Haddon Robinson." *Preaching Magazine.* September 21. http://www.preaching.com/resources/articles/11565763/.

Earth Bible Team, the. 2000. "Guiding Ecojustice Principles." In *Readings from the Perspective of Earth*, ed. Norman C. Habel, 38–53. Sheffield: Sheffield Academic.

Edwards, Denis. 2004. *Breath of Life: A Theology of the Creator Spirit.* Maryknoll, NY: Orbis.

———. 2005. *Jesus the Wisdom of God: An Ecological Theology*. Eugene: Wipf & Stock.

———. 2010. *How God Acts: Creation, Redemption and Special Divine Action*. Hindmarsh: ATF.

Ehrman, Bart D. 2008. *The New Testament: A Historical Introduction to the Early Christian Writings*. New York: Oxford University Press.

Elvey, Anne F. 2005. *An Ecological Feminist Reading of the Gospel of Luke: A Gestational Paradigm*. Studies in Women and Religion. Lewiston, NY: Edwin Mellen.

———. 2011. *The Matter of the Text: Material Engagements between Luke and the Five Senses*. Bible in the Modern World 37. Sheffield: Sheffield Phoenix.

Emerson, Michael O., and Christian Smith. 2000. *Divided by Faith: Evangelical Religion and the Problem of Race in America*. Oxford: Oxford University Press.

Essex, Barbara J. 1997. "Some Kind of Woman: The Making of a Strong Black Woman." In *Embracing the Spirit: Womanist Perspectives on Hope, Salvation and Transformation*, ed. Emilie Townes, 203–11. Maryknoll, NY: Orbis.

Fei, Michelle. 2011. "Cost of Giving Birth May Rise for Mainland Mothers." *China Daily*. March 5. http://www.cdeclips.com/en/hongkong/fullstory.html?id=61692.

Finnegan, Ruth. 1977. *Oral Poetry: Its Nature, Significance and Social Context*. Cambridge: Cambridge University Press.

Fitzmyer, Joseph A. 1981. *The Gospel According to Luke I–IX: A New Translation with Introduction and Commentary*. AB. Garden City, NY: Doubleday.

Fitzmyer, Joseph A. 1985. *The Gospel According to Luke X–XXIV: A New Translation with Introduction and Commentary*. AB. Garden City, NY: Doubleday.

Fletcher-Louis, Crispin H. T. 1998. "The Gospel Thief Saying (Luke 12:39-40 and Matthew 24:43-44) Reconsidered." In *Understanding, Studying and Reading: New Testament Essays in Honor of John Ashton*, ed. Christopher Roland and Crispin H. T. Fletcher-Louis, 48–68. Sheffield: Sheffield Academic.

Folarin, George O. 2008. "The Parable of the Talents in the African Context: An Inculturation Hermeneutics Approach." *AJT* 22/1 (April): 94–106.

Foley, John Miles. 1995. *The Singer of Tales in Performance*. Bloomington and Indianapolis: Indiana University Press.

France, R. T. 1979. "Herod and the Children in Bethlehem." *NovT* 21/2 (April): 98–120.

———. 2007. *The Gospel of Matthew*. NICNT. Grand Rapids: Eerdmans.

Bibliography | 311

Frankemölle, H. 1984. *Jahwe-Bund und Kirche Christi: Studien zur Form- und Traditionsgeschichte des "Evangeliums" nach Matthäus*. NTAbh 10. Münster: Aschendorff.

Friedman, Milton, and Rose Friedman. 1990. *Free to Choose: A Personal Statement*. San Diego: Harcourt Brace Jovanovich.

Fuze, Magema. 1922. *Abantu Abamnyama: Lapa Bavela Ngakona*. Pietermaritzburg: Private.

———. 1979. *The Black People and Whence They Came*. Trans. H. C. Lugg. Ed. A. T. Cope. Pietermaritzburg: University of Natal Press.

Gadamer, Hans-Georg. 1989. *Truth and Method*. Trans. Joel Weinsheimer and Donald Marshall. 2nd rev. ed. New York: Crossroad.

Garland, David E. 2001. *Reading Matthew: A Literary and Theological Commentary*. Macon, GA: Smyth and Helwys.

Gaston, Lloyd. 1970. *No Stone on Another: Studies in the Significance of the Fall of Jerusalem in the Synoptic Gospels*. NovTSup 23. Leiden: Brill.

Gaventa, Beverly Roberts. 1999. *Mary: Glimpses of the Mother of Jesus*. Minneapolis: Fortress Press.

Gaztambide, D. J. 2008. "Pyschoneuroimmunology and Jesus' Healing Miracles." In *Miracles: God, Science, and Psychology in the Paranormal*. Vol. 2, *Medical and Therapeutic Events*, ed. J. Harold Ellens, 94–113. Westport, CT: Praeger.

Gee, James P. 1996. *Social Linguistics and Literacies: Ideology in Discourses: Critical Perspectives on Literacy and Education*. London: Taylor & Francis.

Getty-Sullivan, Mary Ann. 2001. *Women in the New Testament*. Collegeville, Minn.: Liturgical.

Gilbert, Jeremy. 2008. "Another World Is Possible: The Anti-Capitalist Movement." In *Anticapitalism and Culture: Radical Theory and Popular Politics*, 75–106. Oxford: Berg.

Gnilka, Joachim. 1989. "Apokalyptik und Ethik: die Kategorie der Zukunft als Anweisung für sittliches Handeln." In *Neues Testament und Ethik: für Rudolf Schnackenburg*, ed. Helmut Merklein, 464–81. Freiburg im Breisgau: Herder.

Gordon, Linda. 1994. *Pitied but Not Entitled: Single Mothers and the History of Welfare*. New York: Free.

Gottwald, Norman K. 1993. *The Hebrew Bible in Its Social World and in Ours*. SemeiaSt. Atlanta: Scholars.

Grassi, Joseph A. 1989. *The Hidden Heroes of the Gospel: Female Counterparts of Jesus*. Collegeville: Liturgical.

———. 1992. "Child, Children." In *ABD* 1:904–7.

Gray, Sherman W. 1989. *The Least of My Brothers: Matthew 25:31-46: A History of Interpretation.* Atlanta: Society for Biblical Literature.

Green, Joel B. 1997. *The Gospel of Luke.* NICNT. Grand Rapids: Eerdmans.

Green, Michael. 2000. *The Message of Matthew: The Kingdom of Heaven.* Downers Grove, IL: InterVarsity Press.

Gregory, Susan. 1991. "Deafness in Fiction." In *Constructing Deafness*, ed. Susan Gregory and Gillian Hartley, 294–300. London: Pinter.

Gregory, Susan, and Gillian Hartley, eds. 1991. *Constructing Deafness.* London: Pinter.

Greimas, Algirdas Julien. 1987. "On Anger: A Lexical Semantic Study." In *On Meaning: Selected Writings in Semiotic Theory*, 148–64. Minneapolis: University of Minnesota Press.

Greimas, Algirdas Julien, and Joseph Courtès, eds. 1982. *Semiotics and Language: An Analytical Dictionary.* Advances in Semiotics. Bloomington: Indiana University Press.

Grenholm, Cristina, and Daniel Patte. 2000. "Receptions, Critical Interpretations, and Scriptural Criticism." In *Reading Israel in Romans: Legitimacy and Plausibility of Divergent Interpretations*, ed. Cristina Grenholm and Daniel Patte, 1–54. Harrisburg, PA: Trinity Press International.

Gundry, Robert H. 1982. *Matthew, a Commentary on His Literary and Theological Art.* Grand Rapids: Eerdmans.

Gurtner, Daniel M. 2008. "Matthew's Theology of the Temple and the 'Parting of the Ways': Christian Origins and the First Gospel." In *Built Upon the Rock: Studies in the Gospel of Matthew*, ed. Daniel M. Gurtner and John Nolland, 128–53. Grand Rapids: Eerdmans.

Gutiérrez, Gustavo. 1973. *A Theology of Liberation: History, Politics and Salvation.* Trans. and ed. C. Inda and J. Egaleson. Maryknoll, NY: Orbis.

Gwala, Sibusiso. 2007. "The Impact of Unemployment on the Youth of Pietermaritzburg." Master's thesis, University of KwaZulu-Natal.

Habel, Norman C., ed. 2000. *Readings from the Perspective of Earth.* The Earth Bible 1. Sheffield: Sheffield Academic.

Habel, Norman C., and Shirley Wurst, eds. 2000. *The Earth Story in Genesis.* The Earth Bible 2. Sheffield: Sheffield Academic.

———. 2001a. *The Earth Story in the Psalms and the Prophets.* The Earth Bible 4. Sheffield: Sheffield Academic.

———. 2001b. *The Earth Story in Wisdom Traditions.* The Earth Bible 3. Sheffield: Sheffield Academic.

Habel, Norman C., and Vicky Balabanski, eds. 2002. *The Earth Story in the New Testament*. The Earth Bible 5. London: Sheffield Academic.

Habel, Norman C., and Peter Trudinger, eds. 2008. *Exploring Ecological Hermeneutics*. SBLSymS. Atlanta: Society of Biblical Literature.

Hagner, Donald A. 1995a. *Matthew 1–13*. WBC. Nashville: Nelson Reference and Electronic.

———. 1995b. *Matthew 14–28*. WBC. Dallas: Thomas Nelson.

Hajdinjak, Marko. 2006. "From Organized Oblivion to Forced Remembering: Memory and Identity among Serbs and Croats." Paper presented at the International Symposium, "The Memory of Violence/Genocide: Its Meaning in the Process of Peace Building." University of Tokyo, March 18.

Halapua, Winston. 2008. *Waves of God's Embrace: Sacred Perspectives from the Ocean*. Norwich: Canterbury.

Halbwachs, Maurice. 1925. *Les cadres sociaux de la mémoire*. Paris: Librairie Félix Alcan.

———. 1992. *On Collective Memory*. Trans. and ed. Lewis A. Coser. Chicago: University of Chicago Press.

Hare, Douglas R. A. 2009. *Matthew*. IBC. Louisville: Westminster John Knox.

Harrington, Daniel J. 1991a. *The Gospel of Matthew*. SP 1. Collegeville: Liturgical.

———. 1991b. "Polemical Parables in Matthew 24–25." *Union Seminary Quarterly Review* 44: 287–98.

———. 2007. *The Gospel of Matthew*. Rev. ed. SP 1. Collegeville: Liturgical.

Hauerwas, Stanley. 1981. *A Community of Character: Towards a Constructive Christian Social Ethic*. Notre Dame: University of Notre Dame Press.

———. 2004a. "Community and Diversity: The Tyranny of Normality." In *Critical Reflections on Stanley Hauerwas' Theology of Disability*, ed. J. Swinton, 37–43. Binghamton: Haworth Pastoral Press, 2004.

———. 2004b. *Performing the Faith: Bonhoeffer and the Practice of Nonviolence*. Grand Rapids: Brazos, 2004.

———. 2006. *Matthew*. Brazos Theological Commentary on the Bible. Grand Rapids: Brazos.

Held, David, et al. 1999. *Global Transformations: Politics, Economics, and Culture*. Stanford: Stanford University Press.

Herzog, William R., II. 1994. *Parables as Subversive Speech: Jesus as Pedagogue of the Oppressed*. Louisville: Westminister John Knox.

Hillel, Daniel. 2006. *The Natural History of the Bible: An Environmental Exploration of the Hebrew Scriptures*. New York: Columbia University Press.

Hitching, Roger. 2003. *The Church and Deaf People.* Carlisle, UK: Paternoster.

HKCSS (Hong Kong Council of Social Service). 2009. "Poor Population around 1.24 Million." September 27. http://www.hkcss.org.hk/cm/cc/press/detail.asp?id=386.

HKSAR (Hong Kong Special Administrative Region). 2006. "Summary Results of the 2006 Population By-Census Announced." Census and Statistics Department. http://www.bycensus2006.gov.hk/en/press/070222/index.htm

———. 2007–2008. "Situation Analysis of Sexual and Reproductive Health." The Family Planning Association of Hong Kong Annual Report. http://www.famplan.org.hk/fpahk/common/pdf/ar-07-08/Situ_SandRH.pdf.

———. 2008. *Hong Kong Yearbook 2008.* Information Services Department. http://www.yearbook.gov.hk/2008/en/index.html.

———. 2009a. "Lack of Breastfeeding Policy and Trained Doctors to Advise Mothers on Breastfeeding Management: Breastfeeding Rate Drops Rapidly after Discharge from Hospital." Baby Friendly Hospital Initiative Hong Kong Association. August 1. . http://www.babyfriendly.org.hk/wp-content/uploads/2012/09/WBW2009Press-Release_e.pdf.

———. 2009b. "World Breastfeeding Week Annual Survey Summer 2009." Baby Friendly Hospital Initiative Hong Kong Association. http://www.babyfriendly.org.hk/wp-content/uploads/2012/02/2009WBWReport_E.pdf .

———. 2009c. *Hong Kong Yearbook 2009.* Information Services Department. http://www.yearbook.gov.hk/2009/en/index.html. Accessed 13 January 2013

———. 2009d. "Sharing of Housework." In *Thematic Household Survey: Report No. 14.* Census and Statistics Department, 100–109. http://www.statistics.gov.hk/publication/stat_report/social_data/B11302142003XXXXB0100.pdf.

———. 2010a. *Women and Men in Hong Kong: Key Statistics.* Census and Statistics Department. http://www.statistics.gov.hk/publication/stat_report/social_data/B11303032010AN10B0100.pdf.

———. 2010b. Centre for Health Protection. "Breast Milk: Mother's Best Gift to Babies." *Non-Communicable Diseases (NCD) WATCH* 3/7. http://www.chp.gov.hk/files/pdf/ncd_watch_jul_2010.pdf.

———. 2010c. "Family Council: Family Friendly Company Award Scheme." Family Council Paper FC 4. http://www.familycouncil.gov.hk/english/home/files/FC_Paper_4_Award_Scheme.pdf.

———. 2011. "Statistics on Labour Force, Unemployment and Underemployment." Census and Statistics Department. http://www.censtatd.gov.hk/hong_kong_statistics/statistics_by_subject/index.jsp?subjectID=2&charsetID=1&displayMode=T.

———. 2012a. "Baby-friendly Hospital Initiative: the Right Initiative Then and Now." Baby Friendly Hospital Initiative Hong Kong Association. http://www.babyfriendly.org.hk/e/bfhi-progress.php.

———. 2012b. *This Is Hong Kong*. Information Services Department. http://www.brandhk.gov.hk/en/facts/publications/thisishongkong.html; accessed 20 April 2011

Ho, Serinah. 2011. "Hospital Doctors Driven to Brink." *The Standard*. April 18. http://www.thestandard.com.hk/news_detail.asp?pp_cat=11&art_id=110225&sid=32066035&con_type=1.

Hoggard Creegan, Nicola. 2007. "On Being an Animal and Being Made in the Image of God." *Colloquium* 39/2: 185–203.

———. 2010. "God, Strings, Emergence, and the Future of the World." *The Global Spiral* 4. September 28.

Hollensen, Svend. 2011. *Global Marketing: A Decision-Oriented Approach*. 5th ed. Harlow, UK: Financial Times Prentice Hall.

Hong Kong Statistics on "Labour." 2011. Latest Statistics. April 20.

Horsley, Richard A. 2009. *Covenant Economics: A Biblical Vision of Justice for All*. Louisville: Westminster John Knox.

Horsley, Richard A., Jonathan A. Draper, and John Miles Foley, eds. 2006. *Performing the Gospel: Orality, Memory, and Mark: Essays Dedicated to Werner Kelber*. Minneapolis: Fortress Press.

Hosseini, S. A. Hamed. 2010. "From 'Anti-globalization' to 'Alter-globalization.'" In *Alternative Globalizations: An Integrative Approach to Studying Dissident Knowledge in the Global Justice Movement*, 63–89. New York: Routledge.

Howell, David B. 1990. *Matthew's Inclusive Story: A Study in the Narrative Rhetoric of the First Gospel*. JSNTSup 42. Sheffield: Sheffield Academic.

Hultgren, Arland J. 2000. *The Parables of Jesus: A Commentary*. Grand Rapids: Eerdmans.

ILO (International Labor Organization), Director General. 1999. "Decent Work." Geneva: International Labour Organization.

Immerfall, Stefan, and Jürgen von Hagen, eds. 1998. *Territoriality in the Globalizing Society: One Place or None?* New York: Springer.

Isasi-Díaz, Ada María. 1996. *Mujerista Theology: A Theology for the Twenty First Century*. Maryknoll, NY: Orbis.

Jenkins, Willis. 2008. "Global Ethics, Christian Theology, and the Challenge of Sustainability." *Worldviews: Environment Culture Religion* 12: 197–217.

Jensen, Robin Margaret. 2000. *Understanding Early Christian Art*. New York: Routledge.

Joh, Wonhee Anne. 2004. "The Transgressive Power of Jeong: A Postcolonial Hybridization of Christology." In *Postcolonial Theologies : Divinity and Empire*, ed. Catherine Keller, Michael Nausner, and Mayra Rivera, 149–63. St. Louis: Chalice.

Johnson, Marshall D. 1969. *The Purpose of the Biblical Genealogies with Special Reference to the Setting of the Genealogies of Jesus*. SNTSMS 8. Cambridge: Cambridge University Press.

Johnson, Robert. 1991. "Sign Language, Culture and Community in a Traditional Yucatec Maya Village." *Sign Language Studies* 73: 461–74.

Josephus. 1956. *Antiquities*. Trans. H. St. J. Thackeray. LCL. Cambridge, MA: Harvard University Press.

Joshel, Sandra R. 2010. *Slavery in the Roman World*. Cambridge: Cambridge University Press.

Kairos. 1986. *The Kairos Document: Challenge to the Church*. Rev. 2nd ed. Braamfontein, South Africa: Skotaville, 1986.

Kalu, Ogbu. 2000. "Ancestral Spirituality and Society in Africa." In *African Spirituality: Forms, Meanings and Expressions*, ed. Jacob K. Olupona, 54–84. World Spirituality: An Encyclopedic History of the Religious Quest 3. New York: Crossroad.

Keck, Leander, ed. 1995. *The New Interpreter's Bible*. Vol. 3, *1 and 2 Kings, 1 and 2 Chronicles, Ezra, Nehemiah, Esther, Tobit, Judith*. Ed. Nashville: Abingdon.

Keener, Craig S. 1999. *A Commentary on the Gospel of Matthew*. Grand Rapids: Eerdmans.

Kennedy, Joel. 2008. *The Recapitulation of Israel: Use of Israel's History in Matthew 1:1—4;11* Tübingen: Mohr Siebeck.

Kevern, Peter. 2008. "Translation Theory." In *Searching for Meaning: An Introduction to Interpreting the New Testament*, ed. Paula Gooder, 56–62. Louisville: Westminster John Knox.

Kim, Hai Young. 2005. "Korean Pastoral Kids Form a Pastoral Counselling's Perspective." Master's thesis, Ehwa Women's University.

Kim, Jong Hwan. 2005. "Don't Consider PKs as Pastoral Sacrifice Any More." *Ministry and Theology*. 192: 138–39.

Kingsbury, Jack Dean. 1978. "Observations on the 'Miracle Chapters' of Matthew 8–9." *CBQ* 40: 559–73.

———. 1986. *Matthew as Story.* Philadelphia: Fortress Press.

Kirk, Alan, and Tom Thatcher, eds. 2005. *Memory, Tradition, and Text: Uses of the Past in Early Christianity.* SemeiaSt 52. Atlanta: Society of Biblical Literature.

Klass, G. 2003. "Worldwide Study Exposes Wide Variations in Maternity Benefits." January 16. http://lilt.ilstu.edu/gmklass/pos232/articles/maternity_benefits.html.

Klostermann, Erich, and Hugo Gressmann. 1909. *Matthäus.* HNT 1. Tübingen: Mohr (Paul Siebeck).

Knappett, Carl. 2005. *Thinking through Material Culture: An Interdisciplinary Perspective, Archaeology, Culture, and Society.* Philadelphia: University of Pennsylvania Press.

Knappett, Carl, and Lambros Malafouris. 2008. *Material Agency: Toward a Non-Anthropocentric Approach.* New York: Springer.

Kotabe, Masaaki, and Kristiaan Helsen. 2008. *Global Marketing Management.* 4th ed. Hoboken, NJ: J. Wiley.

Kriegel, Leonard. 1991. *Falling into Life.* San Francisco: North Point.

Krišto, Jure. 2001. "Stare i nove paradigme Hrvatske historiografije (Old and new paradigms of Croatian historiography]." *Društvena istraživanja* (Zagreb) 10: 165–89.

Kupp, D. D. 1996. *Matthew's Immanuel: Divine Presence and God's People in the First Gospel.* SNTSMS 90. Cambridge: Cambridge University Press, 1996.

Kyle, J. G., and B. Woll. 1998. *Sign Language: The Study of Deaf People and Their Language.* Cambridge: Cambridge University Press.

Labour and Welfare Bureau. 2010. "Indicators for Poverty—an Update for 2009." In *Press Releases and Publications,* 5–6. http://www.lwb.gov.hk/eng/other_info/2009%20Poverty%20Indicators_eng.pdf.

Ladd, Paddy. 2003. *Understanding Deaf Culture: In Search of Deafhood.* Clevedon, UK: Multilingual Matters.

Lai, Gloria. 2008. "HK Staff Work Some of Longest Hours in World." *The Standard.* July 18. http://www.thestandard.com.hk/news_detail.asp?sid=19804311&art_id=68784&con_type=1&pp_cat=11.

Lam, Agnes. "HK Fifth Worst on Global Work-hours Scale." *South China Morning Post,* 18 July 2008. Available from http://www.scmp.com/article/645727/hk-fifth-worst-global-work-hours-scale.

Lane, Harlan. 2005. "Ethnicity, Ethics, and the Deaf-World." *Journal of Deaf Studies and Deaf* 10: 291–310.

Lane, H., R. Hoffmeister, and B. A. Bahan. 1996. *Journey into the Deaf-World.* San Diego: DawnSign Press.

Laqueur, Thomas W. 1990. *Making Sex: Body and Gender from the Greeks to Freud.* Cambridge, MA: Harvard University Press.

Lau, Siu-kai. 2003. "Confidence in Hong Kong's Capitalist Society in the Aftermath of the Asian Financial Turnmoil." *Journal of Contemporary China* 12/35 (May): 373–86.

Lawrence, L. J. 2009. *The Word in Place: Reading the New Testament in Contemporary Contexts.* London: SPCK.

Latin-English Booklet Missal for Praying the Traditional Mass. 2009. 4th ed. Illinois: Coalition in Support of Ecclesia Dei.

Leal, Robert Barry. 2004. *Wilderness in the Bible: Toward a Theology of Wilderness.* Studies in Biblical Literature 72. New York: Peter Lang.

Lee, Ada. 2008. "Long Hours Mean Errors in Diagnosis, Doctors Say." *South China Morning Post.* April 18.

Lee, Jung Young. 1999. "A Life in-Between: A Korean-American Journey." In *Journeys at the Margin: Towards an Autobiographical Theology in American-Asian Perspective*, ed. Peter C. Phan and Jung Young Lee, 23–40. Collegeville: Liturgical.

Lee, Kim-ming, and Kam-yee Law. 2010. "The Financial Tsunami: Economic Insecurity and Social Protection in Hong Kong." *Development* 53/1 (March): 83–90.

Lee, Sangheon, Deirdre McCann, and Jon C. Messenger. 2007. *Working Time Around the World: Trends in Working Hours, Laws, and Policies in a Global Comparative Perspective.* New York: Routledge.

Lee, Yoon Joo. 2001. "Survey on Pastoral Kids' Self-Identity." Master's thesis, Ehwa Women's University.

Legassik, Martin. 2007. *Towards Socialist Democracy.* Pietermaritzburg: University of KwaZulu-Natal Press.

Leske, Adrian M. 2002. "Matthew 6.25-34: Human Anxiety and the Natural World." In *The Earth Story in the New Testament*, ed. Norman C. Habel and Vicky Balabanski, 15–27. The Earth Bible 5. Sheffield: Sheffield Academic.

Leveque, James. 2009. "What Is Inscribed in the Book: The Book Motif as a Productive Force in the Apocalypses of Daniel." *The Bible and Critical Theory* 5/3: 38.1–11.

Levine, Amy-Jill. 1988. *The Social and Ethnic Dimensions of Matthean Salvation History*. SBEC 14. Lewiston, NY: Edwin Mellen.

———. 1998. "Matthew." In *Women's Bible Commentary*, ed. Carol A. Newsom and Sharon H. Ringe, 339–49. Louisville: Westminster John Knox.

———. 2001. "Matthew's Advice to a Divided Readership." In *The Gospel of Matthew in Current Study: Studies in Memory of William G. Thompson, S.J.*, ed. David E. Aune, 22–41. Grand Rapids: Eerdmans.

———. 2009. "Jesus, Women and Family Values." Willson Lecture Series, Oklahoma City University, Oklahoma City, Oklahoma, September 24.

Levine, Amy-Jill, with Marianne Blickenstaff, eds. 2001. *A Feminist Companion to Matthew*. Feminist Companion to the New Testament and Early Christian Writings 1. Sheffield: Sheffield Academic.

Lewis, Hannah. 2007. *Deaf Liberation Theology*. Aldershot: Ashgate.

Lewis, Theodore. 1997. *Cults of the Dead in Ancient Israel and Ugarit*. Atlanta: Scholars.

Liddell, H. G., and Robert Scott. 1996. *A Greek-English Lexicon*. 9th ed. Oxford: Clarendon.

Liew, Tat-siong Benny. 2003. "Re-Mark-Able Masculinities: Jesus, the Son of Man, and the (Sad) Sum of Manhood?" In *New Testament Masculinities*, ed. Stephen D. Moore and Janice C. Anderson, 93–135. Atlanta: Society of Biblical Literature.

Lim, Hyang Jin. 2008. "Reflections on the Christian Education for Pks Development of Christian Self-Identity." Ph.D. Diss., Yonsei University.

Lin, Manhong. 2010. *Ethical Reorientation for Christianity in China: The Individual, Community, and Society*. Hong Kong: Christian Study Centre on Chinese Religion & Culture.

Liu, Alfred. 2008. "Yam Feels Legco Heat on Minibonds." *The Standard*. October 14. http://paper.thestandard.com.hk/?href=TheStandard/2008/10/14&pageno=1&view=document.

Liu, T. Y. 2008. "Herodes als Symbol von Fremdherrschaft im Matthäusevangelium." Th.D. diss., University of Heidelberg.

Louw, Johannes, and Eugene Nida. 1988. *Greek-English Lexicon of the New Testament Based on Semantic Domains*. 2 vols. New York: United Bible Societies.

Luhmann, Niklas. 1977. *Funktion der Religion*. Frankfurt am Main: Suhrkamp.

Luther, Martin. 1962. *Luther's Works*. Vol. 45. Ed. Walther I. Brandt. Philadelphia: Muhlenberg.

Luz, Ulrich. 1989. *Matthew 1–7*. Trans. Wilhelm C. Linss. CC. Minneapolis: Fortress Press.

———. 1994. *Matthew in History: Interpretation, Influence, and Effects.* Minneapolis: Fortress Press.

———. 1996. "The Final Judgment (Matt 25:31-46): An Exercise in 'History of Influence' Exegesis." In *Treasures New and Old: Contributions to Matthean Studies*, ed. David R. Bauer and Mark Allan Powell, 271–310. SBLSymS 1. Atlanta: Scholars, 1996.

———. 1997. *Das Evangelium nach Matthäus.* Evangelisch-Katholischer Kommentar I/3. Ostfildern: Patmos.

———. 2005. *Studies in Matthew.* Trans. Rosemary Selle. Grand Rapids: Eerdmans.

———. 2007. *Matthew 1–7: A Commentary.* Rev. ed. Trans. James E. Crouch. Ed. Helmut Koester. Hermeneia. Minneapolis: Fortress Press.

Mafico, Temba L. J. 2000. "The Biblical God of the Fathers and the African Ancestors." In *The Bible in Africa: Transactions, Trajectories and Trends.* Ed. Gerald O. West and Musa W. Dube, 481–89. Leiden: Brill.

Malina, Bruce J., and Richard L. Rohrbaugh. 1993. *Social Science Commentary on the Synoptic Gospels.* Minneapolis, Minnesota: Fortress Press.

Malysz, Piotr. 2007. "Nemo iudex in causa sua as the Basis of Law, Justice, and Justification in Luther's Thought." *Harvard Theological Review* 100/3: 363–86.

Man, Joyce. 2008. "Chief Talks Tough on Minibonds." *South China Morning Post.* October 16.

Mao Zedong. 1967. *Selected Works of Mao Tse-tung.* Peking: Foreign Language Press.

Martínez, Aquiles Ernesto. 2006. "Jesus, the Immigrant Child: A Diasporic Reading of Matthew 2:1-23." *Apuntes: Reflexiones Teológicas Desde el Contexto Hispano-Latino* 26/3 (Fall): 84–114.

Mazlish, Bruce. 2005. "The Global and the Local." *Current Sociology* 53/1: 93–111.

Mbeki, Thabo. 1995. "A National Strategic Vision for South Africa." Address by Deputy President T.M. Mbeki, at the Development Planning Summit, Hosted by the Intergovernmental Forum. http://www.info.gov.za/speeches/1995/457g95.htm.

McDermott, R., and R. Varenne. 1995. "Culture as Disability." *Anthropology & Education Quarterly* 26/3: 324–48.

McFague, Sallie. 1993. *The Body of God: An Ecological Theology*. Minneapolis: Fortress Press.

McVann, Mark. 1993. "One of the Prophets: Matthew's Testing Narrative as a Rite of Passage." *BTB* 23: 14–20.

Meier, John P. 1992. "Matthew, Gospel of." In *ABD* 4:622–41.

Melito. 1979. *On Pascha and Fragments*. Ed. and trans. Stuart George Hall. Oxford Early Christian Texts. Oxford: Clarendon Press.

Melville, Herman. 1999. *Moby-Dick*. New York: Simon & Schuster.

Meyers, Carol. ed. 2002. *Women in Scripture*. Grand Rapids: Eerdmans.

Miller, Susan. 2004. *Women in Mark's Gospel*. JSNTSup 259. London: T&T Clark.

Miller-McLemore, Bonnie. 1999. "Ideals and Realities of Motherhood: A Theological Perspective." In *Mother Troubles: Rethinking Contemporary Maternal Dilemmas*. Boston: Beacon.

———. 2002. *Also a Mother: Work and Family as Theological Dilemma*. Nashville: Abingdon.

Mitchell, David T., and Sharon Snyder. 2007. "'Jesus Thrown Everything Off Balance': Disability and Redemption in Biblical Literature." In *This Abled Body: Rethinking Disability in Biblical Studies*, ed. H. Avalos, S. J. Melcher, and J. Schipper, 173–83. Atlanta: Society of Biblical Literature.

Mitchem, Stephanie Y. 2002. *Womanist Theology*. Maryknoll, NY: Orbis.

Mofokeng, T. 1988. "Black Christians, the Bible and Liberation." *Journal of Black Theology* 2: 34–42.

Mokoena, Hlonipha. 2010. *Magema Fuze: The Making of a Kholwa Intellectual*. Pietermaritzburg: University of KwaZulu-Natal Press.

Moore, Stephen D. 1996. *God's Gym: Divine Male Bodies of the Bible*. New York: Routledge.

Morris, Wayne. 2008. *Theology without Words: Theology in the Deaf Community*. Aldershot: Ashgate.

Morton, Adam. 2009. "First Climate Refugees Start Move to New Island Home." *The Age*. July 29. http://www.theage.com.au/national/first-climate-refugees-start-move-to-new-island-home-20090728-e06x.html.

Morton, Timothy. 2007. *Ecology without Nature: Rethinking Environmental Aesthetics*. Cambridge, MA: Harvard University Press.

Mosala, Itumeleng J. 1986. "The Use of the Bible in Black Theology." In *The Unquestionable Right to Be Free: Essays in Black Theology*, ed. Itumeleng J. Mosala and Buti Tlhagale, 175–99. Johannesburg: Skotaville.

————. 1989. *Biblical Hermeneutics and Black Theology in South Africa*. Grand Rapids: Eerdmans.

Mounce, William D. 1993. *The Analytical Lexicon to the Greek New Testament*. Grand Rapids: Zondervan.

Moxnes, Halvor. 2003. *Putting Jesus in His Place: A Radical Vision of Household and Kingdom*. Louisville: Westminster John Knox.

Nason, David. 2008. "'I Made a Mistake' Admits Alan Greenspan." *The Australian* [online archives]. 25 October; available from http://www.theaustralian.com.au/business/opinion/i-made-a-mistake-says-greenspan/story-e6frg9mf-1111117848644.

National Alliance for Caregiving. 2009. "Caregiving in the U.S. 2009." http://www.caregiving.org/data/ Caregiving_in_the_US_2009_full_report.pdf.

Ng, Shi-hung. 2010. *Social Capital in Hong Kong: Connectivities and Social Enterprise*. Hong Kong: City University of Hong Kong Press.

Ng, Winnie. 2011. *The State of Work-Life Balance in Hong Kong 2010: A Summary of Research Findings*. Online e-book. http://www.communitybusiness.org/images/cb/publications/2010/ WLB%20eng%20R3.pdf.

Ng, Winnie, and Shaun Bernier. 2009. *The State of Work-Life Balance in Hong Kong 2009 Survey*. http://www.communitybusiness.org/images/cb/ publications/2009/WLB09.pdf.

Nielsen, Kai. 1992. "Global Justice, Capitalism and the Third World." In *International Justice and the Third World*, ed. Robin Attfield and Barry Wilkins, 17–34. New York: Routledge.

Nolan, Albert. 1988. *God in South Africa: The Challenge of the Gospel*. Cape Town: David Philip.

————. 1996. "Work, the Bible, Workers, and Theologians: Elements of a Workers' Theology." *Semeia* 73: 213–20.

Nolland, John. 1997. "The Four (Five) Women and Other Annotations in Matthew's Genealogy." *NTS* 43/4: 527–39.

Novakovic, Lidija. 2003. *Messiah, the Healer of the Sick*. WUNT II.170. Tübingen: Mohr Siebeck.

Nowell, Irene. 2008. "Jesus' Great-Grandmothers: Matthew's Four and More." *CBQ* 70/1: 1–15.

Nunn, Patrick D. 1997. *Keimami Sa Vakila Na Liga Ni Kalou (Feeling the Hand of God): Human and Nonhuman Impacts on Pacific Island Environments*. 3rd ed. Suva, Fiji: University of the South Pacific.

O'Connor, Kathleen M. 1998. "Crossing Borders: Biblical Studies in a Trans-cultural World." In *Teaching the Bible: The Discourses and Politics of Biblical Pedagogy*, ed. Fernando Segovia and Mary Ann Tolbert, 322–37. Maryknoll, NY: Orbis.

Opland, Jeff. 1983. *Xhosa Oral Poetry: Aspects of a Black South African Tradition.* Cambridge: Cambridge University Press.

Origen. *Commentariorum Series in Matthaeum.* 141 (GCS 38, 293).

Orton, David E. 2003. "We Felt Like Grasshoppers: The Little Ones in Biblical Interpretation," *BibInt* 11: 488–502.

Osiek, Carolyn, and Margaret Y. MacDonald. 2006. *A Woman's Place: House Churches in Earliest Christianity.* Minneapolis: Fortress Press.

Overman, J. Andrew. 1990. *Matthew's Gospel and Formative Judaism: The Social World of the Matthean Community.* Minneapolis: Fortress Press.

Padden, Carol. 1991. "The Deaf Community and the Culture of Deaf People." In *Constructing Deafness*, ed. Susan Gregory and Gillian Hartley, 40–45. London: Pinter.

Padden, Carol, and Tom Humphries. 1988. *Deaf in America: Voices from a Culture.* Cambridge, MA: Harvard University Press.

Panel on Welfare Services. 2011. "Paper on Definition of 'Poverty' Prepared by the Legislative Council Secretariat (Background Brief)." LC Paper no. CB(2)179/09–10(08), 3. http://www.legco.gov.hk/yr09-10/english/panels/ws/papers/ws1109cb2-179-8-e.pdf.

Park, Andrew Sung. 1993. *The Wounded Heart of God: The Asian Concept of Han and the Christian Doctrine of Sin.* Nashville: Abingdon.

Parker, Lonnae O'Neal. 2005. *I'm Every Woman: Remixed Stories of Marriage, Motherhood and Work.* New York: HarperCollins.

Patte, Daniel. 1987. *The Gospel According to Matthew: A Structural Commentary on Matthew's Faith.* Philadelphia: Fortress Press.

———. 1990. *The Religious Dimensions of Biblical Texts: Greimas's Structural Semiotics and Biblical Exegesis.* SemeiaSt. Atlanta: Scholars.

———. 1999. *The Challenge of Discipleship: A Critical Study of the Sermon on the Mount as Scripture.* Harrisburg, PA: Trinity Press International.

———. 2004. Introduction to *Global Bible Commentary*, ed. Daniel Patte, xxi–xxxii. Nashville: Abingdon.

———, ed. 2010. *Cambridge Dictionary of Christianity.* Cambridge: Cambridge University Press.

Perissinotto, Giorgio. 2003. "Linguistic Constraints, Programmatic Fit, and Political Correctness: The Case of Spanish in the United States." In *Critical*

Latin American and Latino Studies, ed. Juan Poblete, 171–87. Minneapolis: University of Minnesota Press.

Philippine Commission on Women. 2012. "Factsheet on Filipino Women and Men." http://pcw.gov.ph/sites/default/files/documents/resources/factsheet_filipino_women_men_march_2012.pdf.

Pilch, John. 2000. *Healing in the New Testament: Insights from Medical and Mediterranean Anthropology*. Minneapolis: Fortress Press.

Pollack, Mark A., and Gregory C. Shaffer. 2001. "Who Governs?" In *Transatlantic Governance in the Global Economy*, 287–305. ed. Mark A. Pollack. Lanham, MD: Rowman and Littlefield.

Pomeroy, Sarah B. 1999. "Reflections on Plutarch, Consolation to His Wife." In *Plutarch's Advice to the Bride and Groom and A Consolation to His Wife*. Trans. and ed. Sarah B. Pomeroy, 33–57. Oxford: Oxford University Press.

Powell, Mark Allan. 2003. "Binding and Loosing: A Paradigm of Ethical Discernment from the Gospel of Matthew." *CurTM* 30: 438–45.

Price, Reynolds. 1994. *A Whole New Life*. New York: Atheneum.

Quinn, Jerome D. 1981. "Is `PAXÁB in Mat 1:5 Rahab of Jericho?" *Bib* 62/2: 225–28.

Rae, John. 1894. *Eight Hours for Work*. London: Macmillan.

Ragaz, Leonhard. 1945. *Die Bergpredigt Jesu*. Bern: Herbert Lang.

Raheb, Mitri. 1995. *I Am a Palestinian Christian*. Minneapolis: Fortress Press.

———. 2004. *Bethlehem Besieged: Stories of Hope in Times of Trouble*. Minneapolis: Fortress Press.

Reicke, Bo. 1972. "Synoptic Prophecies on the Destruction of Jerusalem." *Studies in New Testament and Early Christian Literature*, ed. David E. Aune, 121–34. NovTSup 33. Leiden: Brill.

Reynolds, Thomas. 2008. *Vulnerable Communion: A Theology of Disability and Hospitality*. Grand Rapids: Brazos.

Rhoads, David, and Donald Michie. 1982. *Mark as Story: An Introduction to the Narrative of a Gospel*. Minneapolis: Fortress.

Ricoeur, Paul. 1974. *The Conflict of Interpretations*. Evanston: Northwestern University Press.

Rigby, Kate. 2004. "Earth, World, Text: On the (Im)Possibility of Ecopoiesis." *New Literary History* 35/3: 427–42.

Riggs, Marcia. 2003. *Plenty Good Room: Women Versus Black Male Power*. Cleveland: Pilgrim.

Roberts, Mary Louise. 2002. "True Womanhood Revisited." *Journal of Women's History* 14/1: 150–55.

Robertson, Robert Thomas. 2003. *The Three Waves of Globalization: A History of a Developing Global Consciousness.* New York: Palgrave.

Robertson, Roland. 1992. *Globalization: Social Theory and Global Culture.* London: Sage.

Robbins, Vernon K. 1996. *Exploring the Texture of Texts: A Guide to Socio-Rhetorical Interpretation.* Valley Forge, PA: Trinity Press International.

Robinson, Haddon. H. 2000. "Surprises at the Judgment." In *Creative Styles of Preaching,* ed. Mark Barger Elliott, 141–45. Louisville: Westminster John Knox.

Roth, Ulrike. 2010. *By the Sweat of Your Brow: Roman Slavery in its Socio-Economic Settings.* London: Institute of Classical Studies, University of London.

Roudometof, Victor. 2005. "Transnationalism, Cosmopolitanism, and Glocalization." *Current Sociology* 53/1: 113–35.

Rychlak, Ronald J. 2009. "Cardinal Stepinac, Pope Pius XII, and the Roman Catholic Church during the Second World War." *Catholic Social Science Review* 14: 367–83.

Ryken, Leland, et al, eds. 1998. *Dictionary of Biblical Imagery.* Downers Grove, IL: Intervarsity Press.

SACP (South African Communist Party). 2006. "Special Edition." *Bua Komanisi!: Information Bulletin of the Central Committee of the South African Communist Party*: 31.

Safrai, S., and M. Stern, with D. Flusser and W. C. van Unnik. 1974. *The Jewish People in the First Century: Historical Geography, Political History, Social, Cultural and Religious Life and Institutions.* Assen: van Gorcum; Philadelphia: Fortress Press.

Sainsbury, Sally. 1986. *Deaf Worlds: A Study of Integration, Segregation and Disability.* London, Hutchinson.

Saldarini, Anthony. 1995. "Boundaries and Polemics in the Gospel of Matthew." *BibInt* 3: 239–65.

Saul, John S. 2005. *The Next Liberation Struggle: Capitalism, Socialism and Democracy in Southern Africa.* Pietermartizburg: University of KwaZulu-Natal Press.

Sawicki, Marianne. 1994. *Seeing the Lord: Resurrection and Early Christian Practices.* Minneapolis: Fortress Press.

Scarry, Elaine. 1985. *The Body in Pain: The Making and the Unmaking of the World.* New York: Oxford University Press.

Schaberg, Jane. 1990. *The Illegitimacy of Jesus: A Feminist Theological Interpretation of the Infancy Narratives.* New York: Crossroad.

Scheidel, Walter, and Steven J. Friesen. 2009. "The Size of the Economy and the Distribution of Income in the Roman Empire." *JRS* 99: 61–91.

Schellnhuber, Hans Joachim, et al., eds. 2010. *Global Sustainability: A Nobel Cause.* Cambridge: Cambridge University Press.

Schleiermacher, Friedrich. 1997. *Hermeneutics: The Handwritten Manuscripts.* Ed. H. Kimmerle. Missoula: Scholars.

Schnackenburg, Rudolf. 2002. *The Gospel of Matthew.* Trans. R. R. Barr. Grand Rapids: Eerdmans.

Schottroff, Luisa. 1995. *Lydia's Impatient Sisters: A Feminist Social History of Early Christianity.* Louisville: Westminister John Knox.

Schröter, Jens. 1997. *Erinnerung an Jesu Worte: Studien zur Rezeption der Logienüberlieferung in Markus, Q und Thomas.* WMANT 76. Neukirchen-Vluyn: Neukirchener.

Schüssler Fiorenza, Elisabeth. 1984. *Bread Not Stone: The Challenge of Feminist Biblical Interpretation.* Boston: Beacon.

Schweickart, David. 2009. "Is Sustainable Capitalism an Oxymoron?" In *The Nation in the Global Era: Conflict and Transformation*, ed. Jerry Harris, 449–67. Leiden: Brill.

Schweitzer, Albert. 1950. *The Mystery of the Kingdom of God.* Trans. Walter Lowrie. New York: Macmillan.

Scott, James C. 1977. "Protest and Profanation: Agrarian Revolt and the Little Tradition." *Theory and Society* 4: 1–38, 211–46.

Segal, Alan F. 1990. *Paul the Convert: The Apostolate and Apostasy of Saul the Pharisee.* New Haven: Yale University Press.

Sem, Graham. 2006. "Climate Change and Development in Pacific Island Countries." *Pacific Futures*, ed. Michael Powles, 164–81. Canberra, Australia: Pandanus.

Seneca. 1928. "On Anger." In *Moral Essays.* Vol. 1. Trans. John W. Basore. LCL. Cambridge, MA: Harvard University Press.

Senghas, Richard, and Leila Monaghan. 2002. "Signs of Their Times: Deaf Communities and the Culture of Language." *Annual Review of Anthropology* 31: 69–97.

Senior, Donald. 1995. "Beware of the Canaanite Woman: Disability and the Bible." In *Religion and Disability*, ed. M. Bishop, 1–26. Kansas City: Sheed and Ward.

———. 1998. *Matthew.* ANTC. Nashville: Abingdon.

Senjković, Reana. 2002. *Lica društva, likovi države* (Faces of society, reflections of the state). Zagreb: Institut za etnologiju i folkloristiku.

Shakespeare, Tom. 2006. "The Social Model of Disability." In *The Disability Studies Reader*, ed. Lennard J. Davis, 197–203. New York: Routledge.

Shroer, Silvia. 2000. *Wisdom Has Built Her House: Studies on the Figure of Sophia in the Bible*. Trans. Linda M. Maloney. Collegeville: Liturgical.

Sibinga, Joost Smit. 1975. "Structure of the Apocalyptic Discourse, Matthew 24-25." *Studia theologica* 29/1: 71–79.

Siebers, T. 2006. "Disability in Theory: From Social Constructionism to the New Realism of the Body." In *The Disability Studies Reader*, ed. L. J. Davis, 173–82. New York: Routledge.

Siker, Jeffrey S. 1997. *Scripture and Ethics: Twentieth Century Portraits*. Oxford: Oxford University Press.

Sirico, Robert A. 2000. "The Entrepreneurial Vision." *Journal of Markets and Morality* 3/1 (Spring): 1–21.

Smit, Peter-Ben. 2010. "Something about Mary? Remarks about the Five Women in the Matthean Genealogy." *NTS* 56/2: 191–207.

Smith, Anthony D. 1986. *The Ethnic Origins of Nations*. Malden, MA: Blackwell.

———. 1997. "The 'Golden Age' and National Renewal." In *Myths and Nationhood*, ed. Geoffrey Hosking and George Schöpflin, 36–59. London: Hurst & Company.

Smith, Daniel A. 2009. "Matthew and Q: the Matthean Deployment of Q and Mark in the Apocalyptic Discourse." *ETL* 85/1: 99–116.

Smith, Tony. 2006. *Globalisation: A Systematic Marxian Account*. Leiden: Brill.

Soja, Edward W. 1999. "Thirdspace: Expanding the Scope of the Geographical Imagination." In *Human Geography Today*, ed. Doreen Massey, John Allen, and Philip Sarre, 260–78. Cambridge: Polity.

Spoor, Max, ed. 2004. *Globalisation, Poverty and Conflict: A Critical "Development" Reader*. Dordrecht; London: Kluwer Academic.

Sri, E. P. 2005. *Queen Mother: A Biblical Theology of Mary's Queenship*. Steubenville, OH: Emmaus Road.

Stanley, Christopher D. 2002. "Who's Afraid of a Thief in the Night?" *NTS* 48/4: 468–86.

Stanton, Graham. 1992. *Gospel for a New People: Studies in Matthew*. Edinburgh: T&T Clark.

Stavans, Ilan. 2003. *Spanglish: The Making of a New American Language*. New York: HarperCollins.

Stendahl, Krister. 1960. "Quis et Unde? An Analysis of Mt, 1–2." In *Judentum, Urchristentum, Kirche: Festschrift für Joachim Jeremias*, ed. Walther Eltester, 96–105. BZNW 26. Berlin: Alfred Töpelmann.

Stephenson, John R. 1981. "The Two Governments and the Two Kingdoms in Luther's Thought." *SJT* 34/4: 321–37.

Stiglitz, Joseph E. 2006. *Making Globalization Work*. New York: W. W. Norton.

Strack, Hermann L., and Paul Billerbeck. 1922. *Das Evangelium nach Matthäus erläutert aus Talmud und Midrash*. Munich: Beck'sche.

Strauss, Barry S. 2009. *The Spartacus War*. New York: Simon & Schuster.

Sugirtharajah, R. S. 2002. "Blotting the Master's Copy: Locating Bible Translations." In *Postcolonial Criticism and Biblical Interpretation*, 155–78. Oxford: Oxford University Press.

Sumner, Andy, Joe Ballantyne, and Andrew Curry. 2010. "What Are the Implications of the Global Crisis and Its Aftermath for Developing Countries, 2010–2020?" International Policy Center for Inclusive Growth. http://www.ipc-undp.org/pub/IPCWorkingPaper68.pdf

Tamez, Elsa, et al. 1987. *Against Machismo*. Yorktown Heights, NY: Meyer-Stone.

Tannehill, Robert. 1975. *The Sword of His Mouth: Forceful and Imaginative Language in Synoptic Sayings*. SBL Semeia Supplements 1. Missoula: Scholars.

Tanner, Marcus. 1997. *Croatia: A Nation Forged in War*. New Haven: Yale University Press.

Teng-Cheung, K. Y. 2009. "Hong Kong Church Female Minister Questionnaire Survey in 2009." (trans. from the Chinese). Database online; available http://www.abs.edu/fckeditor/userfiles/PDF.pdf.

Terreblanche, Sampie. 2002. *A History of Inequality in South Africa, 1652–2002*. Pietermaritzburg: University of Natal Press.

Theissen, Gerd. 1992. *The Gospels in Context: Social and Political History in the Synoptic Tradition*. Trans. Linda M. Maloney. Edinburgh: T&T Clark.

———. 1995. "Die Erforschung der synoptischen Tradition seit R. Bultmann: Ein Überblick über die formgeschichtliche Arbeit im 20. Jahrhundert." In Rudolf Bultmann. *Die Geschichte der synoptischen Tradition*, 409–52. Göttingen: Vandenhoeck und Ruprecht.

Thompson, Edward H., Jr. 2002. "What's Unique About Men's Caregiving." In *Men as Caregivers: Theory, Research, and Service Implications*, ed. Betty J. Kramer and Edward H. Thompson, 20–48. New York: Springer.

Thomson, Rosemarie Garland. 1997a. *Extraordinary Bodies: Figuring Physical Disability in American Culture and Literature.* New York: Columbia University Press.

———. 1997b. "Feminist Theory, the Body, and the Disabled Figure." In *The Disability Studies Reader,* ed. Lennard J. Davis, 279–292. New York: Routledge, 1997.

Tofaeono, Ama'amalele. 2000. *Eco-Theology: Aiga—the Household of Life—a Perspective from Living Myths and Traditions of Samoa.* World Mission Script 7. Erlangen: Erlanger Verlag für Mission und Ökumene.

Tolbert, Mary Ann. 1995. "Reading for Liberation." In *Reading from This Place.* Vol. 1, *Social Location and Biblical Interpretation in the United States,* ed. Fernando F. Segovia and Mary Ann Tolbert, 263–76. Minneapolis: Fortress Press.

Tolstoy, Leo. 2008. *The Forged Coupon & Other Stories by Leo Tolstoy.* Rockville, MD: Arc Manor.

Tremain, S. 2002. "On the Subject of Impairment." In *Disability/Postmodernity: Embodying Disability Theory,* ed. M. Corker and T. Shakespeare, 32–47. New York: Continuum.

Trifunovska, Snežana, ed. 1994. *Yugoslavia through Documents: From Its Creation to Its Dissolution.* Dordrecht: M. Nijhoff.

Trilling, Wolfgang. 1969. *The Gospel According to St. Matthew.* 2 vols. New York: Herder and Herder.

Tsang, Donald. 2011. "Big Market, Small Government." http://archive.news.gov.hk/isd/ebulletin/en/category/ontherecord/060919/html/060919en11001.htm.

Turner, David L. 2008. *Matthew.* Baker Exegetical Commentary on the New Testament. Grand Rapids: Baker Academic.

Turner, Victor. 1969. *The Ritual Process: Structure and Anti-Structure.* New York: Aldine de Gruyter.

Tuwere, Ilaitia S. 2002. *Vanua: Towards a Fijian Theology of Place.* Suva, Fiji: Institute of Pacific Studies.

Ukpong, Justin S. 2000. "Developments in Biblical Interpretation in Africa: Historical and Hermeneutical Directions." *Journal of Theology for Southern Africa* 108: 3–18.

Ulrich, Daniel W. 2007. "The Missional Audience of the Gospel of Matthew." *CBQ* 69/1: 64–83.

UNDESA (United Nations Department of Economic and Social Affairs. 2010. *The Millennium Development Goals Report 2010.* http://www.un.org/

millenniumgoals/pdf/MDG%20Report%202010%20En%20r15%20-low
%20res%2020100615%20-.pdf.

UNDP (United Nations Development Programme). 2009. *Human Development Report 2009: Overcoming Barriers: Human Mobility and Development.* New York: Palgrave Macmillam.

————. 2010. *Human Development Report 2010: Real Wealth of Nations: Pathways to Human Development.* New York: Palgrave Macmillam.

United Nations General Assembly. 2000. "United Nations Millennium Declaration." http://www.un.org/millennium/declaration/ares552e.htm.

U.S. Central Intelligence Agency. "Country Comparison: Total Fertility Rate." *The World Factbook.* https://www.cia.gov/library/publications/the-world-factbook/rankorder/
2127rank.html?countryName=Hong%20Kong&country
Code=hk&regionCode=eas&rank=222#top.

Vaka'uta, Nasili. 2010. "Fale-'O-Kāinga: Rethinking Biblical Interpretation Eco-Wise." Paper delivered at the Second Conference of the Society of Asian Biblical Studies. Chinese University of Hong Kong, June 14–16.

Vansina, Jan. 1985. *Oral Tradition as History.* Madison: University of Wisconsin Press.

Vermès, Géza. 1961. *Scripture and Tradition in Judaism.* StPB. Leiden: E. J. Brill.

Via, Dan O., Jr. 1987. "Ethical Responsibility and Human Wholeness in Matthew 25:31-46." *HTR* 80: 79–100.

Volf, Miroslav. 1996. *Exclusion and Embrace: A Theological Exploration of Identity, Otherness, and Reconciliation.* Nashville: Abingdon.

Waetjen, Herman C. 1976. "The Genealogy as the Key to the Gospel according to Matthew." *JBL* 95/2: 205–30.

————. 1989. *A Reordering of Power: A Socio-Political Reading of Mark's Gospel.* Minneapolis: Fortress Press.

Wainwright, Elaine M. 1991. *Towards a Feminist Critical Reading of the Gospel according to Matthew.* BZNW 60. Berlin: de Gruyter.

————. 1997. "Rachel Weeping for Her Children: Intertextuality and the Biblical Testaments—A Feminist Approach." In *A Feminist Companion to Reading the Bible: Approaches, Methods and Strategies,* ed. Athalya Brenner and Carole Fontaine, 452–69. Sheffield: Sheffield Academic.

————. 1998. *Shall We Look for Another? A Feminist Rereading of the Matthean Jesus.* Maryknoll, NY: Orbis.

————. 2000a. "Reading Matthew 3–4: Jesus—Sage, Seer, Sophia, Son of God." *JSNT* 77: 25–43.

———. 2000b. "A Transformative Struggle Towards the Divine Dream: An Ecofeminist Reading of Matthew 11." In *Readings from the Perspective of Earth*, ed. Norman C. Habel, 162–73. The Earth Bible 1. Sheffield: Sheffield Academic.

———. 2006. *Women Healing/Healing Women: The Genderization of Healing in Early Christianity*. London: Equinox.

———. 2008a. "Healing Ointment/Healing Bodies: Gift and Identification in an Ecofeminist Reading of Mark 14:3-9." In *Exploring Ecological Hermeneutics*, ed. Norman C. Habel and Peter Trudinger, 131–40. Atlanta: Society of Biblical Literature.

———. 2008b. "Unbound Hair and Ointmented Feet: An Ecofeminist Reading of Luke 7:36-50." In *Exchanges of Grace: Essays in Honour of Ann Loades*, ed. Natalie K. Watson and Stephen Burns, 178–89. London: SCM.

———. 2010. "Place, Power and Potentiality: Reading Matthew 2:1-12 Ecologically." *ExpTim* 121/4: 159–67.

Walsh, J. T. 1996. *1 Kings*. Berit Olam: Studies in Hebrew Narrative and Poetry. Collegeville: Liturgical.

Warren, Rick. 1995. *The Purpose Driven Church: Growth Without Compromising Your Message and Mission*. Grand Rapids: Zondervan.

Weaver, Dorothy Jean. 1990. *Matthew's Missionary Discourse: A Literary Critical Analysis*. JSNTSup 38. Sheffield: Sheffield Academic.

———. 1992. "Transforming Nonresistance: from Lex Talionis to 'Do Not Resist the Evil One.'" In *The Love of Enemy and Nonretaliation in the New Testament*, ed. Willard M. Swartley, 32–71. Louisville: Westminster John Knox.

Weems, Renita J. 2002. "My Mother, My Self." In *Showing Mary: How Women Can Share Prayers, Wisdom, and the Blessings of God*, 117–25. West Bloomfield, MI: Walk Worthy Press.

———. 2006. "Re-Reading for Liberation: African American Women and the Bible." In *Voices from the Margins: Interpreting the Bible in the Third World*, ed. R. S. Sugirtharajah, 27–39. Rev. and exp. 3rd ed. Maryknoll, NY: Orbis, 2006.

Weiser, A. 1971. *Die Knechtsgleichnisse der synoptischen Evangelien*. SANT 29. München: Kösel.

Welter, Barbara. 1966. "The Cult of True Womanhood: 1820–1860." *American Quarterly* 18/2: 151–74.

Wenham, David. 1984. *The Rediscovery of Jesus' Eschatological Discourse*. Sheffield: JSOT Press.

———. 1989. *The Parables of Jesus.* Downers Grove, IL: InterVarsity.

Wesley, John. 2002a. "Sermon 28. Upon Our Lord's Sermon on the Mount, Discourse 8." In *The Standard Sermons in Modern English.* Vol 2, *On the Sermon on the Mount.* Ed. Kenneth Cain Kinghorn, 21–33, 199–218. Nashville: Abingdon.

———. 2002b. *The Standard Sermons in Modern English.* Vol. 2, *On the Sermon on the Mount.* Ed. Kenneth Cain Kinghorn. Nashville: Abingdon.

West, Gerald O. 1995. *Biblical Hermeneutics of Liberation: Modes of Reading the Bible in the South African Context.* 2nd ed. Maryknoll, NY: Orbis; Pietermaritzburg: Cluster.

———. 2004. "Early Encounters with the Bible among the Batlhaping: Historical and Hermeneutical Signs." *BibInt* 12/3: 251–81.

———. 2005. "Articulating, Owning and Mainstreaming Local Theologies: The Contribution of Contextual Bible Study." *Journal of Theology for Southern Africa* 122: 23–35.

———. 2006a. "Contextual Bible Reading: A South African Case Study." *Analecta Bruxellensia* 11: 131–48.

———. 2006b. "Contextuality." In *The Blackwell Companion to the Bible and Culture,* ed. John F. A. Sawyer, 399–413. Oxford: Blackwell.

———. 2009. "Interpreting 'the Exile' in African Biblical Scholarship: An Ideo-Theological Dilemma in Post-Colonial South Africa." In *Exile and Suffering: A Selection of Papers Read at the 50th Anniversary Meeting of the Old Testament Society of South Africa OTWSA/OTSSA, Pretoria August 2007,* ed. Bob Becking and Dirk Human, 247–67. Leiden: Brill.

Westfield, Nancy Lynne. 2008. *Being Black Teaching Black: Politics and Pedagogy in Religious Studies.* Nashville: Abingdon.

White, Keith J. 2008. "'He Placed a Little Child in the Midst': Jesus, the Kingdom and Children." *The Child in the Bible,* ed. Marcia J. Bunge, 353–74. Grand Rapids: Eerdmans.

Whitehead, Raymond. 1977. *Love and Struggle in Mao's Thought.* Maryknoll, NY: Orbis.

Williams, Delores S. 1993. *Sisters in the Wilderness: The Challenge of Womanist God-Talk.* Maryknoll, NY: Orbis.

Williams, Ritva H. 2002. "An Illustration of Historical Inquiry: Histories of Jesus and Matthew I.I–25." In *Handbook of Early Christianity: Social Science Approaches,* ed. Anthony J. Blasi, Jean Duhaime, and Paul-André Turcotte, 105–23. Walnut Creek, CA: AltaMira.

Witherington, Ben, III. 1984. *Women in the Ministry: A Study of Jesus' Attitudes to Women and Their Roles as Reflected in His Earthly Life.* SNTSMS 51. Cambridge: Cambridge University Press, 1984.

Wittenberg, Gunther. 1993. *Prophecy and Protest: A Contextual Introduction to Israelite Prophecy.* Pietermaritzburg: Cluster.

———. 2007. *Resistance Theology in the Old Testament: Collected Essays.* Pietermaritzburg: Cluster.

Wood, J. Edwin. 1968. "Isaac Typology in the New Testament." *NTS* 14/4: 583–89.

"Working VS Stay At Home." 2006. *Babytalk.* February, 54–56.

World Health Organization. 2009. "World Breastfeeding Week." August 7. http://www.who.int/maternal_child_adolescent/news_events/news/2009/09_08_07/en/index.html.

World Health Organization. 2012. "Baby-friendly Hospital Initiative." http://www.who.int/nutrition/topics/bfhi/en/index.html.

Wu, Leichuan. 1936. *Jidujiao yu zhongguo wenhua* (Christianity and Chinese culture). Shanghai: Youth Association.

———. 1950. *Modi yu yesu* (Motze and Jesus). Shanghai: Youth Association. Reprinted in *Motze dachuan* (Motze collection). Vol. 50. Beijing: Library Press.

Yam, Joseph. 2009. "Reflections Relevant to the Banking Profession in Hong Kong." Central Bankers' Speeches. http://www.bis.org/review/r090930c.pdf.

Yerushalmi, Yosef Hayim. 1982. *Zakhor: Jewish History and Jewish Memory.* The Samuel and Althea Stroum Lectures in Jewish Studies. Seattle: University of Washington Press.

Yieh, John. 2007. *Making Sense of the Sermon on the Mount.* Cambridge: Grove.

Yong, Amos. 2007. *Theology and Down Syndrome: Reimagining Disability in Late Modernity.* Waco: Baylor University Press.

Young, Robert J. C. 2003. *Postcolonialim: A Very Short Introduction.* Oxford: Oxford University Press.

Zerwick, Max, and Mary Grosvenor. 1981. *A Grammatical Analysis of the Greek New Testament.* Rome: Biblical Institute Press.

Ziegler, Dhyana. 1995. "Single Parenting: A Visual Analysis." In *African American Single Mothers: Understanding Their Lives and Families,* ed. Bette J. Dickerson, 80–93. Sage Series on Race and Ethnic Relations. London: Sage.

Author Index

Scripture Index

Ancient and Other Extra-Biblical Sources Index

CPSIA information can be obtained
at www.ICGtesting.com
Printed in the USA
BVHW040812300821
615180BV00052B/72/J

9 780800 699345